COMMUNICATING IN CANADA'S PAST: ESSAYS IN MEDIA HISTORY

Communicating in Canada's Past evolved out of essays presented at the inaugural Conference on Media History in Canada, which brought together media historians from across disciplines and from both French and English Canada. The first collection of its kind, this volume assembles both well-established and up-and-coming scholars to address sizeable gaps in the literature on media history in Canada.

Communicating in Canada's Past includes a substantial introduction to media history as a field of study, historiographical essays by senior scholars Mary Vipond, Paul Rutherford, and Fernande Roy, and original research essays on a range of subjects, including print journalism, radio, television, and advertising. Editors Gene Allen and Daniel J. Robinson have assembled both a sophisticated, wide-ranging introduction for those who are new to media history and a valuable collection of new research and theory for those already familiar with the field.

GENE ALLEN is an associate professor and director of the Master of Journalism program in the School of Journalism at Ryerson University.

DANIEL J. ROBINSON is an associate professor in the Faculty of Information and Media Studies at the University of Western Ontario.

EDITED BY GENE ALLEN AND
DANIEL J. ROBINSON

Communicating in Canada's Past

Essays in Media History

UNIVERSITY OF TORONTO PRESS
Toronto Buffalo London

© University of Toronto Press Incorporated 2009
Toronto Buffalo London
www.utppublishing.com
Printed in Canada

ISBN 978-0-8020-9316-5 (cloth)
ISBN 978-0-8020-9498-8 (paper)

Library and Archives Canada Cataloguing in Publication

Communicating in Canada's past : essays in media history / edited by
Gene Allen and Daniel J. Robinson.

Based on papers presented at the Conference on Media History in
Canada in Toronto in June 2006.
Includes bibliographical references and index.
ISBN 978-0-8020-9316-5 (bound).   ISBN 978-0-8020-9498-8 (pbk.)

1. Mass media and history – Canada – Congresses.   2. Mass media –
Canada – History – Congresses.   I. Allen, Gene, 1952–   II. Robinson,
Daniel J.   III. Conference on Media History in Canada (2006 : Toronto, Ont.)

P92.C3C556 2009   302.230971   C2009-903266-X

University of Toronto Press acknowledges the financial assistance to its
publishing program of the Canada Council for the Arts and the Ontario
Arts Council.

 Canada Council   Conseil des Arts   ONTARIO ARTS COUNCIL
for the Arts   du Canada   CONSEIL DES ARTS DE L'ONTARIO

This book has been published with the help of a grant from the Canadian
Federation for the Humanities and Social Sciences, through the Aid to
Scholarly Publications Programme, using funds provided by the Social Sci-
ences and Humanities Research Council of Canada.

University of Toronto Press acknowledges the financial support for its publishing activities of the Government of Canada through the Book Publishing Industry Development Program (BPIDP).

Contents

vi   Contents

List of Illustrations

Acknowledgments

For their financial and administrative support for the Canadian Media History Conference held at Ryerson University in 2006, the editors would like to thank: Errol Aspevig, Daniel Doz, Paul Knox, and Judith Sandys (all of Ryerson University) and Catherine Ross (University of Western Ontario). We also wish to thank our fellow conference organizers: Josette Brun, Barbara Freeman, Sandra Gabriele, Russell Johnston, Maxine Ruvinsky, Will Straw, and Mary Vipond. Our editors at University of Toronto Press (Stephen Kotowych, Siobhan McMenemy, and Ryan van Huistjee) have offered much support for this project. Funds for translation of chapters 1 and 9 were provided by the Faculty of Communication and Design, Ryerson University, and the Faculty of Information and Media Studies, University of Western Ontario; the Faculty of Communication and Design also provided funds for the printing of colour images in chapter 7. Comments and suggestions provided by two anonymous reviewers for University of Toronto Press were particularly helpful in improving the collection.

COMMUNICATING IN CANADA'S PAST:
ESSAYS IN MEDIA HISTORY

Introduction: Media History as Concept and Practice

GENE ALLEN AND DANIEL J. ROBINSON

The idea and motivation for this essay collection grew out of a conference on Canadian media history held in Toronto in June 2006, an event
which we helped organize. While historical work on Canadian media
and communication systems has a long past – and a celebrated one in
the work of Harold Innis – the field today remains fragmented and only
partially developed.[1] Practitioners are spread across many disciplines,
working (until very recently) without the aid of dedicated scholarly
organizations or journals. The Canadian historical profession includes
groups promoting the historical study of women, Natives, national
politics, labour, business, and children (to name a few), and Canadian
scholars of communications and cultural studies have their own associations as well. Yet only in 2009 was a similar organization established
for the specifically historical study of mass media and communications,
which have greatly influenced Canadian society since the late eighteenth century. The absence of institutional support has not prevented
the appearance of a sizeable body of published works, however,[2] and
the level of scholarly interest is also indicated by the unexpectedly high
attendance at the media history conference, which attracted nearly one
hundred registrants from Canada, Ireland, France, Australia, and the
United States. These researchers spanned many disciplines – history,
communications, media studies, journalism, film studies, and literary
studies, among others – and their papers dealt with a wide array of topics, empirical approaches, and theoretical standpoints.

The essays collected in this volume address historiographical, theoretical, and empirical questions concerning Canadian media history.
With one exception, they originated as presentations at the Toronto
conference and, in published form, constitute the first collection of

original essays on Canadian media history. We hope that this will be the first of many such volumes. The papers herein deal primarily with print and broadcast media, which, in part, reflects the predominance of these media within the overall field of study. It is our hope, however, that future research will tackle less explored topics like popular music, film, photography, and multimedia in Canada.

The remainder of this Introduction offers a survey and an assessment of current approaches to the study of media history, as seen in both the Canadian and broader English-language literature. If, as many believe, media are fundamentally constitutive of modernity – by shaping the evolution and structure of societies harbouring them – then it would seem of great importance to understand their history.[3] And that, in turn, requires some clarification of the conceptual and methodological differences that currently characterize the field.

THERE IS A WIDE RANGE of views about the proper scope of media history and the best ways to approach it. British scholar James Curran calls for the analysis of media within the broadest historical context, in essence crafting a 'general account of the development of modern British society in which the history of the British media is inserted.'[4] In such a framework, the commonalities, not differences, of individual media are emphasized. Conversely, Lisa Gitelman argues that detailed case studies of individual media, especially during their early years and attuned to their social and cultural contexts, offer the most promising pathways for critical insight and analytical rigour.[5] Thomas O'Malley has noted media history's extreme interdisciplinarity, including practitioners from anthropology, sociology, history, communications, and cultural studies, to name a few. (The list of disciplinary influences can be expanded further to include political and social theorists like Jürgen Habermas and Michel Foucault, feminist scholars such as Judith Butler, and economic and business historians such as Innis, G.R. Taylor, and Alfred D. Chandler Jr.)[6] This has brought theoretical innovation and empirical diversity but also highlights 'problems of definition, methodology and ... difficulties of crossing disciplinary boundaries in order to determine an adequate set of interdisciplinary tools for studying the subject.'[7] To complicate matters further, book history and film history – which ostensibly would seem part of media history – have largely developed as separate fields of study.[8] For some, this wide-ranging 'interdiscipline' holds the promise of a vibrant, expansive topic of study; others see disciplinary incoherence and patchwork methodology.[9]

What does it mean to speak about 'media' in a specifically historical sense? Hans Fredrick Dahl has pointed out that the term 'mass media' did not appear until the 1920s and did not enter academic parlance for another twenty years.[10] Indeed, Dahl argues that the term was not commonly used until much later: 'The aggregation of disparate media of communication (newspapers, newsreels, radio, television) into a synthetic whole – "the media" – is a very recent phenomenon, perhaps coinciding with the rise of television in the 1960s as *the* dominant information and entertainment medium.'[11] John Nerone suggests that one common usage of the term first appeared in the early twentieth-century advertising industry – 'media' being a useful shorthand term for the various print, broadcast, and outdoor venues where advertisements could be placed – and agrees that our ways of thinking about what 'media' means are fundamentally, if fortuitously, linked to our experience of television.[12] In considering media historically, one must guard against casting early media forms into a twentieth-century 'mass media' framework.[13]

More broadly, it is important to recognize that electronic media, such as the telegraph or broadcasting, are not typical of media generally. Communication may be separated from transportation, but this is not always or necessarily so.[14] Consider, for example, what the telegraph and pre-electronic postal systems have in common. If the telegraph is considered a medium because it transmitted messages, early postal networks must be media too, since they accomplished a very similar function.[15] Here the term 'medium' applies not only to those objects containing postal messages, the transported letters (which are physically distinct from the network that carries them), but to the entire postal system itself. With the telegraph, by contrast, messages consist of electrical signals that do not exist independently of the transmission channel, making it easier to see channel and message as co-terminous. Many other media products, such as newspapers and magazines, are no less material than letters, and the physical transportation networks that deliver them to their audiences are central to the job they do. Media, then, should be understood as more than end products or content, but rather as integrated, complex systems involving production and dissemination (along with, as is noted below, audience uptake and cultural circulation).

One common approach to media history focuses mainly on technology. If pursued uncritically, this type of media history can end up as the treatment of successive technologies ('from the printing press to the modem'), characterized by teleological notions of progress and 'winning' outcomes.[16] The caveats here are many. For example, books, magazines, and newspapers are different media, but they all rely on the same underlying technology, the printing press. Media are multidimensional, involving complex combinations of technology (frequently, multiple technologies, such as printing press and linotype, in the case of newspapers); forms of economic organization (reliance on advertising, for example); audience characteristics; distribution networks; institutional structures (for newspapers, the international supply of news); and conventional practices (journalistic objectivity).[17] On this last point, Gitelman highlights the social conventions, or 'protocols,' accompanying the use of media, like saying 'Hello' when answering the telephone. For Gitelman, the great benefit of a historical approach is that it allows one to study individual media before the conventions that surround them become firmly established – at which point the protocols tend to seem inevitable and even invisible. If one adopts this approach, the telephone, for example, is seen as a historically contingent phenomenon that can only be understood in relation to the changing sets of social practices in which it is embedded, rather than something with a fixed identity that derives from its underlying technology.[18] Similarly, Rudolph Stöber offers a two-stage model of media evolution in which new communication technologies are soon after accompanied by their social institutionalization, which in turn 'changes the invented media fundamentally.'[19] Media, then, not merely are the sum total of their implementing technologies, but represent a complex composite of economic, social, political, and technological elements.

Besides technology, what other concepts can help us think systematically about media history? Some scholars have focused on the institutional aspects of media, incorporating approaches from business history and political economy in order to examine individual institutions (such as *The Globe and Mail*) or larger media systems (the federally regulated broadcasting sector in Canada). Often concerned with questions of ownership and power, this approach is informed by the view that modern media stand 'at the intersection of two grand distributive systems, politics and the marketplace.'[20] Networks are among the most important of these institutional structures of media, and they are firmly embedded in political and economic contexts: the creation of broadcast networks in the twentieth century, telegraphic networks in the nineteenth, or even early European postal networks typically involved the exercise of (or the struggle for) political and economic power.[21] Joad

Raymond's work on media history embraces networks as a key conceptual tool. While his framework incorporates political, patronage, and ideological networks, the primary emphasis is on media as articulated structures of *dissemination*, for nearly all media share this function of spreading information beyond its points of origin.[22]

So far we have considered media largely in terms of production: technologies for producing and disseminating messages, and the networks and institutions (states, corporations, capital markets) that enable this process. But in cautioning against a narrowly transmission-based approach, James Carey reminds us that media are more than systems, products, or commodities.[23] One of the main reasons for being interested in media is that they carry messages and meaning: they must, therefore, be understood in terms of their content and especially the different ways in which people interpret media content and media forms to construct personal meanings and social identities. Coming originally from literary theory, the audience-response approach asserts that meaning is variable and that the question of a text's meaning always raises the question, 'Meaning for whom?'[24] While recovering reliable information about how past audiences used and responded to media can be difficult, many scholars have found ways of doing so, adding a crucial dimension to our understanding.[25]

Media content and the various ways it is understood can also be seen through the prism of culture. Increasingly since the 1980s, scholars have placed questions of culture at the centre of historical research and explanation. This 'cultural turn' is characterized by concern for what historical events and actions meant to people caught up in them, while acknowledging the embeddedness of such meanings in broader socio-economic contexts. Historical actions are interpreted in terms of performance and symbolism: the actions of a crowd during Carnival, for example, or a demonstration by partisan supporters, become texts for the historian to interpret. This is history, in the words of Robert Darnton, 'in the ethnographic grain.' Inspired largely by the work of cultural anthropologist Clifford Geertz,[26] this approach affirms culture as the primary concept for thinking historically about media. Linked to this paradigmatic shift is the 'linguistic turn,' which posits that understanding of the world occurs primarily through its expression in language, contrary to the view that language is merely a convenient way of describing things that we already know in a pre- or non-linguistic way. In these approaches, media representations of the world – that is, media texts – serve as rich sources for understanding popular meanings and *mentalités* in the past; and concepts and methods derived from cultural anthropology, cultural studies, and communication studies provide sophisticated ways for interrogating these texts.[27] The cultural approach to media is sharply in opposition to what might be called the literalist view that the meaning of historical media texts, like newspaper articles or radio broadcasts, is transparent and self-evident, and can be determined by a simple recounting of the manifest content.[28]

Carey has played a key role in promoting a Geertzian approach to the study of media history.[29] He is concerned with symbolic and social meanings, emphasizing the community-binding, ritualized aspects of communication. In a well-known passage, he describes reading a newspaper

> less as sending or gaining information and more as attending a mass, a situation in which nothing new is learned but in which a particular view of the world is portrayed and confirmed … We recognize, as with religious rituals, that news changes little and yet is intrinsically satisfying; it performs few functions yet is habitually consumed. Newspapers do not operate as a source of effects or functions but as dramatically satisfying, which is not to say pleasing, presentations of what the world at root is. And it is in this role – that of a text – that a newspaper is seen; like a Balinese cockfight, a Dickens novel, an Elizabethan drama, a student rally, it is a presentation of reality that gives life an overall form, order, and tone.[30]

For Carey, communication is a 'symbolic process whereby reality is produced, maintained, repaired, and transformed.'[31] It also transpires in 'historical time,' making it especially suitable for historical modes of inquiry.

While also socio-cultural in orientation, other historical approaches stress structural over symbolic factors, being primarily concerned with how media establish and inform modes of social perception more broadly. One key contribution is Jürgen Habermas's theory of the public sphere.[32] Habermas argues that the very idea of 'the public' – a body of citizens set apart from the domains of family and state – developed in conjunction with the spread of newspapers in eighteenth- and nineteenth-century Europe. Without this forum for information-sharing and discussion among various social groups, often occurring in coffee houses, the idea of 'the public' would not have emerged when and as it did.[33] For Habermas, the concept of 'publicness' is fundamentally historical, being temporally and geographically specific and, in large part, an outgrowth of media development.[34] Benedict Anderson highlights a different connection between media and changing categories of social perception; he argues that the simultaneous consumption of identical media accounts by people who would never meet in person served to create an 'imagined community' that formed the basis of modern nationalism.[35] The public sphere and the nation constitute different types of socio-political spaces,[36] and both may be usefully linked back to the idea of dissemination. They are not only spaces to which messages are disseminated by particular media, but spaces that are *brought into existence* by this dissemination.[37]

The idea of 'publicness' in relation to media – that different media make possible the emergence, disappearance, and reconstitution of different types of publics – offers one promising way to think about media history generally. It potentially brings together approaches involving dissemination and its technological, political-economic, and institutional dimensions; the structural shaping of social consciousness as seen with Habermas and Anderson; and the anthropological view of culture as a symbolic system, one that is often a public or collective phenomenon.[38] These different publics, of course, may be more or less exclusive along lines of class, gender, or ethnicity, and more or less oriented to consumption, local identity, communitarianism, and many other possible variables. We are thus proposing a broader and more descriptive notion of publicness than that advanced by Nerone, who insists that the public, properly understood, is an explicitly represented body of *citizens*, and not merely the aggregate audience for any particular medium.[39]

As we have seen throughout this Introduction, media history is essentially caught up in theories of what media are and how they operate. More then ten years ago, Hans Frederick Dahl noted that this can be problematic for empirically minded historians, who are often sceptical of theory.[40] When we were PhD students in history during the 1980s and 1990s, our training involved little in the way of social and cultural theory, whose importance was not impressed upon us. One could earn doctorates in history, as we did, knowing little about Michel Foucault or Raymond Williams. While there are numerous exceptions, there is some truth in what Canadian historian Adele Perry has characterized as the 'knee-jerk anti-theoretical stance nurtured in history departments.'[41] We currently teach in interdisciplinary, media-related programs and have become more receptive to integrating empiricism with relevant theory, a view also reflected throughout this volume. Theory functions as both passport and lingua franca in a world of fragmenting disciplines and academic specialization. We may not fully understand the technical changes in recording hardware which contributed to the rise of the rock 'concept album' during the 1960s, but if we situate that topic within a theoretical discussion of taste, distinction, and cultural capital inspired by the ideas of Pierre Bourdieu we acquire a template for understanding and a basis for constructive feedback.[42]

While being receptive to theoretical approaches, the study of past media should also constitute an intrinsically historical enterprise. Historians recognize the incompleteness of the historical record and the impossibility of recovering the past 'as it actually was,' pursuing what might be called an enlightened empiricism.[43] Constructive engagement with primary sources, archival or otherwise, remains the sine qua non of the historical approach. Theoretical insight must reflect the weight of empirical evidence, and the 'archive,' then, becomes a testing ground for competing theoretical frameworks.[44] A historical approach, with its regard for the specificities of time and place, can reveal that what may seem universal categories for understanding media (e.g., publicness, or the taken-for-granted protocols that govern how particular media are used) are in fact historically conditioned and subject to change. David Paul Nord has also observed that postmodernism favours a specifically historical approach to media, since it sees meanings as inherently variable, rather than fixed: 'meaning is necessarily situated in the contexts of time and place. It is historical.'[45] In these senses, the historicity of media history represents a vital and enduring characteristic of the field.

MANY OF THE ABOVE themes (interdisciplinarity, empiricism-cum-theory, technology's effects on politics and culture) are defining features in the work of Harold Innis, Canada's most enduring theorist and historian of media. After joining the University of Toronto in 1920, Innis published influential works on the history of 'staples' industries like the cod fisheries and the fur trade in Canada, highlighting their impact on social and political development. Beginning in the 1940s, he turned to information and communication questions, eventually completing two books that explained world history in light of media technologies and systems of communication.[46] These macro-historical accounts plotted communication developments from the ancient Sumerians to Hearst's Yellow Press. Innis defined historical epochs according to their dominant mode of communication and resultant biases (temporal or spatial), which in turn influenced social and political organization and cultural values. If left unchecked, these biases (more tendency than determinism) fostered centralizing 'monopolies of knowledge,' whether among medieval Catholic oligarchs or twentieth-century newspaper oligopolists. Innis also sought to rekindle the spirit and democratizing thrust of orality, which he saw as a brake on commercialization and the 'mechanization of knowledge' characteristic of space-biased societies.

Innis died prematurely in 1952, but his influence later spread. By the 1980s, 'Innisology' was said to have imbued a number of areas of communications, cultural studies, and 'dependency' political economy.[47] Few historians were among these enthusiasts, since much of the interest centred on Innis's communication-era writings, which historians generally saw as 'irrelevant to the writing of Canadian history.'[48] Carl Berger's award-winning study of Canadian historiography examined at length Innis's staples works but largely ignored *Empire and Communications* and *The Bias of Communication*.[49] There were no historians among the twenty-three contributors to an academic collection commemorating the centenary of Innis's birth, most of whom came from the ranks of communications, sociology, and political science.[50] A type of 'two solitudes' has come to characterize academic reception of Innis scholarship, with historians drawn mainly to staples economies and resultant transportation systems and political systems, and media scholars focused on topics like medium theory, asymmetrical information flows, and the trade in 'cultural' goods. This division is unfortunate since conceptual and empirical similarities exist in both bodies of works, notably so with respect to metropole–hinterland power relations.[51] Common analytical threads can be seen in such Innis findings – made decades apart – as that the 'spread of Western civilization' in North America was a function of fur trade–related river systems and that papyrus as a writing medium enabled the advance of Roman rule throughout the Mediterranean basin.

Innis, as Robert Babe has noted, stood outside the mainstream of American communication studies after the Second World War.[52] He was part of a 'quintessentially Canadian' school of communication thought, along with other 'foundational' figures like Marshall McLuhan and George Grant, which dealt with dialectical and ontological inquiry, political economy, and the role of technology in shaping cultural practices. They were 'critical' communication theorists, in contrast to 'administrative' American counterparts like Paul Lazarsfeld and Harold Lasswell, who addressed methodological questions and their administrative applications. McLuhan adapted Innisian concepts to articulate how communication technologies shaped cognitive structures and human social relations. George Grant explored how communication technologies like computers were bound up in the 'civilizational destiny' of Western societies and not value-free outcomes of technological progress. Maurice Charland's concept of 'technological nationalism,' in which communication and transportation technologies served as central metaphors for Canadian national identity and collective purpose, similarly drew on Innis.[53] Innis remains important not only for practitioners of media history, but for interpreters of Canadian identity and nationalism and technology's role in shaping people's sense of themselves.

A recent and highly accomplished work employing Innisian theory is Gerald Friesen's *Citizens and Nation*. He draws on Innis's ideas of time and space to produce a historical synthesis of Canada framed by changing modes of communication and people's attempts to make sense of and to exercise control over these changes. Canada's history is divided into four eras, each defined by a 'dominant' communication system: oral-traditional, textual-settler, print-capitalist, and screen-capitalist. The oral societies of aboriginal Canada emphasized the transcendent nature of time and the melding of human, natural, and spiritual worlds. European settlers introduced literary norms, which co-existed with aboriginal notions of ecological and generational time. Industrialization in the nineteenth century, along with the advent of such communication innovations as the telegraph and mass dailies, replaced localist ties with mediated articulations of national identity. The screen-capitalist era, beginning after the Second World War, further solidified the time-as-money ethos in the midst of accelerated information flows tied to television, computers, and digital telecommunications. These media helped transform social organization, while weakening Canadian identity in the face of consumerism and the rapid influx of U.S. cultural content. Throughout these four eras, Friesen argues, changes to the dominant modes of communication engendered new social and cultural contexts, providing a 'framework for citizenship and nationality and thus for Canada.'[54]

Much of this is convincing, except for the post-1945 era, when, arguably, no single mode of communication predominates. Rather, the mediascape then is characterized by a complex amalgam of pre-existing forms (newspapers, magazines, film, radio) alongside newer ones like television, computers, digital telephony, and, finally, the internet. Can Innisian time-space theory linked to 'dominant' modes of communication still be useful for societies laden with multiple types of print, electronic, and digital media? Or does this question reveal more our own presentist conceit, an inability to imagine the 'media clutter' affecting Canadians a century ago as they charted their world and constructed their identities amid newspapers, magazines, film, and telephones?

MEDIA HISTORY CAN be an important vehicle for reassessing conventional understandings of contemporary media. It also serves to interpret past societies in novel ways, as the essays in this collection demonstrate. Dominique Marquis, in her institutional history of *L'Action catholique*, reassesses widely accepted interpretations of newspaper development during the early twentieth century. Established by Quebec's Roman Catholic Church in 1907, *L'Action catholique* embraced many features of mass-market newspapers while at the same time presenting a Catholic voice in news coverage and commentary. For example, the paper refused advertisements promoting films, plays, or alcoholic beverages[55] as well as advertising from Jewish merchants. Proceeding from a solid theoretical foundation, Marquis provides a comparative analysis of *L'Action catholique*'s content and operations in the context of a wider journalistic system marked by competition with other mass dailies. Her article is a strong example of the productive interplay between theoretical sophistication and empirical rigour characteristic of much recent work in media history.

In his analysis of the emergence of radio news in Canada, Gene Allen addresses larger questions about the relationship between new and preexisting media. Drawing on records of the Canadian Press (CP) news agency, Allen takes issue with received accounts claiming that a 'press–radio war' occurred during the 1920s and 1930s. Instead, he argues, the changing positions of newspaper owners toward radio competition are best explained by the complex competitive ecologies that operated at the local, national, and supranational levels. Allen draws on Innis's concept of time- and space-biased media to illustrate the evolution of these competitive frameworks. With the emergence of the Canadian Radio Broadcasting Commission in 1932, political and regulatory considerations came to the fore, and CP formed a strategic alliance with the public broadcaster. By the early 1940s, newspaper owners had abandoned long-standing attempts to limit CP news on radio, and the press agency began selling news to radio stations with few restrictions. This study underscores the historically contingent way in which print and broadcast news interests both cooperated and competed with one another.

Simon Potter's account of the British Broadcasting Corporation's influence on the formation of public broadcasting in Canada in the 1930s embodies Mary Vipond's call (see p. 15) to situate national media history within transnational contexts. Potter's archival research provides ample evidence for questioning previous accounts of interwar Canadian broadcasting which downplayed the British influence; rather, Canadian nationalists like Graham Spry and Alan Plaunt tapped into British broadcasting circles for ideas and resources while lobbying for a BBC-type service in Canada. Potter illustrates how ideas about 'national and transnational identities' were deployed in support of competing visions of radio, as well as the varied and shifting ways in which 'British influence worked with various home-grown interests' to establish public broadcasting in Canada.

Daniel Robinson explores the first two decades of one of North America's oldest marketing campaigns: Seagram's moderation advertising for responsible alcohol use. The popularity and longevity of this social responsibility campaign, Robinson argues, derived from many factors. The moderation campaign, launched in 1934, fitted well with Seagram's broader strategy of marketing high-end, premium whiskies, meant to be sipped sparingly. In Canada, most provinces banned brand advertising by distillers, but not institutional advertising such as moderation appeals. Moderation advertising proved highly adaptive, eventually branching out to make virtues of the moderate personality, restrained consumption during wartime, and middle-of-the-road politics. What began as a moral imperative concerning responsible alcohol use had by the 1950s colonized the broader domains of psyche, society, and polity.

Before Karla Homolka there was Evelyn Dick, the Hamilton homemaker who was tried three times in the late 1940s for murdering her husband and infant son. In her chapter, Alison Jacques is less concerned with the facts and legal arguments involving guilt or innocence than with media representations of Dick and the trials themselves. Employing gender analysis, Jacques highlights the preoccupation of newspaper reporters with Dick's body, mannerisms, and attractiveness, underscoring her rhetorical transformation from 'comely young widow' to 'short, fat Evelyn.' Jacques explores at length newspaper depictions of spectatorship, both the reserved and orderly attendees inside the courtroom and the boisterous, 'feminized' crowds gathered daily outside the court house. While recent film and television depictions of Evelyn Dick employ the genre of film noir, Jacques argues that press coverage in the 1940s adopted the narrative conventions of melodrama and soap opera.

Informed by Benedict Anderson's concept of the imagined community, Mathew Hayday explores the relationship between broadcasting and national identity in his essay on Dominion Day celebrations organized by the federal government and broadcast by the CBC from 1958 to 1980. His empirical account documents the transition from a 'British-centric model of Canadian identity' to a more pluralistic one incorporating French–English duality, multiculturalism, aboriginal cultures, and regional identities. Certain thematic and stylistic changes occurred over the years. Over time, an emphasis on belonging replaced overt political statements about the nation. By the 1970s, satellite transmission enabled broadcasts that were both centralizing and decentring: the 'live' broadcasts promoted simultaneity of experience from coast to coast, while the enhanced capacity to broadcast from different locations provided greater regional representation.

Scholars of political marketing typically focus on television advertising. James Cairns, however, explores the modern campaign pamphlet, in this case one promoting Ontario Premier William Davis during the 1971 provincial election. The pamphlet was historic for its pioneering and prolific use of colour photography depicting a multi-personae Davis in various work and leisure settings. Employing the semiotic theory of Roland Barthes, Cairns analyses the pamphlet's linguistic, denotative, and connotative meanings engendered by the interplay of text and imagery. As such, he reconfigures the document as a cultural artefact, a multi-voiced promulgator of ideological messages concerning 'acceptable political activity' and the 'normative boundaries of a political community.'

In her essay, broadcast historian Mary Vipond offers a far-ranging historiographical survey of Canadian broadcasting since the 1960s. She describes how Canadian broadcasting history has changed from its initial focus on policy at the national level, and the CBC in particular, to greater concern with cultural questions, private broadcasting, and regional and local patterns of development. Vipond assesses the strengths and shortcomings of the field, arguing that the scarcity of broadcasting history limits our understanding of modern Canadian society, which is heavily influenced by electronic media. She concludes with a call for broadcasting historians to situate their work within larger analytical frameworks such as social history or transnational and global communications.

Fernande Roy has written widely on Quebec intellectual and cultural history, including the history of journalism. She provides here a systematic overview of recent research on the history of newspapers in Quebec, updating a survey that she co-published in 2000.[56] Echoing Vipond, Roy argues that few historians have treated newspapers as primary objects of study, instead employing them as research sources for other topics. She describes how journalism-related subjects have broadened to include such areas as the representation of women and the experiences of gays and lesbians. Interest in Quebec nationalism has waned, while the pace of historical work on Quebec media remains comparatively slow. Calling for additional research, Roy emphasizes the need for cultural accounts of the press to incorporate the newspaper's social presence, economic importance, and its role in power relations.

Pioneering Canadian media historian Paul Rutherford recounts the intellectual odyssey underpinning his research and writing since the 1970s. Following his initial works on newspapers and broadcasting, Rutherford reconfigured his approach to media in response to the emergence of cultural history and its emphasis on the meanings and signification systems of everyday life. He turned to theory to stock his 'intellectual toolbox,' describing his evolving embraces, both brief and protracted, of theorists like Innis, Barthes, Gramsci, Habermas, Baudrillard, and, above all, Foucault. Theory became a primary force in shaping Rutherford's research projects, offering practical and intellectual benefits; it provided a framework for the meaningful organization of archival evidence, while helping to situate findings within broader cultural and social contexts. Theory promotes, too, the cross-pollination of research via shared theoretical bridging among scholars working on otherwise unrelated topics.

The field of media history in Canada has entered a propitious period owing to recent institutional changes and intellectual currents. The 1990s and early 2000s saw the creation (and rapid expansion) of many undergraduate and graduate programs in media and communications, for which introductory history courses are often required.[57] Many of those hired to teach in these programs have historical research interests, and thus the field counts many emerging scholars, a fact demonstrated by the strong complement of junior faculty and graduate students at the 2006 conference. Half of this volume's contributors have worked in academe for less than ten years. Canadian media history, as shown by the essays below, has drawn liberally from both the cultural turn of the humanities and the older tradition of political economy highlighting the centrality of transportation and communication systems in Canada's development. The range of topics and diversity of empirical and theoretical approaches in these essays, we believe, serves to underscore the varied richness of the field to date while promising to open up new lines of inquiry and scholarly debate among media historians in the years ahead.

NOTES

1 On the underdevelopment of broadcasting history in Canada and newspaper history in Quebec, see the essays by Mary Vipond (chapter 8) and Fernande Roy (chapter 9) in this volume.
2 For a selection of previously published articles, see Daniel J. Robinson, ed., *Communication History in Canada* (Toronto: Oxford University Press, 2004).
3 John B. Thompson, *The Media and Modernity: A Social Theory of the Media* (Stanford, CA: Stanford University Press, 1995). The entire book is, in effect, an argument for this conclusion, but see in particular pp. vii, 4, 5, 46. See also Mary Vipond, 'The Mass Media in Canadian History: The Empire Day Broadcast in 1939,' *Journal of the Canadian Historical Association*, n.s., 14 (2003): 1–22. Speaking more narrowly of journalism, John Hartley describes it as '*the* sense-making practice of modernity (the condition) and the popularizer of modernity (the ideology.) ... Journalism is caught up in all the institutions, struggles and practices of modernity; contemporary politics is unthinkable without it, as is contemporary consumer society, to such an extent that in the end it is difficult to decide whether journalism is a product of modernity, or modernity a product of journalism.' Hartley, *Popular Reality: Journalism, Modernity, Popular Culture* (London and New York: Arnold, 1996), 33–4. For a recent debate about the significance of the printing press in particular, see Elizabeth L. Eisenstein, 'AHR Forum: An Unacknowledged Revolution Revisited,' *American Historical Review* 107, no. 1 (Feb. 2002): 87–105, and Adrian Johns, 'AHR Forum: How to Acknowledge a Revolution,' *American Historical Review* 107, no. 1 (February 2002): 106–25.
4 James Curran, 'Media and the Making of British Society, c. 1700–2000,' *Media History* 8, no. 2 (2002): 149.
5 Lisa Gitelman, *Always Already New: Media, History and the Data of Culture* (Cambridge, MA: MIT Press, 2006), 11.
6 John Nerone, 'Approaches to Media History,' in Angharad N. Valdivia,

ed., *A Companion to Media Studies* (Malden, MA: Blackwell, 2005), 96; Maria DiCenzo, 'Feminist Media and History: A Response to James Curran,' *Media History* 10, no. 1 (2004): 43–9.

7 Thomas O'Malley, 'Media History and Media Studies: Aspects of the Development of the Study of Media History in the UK, 1945–2000,' *Media History* 8, no. 2 (2002): 169–70. See also David Paul Nord's valuable methodological guide to communication history, 'The Practice of Historical Research,' in Guido H. Stempel III, David Weaver, and G. Cleveland Wilhoit, eds, *Mass Communication Research and Theory* (Boston and New York: Allyn and Bacon, 2003), 362–85.

8 The work of Robert Darnton is one of the clearest links among book history, media history, and the mainstream historical profession. See, for example, his presidential address to the American Historical Association, 'An Early Information Society: News and the Media in Eighteenth-Century Paris,' *American Historical Review* 105, no. 1 (February 2000): 1–35.

9 For a more hopeful view based on some recent contributions to the field, see the review essay by Mark Hampton, 'Media Studies and the Mainstreaming of Media History,' *Media History* 11, no. 3 (2005): 239–46. A few years earlier, though, Curran described media history as 'the neglected grandparent of media studies: isolated, ignored, rarely visited by her offspring'; James Curran, *Media and Power* (London and New York: Routledge, 2002), 3.

10 Hans Fredrick Dahl, 'The Pursuit of Media History,' *Media, Culture and Society* 16 (1994): 553.

11 Ibid. Michael Schudson suggests that the omnibus term 'the media' came into common usage even later (the 1970s), partly as a result of the Nixon administration's campaign against the press and television news; Schudson, 'National News Culture and the Informational Citizen,' in Schudson, *The Power of News* (Cambridge, MA, and London: Harvard University Press, 1995), 171.

12 Nerone, 'Approaches to Media History,' 99–100. See also Jon Agar, 'Medium Meets Message: Can Media History and the History of Technology Communicate?' *Journal of Contemporary History* 40, no. 4 (2005): 803.

13 See also John Durham Peters, *Speaking into the Air: A History of the Idea of Communication* (Chicago: University of Chicago Press, 1999), 22. For a recent warning about the anachronistic use of the term 'propaganda' to describe seventeenth-century pamphlets and newsbooks, see Joad Raymond, 'Introduction: Networks, Communication, Practice,' *Media History* 11, no. 1/2 (2005): 3–19

14 James Carey has noted that the telegraph was revolutionary precisely because it separated transportation and communication for the first time. See 'Technology and Ideology: The Case of the Telegraph,' in Carey, *Communication as Culture: Essays on Media and Society* (New York: Routledge, 1992; first published 1989), 203. For two recent assessments of the importance of pre-telegraphic transportation improvements to information flows, see Yrjö Kaukiainen, 'Shrinking the World: Improvements in the Speed of Information Transmission, c. 1820–1870,' *European Review of Economic History* 5, no. 1 (2001): 1–28; and Richard D. Brown, 'Early American Origins of the Information Age,' in Alfred D. Chandler, Jr, and James W. Cortada, eds, *A Nation Transformed by Information: How Information Has Shaped the United States from Colonial Times to the Present* (New York: Oxford University Press, 2000).

15 For postal history, see, for example, John Willis, ed., *More Than Words: Readings in Transport, Communication and the History of Postal Communication* (Gatineau: Canadian Museum of Civilization, 2007); Richard B. Kielbowicz, *News in the Mail: The Press, Post Office, and Public Information, 1700–1860s* (New York: Greenwood Press, 1989); Richard R. John, *Spreading the News: The American Postal System from Franklin to Morse* (Cambridge, MA: Harvard University Press, 1998).

16 Nerone, 'Approaches to Media History,' 100.

17 It should also be noted that technologies are not necessarily material, but can be intellectual and organizational too. For example, theorists as diverse as Michel Foucault and James Beniger have stressed the importance of quantitative approaches and systematic record-keeping as social and economic technologies; see Foucault, *Discipline and Punish: The Birth of the Prison*, trans. Alan Sheridan, 2nd ed. (New York: Vintage Books, 1995); and James R. Beninger, *The Control Revolution: Technological and Economic Origins of the Information Society* (Cambridge, MA: Harvard University Press, 1986). Beniger's history of information processing in the nineteenth and twentieth centuries illustrates the interweaving of intellectual and material technologies. A 'crisis of control' during the Industrial Revolution created a need for effective data management by governments and corporations, as seen in such inventions as the Hollerith data-processing machine, representative sampling, and, later, computer networks. For an approach that emphasizes the social and political organization of communication, see Armand Mattelart, *The Invention of Communication*, trans. Susan Emanual (Minneapolis: University of Minnesota Press, 1996).

18 Gitelman, *Always Already New*, 5–8.

19 Rudolph Stöber, 'What Media Evolution Is: A Theoretical Approach to the History of New Media,' *European Journal of Communication* 19, no.4 (2004): 483.

20 Nerone, 'Approaches to Media History,' 103.

21 For broadcasting, see, for example, Robert McChesney, *Telecommunications, Mass Media, and Democracy: The Battle for the Control of U.S. Broadcasting, 1928–1935* (New York: Oxford University Press, 1993); Mary Vipond, *Listening In: The First Decade of Canadian Broadcasting, 1922–1932* (Montreal and Kingston: McGill-Queen's University Press, 1992). For the telegraph, see Menahem Blondheim, *News over the Wires: The Telegraph and the Flow of Public Information in America, 1844–1897* (Cambridge, MA, and London: Harvard University Press, 1994); for early postal networks, Paul Arblaster, 'Posts, Newsletters, Newspapers: England in a European System of Communications,' *Media History* 11, no. 1/2 (2005): 21–36.

22 Raymond, 'Introduction: Networks, Communication, Practice,' 14; Beninger, *The Control Revolution.*

23 James Carey, 'A Cultural Approach to Communication,' in Carey, *Communication as Culture*, 15.

24 See, for example, Stanley Fish, *Is There a Text in This Class? The Authority of Interpretive Communities* (Cambridge, MA: Harvard University Press, 1980); Jane Tompkins, 'Introduction to Reader-Response Criticism,' in Jane Tompkins, ed., *Reader-Response Criticism: From Formalism to Post-Structuralism* (Baltimore: Johns Hopkins University Press, 1980).

25 For examples, see the essays in Part 2 of David Paul Nord, *Communities of Journalism: A History of American Newspapers and Their Readers* (Urbana and Chicago: University of Illinois Press, 2001); Darnton, 'An Early Information Society'; James Huffman, *Creating a Public: People and Press in Meiji Japan* (Honolulu, 1997); Jeremy D. Popkin, *Revolutionary News: The Press in France, 1789–1799* (Durham, NC: Duke University Press, 1990), especially chap. 2, 'Writers, Publishers and Readers,' 35–95; Charles E. Clark, *The Public Prints: The Newspaper in Anglo-American Culture, 1665–1740* (New York: Oxford University Press, 1994); Thomas C. Leonard, *News for All: America's Coming-of-Age with the Press* (New York and Toronto: Oxford University Press, 1995); Mary Vipond, 'Desperately Seeking the Audience for Early Canadian Radio,' in M. Behiels and M. Martel, eds, *Nations, Ideas, Identities: Essays in Honour of Ramsay Cook* (Toronto: Oxford University Press, 2000), 86–96; Lynn Spigel, *Make Room for TV: Television and the Family Ideal in Postwar America* (Chicago: University of Chicago Press, 1992); Richard Butsch, *The Making of American Audiences: From Stage to Television, 1750–1990* (New York: Cambridge University Press, 2000); Michele Hilmes,

ed., *The Television History Book* (London: British Film Institute, 2003), section on 'Audiences'; Hilmes, *Radio Voices: American Broadcasting, 1922–1952* (Minneapolis: University of Minnesota Press, 1997).

26 Geertz's well-known formulation is as follows: 'Believing, with Max Weber, that man is an animal suspended in webs of significance he himself has spun, I take culture to be those webs, and the analysis of it to be therefore not an experimental science in search of law but an interpretive one in search of meaning.' Clifford Geertz, *The Interpretation of Cultures: Selected Essays* (New York: Basic Books, 1973), 5. For a succinct and thoughtful account of the cultural turn, see Victoria E. Bonnell and Lynn Hunt, 'Introduction,' in Bonnell and Hunt, eds, *Beyond the Cultural Turn: New Directions in the Study of Society and Culture* (Berkeley and Los Angeles: University of California Press, 1999), 1–32. See also the essays in Lynn Hunt, ed., *The New Cultural History* (Berkeley and Los Angeles: University of California Press, 1989).

27 For an excellent guide to historical, anthropological, sociological, and literary-critical approaches to the analysis of popular culture, see Chandra Mukerji and Michael Schudson, 'Introduction: Rethinking Popular Culture,' in Mukerji and Schudson, eds, *Rethinking Popular Culture: Contemporary Perspectives in Cultural Studies* (Berkeley and Los Angeles: University of California Press, 1991), 1–61. See also Nord, 'The Practice of Historical Research.' Schudson cautions against the tendency to overstate media influence; 'Introduction: News as Public Knowledge,' in Schudson, *The Power of News*, 17; and Schudson, 'Toward a Troubleshooting Manual for Journalism History,' *Journalism and Mass Communication Quarterly* 74, no. 3 (Autumn 1997): 463–6.

28 See, for example, Vipond, 'The Mass Media in Canadian History,' 4.

29 Carey, 'Cultural Approach to Communication.'

30 Ibid., 20–1.

31 Ibid., 23.

32 Jürgen Habermas, *The Structural Transformation of the Public Sphere: An Inquiry into a Category of Bourgeois Society*, trans. Thomas Burger (Cambridge, MA: MIT Press, 1989).

33 Much of the debate about Habermas's notion of the public sphere has focused on its limited membership, especially in terms of class and gender. For an introduction to this debate, see the essays in Craig Calhoun, ed., *Habermas and the Public Sphere* (Cambridge, MA: MIT Press, 1992).

34 Michael Schudson has raised questions about how much Habermasian rational-critical debate actually took place in the past, but acknowledges media's capacity to '*publicly include*' as 'their most important feature'; whether the audience is actually paying attention or not, 'the assumption

of the *public* presence makes all the difference.' Schudson, 'Was There Ever a Public Sphere?' in Calhoun, ed., *Habermas and the Public Sphere*, 143–63 , and 'News as Public Knowledge,' 25 (our emphasis).

35 Benedict Anderson, *Imagined Communities: Reflections on the Origin and Spread of Nationalism*, rev. ed. (New York and London: Verso, 1991). The nation is not the only kind of imagined community that can arise; for an argument that a similar sense of cultural affinity applied to the British Empire, see Simon Potter, *News and the British World: The Emergence of an Imperial Press System, 1876–1922* (New York: Oxford University Press, 2003). Other scholars have stressed how printed news gave rise to scepticism about the rulers of early modern societies or how regular periodical publication led to the relative privileging of politics over other aspects of social life. See, respectively, Brendan Dooley, *The Social History of Skepticism: Experience and Doubt in Early Modern Culture* (Baltimore and London: Johns Hopkins University Press, 1999); and John Sommerville, *The News Revolution in England: Cultural Dynamics of Daily Information* (New York and Oxford: Oxford University Press, 1996).

36 The nation as seen by Anderson is, of course, also spatial in a straightforward geographical sense, but Anderson's accomplishment is to stress its status as a cultural creation. Nerone suggests that thinking of media in relation to different kinds of space (public space, urban space, etc.) can be a unifying idea: 'Like the virtual space of the public sphere, the actual spaces that communication operates in and constructs can frame a broad history of media' ('Approaches to Media History,' 110).

37 See also Hartley, *Popular Reality*, 35: a key component of the news system 'is the creation of readers as publics, and the connection of those readerships to other systems, such as those of politics, economics and social control.' He also argues that 'publics and consumers are not simply people waiting passively out there for something to consume, but on the contrary that they are brought into being *as* consumers and publics by the process of cultural production itself. By this formula, then, journalism cannot be thought of as an industry which produces a throwaway commodity (printed paper), but as a form of cultural production which produces its own consuming subjects – the public, the consumer' (47).

38 The notion of 'mediated publicness' as a central characteristic of modern societies is elaborated most clearly in Thompson, *The Media and Modernity*. Schudson concludes that in seeking to explain the development of news media (and, by extension, media more generally), 'political economy, geography, social systems and culture [interact] in the usual complex ways that only the best narrative history seems able to capture.' 'News as Public Knowledge,' 15.

39 On the related question whether the meaning that media messages carry is best understood as primarily social and communal or individual and idiosyncratic, see also Lynn Hunt, 'Introduction,' in *The New Cultural History*, 12–16.

40 Dahl, 'The Pursuit of Media History,' 560.

41 Adele Perry, 'The Historian and the Theorist Revisited,' *Histoire sociale / Social History* 65 (2000): 146.

42 Pierre Bourdieu, *Distinction: A Social Critique of the Judgment of Taste*, trans. Richard Nice (Cambridge, MA: Harvard University Press, 1984). See, too, Keir Keightley, 'Long Play: Adult-Oriented Popular Music and the Temporal Logics of the Post-War Sound Recording Industry in the USA,' *Media, Culture and Society* 26, no. 3 (2004): 375–91.

43 See Nord, 'The Practice of Historical Research,' 365.

44 Nerone, 'Approaches to Media History,' 99, 111: 'Historians insist on the reality of the past – not a simple, objective reality, but a reality that resists the present in ways that historians are bound to honor.'

45 Nord, 'The Practice of Historical Research,' 366. In his view, 'communication history seems to be moving to center stage of mainstream historical practice' (364).

46 Innis, *Empire and Communications* (Oxford: Clarendon, 1950); *The Bias of Communication* (Toronto: University of Toronto Press, 1951).

47 Daniel Drache, 'Harold Innis and Canadian Capitalist Development,' *Canadian Journal of Political and Social Theory* 6, no. 1/2 (winter/spring 1982): 35; Charles R. Acland, 'Histories of Place and Power: Innis in Canadian Cultural Studies,' in Charles R. Acland and William J. Buxton, eds, *Harold Innis in the New Century: Reflections and Refractions* (Montreal: McGill-Queen's University Press, 1999), 243–51. Innis's notoriously opaque and elliptical prose style also fitted with postmodernist rejections of 'rational,' linear prose.

48 Graeme Patterson, *History and Communications: Harold Innis, Marshall McLuhan, the Interpretation of History* (Toronto: University of Toronto Press, 1990), 49, 59.

49 Carl Berger, *The Writing of Canadian History: Aspects of English-Canadian Historical Writing 1900–1970*, 2nd ed. (Toronto: University of Toronto Press, 1986).

50 Acland and Buxton, eds, *Harold Innis*.

51 One exception, which explores many parallels between Innis's staples and communication writings, is Paul Heyer's *Harold Innis* (Lanham, MD: Rowman and Littlefield, 2003). See especially chaps 2 and 3.

52 Robert E. Babe, *Canadian Communication Thought: Ten Foundational Writers* (Toronto: University of Toronto Press, 2000).

53 McLuhan, *Understanding Media: The Extensions of Man* (New York: McGraw-Hill, 1964); George Grant, *Technology and Justice* (Toronto: Anansi, 1986); Maurice Charland, 'Technological Nationalism,' *Canadian Journal of Political and Social Theory* 10, no. 1/2 (1986): 196–220.

54 Gerald Friesen, *Citizens and Nation: An Essay on History, Communication, and Canada* (Toronto: University of Toronto Press, 2000), 3 and passim.

55 For an account of alcohol advertising, see the essay by Daniel Robinson in this volume.

56 Fernande Roy and Jean de Bonville, 'La recherche sur l'histoire de la presse québécoise: Bilan et perspectives,' *Recherches Sociographiques* 41, no. 1 (2000): 15–51.

57 Examples at the undergraduate level include University of Western Ontario, McMaster University, Wilfrid Laurier University, University of Calgary, and University of Toronto-Mississauga. Graduate school examples include UWO, University of Windsor, Wilfrid Laurier, and the combined program at York and Ryerson universities.

PART ONE

New Research in Canadian Media History

1 The Catholic Press: A Challenge to the 'Journalism of Information' Paradigm

DOMINIQUE MARQUIS

(TRANSLATED BY PATRICIA SMART)

Newspapers and specialized magazines are part of daily life for thousands of people: they inform us about current events, they satisfy our curiosity, they nourish our reflections. Very few readers of these publications have questions about how the press operates, however, which is a perfectly normal state of affairs. Journalists sometimes ask themselves about the nature of their work, but they are primarily preoccupied with ethical questions and leave the task of looking at the media in an analytical and theoretical way to communications specialists.

Because there is no doubt about their relevance as historical sources, newspapers are now frequently used by many researchers (historians, political scientists, sociologists, etc.). As concrete evidence of a past that has more or less disappeared, they are recognized as rich sources of information: they reveal what were the important events of their period and – through their editorials, commentaries, and even advertisements – they are valuable indicators of the ideologies and *mentalités* that marked their era. Newspapers are studied more for the copious information they can provide on a given subject than for themselves; there is far more history written *with the aid of* the press than history *about* the press.

There is, however, a small number of researchers who are interested in the history of the Quebec press. The journalism of opinion, the journalism of information, the specialized press, as well as press personnel and associations of journalists make up some of the various topics treated in these studies.[1] For example, the move from the journalism of opinion to information-based journalism around the turn of the twentieth century is the topic of an excellent study by Jean de Bonville, in which he emphasizes the important role played by advertising and the economy in the evolution of the Quebec press.[2] For this author, the development of the market economy was the determining factor in the changes that affected not only the business of journalism, but the entire content of newspapers. This study, along with a few others, makes clear the importance of placing the evolution of the press in the larger context of the development of society as a whole and its relationships with other institutions.

The present article will look at some of these complex relationships and also at the theoretical framework within which some authors analyse the press and journalistic practice. After stressing the importance of situating the press within its larger environment, we will present two theoretical proposals intended to explain its evolution. Our study of the Catholic press will subsequently allow us to verify whether or not one can apply to the entire category of the 'journalism of information' a model based on a theory of journalistic paradigms.

The Press, at the Centre of a Complex Network of Relationships

Because the press exists within a complex ensemble of relationships, studies of it become much more interesting when they go beyond simple analyses of newspaper content (which ignore the context of production) and place the newspaper within a larger network. The press does not evolve in isolation; it only exists when it is connected to the world around it. Current events from all spheres of society are its raw material; its pages are open to a whole range of differing opinions; and in turn it redistributes information on all sorts of topics and offers that same society a variety of subjects for reflection. Both a receiver and a transmitter of information, the press is in a constant relationship with other institutions like the state or the churches and benefits considerably from these exchanges. These relationships are often fraught, but without them the press would simply not exist: they force the newspaper out of isolation and into an interaction with the institutions that surround it, and with its competitors. Studies on the press also benefit from the richness of these relationships because they open up new areas for analysis and lead to the possibility of developing original theoretical approaches.

No newspaper can ignore the presence of its competitors: you always have to keep an eye on what your neighbour is doing, even if he has a different political allegiance or mission than you do. This was equally true of the nineteenth-century press of opinion, which, even as it emphasized commentary over information, sought arguments to 'attack the enemy' and defend its own positions in the material present-ed by its rivals. Even though the situation of twentieth-century news-papers is quite different, the presence of competitors is something that must always be considered.

Since the end of the nineteenth century the press has in fact under-gone considerable transformation. Influenced by numerous external factors like technological advances in printing, the development of new methods of transportation, the progress of literacy and (as Jean de Bon-ville points out) the growth of industrial activity,[3] the press has opened itself up to a much broader readership, less literate than before but avid for information of all kinds. The information-based press responds to very different needs than the nineteenth-century press of opinion. The new newspaper concentrates on the news and moves away from politi-cal commentary that would risk creating divisions among its readers. It sees itself as more of a unifying force: even if it still offers commentary and editorial opinions, it no longer aims solely at defending a particu-lar idea and attacking those of other newspapers. The new commer-cial logic that drives it obliges it to diversify its content. And while the news-based press can evolve, it remains constrained by the structure of which it is now a part.

The Journalistic System

The news-based or information press in fact belongs within a 'journal-istic system.'[4] This concept, elaborated by Maurice Mouillaud several years ago, allows us to understand the links that exist among various newspapers as well as the rules that are shared by all journalists in the information-based press. This journalistic system is divided into sev-eral fields, including an inter-journalistic field (the obligatory links among newspapers) and an intra-journalistic one (the connections that characterize the internal functioning of the newspaper). News-based dailies share common characteristics and objectives: they seek to enter-tain and, to a lesser extent, to educate the population, but above all they seek to inform it. They all operate within the same rhythm of events and face the same realities. Because of this, and because they generally rely on identical sources of information, they end up offering a very similar product. These conditions allow them very little room to dis-tinguish themselves from each other, yet they aim for distinctiveness because they are in competition with each other. Each seeks to 'scoop' its opponents, and they are all constantly in search of the 'exclusive' article or interview. Since scoops are not always possible, other means are used to attain distinctiveness: for example, the adoption of certain formats or different ways of using illustrations or photographs.[5]

. According to Mouillaud, 'the field of information organizes in turn a field of readers that did not exist previously.'[6] These readers have an important role to play, as newspapers are subject to what Mouillaud calls a 'double pressure.' Since newspaper content must appeal to a vast public, the tastes of these readers (or what their tastes are seen to be) must be taken into account. Thus the system of the daily press is bidirectional in that its content must satisfy the expectations of readers even as it exerts an influence on these expectations. Even if it can be difficult for readers to make their expectations clear, certain markers like changes in circulation send a message to publishers, who can then make corresponding changes in their publications. Declining circulation generally indicates reader dissatisfaction, and therefore the publishers, taking a good look at the operations of their more successful competitors, will make changes in their layout and content in order to make their paper more attractive and to regain the ground they have lost in the circulation wars.

The competition for circulation matters all the more because within this system advertising has become the principal financial motor of the press. The old forms of financing are no longer adequate for these huge newspaper corporations, which have considerably greater needs than their predecessors and in addition have tried to break free of the constraints that the partisan press was subject to. One of the rules of this new method of financing is that newspapers must increase their circulation, as increased circulation means better advertising contracts. Journalistic practice is thus modified: its aim is no longer, as in the nineteenth century, solely to convince or educate a small group of readers, but rather to inform as large a number as possible. To avoid controversy, objectivity has become the norm, summed up by the mantra 'The facts, just the facts.' In reality this objectivity consists mainly of a refusal to take a position on the events being reported, but in a broader sense opinion is being replaced more and more by raw information.

The schema developed by Maurice Mouillaud puts the emphasis on the news, and since news in the present-day system is no longer an 'autonomous and inert entity,'[7] he stresses the importance of analysing its articulation in the form of the newspaper. He proposes several methodological tools for uncovering the attitudes that allow individual newspapers to differentiate themselves from others within the system. The whole process of page layout thus becomes as important as the newspaper's content.

Mouillaud's approach was favourably received by specialists, who found it a useful way of thinking about the press. By situating each newspaper within a space shared by several others, it invites the analyst to take all the components of this space into account. While specialists have picked up on this new way of looking at the press, non-specialists still tend to limit themselves to the analysis of a single newspaper without paying attention to the fact that it belongs within a system. By treating papers as isolated objects, they miss out on the complexity and richness of the networks they exist within, and their analyses are often cut off from elements that are essential to a true understanding of the nature and function not only of the individual newspaper but also of the press in general.

Maurice Mouillaud's theory is thus a useful means of better understanding the evolution of the press, and researchers stimulated by this approach have followed up on it, developing new explanations of the changes that took place in the twentieth-century press.

The Paradigm of the 'Information Press'

Inspired by the theory of journalistic systems, Jean de Bonville and Jean Charron looked at the transition from the press of opinion to the information press in terms of the evolution of journalistic paradigms. Their first reflections on this question were published in 1996,[8] and the two authors have subsequently revised and enriched their approach.[9]

They distinguish three main periods in Quebec journalism, related to three different journalistic paradigms: journalism of opinion, news-based or information journalism, and journalism of communication. Between these moments, periods of transition are characterized as 'paradigmatic crises,' when the norms dominating a given period give way under the pressure of new ones. We are particularly interested here in the paradigm of news-based journalism because it is this category, according to the authors, that includes the majority of newspapers published in the twentieth century (more specifically, between 1920 and 1980).

Charron and de Bonville situate the first 'paradigmatic crisis' of the press between 1880 and 1920. During this period journalism of opinion, which insisted on subjectivity, gradually gave way to information journalism, with its claims of objectivity. According to them, different news-papers increasingly became vehicles for transmission of the same news items. They also had to publish numerous and varied news items and confined opinion to a very limited space within the newspaper. Outside this space all forms of subjectivity were deemed unacceptable. The role of the journalist was to be 'a witness of world events, responsible for transmitting his observations in the forms permitted by the rhetoric of objectivity.'[10]

Because newspapers in this period were less and less dependent on the traditional sources of financing of the press of opinion (the political parties and the Church), they began to distinguish themselves from the institutions around them.[11] While the ideological spectrum of the opin-ion-based press was quite subtle and nuanced, that of the information press tended to be more uniform, with internal diversity diminishing as all newspapers came to transmit the same news. The authors point out that even the variety that formerly existed in the criteria for the presen-tation and selection of news items (often a mark of the distinctiveness of a newspaper) became more and more 'subject to a universalist and objective approach to the news.'[12]

The paradigm of news-based journalism is thus centred around objectivity and universality, and this new norm influenced all aspects of the information press. Based on Mouillaud's theory of journalistic systems, a model of the information press has been elaborated: that of a universal, objective press focused on reaching certain commercial objectives. But is this model reflected in reality? Do all information-centred newspapers correspond to the proposed model? Or does the great variety of Québécois newspapers published in the twentieth cen-tury not lead us on the contrary to take another look at this theoretical proposal, which tends to minimize differences?

The theory of the paradigm of the information press needs evalua-tion, and the example of the Catholic press is an ideal case in point to put the theory to the test. There are several justifications for choosing the newspaper L'Action catholique to analyse. First, there is absolutely no doubt that the newspaper demonstrated all the characteristics of an information newspaper: it offered various news items to its readers; it sought to entertain them by means of serialized novels and numerous columns; the editorial and accompanying commentaries filled only a small amount of space in its pages; and it had a substantial number of advertisements. As well, the newspaper's close ties to the Catholic Church give us the opportunity to analyse a news-based publication that, rather than evolving in isolation from other social actors, proudly displayed its links with another institution.

The Catholic Information Press

As a first step, in order to understand why the Church saw fit to involve itself in such a venture, it is necessary to briefly describe the origins of *L'Action catholique*. The first experiences of the Catholic Church in the journalistic realm date to the nineteenth century, when the press of opinion was the dominant model – a state of affairs that suited the Church's needs perfectly well, given that education and influencing opinion were the main aims of this type of journalism.[13] The unidirectional character of the press of opinion – from the newspaper to the reader – corresponded perfectly to the Church's way of dealing with the faithful: as the absolute possessor of Truth, it would guide them on the correct path. The mode of operation of the press of opinion was thus one that the Church was familiar with, and it could follow the same course in the press as it did in other areas of society. And in fact the Church did publish a large variety of periodicals and journals: missionary accounts, magazines focused on piety and spirituality, journals of combat. All these publications were part of the spiritual and moral mission of the Church and offered the institution great visibility within society.

However, the arrival of the new daily press in the twentieth century seriously undermined Church practices involving the press, making obsolete the journals of combat that had been delivering the Catholic message to their readers week after week or month after month. As well, the territory occupied by the large-circulation press was becoming more extensive and more threatening for the Church: the news-based paper was now reaching a very large public and its influence was making it possible for ideas to spread much more rapidly. The new information press had expanded so rapidly that the Church had to try to reach this large audience.

In order to maintain its influence, the Church thus decided to move into the domain of the information press. Without abandoning the publication of missionary annals, pious magazines, or newsletters, it had to react to what it considered a new danger: the large circulation press. The period of apprenticeship would be difficult, for while the information press is attentive to the tastes and expectations of its readers, the Church still perceived the function of the press in a unidirectional way. But the system in which it was now beginning to situate itself exerted strong pressure on all its members to respect certain norms if they hoped to succeed within it. Would it be possible for the Catholic information-based newspaper to resist these pressures?

The above question is a legitimate one for researchers, but it is far from the questions that were preoccupying the Archbishop of Quebec, Monseigneur Bégin, when he created L'Action Sociale Catholique and L'Oeuvre de la Presse Catholique, the two bodies that began publishing the daily newspaper *L'Action catholique* in 1907. Bégin specified at the time that a Catholic newspaper was indispensable so that 'the people may also read newspapers that are specially charged with the mission of educating them about the religious and social issues that arise each day within the development of our public life.'[14] And he added: 'The Catholic newspaper must deal with religious questions in order to refute error and to encourage by its influence the spread of healthy doctrine.'[15] In thus defining the role of the press, the archbishop of Quebec was perpetuating the idea of unidirectional communication between the newspaper and its readers. For him, the creation of a newspaper, even one that hoped to compete within the larger sphere of the information press, remained a work of education and of exerting influence.

L'Action catholique, a daily founded in Quebec in 1907, was the vehicle chosen to pursue these objectives. Although the archbishopric was its principal source of financing, the paper belonged legally to a diocesan organization called L'Action Sociale Catholique, whose director was always a member of the clergy named by the archbishop.[16] The links between the newspaper and the archbishop were nonetheless extremely close, with the archbishop giving himself the authority to keep a 'kindly eye' on the publication.

L'Action catholique was founded with the explicit aim of offering the population a newspaper where the reader could find national, international, and local news, reflections on current events, and even entertainment, but above all content in which Church doctrine would be respected and Catholic values promoted. In other words, the newspaper was meant to offer an alternative to the dangerous ideas presented in the large-circulation press and not to betray the ideas of the Church even as it sought economic success.

The first managing editor of the daily, Dr Jules Dorion, was given the mandate to blend news with Catholic values from all points of view. Surrounded by a team made up of some members of the clergy but mostly of lay people, he continued to fulfil his mission until his death in 1939, at which point other managing editors, equally convinced of the value of their mission, replaced him at the helm. On several occasions these editors were challenged by criticism from all sides, not only from rival newspapers which accused them of partisanship, but also from Catholics and nationalists who reproached them, sometimes for their lukewarm attitudes and sometimes for their intransigence.

In spite of these difficulties, and thanks to the indefatigable support of Quebec's archbishop, who frequently had to dip into his coffers to save the newspaper from financial disaster, L'Action catholique was published for almost sixty-five years. In fact it was only in 1971 that the archbishop of Quebec finally admitted defeat and sold the paper to a group of Quebec businessmen. The final issue of what was undoubtedly the most important Catholic daily in Quebec appeared in 1973.

Throughout all these years L'Action catholique had a daily rendezvous with its readers and never deviated from the line of conduct laid out by Monseigneur Bégin in 1907: to offer a Catholic point of view on the news of the day. Was its success a model of successful integration into the newspaper system or, on the contrary, an example of resistance to the pressures exercised by the system? Only a content analysis, the ideal tool for understanding what place a newspaper occupies within the system, allows us to measure the degree of the newspaper's integration or resistance while enabling us at the same time to assess the relevance of the paradigm of information journalism.

Content Analysis: A Means of Evaluating the Paradigm

We chose to concentrate our analysis on the first thirty years of L'Action catholique, the years that led from apprenticeship to maturity. This was the period during which the paper was seeking the formula that would best correspond to its objectives even as it remained conscious of its competitors' presence. We focused in particular on news and advertising content, as well as on the paper's layout. We not only analysed the evolution of the paper, but also situated this evolution within the journalistic system by comparing the Catholic daily to two other daily newspapers published during the same period: Le Soleil, which was its principal rival in the city of Quebec and the surrounding region, and Montreal's La Presse, which had already attained the status of 'the largest French-language daily in America.' Since a newspaper never evolves in isolation, comparative analysis offers an essential tool for better understanding the transformations that mark the life of a publication linked by necessity to other newspapers.

The method of content analysis that was developed to better understand the evolution of the three papers in question was inspired by the model proposed by Jacques Kayser in his book *Le quotidien français*,[17] a model that, while somewhat dated, remains extremely relevant. We carried out a thematic analysis of the content by measuring the space allotted to the different sections of the paper. News, advertising, service articles, serials, and the various columns were identified and measured in order to determine what proportion of print space each occupied.

The news section, the heart of the newspaper, was subjected to a more detailed analysis, and a comparison of the themes and geographic areas covered in each article allowed us not only to measure the relative amount of space allotted to news in the three papers over the period in question but, more importantly, to observe the evolution of the topics selected by the editor in chief and the desk editors in the makeup of the paper. Obviously the close links between an information daily and the news of the day shape this thematic field, but choices are always made and an analysis of this type allows us to bring them to light.

In addition to this content analysis, an examination of the paper's layout and of the relative importance of the various news items on the front page – the newspaper's display window, which invites the reader to buy it – was carried out. Few historical studies have been done of the presentation of news in the Quebec press. Following Jean de Bonville, one of the rare researchers to have shown an interest in such questions,[18] we developed an original method that brings together French, British, and American approaches.

The method examines most of the constituent parts of the newspaper's front page, such as headlines, illustrations, and photos; the appearance of banner headlines and the use of turns to inside pages were also considered. We also looked at the general layout of the page and at the hierarchy of news.[19] The type of headline used is also extremely important in the process of assigning value to various items. The shape, height, and style of the characters vary, and the analysis must take all these factors into account. Covering a period of thirty years and including a comparative dimension as well, the study of these more 'physical' aspects of the newspaper helps to identify the cycles of innovation and catching up that characterize the relationships between newspapers. And it is then that the full meaning of Maurice Mouillaud's proposition concerning the existence of an 'inter-newspaper' field is revealed.

The Evolution of the Catholic Daily

What did these analyses of *L'Action catholique* uncover? At first (that is, during its first decade of existence), the product provided by the managing editors of the newspaper was very similar to the model of nineteenth-century newspapers. Not surprisingly, religious news items concerning the Catholic world took up a large amount of space in the paper. The content was dominated by political news, both national and international, these being the years of the First World War and, on the national scene, of the conscription crisis of 1917.

As in the nineteenth century, the paper's editors relied on input from pastors in outlying regions to fill them in on parish news. These local news items brought in readers from outside Quebec City proper, who were glad to find news of their communities in the newspaper. This practice tended to disappear fairly early on from the other daily newspapers under study, but *L'Action catholique* considered it a duty to offer such a service. While *La Presse* and *Le Soleil* understood that readers are thirsty for *faits divers*,[20] the Church, which had always denounced such items as frivolous, was not yet ready to soften its stance. So *L'Action catholique* offered very few *faits divers*; when it did, these articles never went beyond the limits of good taste and were, for that reason, concisely presented.

The paper's layout was also very conservative: a page consisted of seven columns, making for a very 'dense' reading experience, and there were no banner headlines or illustrations to liven up the front page. It should be mentioned, however, that *Le Soleil* in the same period also lacked an inviting layout, and the two papers clearly seemed to belong to the same era. During these same years, *La Presse* in Montreal adopted a much more modern page layout, inspired by the American press, with large headlines and illustrations giving more and more distinctiveness to the front page.

In the 1920s there was little change in the content of *L'Action catholique*: the paper continued its 'program of education and of patriotic and religious defence,'[21] discussing causes dear to its heart like temperance, education, the family, social assistance, work, and, obviously, religion. All of this information was presented from the Catholic point of view, so that the reader was always in contact with the Truth. *Faits divers* and sports items, two very important elements in the popular appeal of the information press, were given little space in the paper, in contrast to *Le Soleil* and *La Presse*. Evidently sports were considered by the managing editors of *L'Action catholique* to be a secondary component of the paper rather than an element that might attract and retain a large readership.

Even if the news offered to readers of *L'Action catholique* did not correspond to what was being offered in other large daily newspapers of the period, the 1920s nonetheless marked a turning point in the paper's presentation. It gradually lost its austere, nineteenth-century look and took on a more modern appearance. An effort was made to break up the uniformity of the reading experience. The front page was still very dense, but the headlines began to stretch over two or three columns and several lines of type; illustrations were added, and one saw more and more use of the turn to indicate continuation of the articles on subsequent pages. We are still far from American-style layout, but there was clearly an effort towards modernization. The paper kept its Catholic character by offering its readers a large number of religious news items from around the world, as well as commentaries and editorials closely aligned with Catholic doctrine.

In the 1930s *L'Action catholique* finally gave in to pressure from the system and began to take the tastes of its readers more into account. The newspaper's situation was obvious: if its managers wanted it to influence the population it would have to be read, and in order for it to be read it would have to be made as attractive as its competitors. As the newspaper's circulation had decreased in the 1920s, the need for action was clear. The arrival on the scene of a new editor-in-chief, Eugène L'Heureux, was an important factor in the newspaper's success in turning this situation around and substantially renewing its content and layout. L'Heureux was an experienced journalist, convinced that the popularity of a newspaper could be significantly enhanced by improving its appearance and by being more responsive to the tastes of its readers.

A well-organized sports section now became an important part of the paper. The results of the different professional and semi-professional baseball and hockey leagues were always included, and boxing and wrestling were also well covered. More detailed articles on important sporting events were presented. By the end of the 1930s, the daily paper founded by the archbishop of Quebec was looking more and more like the other information journals. Even *faits divers* now made up almost 20 per cent of the space in the newspaper. Formerly disapproved of by the Church, they were now as plentiful in *L'Action catholique* as in either *Le Soleil* or *La Presse*. The newspaper's editors had finally understood that such news items, when presented in a sober and dignified fashion, could enhance the paper's mission by attracting new readers, who, in addition to reading the *faits divers* and sports articles, would appreciate the value of the newspaper in its entirety.

The front page also underwent rejuvenation during these years, with *L'Action catholique* coming to look more and more like *Le Soleil* and *La Presse* (see figures 1.1 and 1.2). The procedure for establishing a hierarchy of news items was refined: the size and choice of typefaces displayed more diversity, thus drawing attention to more important items. However, despite these changes in form and content, it would be impossible to remove the adjective 'Catholic' from the newspaper's title. *L'Action catholique* was still very Catholic, as evidenced by the strong presence of religious news items in its pages, commentaries, and editorials that communicate Catholic thought, and even a front-page layout that insisted on the newspaper's Catholic character by an illustration of Saint Peter's Basilica as part of the paper's masthead.

Advertising: Another Area of Distinctiveness

Another important area in which *L'Action catholique* distinguished itself from its competitors was advertising. If it is true that advertising was a determining factor in the evolution of the information press, then it is all the more important to analyse it. What we are interested in here is not pointing out the values associated with different advertising messages, but rather measuring the amount of space allotted to the different types of advertising in the paper: local, national, service-related, and classified. By measuring these items we can determine the nature of the financial support received by the paper (which businesses are contributing to it and which products it agrees to promote).

In the area of advertising *L'Action catholique* displayed several attitudes typical of the information press. One finds in its pages many ads from local merchants announcing their new products and upcoming sales. Grocery stores, furniture dealers, and department stores were directly approached by agents hired by the newspaper to negotiate these valuable contracts. 'National' advertisements – that is, for major brand-name products – were also present and indicated that the newspaper had succeeded in positioning itself well in relation to the large advertising agencies that linked the press to industry and manufacturing.

The classified ads, considered to be one of the distinctive characteristics of the information press,[22] made up a larger and larger proportion of the advertising space in *L'Action catholique*. Up until the beginning

Figure 1.1: Front page of *L'Action catholique*, 19 November 1938

Figure 1.2: Front page of *La Presse*, 16 September 1938. Courtesy of *La Presse*.

of the 1930s classified ads were badly organized; they were dispersed throughout the paper and their presentation did not suggest a clear intention on the part of the newspaper's management to provide a coherent and efficient service to readers. After 1930 – indicating that the paper was finally responding to its readers' wishes – they were grouped together and organized under thematic headings, as *Le Soleil* and *La Presse* had already been doing for several years.

Service-related advertising was an important feature of the Catholic daily. Generally local in nature, it offered readers a variety of services (teaching, legal services, health services, etc.), and included advertisements for cultural products as well. *La Presse* and *Le Soleil* both took advantage of popular enthusiasm for movies and theatre and published a large number of movie ads and theatre reviews. These ads were very lucrative and made up a significant part of the advertising revenues of these papers. *L'Action catholique* was very different from its rivals in this regard, as the stars of the big screen were not welcome in its pages. It systematically refused theatre and movie ads – a refusal that would cost it thousands of dollars – because they were judged to be pernicious and a dangerous threat to the maintenance of moral values.

Thus, while *L'Action catholique* did conform to a large number of the rules inherent in the newspaper system, most notably in the areas of *faits divers* and sports news, as far as content is concerned, and in the modernization of its front-page layout, an analysis of its advertising content reveals that this capacity for adaptation was not limitless and that certain boundaries could not be crossed. The paper was based on major ideological principles that deprived it of important revenues. A directive issued by the management of L'Action Sociale Catholique, the paper's owner, made it clear that it was out of the question to encourage businesses or products judged to be dangerous by publishing advertisements for them. Not only was the paper not allowed to publicize movies and theatrical events, but ads for Jewish merchants and for alcoholic beverages were also absent from its pages. Advertising represented an important material resource for the information-based newspaper, but the financial independence it provided demanded a price that *L'Action catholique* was unwilling to pay. By accepting these ads, the management would be denying its own raison d'être, and sacrificing its objectives on the altar of financial viability.

L'Action catholique therefore had to count on other sources of revenue, and its ties to the Church became all the more valuable since the Church made available a multitude of resources which were out of the question for rival newspapers. For example, the Church organized special collections during some of its Sunday services, it strongly encouraged Catholic organizations and religious communities to use the newspaper's printing services, and it set up large promotional contests for readers and vendors of the newspaper. Without these resources, and above all the direct financial support of the archbishopric, *L'Action catholique*, given its advertising policies, would obviously have been unable to survive for long.

The analysis of advertising in the paper is thus very rich: it illustrates the fact that a newspaper is not just a vehicle for the transmission of news, but also a showcase for products and services. The study of this showcase, especially when compared with rival newspapers, can be as useful a tool in understanding the character of a newspaper as its news or editorial content. In the case of *L'Action catholique*, it allows us to measure the boundaries of the editorial board's comfort zone in relation to the rules of the information press system.

Conclusion

In spite of a certain amount of resistance, it must be concluded that *L'Action catholique* adapted to the new rules and finally accepted the principle of exchange with its readers – the 'double pressure' described by Maurice Mouillaud. Within the larger space created by the journalistic system it carved out a place where it could be distinctive by maintaining its clearly Catholic character. This allowed the Church to move into the territory of the daily press even as it created its own space within the territory.

The Church was perfectly willing to create an information-based paper, but it refused to conform to the existing model and proposed a new one, based more on patronage than on advertising. This allowed it to free itself to some extent from the existing rules and to continue to transmit a doctrinal message. It is true that the case of *L'Action catholique* is atypical because it was created and financed by a powerful institution that possessed the financial means to sustain it; but other, similar cases exist in the history of the Quebec press.

As a result of this study, the news-based press in Quebec no longer appears as a homogeneous ensemble of daily publications: it is possible to distinguish two categories within it. First there are the papers like *La Presse* that conformed with no difficulty to the model proposed in the paradigm of the information press. They were in competition with each other, and the stakes of their competition were essentially commercial. In order to win they must acquire the largest possible readership by paying attention to the tastes and expectations of their readers but must at the same time must distinguish themselves from the others by incorporating exclusives and by introducing new elements (for example, new columns) in their content and layout.

On the other hand, there were the dailies that acted outside the paradigm. It cannot be denied that they were true news-based papers, even if they did not respect all the rules imposed by the model. They offered varied news items based on the news of the day and corresponding to the taste of their readers, they dealt with subject areas that were instructive and entertaining, and advertising played an important role in their financing strategies. These papers aimed, however, at more ideological or political goals than their competitors and were less likely to concede to all the expectations of their readers, which might at times contradict their own objectives. Nevertheless, they accepted most of the practices, to the extent that they did not go against the paper's particular mission.

For example, Montreal dailies like *Le Devoir* (1910–) or *Le Canada* (1903–53) did not have large circulations but managed to survive for long periods of time.[23] Created with very specific objectives – the defence of the Catholic religion and Canadian nationalism in the first case and an unconditional support for the Liberal Party in the second – they deviated to some extent from the model of news-based journalism. The pressures exercised by the system of the information press made it necessary for them to receive financial support from other sources, however: the first from the group 'Les Amis du Devoir' and the second from the Liberal Party.

The Church positioned itself outside the paradigm. It saw in the news-based paper an efficient tool for spreading Catholic values and principles, and it learned to use this weapon, which it referred to as 'queen of the world' (recalling one of the ways the Blessed Virgin Mary was traditionally described). 'Let us oppose writing by writing,' said the Popes. The formula still worked; even when transformed, the press was still a privileged space for getting one's message across. The Church did not choose to involve itself in the information press in order to produce an objective newspaper but because this space offered it an excellent means of exercising its influence. For that matter, there would be little interest for the researcher in studying the news-based press if it was in fact completely uniform and objective: all dailies would end up being identical.

The example of the Catholic press necessitates a re-evaluation of the paradigm of the information-based press. It clearly establishes that the information press was not uniform and that the universality often attributed to it does not correspond to the reality of the newspapers involved. There were obviously some norms shared by all newspapers in the system, and journalists working for them would probably have a fairly similar idea of their craft and the rules that supported it. However, factors other than the journalistic code must be taken into consideration in an analysis of the different newspapers. Ideological goals could often take precedence over the commercial ones associated with the information press, and these objectives gave a different tone or colour to the individual papers. The significance of discovering those tones and colours is that it makes the news-based press a much more dynamic space and invites researchers not to minimize the differences between publications.

By presenting a specific example of a newspaper that deviates from the paradigm and by suggesting the existence of other similar cases, our demonstration has laid out the limits of the theory in question. At the same time, however, it has shown the value of examining the information press in the context of the journalistic system. The press does not evolve in isolation, and *L'Action catholique* is a good example of the relevance of situating a newspaper in this larger space where relationships with competitors and other institutions can be determining factors in the paper's evolution. Other, similar analyses could doubtless enrich our understanding further. The universe of the twentieth-century information press deserves to be looked at more closely, without limiting our perspectives.

NOTES

1 See Fernande Roy's article in this volume (chapter 9) for an overview of the different tendencies in research on the Quebec press.
2 Jean de Bonville, *La presse québécoise de 1884 à 1914. Genèse d'un média de masse* (Quebec: Les Presses de l'Université Laval, 1988).
3 Ibid., 313–47.
4 Maurice Mouillaud, 'Le système des journaux (Théorie et méthodes pour l'analyse de presse),' *Langages* 11 (1968): 61–83.
5 Ibid., 75.
6 Ibid., 68.

7 Ibid., 83.
8 Jean Charron and Jean de Bonville, 'Le paradigme du journalisme de communication: essai de définition,' *Communication* 17, no. 2 (décembre 1996): 51–97.
9 Jean Charron and Jean de Bonville, 'La notion de paradigme journalistique: aspects théorique et empirique,' in Colette Brin, Jean Charron, and Jean de Bonville, eds, *Nature et transformation du journalisme. Théorie et recherches empiriques* (Quebec City: Les Presses de l'Université Laval, 2004), 33–55.
10 Charron and de Bonville, 'Le paradigme du journalisme de communication,' 71.
11 Ibid.
12 Ibid., 74.
13 Christiane Campagna, 'Le rôle de la presse selon les propriétaires et rédacteurs des journaux montréalais (1830–1880)' (MA thesis, Université du Québec à Montréal, 1998).
14 *L'Action sociale catholique et l'oeuvre de la presse catholique* (Quebec City: Imprimerie Éd. Marcotte, 1907).
15 Ibid., 13.
16 For a complete history of the paper's founding, see Dominique Marquis, *Un quotidien pour l'Église: L'Action catholique, 1910–1940* (Montreal: Leméac, 2004).
17 Jacques Kayser, *Le quotidien français* (Paris: Armand Colin, 1963).
18 Jean de Bonville, *Les quotidiens montréalais de 1945 à 1985: Morphologie et contenu* (Quebec City: Institut québécois de recherche sur la culture, 1995).
19 Dominique Marquis, 'La presse catholique au Québec, 1910–1940' (PhD thesis, Université du Québec à Montréal, 1999), chap. 6.
20 There is no simple English translation of *faits divers*. The term refers to short news items about crime, accidents, scandals, oddities, and so forth, that are generally considered as frivolous or non-serious news.
21 'L'année de l'Action Sociale Catholique,' *Almanach de l'Action sociale catholique* 47 (1923): 113.
22 de Bonville, *La presse québécoise de 1884 à 1914*, 231.
23 A detailed study of *Le Canada* remains to be done. *Le Devoir* has been the object of several studies, including my own, which looked at Henri Bourassa's concept of journalism. '*Le Devoir*, un produit unique,' *Les Cahiers du journalisme* 8 (décembre 2000): 60–74.

2 Old Media, New Media, and Competition: Canadian Press and the Emergence of Radio News

GENE ALLEN

The introduction of radio news in the 1920s and 1930s provides a valuable opportunity to study how a new medium affects an established predecessor in the quest for audiences, revenue, and cultural legitimacy. It allows one to address some general questions about media evolution: does the example of radio suggest that new media are necessarily antagonistic to existing ones? In what ways did this new medium present challenges to, or complement, its predecessor, the newspaper industry? Did it develop entirely new functions or mainly fulfil existing functions in new ways? What specific aspects of business strategy, audience response, and changing political-economic structures account for the way radio found its place as a news medium during these years?

This paper examines the introduction of broadcast news in Canada through the actions of the members of the Canadian Press (CP) news agency. CP is a co-operative whose members include virtually every newspaper in Canada. It was formally established in 1917 (although Canadian newspaper publishers had been adopting progressively more systematic arrangements for the exchange of telegraphic news since 1903), and had been in operation for only five years when radio first came to its attention.[1] CP's members dominated the coverage of local news in Canada; through a telegraphic exchange system, this was the backbone of the agency's domestic Canadian news service. In addition, CP as a collective controlled the crucial resource of international telegraphic news through its alliance with the American news agency Associated Press (AP). The new medium of radio had to deal with CP and its members for access to both these kinds of news. Fortunately for the historian, CP kept detailed and candid records of its many discussions and disagreements about radio news, providing an excellent vantage point from which to study how newspapers and radio negotiated this unfamiliar new ground.

Some scholars have used the metaphor of a 'press–radio war' as a way of explaining the relationship between newspapers and broadcast news in the 1920s and 1930s.[2] A careful examination of CP's experience, however, suggests that while the 'war' metaphor captures some important aspects of newspapers' role in the emergence of radio in Canada, it does not provide a good overall explanation. Rather, the conflicts between some (not all) newspapers and radio are better understood by examining the evolution of the competitive environment in which they operated.

To understand a competitive situation clearly, it is important to see how *all* the participants in a particular market interacted with each other. This 'ecological approach' borrows from John Nerone's analysis of the antebellum Cincinnati press. Nerone suggests that a medium should be considered not so much a thing in itself as 'exactly what the word suggests: something in between other things ... a set of relationships within a social and cultural ecology.'[3] The proper unit of study 'is not the individual medium, but the whole set of media within a particular ecology.' While the present study goes beyond the local scale which Nerone suggests is particularly appropriate for an examination of this kind, it attempts to keep the overall ecological context in mind when moving among local, regional, national, and continental scales. In this context, it becomes clear that some of the main methods newspapers adopted to deal with radio competition were very much like the methods they had previously used, and continued to use, to meet competition from other newspapers. Furthermore, many newspapers used radio in an effort to gain competitive ground on their newspaper rivals. The central fact in these circumstances was competition rather than the particular medium in which it was expressed.

Besides the ecological approach suggested by Nerone, this chapter also uses Harold Innis's categories of time and space to seek to understand the nature of the competitive threat that radio presented to newspapers.[4] In terms of time, radio continued the reshaping of the time structure of information that is traditionally associated with the telegraph. The telegraph allowed the virtually instantaneous dissemination of information to a great many recipients simultaneously; in practical terms, this meant that Kingston or Peterborough, Ontario, received the latest London news or Liverpool grain prices at virtually the same time that New York or Toronto did. But the telegraph only took the revolution partway, one might say: rather than disseminating information to individual readers, it disseminated information to newspapers, which published (more or less) once every twenty-four hours[5] and, in Canada, usually no more than six days a week. For readers, then, the time structure of telegraphic news meant that they received a single, quite large block of miscellaneous, up-to-date information at about the same time once every twenty-four hours. As long as a newspaper had a current connection to a telegraphic news agency, its news would generally be as up-to-date as anyone else's.[6]

Radio, in effect, completed the instantaneousness revolution. News bulletins could now be broadcast at any given moment, as soon they were received, and they would reach thousands of listeners directly and immediately. In theory, every piece of news that appeared in the morning edition of the *Globe* or any other paper could have been broadcast earlier, at some point in the previous twenty-four hours.[7] Since newspapers depended heavily on being timely and up-to-date to attract readers, this quite radical shift in the time structure of information was potentially devastating. The ability to broadcast news events live, as they actually unfolded, made radio an even more formidable competitor.[8] There were, then, obvious and pressing grounds for concern.

Radio also changed the way information was disseminated in space. Newspapers have to be physically transported to their readers. Consider the example of a metropolitan newspaper that seeks to expand its circulation among out-of-town readers. It takes at least ninety minutes to transport a newspaper published in Toronto the sixty miles to, say, Kitchener, Ontario. During that ninety minutes, a competing Kitchener-based paper could continue to put later news developments into that day's edition before starting its press run, thus publishing more up-to-date news than its Toronto rival while still reaching readers at the same time. But radio was different: a Toronto station with a sufficiently strong signal could reach Kitchener and Toronto at exactly the same time, which gave the Toronto radio station a spatial reach that the newspaper did not possess, and a stronger competitive position in the distant market. The telegraph had tended to strengthen the position of local newspapers against their metropolitan rivals, but radio worked in the opposite direction.[9] When radio stations were coordinated into networks, the changing spatial reach of information that resulted was revolutionary. Now hundreds of thousands or millions of people in widely distant locations – all across Canada, for example, or all around the British Empire – could receive exactly the same information at exactly the same time.[10] These considerations remind us that many newspapers had strong reasons to feel threatened by radio. The structure of time and the organization of space on which their businesses depended were radically called into question by radio's instantaneousness and its regional, national, and continental reach.

In practical business terms, the basic concern was that radio would cut into newspaper circulation and advertising revenue by being faster with the news. The historical record is full of examples of newspapers in the 1920s and 1930s that tried various measures to stop this feared loss of circulation and advertising revenue. In Canada, the United States, and Britain, one sees the same demands: radio news broadcasts should be restricted to specific times when they would not scoop newspaper coverage; radio must not be allowed to gather news on its own; radio stations should not be allowed simply to read news from newspapers over the air without permission.[11] Even newspapers that embraced radio often did so in ways that were intended to limit the full exploitation of its temporal and spatial advantages in disseminating news. In short, there were systematic attempts to make radio depend on newspapers for its news, which in turn would allow the newspapers to impose restrictions that nullified radio's competitive advantages. In Innis's terms, some (but not all) newspapers wanted to maintain a monopoly of knowledge by restricting radio's capacity to operate as a medium for news.[12]

This, broadly, seems consistent with the assessment that something like a press–radio war was indeed going on. But when one looks in detail at how the members of Canadian Press responded to the emergence of radio news, the picture quickly becomes more complicated.

Although there were significant continuities throughout the whole period under study, it is useful to distinguish three main phases. The first period, from 1922 until 1931, was characterized by tremendous disarray. CP adopted a series of ad hoc, often contradictory policies about radio, and even these were often ignored by its members. Local and regional competition was the key underlying factor. The second phase began in 1931, as radio became a more serious competitor for advertising revenue and the Canadian regulatory environment underwent radical changes with the advent of the Canadian Radio Broadcasting Commission (CRBC). CP now began to approach radio much more systematically, and at a national level. The crucial decision came in 1933, when the formation of a strategic alliance with the CRBC saw CP as an organization become a provider of radio news for the first time. In the third period, from 1935 to 1941, U.S.-based radio news services began expanding aggressively into Canada. This inexorably forced CP, which was now committed to the radio news business for better or worse, into a series of retreats from what had previously been considered the bedrock of its approach, notably strict time limits on when radio news could be broadcast and a ban on commercial sponsorship. By 1941, these competitive pressures effectively left CP with no choice but to become one of several commercial suppliers of radio news, imposing very few restrictions on its clients.

Throughout these years, competition of different kinds and at different levels ebbed, flowed, and overlapped. At least seven distinct competitive relationships can be identified: (1) between newspapers that owned (or otherwise had connections with) radio stations and those that did not; (2) between radio stations that had newspaper connections and those that did not; (3) among news organizations (newspapers and radio stations) within cities; (4) among news organizations in cities and those in their surrounding regions; (5) between public and commercial radio stations after 1933; (6) between CP as a provider of news to radio and other radio news services after 1935; and (7) between Canadian and American sources of news. With all these different currents in operation, the overall competitive ecology at any point was highly complex. An Innisian focus on the changing temporal and spatial dynamics of the Canadian market for news helps explain how radio as a new journalistic medium took shape in these decades.

A Decade of Disarray: 1922–1931

Right from the beginning, CP's members had great difficulty coming up with rules governing the use of the agency's news on the air that would command general support. For a wide range of reasons, some CP members actively wanted to be involved in radio broadcasting, either as station owners or as regular news providers to stations they did not own. Their reasons were often promotional, using radio, in effect, as an advertising vehicle for their newspapers. Some were more aggressive, seeing radio news as a way to gain competitive ground on their rivals in timeliness of coverage, circulation, and advertising; and this prompted others to adopt radio for defensive reasons. For one or another of these reasons, many of the largest and most powerful newspapers in Canada embraced radio in the 1920s: *La Presse* of Montreal; the *Toronto Daily Star, Globe, Mail and Empire,* and *Telegram*; the *Van-*

couver Sun and *Province*; the *Calgary Herald* and *Edmonton Journal*; the *Halifax Herald*; the *London Free Press*, and many others (including smaller papers). In many situations these radio-affiliated newspapers were prepared to support some restrictions on the use of CP news on the air, but they were hardly dyed-in-the-wool opponents of broadcast news.[13]

On the other side of the issue stood a large number of mostly smaller newspapers (such as the *Stratford Beacon-Herald* and the *Oshawa Times*) which, particularly in the early years, were not involved with broadcasting. Many in this group were prepared to ban the use of CP news on the air entirely or restrict it severely, but they did not have sufficient collective weight within the organization to impose their wishes on the others. Even when restrictive policies were adopted, many papers ignored them with relative impunity.

The subject of radio news first came before CP's board of directors in March 1922, and the initial impulse was restrictive: a blanket ban on CP news being broadcast was proposed. At the annual general meeting two months later, however, the members decided to do nothing until they had a clearer idea of how radio would affect them. The tension between prohibition and tolerance that emerged at this early date would persist through the 1920s and 1930s.[14]

The following year, representatives of several western Canadian newspapers explained why they wanted to be involved with radio. John Imrie of the *Edmonton Journal* said radio was more important in the west than the east because of the long distances between settlements: 'The obligations of a daily newspaper to subscribers reached by the paper a day or even two days later than publication involved some departures from former ideas of publication and circulation.'[15] Farmers taking their grain to market needed to know the current price by early afternoon, well before that day's newspaper could reach them. The availability of radio could also promote settlement: 'Settlers were no longer isolated if they put radio sets in their homes.' For Burford Hooke of the *Regina Leader*, a mixed-media form called radiographing – sending radio reports to remote locations, where they were transcribed and posted on bulletin boards – was producing good results: 'The policy of this paper was to radiograph just enough to leave the people in suspense and make them buy papers.'[16] The notion that radio could 'whet, but not satiate' listeners' appetite for news was one that newspaper proponents of broadcasting asserted throughout the period.

The 1923 meeting also heard arguments about how and why radio news should be restricted. Arthur Penny of the *Quebec Chronicle* said restrictions should apply only when radio news altered the competitive balance in a particular location, but not otherwise. Stewart Lyon of the *Globe* insisted that radio stations be allowed to broadcast election returns supplied by CP only after the results had been printed in every newspaper in the city or region in question. The broadcasting of election results after 10 p.m. on an election night was accordingly banned, guaranteeing that those eager to know the outcome would have to turn to their morning or afternoon newspaper the following day.

The general policy that CP adopted that year on news broadcasting was restrictive, but not an outright prohibition. It specified that any news already published in a CP member's newspaper could be broadcast on a radio station which the newspaper owned or which it regularly supplied with news. (Several newspapers had regular supplier arrangements of this kind, which gave them on-air credit for the news broadcasts and thus had clear promotional value. The *Globe's* arrangement with CFRB in Toronto and the *Telegram's* alliance with CKGW were two prominent examples of this approach.) The purpose of this restriction was clearly to limit the disruption caused by the unprecedented speed of radio news, making sure that newspaper readers would not hear news on the air before they had a chance to read it. The only exceptions were bulletins specifically designated by CP management for radio broadcast, or news of overwhelming importance. It was generally agreed that bulletins about major accidents or natural disasters, for example, could not reasonably be withheld; these, known as extraordinary service, or EOS, bulletins, could be broadcast at any time.[17]

It is important to recognize that in imposing these time restrictions, the members of CP were not doing anything new. Co-operative news agencies such as Associated Press and Canadian Press are in some respects very unusual organizations. Their purpose is to allow extensive and valuable cooperation in newsgathering among member newspapers which are, in many cases, direct and bitter competitors. Therefore, the rules of these organizations included explicit and binding provisions to control competition, especially in relation to time.

The designation of every CP member as either a morning or afternoon paper was central to the time-based control of competition that was embedded in the agency's structure. Morning papers were allowed to publish only between the hours of 11 p.m. and 11 a.m., while afternoon papers were restricted to publishing between 11 a.m. and 11 p.m. The agency distributed its telegraphic news accordingly: a substantial news story would typically be transmitted once for all papers in the twelve-hour 'a.m.' publication cycle, with an updated version being sent once during the 'p.m.' cycle. In a city with one morning and one afternoon paper, this meant that they interfered with each other, competitively speaking, as little as possible – the morning paper could go out to its readers secure in the knowledge that the CP news it published was substantially fresher than anything that had appeared in the previous day's afternoon paper, and the afternoon paper had the same assurance. These rules were strictly enforced.[18] Thus when the members of CP imposed time limits on radio news broadcasts to limit the competitive threat, they were simply applying rules of a kind they all accepted already. Radio was not treated as something requiring a radically new response; instead, the very real competitive pressures it represented were incorporated into a well-established structure for controlling competition among newspapers.[19]

In any case, this restrictive approach to radio news did not last long. In 1925, CP decided that members could broadcast CP news at any time during their approved hours of publication, which left open the possibility that stories could be broadcast before they were physically printed.[20] Radio news was now controlled in relation to time in exactly the same way that printed news was controlled. This was much less restrictive than Associated Press's approach at the time, which was close to an outright ban on the use of its news for broadcast.[21] The adoption of different approaches by the Canadian and American news agencies makes it clear that the inherent characteristics of newspapers and radio as media were not the only factors involved.

However, even CP's relatively liberal 1925 policy was difficult to enforce. Two Toronto morning newspapers, the *Globe* and the *Mail and Empire* – both involved in broadcasting news through continuing arrangements with independent radio stations – were the prime focus of complaint. These stations were including CP news from nearby Ontario towns on their noon radio broadcasts, which was outside their approved hours of publication as morning papers.

The problem (evidently a persistent one) was discussed at length during CP meetings in 1930, illustrating the complexity of the underlying competitive situation. H.W. Anderson of the *Globe* said the news being broadcast was lifted from the noon editions of the Toronto evening papers, not taken directly from CP; the *Globe* had a right to broadcast it 'because it was public property when published.'[22] But if this practice was allowed to continue, it would threaten one of CP's main organi-

zational characteristics: the requirement that all members provide the
local news they gathered to the co-operative, which then disseminated
it to other members. This obligation to provide 'return news,' as it was
called, was one of the great competitive strengths of co-operative agencies like CP and Associated Press, which thereby could offer extremely
broad geographical coverage without a large staff. However, problems
arose when competing newspapers – often metropolitan papers seeking additional circulation in nearby towns and cities – used the return
news supplied by a member to make inroads in its circulation area,
and the spatial reach of radio made this problem more acute. Many of
the elaborate rules that specified when and under what circumstances
members could use the co-operative's news were intended to assuage
such concerns about unfair competition.[23] Fred Livesay, CP's general
manager, pointed out to Anderson that Ontario papers outside Toronto
would simply withhold their return news if they risked being scooped
by Toronto-based broadcasts, and others supported this view. A.R.
Alloway of the *Oshawa Times* (Oshawa is thirty miles east of Toronto)
said that when news was broadcast before it could be published locally,
it 'decreased the value of that news and lowered the prestige of the
newspaper.'[24]

> It was embarrassing to be told by people on the street that certain things
> had happened that morning in Oshawa, for instance. Radio listeners
> thought they were giving the paper a tip, whereas the paper had the story
> in type waiting for presses to run. The practice knocked the props from
> under the smaller Ontario papers, who were subjected to enough legiti-
> mate penetration by Toronto papers in their home circulation field, with-
> out radio aggravating it.[25]

To satisfy the complaining members, both the *Globe* and *Mail and Empire*
promised to cease broadcasting CP news from Toronto noon editions.

Not all newspapers agreed with this solution, however. Thomas
Miller of the *Moose Jaw Times-Herald* said his paper was mainly concerned about competition from commercial broadcasters that had no
newspaper affiliation, not other newspapers that were involved with
broadcasting. The unaffiliated commercial stations simply read on the
air the news that appeared in the noon editions of the Winnipeg papers;
since CP had no way of controlling these private broadcasters, 'it hardly seemed fair to penalize newspaper broadcasting stations' that competed with them by restricting what the newspaper-affiliated stations

could broadcast and when.[26] The presence of private broadcasters who could operate entirely independently of CP meant that limiting radio news on stations affiliated with CP members would simply weaken their competitive position.

In any case, it soon became apparent that the Toronto newspapers had no intention of honouring the agreement. John Scott of the *Mail and Empire* admitted that 'all the Toronto papers were broadcasting news in self-defence, because commercial broadcasting organizations picked up Canadian Press news and broadcast it after it was published without any interference.'[27] Livesay concluded that the regulation restricting the hours of broadcasting had been brought into contempt by 'the failure of the Toronto members to respect it in any way, shape, or form' and should therefore be rescinded. Yet another new approach was now proposed: members could not broadcast CP news at all unless it was classified 'Bulletin MBB (May Be Broadcast).'[28] This would explicitly leave all decisions about what could be broadcast to CP's management. But if the new restrictions were to be effective, Livesay warned, the board of directors must be prepared to 'drastically deal with all breaches.'

The rules under which Associated Press made its news available to U.S. stations also affected the competitive situation in Canada. Many American stations could be heard in Canada, and powerful stations like CFRB in Toronto and CKAC in Montreal were affiliates of American networks. Similarly, Canadian broadcasts could reach U.S. listeners. In March 1925, AP's general manager, Kent Cooper, complained to Livesay that a Montreal station had broadcast an AP news item about recent tornadoes. These reports, which violated AP's ban on the use of its news on the air at the time, could be heard throughout the U.S. northeast. Cooper urged CP to seek a Canadian court ruling establishing property right in news, which had been recognized in the United States by the Supreme Court in 1918 and could therefore be used to stop the unauthorized use of AP news by U.S. broadcasters. CP, however, was never able to obtain such a ruling in Canada. All Livesay could do in this case was to warn CP members that they were not allowed to broadcast AP news.[29]

Soon, however, the situation was reversed. CP's initial approach to covering the federal election of 29 October 1925 was to reiterate the existing ban on the broadcasting of CP-provided election returns after 10 p.m. on voting day.[30] Four days after that policy was restated, however, Livesay essentially abandoned it. AP, facing competition from other U.S. news agencies that dealt more liberally with radio, had now dropped its ban on broadcasting election results,[31] and CP quickly followed suit. A special, limited election service would be prepared for radio use only, reflecting the principle that radio news 'should be designed to whet the appetite rather than satiate it.' Overall national and provincial results would be reported along with summaries from the larger cities, and the election or defeat of prominent candidates, but no individual constituency results beyond that.[32] Only those broadcasters owned by or otherwise connected with a local newspaper would be allowed to use the CP service. The intention was to strengthen the competitive position of radio stations allied with CP members against stations without such a connection, not to pit newspapers against radio per se.

This sudden change of heart showed clearly that AP's decisions had to be taken into account in Canada. This was underscored again in 1930, after AP had decided to allow major news bulletins to be broadcast outside the publication hours of member newspapers that supplied news to radio stations. CP's policy at the time was more restrictive, but as Livesay observed candidly, when Canadians could hear such bulletins on American stations (or Canadian affiliates of U.S. networks) but not their own, the Canadian broadcasts 'became jokes.'[33] CP's rules were amended accordingly and promptly. The pervasive continental dynamic of radio, as Mary Vipond has observed, was a permanent feature of the competitive ecology in which Canadian broadcasters (and the newspapers with which some of them were connected) had to operate.[34]

Strategic Alliance with Radio: 1931–1935

For almost a decade after 1922, CP's attitude toward radio was characterized by disagreement and disarray. There had been a rapid succession of changing and sometimes contradictory policies, often improvised to address the most recent problem to arise. Not until April of 1931 did CP decide to address the question of radio in a comprehensive way. Eighteen months had passed since the Royal Commission on Radio Broadcasting had called for the nationalization of radio in Canada, and it was clear that the regulatory framework for broadcasting was about to undergo major and systematic changes, with important consequences for Canadian newspapers. Victor Sifton told CP's board of directors that the time had come for the members of CP to work together with the Canadian Daily Newspapers Association (CDNA) (the newspapers' industrial and lobbying organization), looking into 'all angles' of the radio question. 'If a joint committee decided radio was a great menace, it could decide on a programme. If all members pressed for and obtained the nationalization of radio, their troubles would be ended because broadcasting of news could be controlled and advertising probably would be cut out entirely.'[35] The involvement of the CDNA signalled that radio was no longer simply a matter affecting the supply of news, which was CP's main responsibility; the whole economic basis of the industry was at stake.

The emergence of advertising as a central issue in newspapers' dealings with radio had much to do with the development of a more united front in the early 1930s. As Mary Vipond has noted, advertising was not an established method of financing radio broadcasting until the late 1920s, so newspapers had not previously considered radio a serious competitor in this respect.[36] In 1931, though, M.E. Nichols, general manager of the *Winnipeg Tribune*, told his colleagues that radio advertising revenue in the United States had now reached $50 million annually, about one-quarter of the total advertising revenue of daily newspapers.[37] The situation was not that bad in Canada yet, but radio broadcasting could quickly become 'a serious menace to Canadian newspapers' if no action was taken. A permanent CP-CNDA committee was established whose sole purpose was to study the effect of radio advertising on newspaper revenue and to find ways of limiting it.[38] By 1935, Livesay was reporting to CP's board of directors that commercial radio stations considered news the best seller for advertisers and the cheapest commodity they had to offer.[39] It was reported that commercial broadcasters could get three times as much for advertisements immediately before and after news broadcasts than at any other time.[40]

The sharpening focus on lost advertising revenue marked a major shift in the way CP members approached the problem of radio. For the first time, the radio medium as a whole was seen in opposition to the newspaper medium as a whole, rather than as a new but far from decisive factor overlaid on existing patterns of competition. In this spirit, Nichols urged everyone to put aside local competitive issues, which had dominated CP's approach to radio so far, and concentrate on the threat they faced in common. Frederick Ker of the *Hamilton Spectator* said that Britain's policy of full public ownership offered the 'surest means for safeguarding the great potentialities of radio from exploitation for private profit instead of the welfare of the public.' This would also allow CP to make arrangements with a 'responsible' government body for broadcasting news, leaving newsgathering in the hands of the newspapers.[41]

Joseph Atkinson, publisher of the *Toronto Daily Star*, had been one of the first newspapermen in Canada to operate a radio station; the *Star* still owned CFCA, though it operated at a mere 500 watts.[42] He too agreed that radio was a 'growing menace' to newspapers. Atkinson suggested approaching the subject under four general headings: (1) should broadcasting of news be limited to newspapers; (2) should newspapers broadcast at all; (3) would the interests of the newspaper industry be better guarded if radio broadcasting was nationalized; (4) invasion of radio on advertising revenues. While many newspaper executives were in favour of nationalization, this view was not unanimous. Oswald Mayrand of *La Presse*, which operated one of the largest and most successful newspaper-affiliated radio stations in the country, said he believed the people of Quebec would not support nationalization, though they did favour government regulation of broadcasting.[43]

Unable to reach a common position on nationalization,[44] the CP-CDNA committee decided to focus on a much more limited step that almost everyone could accept: a proposal to stop, or at least limit, the publication of radio stations' broadcast schedules in newspapers. Since many radio programs now included a sponsor's name as part of the title, the publishers considered such listings to be unpaid advertising; even if no brand name was used, publicizing sponsored programs seemed too much like helping a direct competitor for advertising revenue. As a first step, it was agreed to limit radio schedules to announcing programs of outstanding interest, eliminating all trade names. Stations that wished to list sponsored programs would have to purchase advertising space.[45]

As long as every newspaper in a particular market adopted the same approach – that is, if no one took advantage of a competitor's limitations on radio listings by resuming their publication in order to poach readers – this would have few competitive repercussions. Atkinson said he was prepared to eliminate from the *Star*'s news columns all reference to its own radio station and programs, to stop publishing all radio schedules, and even to stop broadcasting news altogether – but only if all the other Toronto papers would do the same. But inducing everyone to adopt the same approach was difficult. With four competing dailies in Toronto, the competitive situation was inherently unstable, as W.B. Preston of the *Brantford Expositor* observed: 'While the Globe,

Mail and Empire and Star were willing to reach a fair agreement [about the broadcasting of news], The Telegraph [*Telegram*] would not as long as The Star operated its own station.'[46]

Besides limiting radio schedule listings, CP also wanted to prevent commercial stations from simply appropriating news that appeared in local newspapers. To have any success in this area, CP would have to explore the possibility of having property rights in news legally recognized, as was the case in the United States.[47] Before anyone could see where this might lead, however, the Canadian radio landscape was radically altered by the establishment of the Canadian Radio Broadcasting Commission in 1932. The CRBC's plan to operate six very powerful, publicly owned stations across Canada, while allowing private stations to continue in operation under its regulations, changed the competitive radio–newspaper ecology dramatically. CP members could now focus their attention on the new national broadcaster-regulator and seek to establish working arrangements for radio news that would apply to most of Canada. The CRBC's determination not to rely on advertising for its stations meant the threat of revenue loss to newspapers was reduced; its regulatory powers might bring a ban on the scalping of newspaper stories by broadcasters. But if CP was to take advantage of the possibilities of greater control over radio news offered by the creation of the CRBC, it would have to become an official and systematic news provider to the national radio service. This was a major change, since previously the authorized use of CP news on radio had been limited to radio stations that were allied with individual CP members. Now, for the first time, CP as an organization was considering providing news to a radio service with which none of its member newspapers had any direct connection.

As soon as Hector Charlesworth, a prominent magazine editor and critic, was appointed chief commissioner of the CRBC, Livesay contacted him to suggest that the commission copy an Australian rule prohibiting the broadcasting of news without consent of the agency or newspaper that supplied it. Charlesworth was sympathetic, inviting CP to send a 'strong delegation' to Ottawa to discuss its request. At this meeting, in February 1933, Charlesworth told the more than twenty CP members present that the CRBC wanted to have daily news broadcasts on its stations, especially to serve remote areas, and that he hoped arrangements to provide these could be worked out with CP.[48]

Soon afterward, the government gave Canadian newspapers much of the protection they had been demanding. An order-in-council prohibited Canadian radio stations from broadcasting news taken from any newspaper or news agency unless it was a bulletin prepared by CP 'for the express use of broadcasting stations,' local news provided by arrangement with a local newspaper, or news gathered directly by the station or any newsgathering agency it employed. This would still allow newspaper-allied stations to broadcast news as they had been doing, but the scalping of newspaper reports by unaffiliated private stations was banned. With this explicit protection, CP's quest to establish property right in news was no longer necessary. Livesay later told CP members that the order-in-council came as 'a complete surprise,' adding that the commission was clearly in earnest with its plans to broadcast news to parts of the country where newspapers were unavailable, 'and if CP refused to supply the bulletins the commission would have to go elsewhere.'[49]

Charlesworth then invited CP to present a proposal for news broadcasts, and a draft agreement was soon reached. CP would provide four news bulletins a day to CRBC stations, each of five minutes' duration (300–400 words), to be broadcast at 8 and 11 a.m. and 4 and 9 p.m. It was to be paid $6,000 annually for this service. The news broadcasts were to be sponsored by the commission, with due credit given to CP. CP news was not under any circumstances to be sold to advertisers; there could be no question of CP itself participating in the siphoning-off of advertising revenue from newspapers. All in all, the quid pro quo could not have been clearer: Charlesworth stressed that once the service began, the commission would deal effectively with complaints from CP members about theft of their news by competing commercial broadcasters.[50]

As usual when radio was involved, the draft agreement with the CRBC provoked heated debate among CP's members. C.O. Knowles of the *Telegram* thought it was a mistake to sell news 'to a rival organization, radio' and suggested nothing more was needed than some effective protection against the 'theft' of news. Moreover, the sample newscasts which Livesay had provided were both too informative and too numerous, 'exactly what shouldn't be put on the air.' Knowles also recommended against accepting any payment from the CRBC, a position that many members agreed with.[51] Some complained that a noon broadcast would bring back the old problem of regional stories being heard on the air before the provincial papers were on the street, while others said a 4 p.m. newscast would hurt the sales of evening papers, and others still said the 10 p.m. broadcast would be bad for morning papers.[52]

Supporters of the CRBC agreement generally presented it as a lesser evil of one kind or another. John McNeil of the *Montreal Gazette* expressed a common view, observing that since news broadcasts appeared inevitable, it was better if they were under CP's control. Ker of the *Hamilton Spectator* urged those who opposed the deal to remember that they were 'shivering in their boots' a year ago. Now, with Canadian radio under public control, Canadian publishers were the envy of their American counterparts. The CRBC agreement gave them real protection against news theft, reduced the frequency and duration of news broadcasts, and ensured that CP controlled their contents. If the agreement was rejected, Ker concluded, it was only a matter of time before Canadian broadcasters set up a rival newsgathering organization, as was already being planned in the United States.

The agreement was accordingly approved, with the provisos that no payment be accepted, that the number of daily newscasts be reduced from four to two, and that they be scheduled so as not to 'prejudice unduly' daily paper publication (6:30 and 10:30 p.m. were eventually decided on).[53] The next year, the two bulletins were consolidated into one ten-minute broadcast at 10:45 p.m.[54] CP's relationship with the CRBC was like a strategic alliance with a powerful and potentially threatening neighbour, an alliance that sought to limit (but not eliminate) the threat and to find ways of working together that were mutually beneficial. Any drawbacks could be justified on the grounds that the alternative – not having an alliance – was likely to be worse. CP, representing nearly all of Canada's newspapers, was now formally and irrevocably in the business of radio news.

Opening the Floodgates: 1935–1941

Having made this fundamental change in orientation, CP soon found that new competition pushed it relentlessly to loosen the restrictions that initially appeared so advantageous. Less than two years after the CRBC agreement was adopted, Livesay was warning the board about a new threat from radio: an 'invasion' of Canada by Transradio and other U.S. radio news services.

Transradio was one of several agencies established in the spring of 1934 to serve independent radio stations in the United States. This was a response to the Biltmore Agreement of December 1933, in which the main U.S. radio networks, CBS and NBC, reached an agreement with AP, United Press, and Hearst's International News Service to accept severe limitations on their broadcasting of news. Many independent stations remained outside the agreement, however, which meant they needed news services to supply them. Transradio was founded by Herbert Moore, a former UP writer who had been news editor for the CBS news division until it was abolished as part of the Biltmore Agreement.[55] Now Transradio was expanding into Canada, where the restrictive rules adopted by the CRBC and CP offered similar opportunities to make money by supplying news to independent stations on more favourable terms. Its presence in the Canadian market as a potential nationwide competitor to CP radically changed the competitive ecology once again.

Transradio offered two major advantages to private broadcasters competing with the CRBC stations supplied by CP: its newscasts could be sold to sponsors, and it offered four broadcasts throughout the day, rather than a single broadcast late in the evening. To meet this competition, Livesay recommended that CP also allow its CRBC news bulletins to be broadcast during the day, putting aside the traditional objection that this would hurt sales of afternoon papers.[56] The board agreed, saying it was now in CP's interest to be 'generous rather than parsimonious' with radio news bulletins. If CP was not prepared to compete aggressively, Transradio – which had already picked up clients in Montreal and western Canada – would spread 'like German measles.'[57]

Livesay also recommended that CP ease the restrictions on commercial radio stations allied with member newspapers – otherwise, the stations would procure their news elsewhere.[58] As matters stood, many CP members were simply ignoring the rules. W.B. Preston of Brantford confessed that for a while his paper 'conformed religiously' to the restrictions on using CP news for broadcasting, but finding that other newspapers' broadcasts were so much more comprehensive, he was 'compelled to follow suit or get off the air.'

The policy that CP adopted in November 1935 was extremely liberal: any member newspaper could broadcast any of the agency's news at any time on a station with which it was connected. The sole limitation was that there could be no more than three broadcasts every twenty-four hours, with each broadcast lasting no longer than ten minutes. The attempt to control the time advantages of broadcast news lay, for the moment at least, in tatters; only the ban on selling CP's news to commercial sponsors remained. As the market for radio news grew – Livesay observed that 'news on the air in one form or another has become such a marketable commodity that the radio listener is deluged with it, good, bad, and indifferent'[59] – and as new competitors entered the market, the CRBC agreement turned out not to be the panacea that many CP members had hoped for.

As Transradio continued making inroads into the Canadian market, the rules were relaxed even further in 1936. Taking a more nationalistic approach than had previously been seen, CP's president told the annual meeting that it was a matter of vital national welfare for radio news to be in the hands of an organization like CP that was devoted to the Canadian and British viewpoint, and 'whose principles of accuracy and impartiality in the preparation of its news have been well established.'[60] It was now recommended that CP prepare and supply four news bulletins a day to *all* radio stations, regardless of CRBC or newspaper affiliation. The only charge would be $10 weekly for distribution by telegraph.[61] Sponsorship was still banned, however; any station using the CP material had to give credit to CP and the local newspaper. Livesay acknowledged that this was a radical departure from past practice but defended it as the only way to meet the competition from Transradio, by now 'strongly entrenched' in western Canada and northern Ontario and making headway in Quebec and the Maritimes.

Once again, there was substantial dissension over the new approach. Although the *Toronto Daily Star* had been involved with broadcasting since 1922 (and still was), Joseph Atkinson now concluded that 'news on the air took the edge off the public appetite for news. Broadcasting was not worth what it cost.' While the Moose River mine collapse story was unfolding in April, the *Star* had sold 10,000 extras but would have sold 60,000 if not for radio competition. Atkinson repeated that if others stopped broadcasting news, he would do the same, and would be quite happy to see no CP news being broadcast.[62] Knowles of the *Telegram* described the new arrangement as 'vicious'; the argument that the new policy was the only way to stop Transradio was rather like saying, 'We shoot ourselves rather than let Transradio shoot us.' H.P. Duchemin of the *Sydney Post* disagreed with both Torontonians. His paper, like most CP members, was not 'as happily situated as the Toronto Star and the Toronto Telegram with radio stations of their own'; since the new contract meant that news on the air had to be credited to CP and the local newspaper, it provided valuable free publicity.

The underlying competitive situation did not change much during the remaining years of the 1930s. The transformation of the CRBC into the CBC in 1936 promised a larger network of stations and expanded hours of daytime broadcasting, which CP members had seen in the past as ways of strengthening the position of their non-commercialized news against sponsored competitors. But even this did not have the hoped-for effect; if CP's noon news broadcast was made available on the new, broader network of CBC stations, many competing private stations that now used the free CP service would drop it for Transradio or another competitor, British United Press (BUP).[63] (As of 1938, Transradio was serving twenty-one stations across Canada and British United Press six, with contracts for six more.)[64] The fact that competing agencies' broadcasts could be sold for sponsorship, important as it was, was not the only consideration. The managers of stations affiliated with the *Edmonton Journal* and *Calgary Herald* said that even without advertising revenue, they would be willing to pay three times more to receive BUP's service than the $10 a week that CP charged, citing the limited amount of western news in the CP daytime bulletins, their inferior radio style, duplication of items in the three bulletins, and the absence of special news flashes.[65] A more serious threat was that BUP was using its connections with radio stations to offer an inexpensive print news service to the newspapers affiliated with them, directly challenging CP in its core business. CP was clearly not keeping up with the competition, and positions that until now had been summarily rejected, such as allowing sponsorship of CP news, or charging a realistic fee to the CBC for its CP bulletins, were increasingly put forward.[66]

The outbreak of war in September 1939 seemed to give CP one more opportunity to realize its long-held goal of being designated the sole provider of national radio news (or at least of obtaining a ban on the sponsorship of news broadcasts, which would severely weaken its Transradio and BUP competitors). C.D. Howe, the minister of transport, was asked in October 1939 to grant CP a monopoly on the provision of radio news. When Howe noted that not all CP members supported this position, the request was amended to a ban on the sponsorship of news. But fifteen of eighty-nine CP members opposed this position too; dissenters included the *Telegram*; the *Montreal Gazette*; *La Presse* and five other French-language newspapers in Quebec; Roy Thomson's papers in North Bay, Sudbury, and Timmins; the *London Free Press*; and the *Victoria Times*.[67] The division between CP members that sought severe restrictions on radio news and those that did not was as persistent as ever. In fact, the later 1930s saw an increase in the number of newspapers owning radio stations, as also happened in the United States:

by 1939, more than one-third of Canadian private radio stations were either owned by or had affiliations with newspapers.[68]

In 1939, AP lifted the long-standing ban on allowing its newscasts to be sold for sponsorship,[69] and in the absence of a favourable government response to its latest request, CP decided it had to follow suit. With BUP using its growing radio connections and profits to offer newspapers a service that was much cheaper than CP's, the organization's very survival was at stake. The long battle to prevent sponsorship of CP news on the air was finally given up in March 1941;[70] this marked the emergence of CP's commercial broadcasting subsidiary, Press News, now known as Broadcast News or BN. (Two months earlier, CP had lost its position as the exclusive supplier of news to the CBC, which, no doubt, played a role in the decision too.)[71] In a memorandum summing up the tortuous path that had led to this point, CP's new general manager referred to 'the years of [CP's] struggle with the radio problem' – which summed up the experience in a phrase.[72]

Conclusion

While the version of events given here highlights the difficulties of adopting a 'press–radio war' interpretation, it does not differ radically from what some others have concluded. Mary Vipond, for example, has warned against adopting a 'black-and-white picture of a press-versus-radio battle.'[73] M.E. Nichols, who was a participant in many of these events and wrote the sole published history of CP, observed that radio 'provoked acute internal dissensions' inside the organization for fifteen years and that 'while carrying on collectively against the common foe, [CP members] also fought among themselves.'[74] Rather than belabouring these factual findings, I would like to address some methodological and conceptual points in conclusion and offer some suggestions about how to consider the relations between different media during periods of change.

First, the long and complicated story of how the members of Canadian Press responded to the emergence of radio news shows clearly the importance of keeping the competitive ecology of different markets in mind when explaining the emergence of a new medium. In this case, it is striking how many competitive cross-currents were at work more or less simultaneously. For example, the big Toronto newspapers competed vigorously with each other. If one had a radio outlet, most or all of the others felt they needed one too, if only for defensive reasons.

Overlaid on top of this was the metropolis–hinterland competition between big-city papers and those in nearby smaller towns. In this case, the adoption of radio built on (and made more acute) existing patterns of competition. Another important fault line separated *all* newspapers that had affiliations with radio stations, whether in big cities or smaller towns, from those that did not. These two groups were not necessarily direct competitors as in the previous case, but were nonetheless in quite persistent conflict, with radio-affiliated newspapers wanting fewer, and non-allied generally wanting more, restrictions on radio news.

From the point of view of broadcasters rather than publishers, there were competitive conflicts between stations that were allied with newspapers (and therefore operated under CP's relatively restrictive rules) and those without such connections. The non-allied stations, as we have seen, were free to take news from other suppliers that did not impose CP-like restrictions. This aspect of the competitive situation constantly militated against CP's adopting the highly restrictive approach to radio that many of its members wanted. Later, when CP became a provider of radio news in its own right, it had no choice but to respond to competition from Transradio and British United Press. If CP's newscasts were too few, too late, too dull, or did not allow commercial sponsorship, they would lose customers.

Finally, there was the competition between Canadian and American radio stations or networks. Since radio waves travelled easily across the border, and since several of the larger Canadian stations had U.S. network connections, CP had to take account of American rules and practices when adopting restrictions in Canada (and vice versa). Recall Livesay's comment that if U.S. stations were broadcasting major bulletins and their Canadian counterparts were not, the Canadian broadcasts 'became jokes.'

This competitive ecology was highly complex and dynamic. Some forms of competition had greater prominence in the early years of radio, while others became more important later. Before 1930, radio was mainly assimilated into structures of competition that were already well established among newspapers. These underlying local and regional tensions never disappeared, but with the establishment of the CRBC and CBC, competitive pressures also operated on a larger, national and continental, scale. Fundamental political decisions about the shape of Canadian broadcasting in the 1930s also brought new elements – notably the conflict between non-commercial and commercial broadcasters and an explicitly national framework – into the competitive mix. Over all, a focus on the changing competitive ecology of news media allows a more nuanced and persuasive account of how and why change occurred than such medium-centric notions as a 'press–radio war.' Conflict between newspapers and radio was an important part of the story, but it cannot explain everything. At times, the situation had the character of a civil war among newspapers as much as a war between different media.

A second point to consider is the usefulness of approaching these processes of change through the Innisian categories of time and space. Radio radically changed the time structure of news, and this threatened newspapers without radio outlets. CP's attempts to control the time structure of radio news to minimize its competitive advantages were simply an extension of its own well-established rules intended to control competition among its newspaper members. The imposition of time restrictions was not something new that emerged only in relation to radio.

In terms of space, radio disrupted the (already unstable) metropolis–hinterland relationship between big-city dailies and nearby small-town papers and thus put pressure on the always-vulnerable return news practices that CP depended on for a great deal of its news. At a broader level, the new spatial patterns of news that broadcasting established tended to bring American and Canadian news providers into a common framework. Newspapers, with their territorially restricted circulation areas, had not previously had to take account of competition on this scale.

Finally, this examination of how Canadian newspapers responded to the emergence of radio news raises a more general conceptual question: what exactly does it mean to speak of a medium or a new medium? Even with the best will in the world, it is difficult to avoid falling back on a definition of 'medium' that is implicitly technological or material. Thus, 'the press' is seen as one thing, defined by its use of newsprint and printing presses, a certain configuration of items on the page, and a particular range of sources and types of stories, while 'radio' is primarily understood as the technical capacity to broadcast sound over the air to a potentially unlimited number of receiving sets at a distance.

This is not to suggest that the technical characteristics of newspapers or radio do not matter or to deny that radio as a technology disrupted existing patterns of communication in important and lasting ways. But when one looks closely at how Canadian Press responded to the emergence of radio as a news medium, the striking thing is that 'newspapers' simply did not function as one entity – as one medium. They were, in fact, profoundly divided by different aspects of the competitive matrix in which they were jointly enmeshed, and as a result they adopted quite different (and changing) positions toward radio. Although the actual functioning of the competitive environment changed substantially during these years, the fact of division was fundamental and long-lasting.

The slipperiness of the term 'medium' emerges particularly strongly when one looks at radio in the 1920s and 1930s. The medium of radio that actually took shape in Canada was one very specific subset of a much wider range of possibilities that might have emerged out of the basic technology; it was shaped fundamentally by economic structures and political decisions. The introduction of limited public ownership and a non-commercial form of radio in the early 1930s sent the competitive dynamic, and hence the nature of the conflict between newspapers and radio, into different directions in Canada than in the United States. The nature of the conflict was changed yet again, not by the characteristics of radio per se, but by CP's decision to become systematically a provider of radio news and the ensuing conflict with Transradio (which was itself a very specific exploitation of the possibilities of the medium that arose in response to a specific competitive situation in the United States). In effect, the 'medium' that newspapers confronted was something quite different in Canada and the United States (and, one might add, in Britain). Some newspaper owners did attempt to enforce an Innisian monopoly of knowledge in relation to news, but the monopolistic impulse reflected particular and variable business strategies and did not inhere in the technology itself.

In the Epilogue to her study of press–radio relations in the United States, Gwenyth Jackaway quotes the historian of technology Carolyn Marvin: 'The history of media is never more or less than a history of their uses, which always leads us away from them to the social practices and conflicts they illuminate.'[75] In this case – and, I would suggest, in others – these practices and conflicts are usefully illuminated if we pay attention to patterns of competition, an approach that draws attention both to the divisions among owners of one medium (newspapers) and to the frequent overlapping of interests among different media (newspapers and radio).

Focusing on competition also helps explain why newspapers' embrace of radio was rarely whole-hearted. Most newspapers initially became involved with radio for promotional reasons and were not necessarily interested enough in the new medium for its own sake to commit the resources that a full-fledged involvement in broadcasting would require. A few, like *La Presse*, or the *London Free Press*, did make such a commitment; over all, though, it is striking how frequently newspaper publishers and editors became involved with radio, or remained involved, only because of what their competitors were doing or might do. Once any newspaper in a competitive market started using radio, for whatever reason, everyone else had to take account of the changed landscape. As more newspapers became drawn into this new form of competition, and as the spatial reach of radio became more extensive – moving from local, to regional, to national and continental scale – it became progressively harder for anyone to remain aloof. Over time, the impetus toward involvement with radio was cumulative. CP's decision to become a systematic provider of news to the CRBC in 1933 meant that every member of the co-operative – even those that as individual newspapers had no local involvement – was now implicated in radio.

The precise way in which the newspaper–radio relationship took shape in Canada reflected the interplay of economic, political, institutional, technological (and sometimes idiosyncratically personal)[76] factors. No predictive model could possibly capture the variations in how these factors interacted. As this chapter has attempted to show, however, that does not rule out systematic explanation and analysis of how and why the members of Canadian Press responded to the emergence of radio news in the 1920s and 1930s. A focus on the changing competitive ecology of markets – local, regional, national, continental (and eventually global) – is essential if we are to understand clearly the relations between new and older media.

NOTES

I am grateful to Daniel Robinson, Mary Vipond, and the anonymous reviewers for University of Toronto Press for their helpful comments. Research assistance was provided by June Morrow, Dafna Izenberg, Martin Kuebler, and Sarah Petrescu.

1 For the origins of CP, see Gene Allen, 'News across the Border: Associated Press in Canada, 1894–1917,' *Journalism History* 31, no. 4 (Winter 2006): 206–16, and M.E. Nichols, *(CP): The Story of The Canadian Press* (Toronto: Ryerson Press, 1948), 1–135.
2 For recent examples of this argument, see Gwenyth L. Jackaway, *Media at*

War: Radio's Challenge to the Newspapers, 1924–1939 (Westport, CT: Praeger, 1995); Sian Nicholas, 'All the News That's Fit to Broadcast: The Popular Press Versus the BBC, 1922–45,' in Peter Catterall, Colin Seymour-Ure, and Adrian Smith, eds, *Northcliffe's Legacy: Aspects of the British Popular Press, 1896–1996* (London: Macmillan, 2000), 121–48. In a recent survey history – Michael Emery, Edwin Emery, and Nancy Roberts, *The Press and America: An Interpretive History of the Mass Media* (Needham Heights, MA: Allyn and Bacon, 2000), 320–1 – the term 'newspaper–radio war' is used but is limited to the period of acute conflict in the mid-1930s. The Canadian literature is more nuanced on this point; see Mary Vipond, 'The Continental Marketplace: Authority, Advertisers and Audiences in Canadian News Broadcasting, 1932–1936,' *Journal of Radio Studies* 6, no. 1 (1999): 169–84. One U.S. scholar has explicitly questioned the press–radio war interpretation; see Alf Pratte, 'Going along for the Ride on the Prosperity Bandwagon: Peaceful Annexation, Not War, between the Editors and Radio, 1923–1941,' *Journal of Radio Studies* 2 (1993): 123–39.

3 John C. Nerone, 'A Local History of the U.S. Press: Cincinnati, 1793–1858,' in William S. Solomon and Robert W. McChesney, eds, *Ruthless Criticism: New Perspectives in U.S. Communication History* (Minneapolis and London: University of Minnesota Press, 1993), 39. See also Richard L. Kaplan, *Politics and the American Press: The Rise of Objectivity, 1865–1920* (Cambridge: Cambridge University Press, 2002), 56, 67; Thomas L. Walkom, 'The Daily Newspaper Industry in Ontario's Developing Capitalistic Economy: Toronto and Ottawa, 1871–1911' (PhD diss., University of Toronto, 1983). Dominique Marquis, in chapter 1 of this volume, adopts a similar approach.

4 For an account of Innis's use of these concepts in relation to telegraphic news and news agencies, see Gene Allen, 'Monopolies of News: Harold Innis, the Telegraph and Wire Services,' in Menaham Blondheim and Rita Watson, eds, *The Toronto School of Communications Theory: Interpretations, Extensions, Applications* (Toronto and Jerusalem: University of Toronto Press/Magnes Press, 2008), 170–98. See also James Carey, 'Technology and Ideology: The Case of the Telegraph,' and 'Space, Time and Communications: A Tribute to Harold Innis,' in Carey, *Communication as Culture: Essays on Media and Society* (New York: Routledge, 1992; first published 1989); and Dwayne Winseck, 'Back to the Future: Telecommunications, Online Information Services and Convergence from 1840 to 1910,' *Media History* 5, no. 2 (1999): 137–57.

5 In big cities particularly, newspapers published multiple editions and often published extras outside their usual edition times for very big stories.

There was thus some modification of the twenty-four-hour cycle, but this remained the basic form.

6 In view of this essay's questioning of the 'press–radio war' metaphor and its emphasis on points of continuity between the two media, it is interesting to note that a recent overview of the introduction of the telegraph similarly questions its revolutionary character. See Richard D. Brown, 'Early American Origins of the Information Age,' in Alfred D. Chandler, Jr, and James W. Cortada, eds, *A Nation Transformed by Information: How Information Has Shaped the United States from Colonial Times to the Present* (New York: Oxford University Press, 2000).

7 Radio bulletins were, of course, much shorter than newspaper articles, so that radio functioned somewhat as a headline service and generally did not compete with newspapers in depth and breadth of coverage.

8 See, for example, Jeff Webb, 'Canada's Moose River Mine Disaster (1936): Radio–Newspaper Competition in the Business of News,' *Historical Journal of Film, Radio and Television* 16, no. 3 (August 1996): 365–77.

9 Allen, 'Monopolies of News.'

10 As Jeff Webb has suggested with reference to the Moose River mine disaster of 1936 and Mary Vipond has done with the Empire Day broadcast of 1939, this experience of simultaneity across long distances had a powerful effect on listeners' sense of being connected to a larger social reality. Radio thus created even stronger 'imagined communities' than print. See Webb, 'Canada's Moose River Mine Disaster,' and Mary Vipond, 'The Mass Media in Canadian History: The Empire Day Broadcast in 1939,' *Journal of the Canadian Historical Association*, n.s., 14 (2003): 1–22. The widely used term 'imagined communities' was coined by Benedict Anderson, *Imagined Communities: Reflections on the Origin and Spread of Nationalism*, rev. ed. (New York and London: Verso, 1991).

11 For details of these demands in the United States, see Jackaway, *Media at War*; for Britain, see Nicholas, 'All the News That's Fit to Broadcast.'

12 As Paul Heyer and David Crowley have observed, Innis's notion of the monopoly of knowledge is complicated. At some points in his writing, Innis emphasizes the social basis of the monopoly of knowledge, describing it as a strategy by a particular class or social group to maintain its primacy, based on control of a particular mode or technology of communication; for an example, see Innis, *Empire and Communications*, rev. ed. (Toronto: University of Toronto Press, 1972), 24–5. In other places, however, the tendency toward a monopoly of knowledge is seen as inhering in the technology itself. See Heyer and Crowley, 'Introduction,' in Harold A. Innis, *The Bias of Communication* (Toronto: University of Toronto Press, 1991), xix–xx; Allen,

'Monopolies of News.' There are numerous references to the concept in Innis's work; see in particular 'The Concept of Monopoly and Civilization' in Harold A. Innis, *Staples, Markets and Cultural Change: Selected Essays*, ed. Daniel Drache (Montreal and Kingston: McGill-Queen's University Press, 1995), 384–9. With its emphasis on divisions among newspaper owners about how to respond to radio, the present essay interprets the effort to assert a monopoly of knowledge in the context of competing economic interests rather than the technologies involved.

13 There were similar divisions among newspapers in the United States; Jackaway, *Media at War*, 11, 15, 19. While Jackaway recognizes that conflict within the newspaper industry about how to respond to radio was wide-spread before 1933, she interprets this as a first, intra-industry, stage in a broader press–radio war.

14 Canadian Press documents, circular no. 4, J.F.B. Livesay (general manager of Canadian Press), to all members of Canadian Press Limited, 22 March 1922; minutes of the annual general meeting, 2 May 1922.

15 CP documents, minutes of the annual general meeting, 1 May 1923.

16 Ibid.

17 The assassination of a political leader or a major disaster are examples of EOS news – events of such great news value that the normal time restrictions on publication did not apply. Member newspapers were also permitted to publish extras containing EOS news outside their regular publication hours. It is noteworthy that in this instance, radio was assimilated to organizational rules that were already in general use for newspapers.

18 For a more detailed account of CP's structure and its relation to competition, see Allen, 'News across the Border.'

19 CP's bylaws also restricted competition in relation to space. Although the provision was used less often by the 1930s, every CP member had the right to object to a new CP franchise being awarded in its circulation area, usually defined as being the area within a radius of ten miles from the place of publication. See Allen, 'News across the Border,' 209.

20 CP documents, minutes of board of directors meeting, 29–30 April 1925.

21 The structure of AP's membership, in which smaller papers had a greater relative weight than they did in Canada and no one metropolitan area was dominant, may have contributed to this initially more restrictive policy. For AP's membership circa 1920, see Richard A. Schwarzlose, *The Nation's Newsbrokers*, vol. 2: *The Rush to Institution* (Evanston, IL: Northwestern University Press, 1990), 248–9. While AP was a co-operative like CP, its position was complicated by the fact that two competing, commercially

based news agencies in the United States (United Press and Hearst's International News Service) were entirely willing to sell their news to radio stations; Jackaway, 16–18. Under these circumstances, AP's more restrictive approach did not last; see pp. 56–7 below.

22 CP documents, minutes of board of directors meeting, 28 April 1930. Mary Vipond has noted that most news broadcasting during the 1920s consisted of reading items directly from newspapers. See Vipond, *Listening In: The First Decade of Canadian Broadcasting, 1922–1932* (Montreal and Kingston: McGill-Queen's University Press, 1992), 92–3.

23 Allen, 'News across the Border,' 211–12.

24 CP documents, minutes of board of directors meeting, 28 April 1930.

25 CP documents, minutes of board of directors meeting, 27–8 April 1931.

26 CP documents, minutes of board of directors meeting, 28 April 1930.

27 CP documents, minutes of meeting of Ontario members, 28 January 1931.

28 CP documents, minutes of board of directors meeting, 27–8 April 1931. In 1926, CP members had given Livesay the authority to decide which CP items could be broadcast. It was generally understood that more important news was eligible for broadcast, but not routine local stories. In 1929, the policy was spelled out more clearly: news eligible for broadcast must be of international or national importance, 'namely of wire bulletin value, and such routine news, sports, markets, etc. as the General Manager may from time to time specify.' CP documents, minutes of annual general meeting, 1 May 1929.

29 CP documents, minutes of the annual general meeting, 28 April 1925, Report of the management on radio broadcasts.

30 CP documents, Dominion Elections, 1925, circular no. 6, from J.F.B. Livesay, general manager, to all members and staff of the Canadian Press, 12 October 1925.

31 Jackaway, 18.

32 CP documents, Dominion Elections, 1925, circular no. 8, from J.F.B. Livesay, general manager, to all members of the Canadian Press, 16 October 1925.

33 CP documents, minutes of board of directors meeting, 28 April 1930.

34 Vipond, 'The Continental Marketplace,' 171.

35 CP documents, minutes of board of directors meeting, 27–8 April 1931.

36 Vipond, *Listening In*, 63.

37 According to figures provided by Gwenyth Jackaway, Nichols was exaggerating somewhat: in the United States, she notes, newspaper advertising revenue dropped from around $800 million in 1929 to $450 million in 1933, while radio advertising revenue rose during the same period from $40

million to $80 million, for a ratio that rose from around 5 per cent to 18 per cent. Jackaway, 20.

38 CP documents, minutes of meeting of joint radio committee, 1 June 1931, confidential.

39 CP documents, minutes of board of directors meeting, 4–5 November 1935, memorandum by J.F.B. Livesay, 'News on the Air.'

40 CP documents, minutes of meeting of the radio committee, 19 May 1936. In April 1931, Charles Bowman – editor of the *Ottawa Citizen*, one of the three members of the Royal Commission on Broadcasting, and a strong proponent of nationalization – gave a speech to the CDNA about radio's threat to newspaper revenue. The Canadian Radio League, with help from Joseph Atkinson of the *Toronto Daily Star*, distributed a pamphlet entitled 'Radio Advertising – A Menace to the Newspapers and a Burden to the Public' at around the same time. It stated that advertising revenue for radio stations in Canada and the United States had increased by 74 per cent in 1930, while newspaper ad revenue had dropped by 12 per cent during the same period. Some critics representing private broadcasters asserted that the Radio League was nothing more than a front for the newspaper industry. In fact, though, the newspaper industry was far from monolithic on the question of nationalizing radio: a survey of newspaper opinion in 1930 showed 34 in favour of nationalization, 16 against, and 14 non-committal. Vipond, *Listening In*, 232, 239.

41 CP documents, minutes of meeting of joint radio committee, 1 June 1931.

42 Mary Vipond has noted that, like the *Star*, many newspapers were unwilling to make the heavy investment required to operate a high-powered station; *Listening In*, 45.

43 CP documents, minutes of meeting of the joint radio committee, 1 June 1931, confidential.

44 CP documents, minutes of meeting of the joint radio committee, 1 June 1931. Many newspapers, especially the *Star* and the Southam and Sifton chains, strongly supported nationalization, while the *Telegram* and *La Presse* were strongly opposed. Other opponents included the *Financial Post*, the *Globe*, *London Free Press*, and *Calgary Albertan*; Vipond, *Listening In*, 232, 239.

45 The two dailies in Winnipeg, the *Free Press* and *Tribune*, took matters further, jointly agreeing in September 1930 to drop radio listings entirely and maintaining this policy until December 1931, when it was abandoned in the face of a threatened boycott of the *Free Press* by a coalition of advertisers representing broadcast stations, radio-equipment manufacturers, and

related businesses. CP documents, Nichols to Livesay, 29 December 1931; memorandum, 'The Winnipeg Newspapers and Radio Programmes,' 16 December 1931, enclosures in Livesay to joint radio committee, 2 January 1932.

46 CP documents, minutes of board of directors meeting, 6 October 1931. The *Telegram* was particularly upset because the *Star* station, CFCA, had been given its own frequency, while CKGW, the *Telegram*'s affiliate, had to share its frequency with another station, allowing it to broadcast only half-time. The *Telegram* asserted that Atkinson's connections with the Liberal government explained the different treatment. See Vipond, *Listening In*, 177–8, 203–4.

47 CP documents, minutes of board of directors meeting, 2 May 1932.

48 CP documents , minutes of meeting of radio subcommittee, 13 June 1933, enclosing memorandum from Livesay about proposed agreement with Canadian Radio Broadcasting Commission, 3 June 1933. The relationship that took shape between CP and the CRBC has been previously, and clearly, described by Vipond; see 'The Continental Marketplace,' 171–4.

49 CP documents, minutes of board of directors meeting, 5 June 1933.

50 CP documents, minutes of meeting of radio subcommittee, 13 June 1933, enclosing memorandum from Livesay about proposed agreement with Canadian Radio Broadcasting Commission, 3 June 1933.

51 CP documents, minutes of board of directors meeting, 5 June 1933.

52 Ibid.

53 CP documents, minutes of meeting of radio subcommittee, 13 June 1933. See also CP documents, minutes of board of directors meeting, 13 November 1933, management report. The Press-Radio Bureau in the United States, established after the Biltmore Agreement of December 1933, ended up adopting a pattern that was similar in many respects to the CP-CRBC agreement. See Jackaway, 27–9.

54 CP documents, minutes of board of directors meeting, 4–5 November 1935, memorandum by J.F.B. Livesay, 'News on the Air.'

55 Jackaway, 29.

56 CP documents, minutes of board of directors meeting, 4–5 November 1935, memorandum by J.F.B. Livesay, 'News on the Air.'

57 The phrase was Livesay's: CP documents, minutes of meeting of the board of directors, 2 November 1936.

58 CP documents, minutes of board of directors meeting, 4–5 November 1935.

59 CP documents, minutes of board of directors meeting, 4–5 November 1935, memorandum by J.F.B. Livesay, 'News on the Air.'

60 CP documents, minutes of annual general meeting, 29 April 1936.

61 CP documents, minutes of annual general meeting, 29 April 1936. Preston added in passing that the number of U.S. radio stations owned by newspapers had more than doubled from 1934 to 1935: 'if the policy of owning or controlling a radio station were generally adopted by Canadian publishers, it would go a long way toward solving the radio problem.'

62 CP documents, minutes of meeting of the radio committee, 19 May 1936.

63 CP documents, minutes of board of directors meeting, 11–12 October 1937. British United Press, an offshoot of United Press in the United States, was intended to provide UP with an entry into the Canadian and British markets.

64 CP documents, minutes of board of directors meeting, 3 October 1938.

65 CP documents, minutes of board of directors meeting, 11 October 1937.

66 CP documents, minutes of board of directors meeting, 11 October 1937 and 3 October 1938; management report, 27 April 1938; minutes of annual general meeting, April 1938.

67 CP documents, minutes of meeting of radio committee, 25 May 1940.

68 Frank W. Peers, *The Politics of Canadian Broadcasting, 1920–1951* (Toronto: University of Toronto Press, 1969), 286. Between 1934 and 1938, the number of U.S. radio stations that were owned by or affiliated with newspapers increased from around 100 to 211, accounting for about 30 per cent of the total; Jackaway, 32.

69 Jackaway, 33.

70 CP documents, minutes of the annual general meeting, 5 March 1941.

71 I am grateful to Mary Vipond for drawing this point to my attention.

72 CP documents, minutes of meeting of the board of directors, 3 March 1941, memorandum from J.A. McNeil on 'Conditional Plan for Sale of CP News for Radio Broadcasting.'

73 Vipond, 'The Continental Marketplace,' 171.

74 Nichols, *(CP)*, 258, 260.

75 Jackaway, 153, quoting from Carolyn Marvin, *When Old Technologies Were New: Thinking about Electric Communication in the Late Nineteenth Century* (New York: Oxford University Press, 1988).

76 For example, it is noteworthy that newspapers in structurally similar competitive positions, such as the *Star* and *Telegram* in Toronto, had different ideas about how best to compete, which led to their adopting quite different approaches to radio – one opposing, and one supporting, the idea of public ownership.

3 Britishness, the BBC, and the Birth of Canadian Public Broadcasting, 1928–1936

SIMON J. POTTER

Historians have paid insufficient attention to the role of British models, British identities, and direct British intervention in the birth of Canadian public broadcasting. This essay seeks to provide a corrective. It does not claim that there existed any centrally directed plan to shackle Canadian broadcasting in imperial chains. The relationships between Britain and Canada, and between British and Canadian identities, were more subtle than this in the interwar years. Rather, the essay argues that in order to understand how British influences shaped the Canadian broadcasting debate in the late 1920s and early 1930s, we need to examine the interplay of a range of domestic and overseas impulses. This involves a careful dissection not only of the roles played by bodies such as the British Broadcasting Corporation (BBC) and the Canadian Radio League (CRL), but also of the activities and motivations of particular people within those organizations. Only in this way can we construct a satisfactory account of how domestic and overseas impulses worked together to determine the outcome of the Canadian broadcasting debate.

Such a re-evaluation of the Canadian broadcasting debate is timely. Historians of the mass media are now widening the geographic scope of their inquiries, moving beyond nationally focused accounts and considering how media institutions became enmeshed in transnational structures.[1] An interest in the role of empires in this regard, particularly the British empire, is marked. While historians now generally shun simplistic arguments about 'media imperialism,' they are increasingly interested in how the mass media helped sustain (and erode) imperial structures of rule and imperial identities.[2] Historians of globalization have similarly emphasized how modern transnational communications technologies and infrastructures developed in the context of, and were shaped by, a world of empires.[3] The emergence of a globalized mass media, with all the inequalities that this entailed, was bound up with the history of empires.[4]

Where might a re-examination of the interwar Canadian broadcasting debate fit into this bigger picture? How can an analysis of this specific Canadian example inform scholars undertaking the broader task of writing imperial and transnational histories of the media? In answering these questions it is possible to build on and revise a rich historiography. The first historians to address the question of the birth of public broadcasting in Canada tended to adopt a nationalist perspective and to portray public broadcasting as a means to limit transnational influences. They suggested a straightforward clash between United States influence on the one hand, and English-Canadian nationalism on the other. According to this interpretation, public broadcasting was introduced as an alternative to the American commercial model, primarily in order to protect Canada's status as 'a separate nation on the North American continent' and to avoid 'cultural annexation' by the United States.[5] Such accounts tended to play down the fact that the idea of public broadcasting was closely connected with the model provided by the BBC and that it thus had transnational and imperial implications of its own.[6] Instead, they preferred to see the establishment of public broadcasting in Canada as a reflection and bulwark of a national identity generated from largely domestic sources. The historian and former Canadian Broadcasting Corporation (CBC) employee Frank W. Peers thus wrote of 'a unique Canadian system of broadcasting [reflecting] values different from those prevailing in the British or American systems.'[7]

Subsequently, historians began to question whether ideas about national identity and interest worked in such a straightforward fashion. New research showed that the motives of those advocating the introduction of public broadcasting in Canada during the 1920s and 1930s could not be reduced to a simple, monolithic nationalism. For a section of Canada's cultural elite, public broadcasting was not only a means to protect a national culture, but also a way of ensuring the ascendancy of a particular type of 'high' culture over the 'lowbrow' fare dished up by commercial stations. Other interest groups saw public broadcasting as a useful means to further their own ends, for example to protect Canadian enterprise against foreign competition (by restricting opportunities for American companies to advertise in Canada), or to help usher in a more progressive and democratic society (by making airtime available for non-commercially oriented programming). While national sentiment had a genuine appeal, it also acted as a useful means to lend legitimacy to these other goals and was deployed in contingent and at times quite cynical ways in the broadcasting debate.[8] Indeed, while playing on national sentiment, advocates of public broadcasting in Canada could also exploit transnational connections when it suited them. Thus, if at times they placed a great deal of emphasis on the American threat, they still remained willing and able to forge links with the public broadcasting lobby in the United States in order to support their campaign at home.[9] Connections with Britain and the BBC were more complex still.

This complexity in part reflected the broader shifts that had transformed the relationship between Britain and Canada during and after the First World War and that had in turn changed how thoughtful Canadians saw themselves and their place in the world. An earlier generation of English Canadians had cherished their British heritage as central to their Canadian identity and had also hoped for greater participation and influence in a more united empire of equal member states, in part as a counterweight to the pull of continentalism. It had seemed possible to be both an 'imperialist' and a 'nationalist,' because the aim of 'imperialists' was to secure a position of influence for Canada as a partner in a powerful global empire.[10] However, this task subsequently proved difficult to achieve. Proposals for an imperial federal parliament or council had all been crippled by the perceived threat of British domination. The greater demographic weight of the UK relative to the self-governing dominions (Canada, Australia, New Zealand, and South Africa), and dominion resistance to any form of closer imperial union that might make it easier for the empire's Asian subjects to migrate to what were then seen as 'white settler' countries, had proved insurmountable obstacles.[11] During the First World War, Canadian hostility to the idea of an imperial federation was expressed most forcefully by the lawyer and constitutional theorist John S. Ewart, who increasingly used the word 'imperialist' to indicate someone who advocated central control by London and who was thus not truly Canadian.[12] Most English Canadians had always been wary of this form of centralization, and an enduring Canadian 'under current of antagonism and suspicion and sometimes even of hostility' towards suspected British 'imperialists' survived into the interwar years.[13]

However, this did not lead to a decisive break with the empire. Instead, during the 1920s it became accepted, both in Britain and in the dominions, that flexible procedures for continued imperial consultation and cooperation offered the best hope for future unity. 'Britannic solutions' to some of Canada's interwar problems still seemed both possible and desirable, as long as the hint of 'imperialist' direction from London could be avoided.[14] Moreover, many English Canadians retained a strong sentimental attachment to Britain, British culture, and the British empire. Indeed, the appeal of this heritage of Britishness to some extent increased in the interwar years, in reaction to the continued growth of U.S. influence.[15] Reflecting these mixed emotions, the Canadian broadcasting debate would involve discussion both of the desirability of exploiting and maintaining Canada's British heritage, and of the dangers of real or imagined 'imperialist' plans to subordinate Canada to Britain.

In terms of the British cultural heritage, public broadcasting could be presented not only as suited to Canadian conditions but also, given its British origins, as a means to cement Canada's continuing connection with the empire. Conversely, U.S.-inspired commercial broadcasting could be portrayed as a threat to Canada's Britishness as well as to more exclusively national identities. Moreover, Britishness implied respectability. Canadian advocates of public broadcasting could stress the British precedent and thus reassure those worried by the departure from the long-established principle of private ownership and control of the mass media that public broadcasting would involve.

Direct, 'imperialist' British influence and intervention were more problematic. In the 1920s and 1930s senior BBC employees were keen to spread the gospel of public broadcasting all around the world, due to a shared conviction that public broadcasting was the best type of broadcasting and a desire to arrest the spread of U.S.-style commercial broadcasting and American cultural influence.[16] Perhaps more significantly, in the case of the colonies and especially the self-governing dominions of the British empire, senior BBC officials believed that cooperation among public broadcasting organizations could help cement imperial unity. Closer imperial connections were to be encouraged by sharing the model of public broadcasting. In Jamaica, South Africa, Newfoundland, and elsewhere, BBC employees intervened to try to ensure that public broadcasting authorities were established.[17] The BBC hoped that such partner organizations would help disseminate its programs around the empire, by rebroadcasting material supplied to them on record and via the BBC's Empire Service of long-range shortwave transmissions, established in 1932. Public broadcasting authorities in the colonies and dominions would also provide the BBC with material. Sir John Reith, director general of the BBC, hoped that the Empire Service would 'have considerable effect in the way of consolidating the Empire.'[18] There was, however, no coherent BBC master plan for drawing broadcasters around the empire into the corporation's orbit. Intervention was more opportunistic, and less well thought out, than this.

A number of BBC officials laboured to encourage the establishment of public broadcasting in Canada. Their efforts interacted with the campaigning of home-grown advocates of public broadcasting in quite complex ways. Individuals and institutions in Canada and Britain sought to work with a range of national and transnational media connections and in the process encouraged and exploited various ideas about identity. In order to understand the results of their diverse activities, this essay discusses in some detail the nature and interests of the different lobby groups and media organizations that were involved and looks at the actions and motives of particular individuals within those bodies.[19] It draws on disparate institutional archives and personal manuscript collections in Canada and in Britain. The widely dispersed nature of the evidence reflects the fact that the campaign for public broadcasting was waged across the internal boundaries of the empire, often in private, and sometimes in a covert fashion. The historian must thus gather evidence from British as well as from Canadian sources, and from the testimony and correspondence of individuals as well as from the collective records of organizations. Even then, some care is necessary in interpreting the results of the archival trawl, for the activities of individuals, and especially of some BBC employees, did not always reflect the agreed policies of the organizations of which they were a part and were not always accurately recorded. Before we can generalize about transnational tendencies or the role of particular institutions, we need to consider the specific roles of individuals, the arguments they deployed, and the decisions they made.

RADIO BROADCASTING initially developed in Canada according to the vagaries of private enterprise, with little government intervention. By 1928, a series of disputes over controversial religious broadcasts by, and allocation of wavelengths to, private stations made a review of regulatory procedures a matter of some urgency.[20] Moreover, given the fact that U.S. commercial stations were winning large Canadian audiences, the introduction of some form of public broadcasting authority that might compete where private Canadian stations had failed seemed increasingly attractive. In contemplating such a move, W.L. Mackenzie King's Liberal government looked to Britain to provide a respectable example of state intervention.[21] King had himself witnessed the activities of the BBC during the 1926 Imperial Conference in London when he had participated in a broadcast and met with Reith, the director general of the corporation. King's broadcast speech on that occasion was written by Charles A. Bowman, the British-born editor of the Liberal *Ottawa Citizen*. King subsequently appointed Bowman to the Royal Commission on Radio Broadcasting that was established at the end of 1928.[22]

Bowman and his fellow commissioners, Dr Augustin Frigon (director of l'École Polytechnique in Montreal and an electrical engineer) and Sir John Aird (president of the Canadian Bank of Commerce and chairman of the Royal Commission), began their investigations in New York. Here, executives of one of the large American commercial networks, the National Broadcasting Company (NBC), openly avowed their belief that Canadian stations would naturally join their network. This had what Bowman later described as 'an amusing effect': Aird, 'a loyal knight of the British connection,' immediately booked passages to Britain for the commissioners, even before they had left New York.[23] By the time the commission arrived in Britain at the beginning of 1929 to start its European investigations, its secretary felt confident enough to announce to the press that Canadian opinion favoured the British model.[24] The commissioners were subsequently welcomed by the BBC 'with an open door to every department,' met with Reith on several occasions, and were shown the varied aspects of the corporation's work.[25] Aird assured Reith that 'the B.B.C. is setting a high standard of public service which may be emulated by the broadcasting authorities in Canada whoever they may prove to be.'[26]

By the time they returned home, the commissioners certainly had an idea of what their final recommendations would be. As they toured Canada, they constantly presented the BBC as a useful model. All three were careful to refute claims that the BBC was unpopular in Britain or that it gave listeners insufficient choice.[27] Aird argued that a carefully adapted Canadian counterpart could import British programs and produce similar ones of its own, thus assisting 'the people in Canada in doing away with a great deal of American material.'[28] The U.S. menace was introduced as a threat to imperial as well as national identity, to 'British loyalty.'[29] Indeed, national and imperial identities were seen to be closely connected: one witness argued that radio could satisfy 'a strong demand for linking up the different points of the empire,' combating American penetration and allowing Canada to 'develop a national spirit.'[30] The idea that the British connection could be used to strengthen Canadian cultural autonomy in the face of U.S. influence recurred throughout the broadcasting debate. As Bowman's *Ottawa Citizen* commented, 'We believe that Canada should be Canadian ... there should be preserved a distinct culture, with preponderant British traditions, on this continent.'[31]

During its overseas tour and provincial hearings, the Aird Commission emphasized Canada's Britishness and stressed the virtues of the British broadcasting model. Its final report praised the BBC and endorsed Reith's emphasis on broadcasting 'as an instrument of education.' It recommended that Canadian broadcasting be publicly owned and run as a domestic monopoly on a 'public service' basis, as in Britain.[32] Only the most explicit appeals to Canada's Britishness were curbed; specifically, Frigon vetoed Bowman's mischievous suggestion that a 'Royal Canadian Broadcasting Corporation' be established, fearing how his fellow French Canadians would react.[33] This reflected an understanding that Britishness and the BBC model had to be deployed with care in Canada, as subsequent events would make clear.

The Aird Report did not suggest the creation of a Canadian clone of the BBC. Canadian conditions and concerns were clearly uppermost in the commissioners' minds. Significant divergences from the British model were apparent in the document, including the recommendation that public broadcasting be funded through advertising and government subsidies as well as licence fees, and that the provinces should be given some sort of power over regional programming. Links with the British model were further obscured by the fact that the report left several key questions unanswered. It did not state clearly how the envisaged public broadcasting authority would relate to the federal or provincial governments, or where ultimate responsibility for broadcasting policy would lie. Reith was worried by this and warned Aird that he could not see in the report 'one real authority anywhere.'[34] This lack of clarity would continue to dog many subsequent attempts to devise a workable Canadian radio policy, to the concern of advocates of public broadcasting both in Britain and in Canada.

The onset of the depression and the fall of the King government meant that the Aird Report was not immediately acted upon. R.B. Bennett's new Conservative government was known to be unfavourable to public ownership of industry. However, the campaign for public broadcasting subsequently gathered momentum under the leadership of Graham Spry, national secretary of the Association of Canadian Clubs and a former Rhodes Scholar, and Alan Plaunt, 'a socially committed philanthropist' who, like Spry, had studied at Oxford, returning to Ottawa to work at Bowman's *Citizen*. Spry and Plaunt formed the nucleus of a new lobby group, the Canadian Radio League (CRL), and used their social and political connections to harness a wide and influential body of support.[35]

Spry and Plaunt were certainly driven by a desire to promote Canadian national interests as they perceived them. However, this imperative interacted with other sentiments in complex ways, manifest in a certain rhetorical elasticity as the CRL sought to appeal to specific groups. Although Spry famously claimed that the alternatives facing Canadian broadcasting were either 'the State or the United States,' both in private and in retrospect he sought to downplay the CRL's anti-Americanism.[36] Britain occupied a similarly ambiguous place in Spry and Plaunt's thinking. To some extent their aim was to use radio to develop a truly autonomous Canadian identity, 'a distinct nation at once different from either Britain or the United States.'[37] Moreover, like the Aird Commission, they recognized that any scheme for public ownership would have to be tailored to Canadian conditions, and they never advocated the adoption of the BBC model in its entirety.[38] Nevertheless, the suggestion that Spry and Plaunt were 'anti-British' is problematic.[39] While they were not slavish Anglophiles, neither were they essentially hostile to the British connection, and both often cited the BBC model with approval in public and in private.[40] As was somewhat traditional in Canada, the CRL drew on the British connection in an opportunistic fashion: concealing it when it could do harm, but brandishing it when it promised to rally additional support, such as when dealing with the Imperial Order Daughters of the Empire or with various sympathetic academics and clerics.[41]

Like the Aird Commission, the CRL established direct, if discreet, links with the BBC from the outset. One of Spry's friends from Oxford, Lindsay Wellington, worked at the BBC. Wellington put Spry in touch with Major William Ewart Gladstone Murray, the BBC's Canadian-born head of publicity. Together, Spry and Murray arranged for the Canadian prime minister to be invited to visit the BBC when he attended the 1930 Imperial Conference in London. Although Bennett failed to acknowledge Murray's offer, on his return to Canada he announced plans to introduce a radio bill.[42]

Gladstone Murray would play a crucial if somewhat enigmatic role in the events that followed. Born in British Columbia, 'of pure High-land stock,' he studied at McGill before taking up a Rhodes Scholar-ship in 1913, when his imagination was fired by a long talk with Lord Milner, one of Cecil Rhodes's trustees. Murray remembered long after Milner's injunction that Rhodes Scholars had 'a moral duty to make afterwards some contribution to the cause of Empire development and cohesion.' Following distinguished wartime service, Murray worked in journalism in London and in 1924 joined the BBC, where he became director of publications and, subsequently, public relations manager.[43] Energetic and charismatic, but also somewhat unstable, for better or worse Murray would occupy prominent positions in broadcasting in both Britain and Canada.

Spry and Plaunt remained in contact with Murray after the Imperial Conference, but, as Wellington noted, it was understood that connec-tions between the CRL and the BBC should not be publicized.

Murray tells me that the chief weapon of the opponents of national Ca-nadian broadcasting is the assertion that it is designed to bring Canada under the influence of the B.B.C. and of Britain. It's an absurd sugges-tion since the whole meaning of the scheme is Canadian broadcasting for Canada, but apparently its absurdity is not universally recognized.[44]

British support needed to be deployed with care. Advocates of public broadcasting wished to avoid the charge that BBC influence threatened Canadian autonomy or that it would bring to Canada an unhelpful set of ideas about radio. Earlier, supporters of commercial broadcast-ing had been quick to criticize the Aird Report's devotion to the British model, claiming that it was unsuited to Canadian conditions and that the BBC was not worth emulating, as it was allegedly open to political manipulation and failed to give listeners sufficient choice.[45] Bowman and Frigon had sought to counter such attacks; Spry likewise defended the BBC's record of service to its listeners.[46]

Nevertheless, the CRL's opponents continued to denigrate the Brit-ish model. Claiming that 'the slogan of the British Broadcasting Cor-poration might well be: "The public be damned!" R.W. Ashcroft, one of the most prominent and persuasive advocates of commercial broad-casting in Canada, recommended the creation of two Canadian radio networks. A state-owned non-commercial system, operating under the auspices of Canadian National Railways (CNR), would complement a privately owned commercial network broadcasting over the facilities of the Canadian Pacific Railway (CPR).[47] The Ashcroft plan was endorsed by John Murray Gibbon, chief public relations officer of the CPR. In an article published in the *Canadian Forum*, Gibbon claimed that the BBC, the 'ideal' of both the Aird Commission and the CRL, was a government propaganda machine, unpopular with listeners, destructive of musical talent, and kept afloat by covert advertisements and revenue from the BBC's weekly magazine, the *Radio Times*. Countering arguments about national and imperial identity, Gibbon stated that a Canadian version of the BBC would merely drown out programs broadcast from the United States that were better suited to the 'North American mentality.'[48]

However, Plaunt and Spry had friends on the editorial board of the *Canadian Forum*, one of whom gave Spry an advance copy of Gibbon's article. In a reply published in the next issue, Spry demolished Gibbon's generally inaccurate criticisms of the BBC and argued that the Ashcroft plan was designed to saddle the taxpayer with the bill for public broadcasting while giving the CPR a highly profitable monopoly of radio advertising and paving the way for American companies to enter the Canadian market.[49] Spry's attack on American influence was supported by British reinforcements. He dispatched an advance copy of Gibbon's article to Gladstone Murray, who thus armed was able to approach the CPR's London office suitably outraged. CPR officials attempted to dissuade Murray from responding with a public statement, claiming that this would add substance to rumours that the BBC was attempting to intervene in the Canadian debate. Murray nevertheless issued a press release, denouncing Gibbon's article as 'a unique combination of inaccuracy and malevolence.' The CPR eventually declared that Gibbon had written the article in a private capacity, and the issue was allowed to drop.[50] Despite the danger of seeming to be too closely associated with the British model, the CRL had successfully drawn on BBC support and played up the danger of U.S. influence in order to neutralize the arguments of powerful opponents.

In May 1931, Bennett suggested to Spry that Reith visit Canada.[51] Although nothing came of the idea (immediately at least) the episode did indicate Bennett's growing support for public broadcasting. An incident that occurred later in the year further strengthened Bennett's resolve. Towards the end of 1931, the BBC attempted to coordinate a round-the-world empire Christmas broadcast. While the CNR agreed to provide the required Canadian relay, part of the arrangement depended on landlines owned by the Bell Telephone Company and the American Telephone and Telegraph Company (AT&T), which owned a substantial interest in Bell. When neither company proved willing to cooperate, the BBC cancelled the entire empire broadcast. Protests followed and, partly due to personal intervention by Bennett, Bell offered to reverse its decision. However, the BBC responded that it was too late to reinstate the broadcast.[52] Both the CRL and the BBC were in fact happy with this outcome, for it demonstrated the need for the establishment of a Canadian public broadcasting authority capable of taking charge of such events. Spry later recalled with special satisfaction the impact that the affair had on Bennett, 'the great imperialist.'[53]

In February 1932 (once a challenge from the Quebec provincial government, questioning the right of the federal authorities to legislate on broadcasting issues, had been overruled by the Judicial Committee of the Privy Council in London) Bennett announced that a Special Commons Committee on Radio Broadcasting would be appointed. He hinted that the committee would find in the Aird Report some 'very helpful information'; soon afterwards, the government raised the radio listener licence fee from $1 to $2, seen by some as a further indication that public broadcasting would soon be introduced.[54] Plaunt and Spry began an intensive lobbying campaign and submitted a brief arguing that without public broadcasting, Canadian radio would come under American control. Again, the CRL drew on British allies, and following exchanges between Reith and Bowman, and among Spry, Plaunt, and Murray, it was arranged that Murray would be invited to give evidence to the committee. Murray's visit was funded privately by supporters of the CRL, including the Canadian businessman, philanthropist, and diplomat Vincent Massey.[55]

In presenting his evidence to the committee, Murray sought to avoid the charge of British interference: he was there to provide information only, 'and in no sense to suggest that what is happening outside Canada should necessarily be a criterion of what Canada should do.' Nevertheless, he outlined the British system in some detail, including the idea that a public authority should enjoy a domestic monopoly of broadcasting. Murray stressed the merits of the BBC model and emphasized in particular the importance of the British principle of 'remote State control,' by which an independent public broadcasting authority would, while remaining responsible to Parliament, in theory at least be free of the direct influence of any government seeking to further its own political ends.[56]

According to Spry and other sympathetic commentators, Murray's testimony helped swing the committee in favour of public broadcasting; however, Bowman later claimed that the result was really due to direct intervention by Bennett.[57] Murray certainly did not persuade the committee that a Canadian version of the BBC was required: the committee's report, while endorsing the idea of public broadcasting, did not suggest either the creation of a domestic broadcasting monopoly or the introduction of the principle of remote state control. The Canadian Radio Broadcasting Commission (CRBC) that was established in line with the committee's recommendations was to build and operate its own stations and produce programs, funded by advertising revenue as well as by monies generated by listener licence fees. However, private stations would remain. They would be regulated by the commission and organized into a network in order to allow them to broadcast a selection of the commission's programs. The government of the day would meanwhile retain significant authority over CRBC finances and appointments.[58]

It was this latter departure from the British model that most concerned observers at the BBC. At a lunch with Sir George McLaren Brown and J. Murray Gibbon of the CPR, C.F. Crandall of the British United Press news agency, and Gladstone Murray, Reith was told that

at the last moment Bennett the Canadian P.M. had switched the Broadcasting Commission over from an autonomous body like [the BBC] to be more or less a Government Department … They say it was arranged at a tea party between two women, the wife of [W. Arthur] Steel, [technical advisor to the committee and subsequently] one of the Commissioners [of the CRBC] and the other Bennett's sister, who married Bennett's political agent [W.D. Herridge] … It is really monstrous.[59]

Although this rumour came from sources that could hardly have been deemed impartial, for Reith it seemed to explain why the British principle of remote state control had been ignored. In an article published in the *London Daily Telegraph*, Reith described the new structure adopted in Canada as 'surprising and, to many, disquieting.'[60]

Despite these significant divergences from the BBC model, the CRBC could still at least in part be seen as the product of successful appeals to British loyalties by Canadian advocates of public broadcasting, and of discussion of the British system. Allegations of 'imperialist' influence had largely been avoided, and the British connection seemed essentially benign. Murray of the BBC had exerted a continuous behind-the-scenes influence over the Canadian debate and at key moments had acted to provide the CRL with public support. Indeed, contemporaries recognized the foundation of the CRBC as an imperial as well as a national achievement. The committee's report argued that radio could act as 'one of the most efficient mediums for developing a greater National and Empire consciousness within the Dominion and the British Commonwealth of Nations.'[61] Bennett subsequently asserted that only public broadcasting could meet Canada's 'national requirements and empire obligations,' and presented the new CRBC as 'a dependable link in a chain of empire communication by which we may be more closely united one with the other.'[62] For Bennett, such rhetoric may have been a means to render a new experiment in public enterprise respectable, but it also reflected his own personal beliefs. Bennett told Spry that 'you have saved Canada for the British Commonwealth.'[63] Plaunt was similarly proud of the imperial ramifications of the CRL's achievement, noting privately that it was not perhaps a coincidence that

> the bill to create a unified Canadian system and another – the final link – in an all Empire chain, was passed on Empire Day, just before the Imperial Economic Conference, just before, it may be, the beginnings of the 'Fourth British Empire.' The CRBC may well be indeed one of the links, to quote Sir Wilfrid Laurier, 'light as air, yet strong as the bonds of steel' that will bind the new empire.[64]

YET BRITISH INFLUENCE did not go unchallenged. The CRL suggested that Gladstone Murray of the BBC be appointed chairman of the new CRBC. Murray was unwilling to accept the pay cut that this would have entailed but subsequently agreed to visit Canada at Bennett's invitation ('There were stirring appeals to my patriotism and my imperialism') to investigate the CRBC's increasingly apparent financial and organizational shortcomings. Between April and June 1933 Murray travelled across Canada at the federal government's expense.[65] His interim report to the Canadian House of Commons reiterated his recommendation of 1932 that the British principle of remote state control of broadcasting be adopted, which would now involve diluting the government's direct authority over CRBC revenue, appointments, and policy. The report led to heated debate in the House, including repeated and aggressive questioning as to whether a visitor from Britain had any business getting involved. Resentment of 'imperialist' intervention was clear. Reith thought the debate 'too dreadful for words.'[66] Murray's final report tactfully emphasized the need to cater to Canadian conditions, but his recommendations were nevertheless largely ignored.[67] Individuals based in Britain would never again intervene so openly in the Canadian broadcasting debate. When, during a trip to New York in November 1933, Reith made a brief excursion to Ottawa, he purposefully avoided seeing Bennett or making any public comments about Canadian broadcasting, even though privately he detested the constitution and operation of the CRBC.[68] However, if overt BBC involvement was henceforth ruled out, covert influence would intensify.

When Murray returned to Britain he advised Reith that the CRBC was disorganized and 'hopelessly incompetent'; he claimed to have told Bennett that no international relay programs from Canada should be considered until 'some semblance of organization' had been achieved.[69] Similar criticisms of the CRBC's programming and administration were also being rehearsed in Canada, and it was rumoured that the authority would be abolished.[70] When a special Commons committee of investigation was appointed, the CRL sought to impress upon it the need for a more effective 'independent public corporation somewhat similar to the BBC,' administered by a BBC-style general manager.[71] The CRL also probably helped secure the testimony of G.A. Grier. Grier was the nephew of the wife of Brooke Claxton; Claxton was a Montreal lawyer and Liberal and one of Plaunt and Spry's closest allies. Grier, a Cambridge undergraduate at the time of the Aird Commission, had studied the workings of the BBC in Britain with Murray's help before returning to Canada.[72] Defending the BBC model, he read the committee 'a résumé which is in accordance with the principle of British control of broadcasting,' arguing for the establishment of a public authority, headed by Murray, that would enjoy a broadcasting monopoly.[73] However, apart from recommending the appointment of a general manager, the report of the 1934 committee did little more than note the difficulties facing the CRBC. Murray told his colleagues at the BBC that Bennett knew he would be out of office soon and had decided to leave his successor to grapple with the intractable issue of broadcasting.[74]

Following the victory of Mackenzie King's Liberals in the 1935 general election, Plaunt began to press upon the new prime minister the case for reform. This task was in some ways made easier by King's chagrin at the CRBC's seemingly partisan programming during the election campaign.[75] However, Brooke Claxton feared that King's annoyance would translate into an attempt to bring broadcasting under even tighter government direction. In order to resist this, Claxton, like Murray, emphasized the British principle of remote state control and urged Plaunt to 'take from Sir John Reith's speeches, etc., everything you can get to support the idea of immediate independence, ultimate responsibility.'[76] In early 1935 Reith had delivered a report on broadcasting to the South African government; Claxton and Plaunt found that this document contained 'many passages which are apposite to the Canadian situation' and 'good material' for a new Canadian broadcasting act. They continued to draw on Reith's South African report over the months that followed.[77]

The BBC model, and particularly the British principle of remote state control, thus remained before the CRL's eyes as it contemplated the future of broadcasting in Canada. Direct, albeit covert, intervention from Britain also continued. Murray began to provide Plaunt with detailed feedback on his proposals, accompanied by surveys of the state of broadcasting in Britain and confidential information about the internal workings of the BBC.[78] Plaunt duly submitted his recommendations, revised in accordance with Murray's suggestions, to C.D. Howe, the new minister of marine, who had responsibility for broadcasting. Plaunt presented the proposals as his own work, written 'in conjunction with members of the group which organized and directed the League.' Murray's role was not mentioned. Howe seemed impressed; he asked Claxton to draft a broadcasting bill and intimated that Plaunt might become a governor of the proposed new authority. While Murray's role in devising the new recommendations remained a secret, Howe had heard of him and suggested that he might be appointed general manager.[79]

Senior officials at the BBC would probably have approved of the line that the CRL was taking with Howe, and of its use of Reith's South African report for guidance. As noted above, Reith had already expressed in private and in public his worries about the Canadian government's failure to take seriously the principle of remote state control of broadcasting. With characteristic candour and condescension, he later lamented in his diary 'What incredible idiots and bunglers they are in Canada.'[80] Moreover, there was growing dissatisfaction at the BBC with what was regarded as the CRBC's uncooperative attitude, particularly regarding rebroadcasting the BBC's Empire Service in Canada.[81] If the Canadian government were to replace the CRBC with an organization more like the BBC, then it might be hoped that closer connections could be forged between broadcasters in Britain and Canada.

However, in advising the CRL and passing on confidential BBC information, Murray did not necessarily have the blessing of his superiors.
Murray himself later acknowledged that although Reith had come to
share his interest in the Canadian situation following the Aird Commission's visit to Britain, they had subsequently only discussed the issue
in a 'desultory' fashion.[82] Indeed, while Murray's early interventions
in the Canadian debate probably had Reith's support, his later actions
should be seen in a quite different light. Here, as discussed at the beginning of this essay, in order to understand British influence on the Canadian broadcasting debate, we need to focus analysis at a personal level
and consider the human factor.

The BBC demanded that its employees adhere to a strict moral code
in their private lives.[83] Murray failed to meet these standards. This was
partly due to a drinking problem, which some believed was the cause
of his frequent, unexplained absences, his 'exaggeration which worries
everyone in the place, his lack of candour and straightforwardness and
his untruthfulness,' and his general 'mysteriousness.' Murray was suspected of leaking confidential information to the press, and when he
returned from his Canadian tour in 1933 Reith considered moving him
to a less responsible position.[84] Murray's enterprising personality also
jarred with the consensus-based decision-making processes characteristic of the BBC at the time. By early 1935, as more general disquiet
within the organization grew following the introduction of new administrative structures, Murray was at loggerheads with senior colleagues
on a number of issues. After being passed over for promotion, he spoke
of leaving the BBC.[85]

Despite the existence of general agreement at the BBC as to the desirability of strengthening public broadcasting in Canada, the advice
given to Plaunt by Murray in 1935 and 1936 thus did not necessarily
reflect consultation with other senior BBC employees. This became
clear when, at the end of 1935, the newly appointed BBC North American representative in New York, Felix Greene, visited Ottawa. Howe,
the minister of marine, asked Greene to submit suggestions as to what
sort of authority might replace the CRBC, which he confided was to
be abolished. However, he warned Greene that 'B.B.C. principles were
not entirely applicable to Canadian conditions.' Reporting this to Cecil
Graves (the former head of the BBC's Empire Service, who had been
promoted to the position of controller of programs in preference to
Murray), Greene emphasized the obstacles in the way of 'any change
along the lines that we would want to see … If I were frank I would say

that the chance ... of any plan of ours being accepted by the Government as a basis of re-organization is very small indeed.' Greene clearly felt that he was operating according to a shared conception of what the BBC desired for Canada. However, he had not been given any specific guidelines to work with. Accordingly, like Plaunt and Claxton, in thinking about broadcasting in Canada he turned to Reith's South African report for inspiration, using it as a source of ideas that could be applied in Canada.[86]

Distance from London, and the fact that his trips to Canada coincided with the festive season, when his superiors back home were out of the office, gave Greene an additional degree of autonomy. Against instructions, he submitted his report (which argued for the creation of a 'Canadian Broadcasting Corporation' under remote state control) to Howe before Graves had a chance to see it or comment on its contents.[87] Greene's activities revealed not just the absence of any specific BBC plan for broadcasting in Canada, but also how this lack of direction made it possible for a BBC employee to play a lone hand. Moreover, Greene's visit to Canada exposed the extent of Murray's isolation within the BBC. Murray admitted to Plaunt that he was being 'studiously left out of the official exchanges' between Greene and his superiors.[88]

Murray nevertheless continued to provide Plaunt and Claxton with detailed comments on their drafts of a new broadcasting bill.[89] However, as Claxton had feared, Howe subsequently announced that he was considering tightening direct government control over broadcasting and that the whole matter was to be referred to a select parliamentary committee. The CRL again emphasized the need for remote state control, and Murray discussed the issue with Vincent Massey, who had been appointed by King as Canadian High Commissioner in London. Together, Murray and Massey sent a long cablegram to Howe, supporting the CRL's position. Howe wavered, and asked Claxton to prepare a revised bill.[90]

Howe also suggested to Greene that he should present his own proposals in person to the parliamentary committee. While Greene was eager to do so, Graves had serious doubts, and Reith (who was less concerned about the propriety of a BBC representative appearing, but doubted whether Greene possessed sufficient knowledge to do the job properly) discussed the matter with the Dominions Office in London.[91] Graves made it clear to Greene that the BBC was prepared to 'wash our hands of the whole business' as it did not like 'the attitude that was being adopted.' He warned Reith that 'it all looks very bad.'[92]

Ultimately, Greene did not appear before the committee, and Plaunt secured King's backing for the proposals that he had devised in consultation with Claxton and Murray.[93] The committee's report duly recommended that the CRBC be replaced by a corporation entrusted with the powers 'now enjoyed by the British Broadcasting Corporation': almost all of the CRL's recommendations were adopted. That these were very similar to Greene's proposals was not surprising, given that both had drawn on Reith's South African report. The new Canadian Broadcasting Corporation (CBC) was to be directed by a general manager answerable to a nine-member board of honorary governors; Plaunt was one of the first appointed.[94] While the CBC was not to enjoy a BBC-style domestic broadcasting monopoly and remained partially reliant on advertising for funding, direct government authority over broadcasting had been much reduced, and something that approximated the British principle of remote state control had been established. The Dominions Office saw the report as a 'definite move in the right direction,' and Greene presented it as a triumph. Although senior BBC officials had not authorized the recommendations made by either Greene or Murray, Graves agreed that 'things seem to have gone unexpectedly well, and we are naturally very glad to see that the Committee has made such definite recommendations along what I think we all feel are the right lines.'[95]

Plaunt immediately began a campaign to have Murray appointed as CBC general manager. While this had been his and Murray's intention for some time, action was rendered urgent by the fear that Reginald Brophy, the Canadian-born head of NBC station relations in New York, and the man favoured by the commercial stations, would get the job. In championing Murray's candidacy, Plaunt had to counter persistent rumours about Murray's drinking and his cavalier attitude to personal expense claims, and allegations that Murray was 'shortly to be eased out of the BBC.'[96] This latter claim was in fact true. Murray continued to be suspected of leaking confidential information to the press, and in February 1936 a rumour even circulated that he was involved with a Canadian-registered company that planned to sell advertising time to English companies on Radio Luxembourg and other European commercial stations that competed with the BBC for British listeners.[97] Shortly thereafter, following orders from Reith, Graves submitted a formal report stating that he did not trust Murray enough to delegate work to him.[98] Reith informed Murray that his position at the BBC was 'in jeopardy,' but noted that if Murray were offered and accepted the Canadian job, then the BBC would not dismiss him publicly.[99] The

BBC hoped to rid itself of Murray at the expense of the infant CBC. It did not seek to have him installed as an agent of British influence in Ottawa.

Plaunt meanwhile also had to combat claims that Murray had become 'too British' to make a success of Canadian broadcasting and that Brophy, as 'a man with Canadian and American training,' would be more suitable. Playing the empire card had worked well when dealing with Bennett. King's attitude to the imperial connection was more ambivalent, and so the CRL changed its tactics. Murray's known imperial enthusiasms were now something of a liability, and Plaunt urged him to demonstrate 'that you are not an imperialist, that you understand and appreciate the growing sentiment in Canada, especially in French Canada, of a quasi-"isolationist" variety.'[100] Murray, who also denied the allegations about his personal life, was keen to oblige. When writing to Plaunt he downplayed his British and imperial loyalties, even though he simultaneously urged the BBC to support his candidacy for the Canadian job on the grounds that it would allow him to 'fulfil the intention of the Founder of the Rhodes Trust in terms of service to my own country in the British Commonwealth.'[101]

Indeed, fearful that the BBC would actively try to scupper his chances in Canada, Murray even sought to convince Plaunt that the BBC had become an untrustworthy ally. Murray had earlier warned Plaunt of a 'fantastic proposal' by NBC to 'take over Canadian broadcasting.'[102] He now hinted that the BBC might acquiesce in any such scheme, due to its recent rapprochement with 'the American commercial "Octopus."' At the same time, and in a rather contradictory fashion, Murray warned Plaunt of a supposed plan by Reith to establish subservient 'satellites' of the BBC around the empire.[103] While it is conceivable that Reith viewed the CBC as a potential BBC 'satellite,' given the available evidence it seems unlikely that the BBC was working in collusion with NBC. Rather, having fallen from grace at the BBC, and being aware of the need to stress his Canadian credentials, Murray was now desperately trying any ploy that would help him get the CBC job.

Murray's worries were further sharpened by his knowledge that Greene and Brophy had become friends and that Greene was likely to support Brophy's candidacy.[104] This concern at least was well founded. While Graves and Reith kept their promise and maintained a policy of silence regarding Murray's unsuitability for the Canadian job, Greene, when visiting London, suggested to the Dominions Office that it should promote Brophy's claims and argued that Brophy could be relied on to 'run things on B.B.C. lines.'[105] In Ottawa, Greene subsequently met with Plaunt. He rubbished Murray's conspiracy theories about the BBC, hinted to Plaunt that Murray's future prospects at the BBC were dim, and, knowing it would do Murray no good, drew attention to Murray's 'imperialistic' beliefs.[106]

Plaunt chose to ignore these veiled warnings, and the CRL continued to press Murray's candidacy. Writing to King, Charles Bowman argued that

> [Murray is] no Imperialist, but truly Canadian, with the right liberal vision ... Some of the efforts to discredit him have doubtless been inspired by imperialist interests. Certain interests in London as well as in New York would much rather see someone with less Canadian vision as executive head of the new Canadian Broadcasting Corporation.[107]

Murray was presented as a candidate with 'worldwide knowledge' of broadcasting but who would not bring to Canada the 'arrogance' of the BBC. Brophy was portrayed as likely to 'sell-out' to American commercial interests.[108] The lobbying worked, and, even though Greene's insinuations reached Howe's ears, Murray was appointed as the first general manager of the CBC.[109] Despite Murray's new nationalist image in Canada, the British press (with which Murray generally enjoyed excellent relations, secured partly through his generous, BBC-funded hospitality) presented the appointment as an imperial triumph: the *Liverpool Daily Post* depicted Murray as 'the Sir John Reith of Canada'; *Wireless World* claimed that his appointment 'sets the seal on another "B.B.C." overseas'; and the *Sunday Times* presented Murray as 'solidly for the imperial connection.'[110]

THROUGHOUT THE DEBATE, Murray drew on a range of different ideas about broadcasting, Britishness, and Canadian identity in an opportunistic and often contradictory manner. His behaviour was undoubtedly increasingly duplicitous, but it also reflected an underlying pattern in the broader controversy. Historians have struggled to explain how perceived identities motivated the proponents of public broadcasting in Canada and have disagreed about how genuinely those sentiments were held. In the end, we may have to accept a pardonably human degree of ambiguity. The CRL deployed arguments about national identity pragmatically so as to bolster a socially radical agenda and maximize wider support for public broadcasting; nevertheless, those arguments probably also reflected sincere beliefs about Canadian interests. The CRL eagerly forged connections with like-minded organizations in the United States; yet, while Plaunt and Spry were not themselves necessarily 'anti-American,' they were wary of the broader economic and cultural influence of the United States and knew that anti-Americanism offered a useful means to generate wider support for their goals. The CRL was cautious in its deployment of British ideas and British reinforcements in the Canadian campaign, particularly when approaching King's Liberal government; however, Plaunt and Spry were ultimately keen to use those resources when it served their broader purposes. They felt some degree of attachment to the British connection themselves.

These ambiguities may have been specifically Canadian, in that they reflected the increasingly unstable nature of the country's triangular relationship with Britain and the United States during the interwar years. However, they may also be of wider interest to historians who wish to consider how, in other countries also, ideas about national and transnational identities were deployed to support different visions of broadcasting during this period. Similarly, the complex way in which British influence worked with various home-grown interests to encourage the establishment of public broadcasting in Canada may tell us something of more general validity about flows of imperial and transnational media influence. If the CRL was at times cautious about leaning too heavily on the BBC model and British sentiment in Canada, then senior BBC employees were equally wary of seeming to intervene too openly in Canadian affairs and remained reluctant to devise or work according to any blueprint of their own for the future of Canadian broadcasting. Both sides sought to avoid any hint of 'imperialist' intent, defined as a desire to exert central control from London. Moreover, for many at the BBC, distracted by their organization's own domestic problems, Canada was simply not a very high priority. As a result, the initiative remained with the CRL in Canada. Certain BBC employees, convinced of the central importance of putting public broadcasting on a sound footing in Canada, were also able to play a lone hand. Greene, the BBC's representative in North America, worked according to his own interpretation of events and BBC priorities, and Murray had a number of reasons, some of them highly self-interested, for intervening to support the establishment of public broadcasting. However, neither Greene nor Murray should be seen as agents of a concerted, detailed BBC plan to establish a client organization in Canada, and Murray was certainly not installed as the BBC's man in Ottawa. Greene was anxious about whether Murray would be willing to cooperate with the BBC after it had, effectively, sacked him; Reith was not overly concerned, as he thought Murray would not last long at the CBC.[111]

British influence on the Canadian debate was thus subtle and limited, perhaps reflecting the highly qualified imperial sway enjoyed by Britain over Canada during this period. There was no simple, direct form of 'media imperialism' at work. Further research is clearly necessary in order to gauge whether this point holds true in relation to BBC influence over broadcasting in other parts of the empire during the twentieth century. Nevertheless, there is probably at least one point of wider significance that arises from this essay. While imperial, transnational forces could clearly be significant in shaping the nature of broadcasting in a country such as Canada, it is difficult to locate any single, formative transnational influence that determined the outcome of local debate. Instead, domestic and overseas impulses interacted in a complex fashion, according to the various motives of the different organizations and individuals involved. Thinking about the birth of public broadcasting in Canada in these terms may help us understand the broader context in which media connections operated within the twentieth-century British empire and highlights the need for detailed case studies that will help add complexity to histories of the media, empire, and globalization.

NOTES

This essay is based on research conducted with the support of a Government of Ireland Research Fellowship and a Small Project Grant, both provided by the Irish Research Council for Humanities and Social Sciences (IRCHSS); an Ireland-Canada University Foundation Scholarship; and an International Council for Canadian Studies Faculty Research Award. For comments on an earlier version of the piece I am grateful to the audience at the National University of Ireland, Galway colloquium on 'Media History in Ireland, Britain and Canada: Connections and Comparisons' (4 November 2005, also supported by the IRCHSS), and to Mark Hampton and Len Kuffert.

1 This clearly builds on the earlier work of scholars such as Harold Innis and Marshall McLuhan. See also John B. Thompson, *The Media and Modernity: A Social Theory of the Media* (Stanford, CA: Stanford University Press, 1995).
2 Lisa Parks and Shanti Kumar, eds, *Planet TV: A Global Television Reader* (New York and London: New York University Press, 2003); Julie F. Codell,

ed., *Imperial Co-Histories: National Identities and the British and Colonial Press* (Madison, NJ: Fairleigh Dickinson University Press, 2003); Chandrika Kaul, *Reporting the Raj: The British Press and India, c. 1880–1922* (Manchester: Manchester University Press, 2003); Simon J. Potter, *News and the British World: The Emergence of an Imperial Press System, 1876–1922* (Oxford: Oxford University Press, 2003); Simon J. Potter, ed., *Newspapers and Empire in Ireland and Britain: Reporting the British Empire, c. 1857–1921* (Dublin: Four Courts, 2004); Simon J. Potter, 'Strengthening the Bonds of the Commonwealth: The Imperial Relations Trust and Australian, New Zealand, and Canadian Broadcasting Personnel in Britain, 1946–52,' *Media History* 11, no. 3 (December 2005): 193–205; Chandrika Kaul, ed., *Media and the British Empire* (Basingstoke and New York: Palgrave Macmillan, 2006).

3   Edward S. Herman and Robert W. McChesney, *The Global Media: The New Missionaries of Corporate Capitalism* (London and New York: Cassell, 1997); David Held, Anthony McGrew, David Goldblatt, and Jonathan Perraton, *Global Transformations: Politics, Economics and Culture* (Stanford, CA: Stanford University Press, 1999); Robert Pike and Dwayne Winseck, 'The Politics of Global Media Reform, 1907–23,' *Media, Culture and Society* 26, no. 5 (September 2004), 643–75; Dwayne R. Winseck and Robert M. Pike, *Communication and Empire: Media, Markets and Globalization, 1860–1930* (Durham, NC, and London: Duke University Press, 2007).

4   James Curran, *Media and Power* (London and New York: Routledge, 2002), 166–82; Simon J. Potter, 'Webs, Networks, and Systems: Globalization and the Mass Media in the Nineteenth- and Twentieth-Century British Empire,' *Journal of British Studies* 46, no. 3 (July 2007): 621–46.

5   John Egli O'Brien, 'A History of the Canadian Radio League, 1930–1936' (PhD dissertation, University of Southern California, 1964), 446; Margaret Prang, 'The Origins of Public Broadcasting in Canada,' *Canadian Historical Review* 46, no. 1 (March 1965): 1–31, esp. 3, 31.

6   On this point see Kenneth C. Dewar, 'The Origins of Public Broadcasting in Canada in Comparative Perspective,' *Canadian Journal of Communication* 8, no. 2 (January 1982): 26–45.

7   Frank W. Peers, *The Politics of Canadian Broadcasting, 1920–1951* (Toronto: University of Toronto Press, 1969), 3. This perhaps reflected a wider change in how Canadian historians dealt with the British imperial connection in the 1960s. See D.R. Owram, 'Canada and the Empire,' in Robin W. Winks, ed., *The Oxford History of the British Empire* vol. 5: *Historiography* (Oxford: Oxford University Press 1999), 157–8.

8   Mary Vipond, 'The Nationalist Network: English Canada's Intellectuals and Artists in the 1920s,' *Canadian Review of Studies in Nationalism* 7,

no. 1 (spring 1980): 32–52; Michael Nolan, 'An Infant Industry: Canadian Private Radio, 1919–36,' *Canadian Historical Review* 70, no. 4 (December 1989): 497–518, esp. 517–18; Marc Raboy, *Missed Opportunities: The Story of Canada's Broadcasting Policy* (Montreal and Kingston: McGill-Queen's University Press, 1990), 31–7; Mary Vipond, *Listening In: The First Decade of Canadian Broadcasting, 1922–1932* (Montreal and Kingston: McGill-Queen's University Press, 1992), 210–11, 247–50; Russell T. Johnston, 'The Origins of Public Broadcasting in Canada Reconsidered: The Radio Branch and Cultural Administration, 1922–1932' (MA thesis, Queen's University, 1992), 34–5; Eric Durocher, 'Critical Interests in Broadcasting Policy: Fashioning the Public Interest in the 1932 Broadcasting Act' (MA thesis, Concordia University, 1995), 122–30.

9 Robert W. McChesney, 'Graham Spry and the Future of Public Broadcasting,' *Canadian Journal of Communication* 24, no. 1 (1999): 25–48.

10 Norman Penlington, *Canada and Imperialism, 1896–1899* (Toronto: University of Toronto Press, 1965); Carl Berger, *The Sense of Power: Studies in the Ideas of Canadian Imperialism, 1867–1914* (Toronto: University of Toronto Press, 1970); Carman Miller, *Painting the Map Red: Canada and the South African War, 1899–1902* (Ottawa: Canadian War Museum, 1993). On the ambiguities of national and imperial identities in Canada and elsewhere see Douglas Cole, 'The Problem of "Nationalism" and "Imperialism" in British Settlement Colonies,' *Journal of British Studies* 10, no. 2 (May 1971): 160–82.

11 See Daniel Gorman, *Imperial Citizenship: Empire and the Question of Belonging* (Manchester: Manchester University Press, 2006).

12 Simon J. Potter, 'Richard Jebb, John S. Ewart, and the Round Table, 1898–1926,' *English Historical Review* 122, no. 495 (Feb. 2007): 105–132.

13 UK National Archives (henceforth UKNA), Kew, DO35/228/2, Sir F. Floud to Sir E. Harding, 17 Jan. 1936.

14 John Darwin, 'A Third British Empire? The Dominion Idea in Imperial Politics' in Judith M. Brown and W. Roger Louis, eds, *The Oxford History of the British Empire*, vol. 4: *The Twentieth Century* (Oxford: Oxford University Press, 1999).

15 David MacKenzie, 'Canada, the North Atlantic Triangle, and the Empire' in Brown and Louis, eds, *The Oxford History of the British Empire*, vol. 4. See also Phillip Buckner, ed., *Canada and the End of Empire* (Vancouver: UBC Press, 2004).

16 Michelle Hilmes, 'Who We Are, Who We Are Not: Battle of the Global Paradigms,' in Parkes and Kumar, eds, *Planet TV*, 65.

17 On Jamaica see BBC Written Archives Centre, Caversham Park, Reading (henceforth WAC), E1/113/3, 'North American Representative's report on

activities of BBC New York Office during the past year,' 6 July 1939. On Newfoundland see WAC, E18/43/4, C.G. Graves, 'Report on broadcasting in Newfoundland submitted to the Commissioner for Finance,' June 1935. On South Africa see WAC, Sir John Reith Diaries, S60/5/4/1 entries on Reith's South African tour.

18 WAC, E1/341/1, Sir J. Reith to H.P. Brown, 22 December 1931.

19 For an analysis of transnational connections framed in similar terms, but looking at social politics, see Daniel T. Rodgers, *Atlantic Crossings: Social Politics in a Progressive Age* (Cambridge, MA: Belknap Press of Harvard University Press, 1998).

20 O'Brien, 'History of the CRL,' 43–4.

21 Vipond, *Listening In*, 205–6. Canada, House of Commons *Debates*, 1 June 1928, 3662.

22 Charles A. Bowman, *Ottawa Editor* (Sidney, BC: Gray's Publishing, 1966), 94–7, 121; Library of the University of British Columbia, Special Collections Division, Vancouver (henceforth UBCSCD), interview conducted by Alan Thomas with Charles A. Bowman, 18 February 1960; David Ellis, *Evolution of the Canadian Broadcasting System: Objectives and Realities, 1928–1968* (Ottawa: Department of Communications, 1979), 2.

23 UBCSCD, Bowman interview. Bowman, *Ottawa Editor*, 124–5.

24 WAC, L2/154/1, Press Association report, 15 January 1929.

25 UBCSCD, Bowman interview; Library and Archives Canada, Ottawa (henceforth LAC), RG42, vol. 1076, file 227-2-4, typescript MSS – 'Activities of the Royal Commission on Radio Broadcasting – fiscal year 1928–1929'; Bowman, *Ottawa Editor*, 123–6.

26 LAC, RG42, vol. 1077, file 227-3-6, copy of Sir John Aird to Reith, 6 February 1929.

27 LAC, RG33 14, vol. 1, file 227–9–5, Summary of public hearings held at Port Arthur, 8 May 1929; file 227-9-9, Summary of public hearings held at Toronto, 17 May 1929; vol. 2, file 227-13-5, Summary of public hearings held at Charlottetown, 20 June 1929; Vipond, *Listening In*, 217.

28 LAC, RG42, vol. 1077, file 227-10-8, summary of public hearings held at Quebec City, 5 June 1929. Bowman's *Citizen* had already made many of the same points: see 'Control of Radio in Canada,' *Ottawa Citizen*, 23 November 1927.

29 LAC, RG 33 14, vol. 1, file 227-9-5, Summary of public hearings held at Port Arthur, 8 May 1929.

30 Ibid., vol. 2, file 227-12-5, Summary of public hearings held at Halifax, 15 May 1929.

31 'Canada's Radio Opportunity,' *Ottawa Citizen*, 13 September 1928.

32 *Report of the Royal Commission on Radio Broadcasting* (Ottawa, 1929).
33 UBCSCD, Bowman interview and LAC, RG41, vol. 303, file 14-2-1 (part 1), copy of Bowman to Donald Manson, 10 January 1949.
34 LAC, RG 33 14, vol. 2, file 227-14-1, copy of Reith to Aird [n.d.].
35 Michael Nolan, *Foundations: Alan Plaunt and the Early Days of CBC Radio* (Toronto: CBC Enterprises, 1986), 13–28, 63–7; Prang, 'Origins of Public Broadcasting,' 7–10; O'Brien, 'History of the CRL,' 73.
36 McChesney, 'Graham Spry and the Future of Public Broadcasting'; Spry, 'The Origins of Public Broadcasting in Canada: A Comment,' *Canadian Historical Review* 46, no. 2 (June 1965): 134–41.
37 Spry, quoted in Vipond, *Listening In*, 228.
38 O'Brien, 'History of the CRL,' 142.
39 Plaunt in particular has sometimes been portrayed as anti-British: see Nolan, *Foundations*, 19, and LAC, R5632-0-4-E, Kenneth Bambrick fonds, 240540 – recording of interview with Ernie Bushnell, 5 October 1978.
40 UBCSCD, Alan Plaunt papers, file 8-9, Plaunt to Leonard Brockington, 12 October 1938; *The Canadian Radio League: Objects, Information, National Support* [Ottawa, 1932]; LAC, Graham Spry papers, vol. 84, file 13, typescript MSS of chapter 4 of Spry's unpublished memoirs.
41 Plaunt papers, file 6-1, copy of Plaunt to W.H. Barker, National Sec., IODE, Toronto, 29 October 1930; file 6-6, Plaunt to Most Revd. Neil McNeil, Archbishop of Toronto, 29 December 1930; file 6-22, Plaunt to Hon. and Rev. H.J. Cody [c. 1931]; file 6-8, Plaunt to Miss Arnoldi, 5 January 1931; file 2-22, A.H. McGreer, Principal, Bishop's University, Lennoxville, Quebec, to Plaunt, 12 February 1931; file 6-25, Plaunt to Rev. W.G. Brown, 17 July 1931; file 2-6, Elizabeth G. Cameron, President of the Federated Women's Institutes of Canada, to Plaunt, 25 August 1931; file 1-15, extract of Carleton Stanley, President, Dalhousie University, Halifax NS, to Plaunt, 1 March 1932; file 4-5, Nellie B. Freeman, President, Nova Scotia Women's Institute, to Plaunt, 1 April 1932; file 2-6 copy of Robert A. Falconer, President Emeritus, University of Toronto, to A.L. Beaubien MP, 8 April 1936; W.A. Mackintosh, Sec., Canadian Universities Conference, to Plaunt, 4 May 1936.
42 Plaunt papers, file 11-15, cable from Spry to Lindsay Wellington, 6 October 1930; file 11-14, Wellington to Spry, 7 October 1930; file 11-6, Spry to W.D. Herridge, 15 October 1930. Prang, 'Origins of Public Broadcasting,' 13. Nolan, *Foundations*, 83–8.
43 LAC, W.E.G. Murray fonds, vol. 6, 'The Place of the British Commonwealth and Empire in the World of the Future – Address by Major Gladstone Murray Given before the Empire Club of Manitoba,' 17 February 1944; vol. 14, scrapbook, cuttings – 'Radio's diplomat' by 'the Private Sec-

retary,' 22 December 1934, and 'A day in my life, by the man who answers the awkward questions,' *Radio Pictorial*, 9 November 1934.

44 Plaunt papers, file 11-14, Wellington to Spry, 7 October 1930.

45 *Aird Project Menaces the Trade and Commerce of Radio – On Guard against the Nationalization of Radio* (Montreal [1929]); *Facts Respecting Radio Broadcasting under Private Ownership – Issued by Canadian Association of Broadcasters* [1929]. For similar arguments see also Frederick Edwards, 'Does Canada Want Government Radio? NO,' *Maclean's Magazine*, 1 May 1930.

46 Charles A. Bowman, *Radio Public Service for Canada: Some Objections Answered* (Ottawa, January 1930); Augustin Frigon, *The Organization of Radio Broadcasting in Canada: Extrait de la Revue Trimestrielle Canadienne, Septembre 1929* (Montreal, 1929); O'Brien, 'History of the CRL,' 168–75.

47 Ashcroft republished an initial article, with minor revisions, as a pamphlet, 'Government vs Private Ownership of Canadian Radio' [Toronto, January 1931].

48 John Murray Gibbon, 'Radio as a Fine Art,' *Canadian Forum*, March 1931.

49 Graham Spry, 'The Canadian Broadcasting Issue,' *Canadian Forum*, April 1931. On the leaking of the draft of Gibbon's article see Plaunt papers, file 11-14, Frank Underhill to Spry, 21 February 1931; Graham Spry, 'Public Policy and Private Pressures: The Canadian Radio League 1930–6 and Countervailing Power,' in Norman Penlington, ed., *On Canada: Essays in Honour of Frank H. Underhill* (Toronto: University of Toronto Press, 1971), 31. Spry also arranged for a lengthy memorandum on Gibbon's article to be sent to various Canadian papers, allowing them to attack Gibbon's proposals in their editorial pages. See Prang, 'Origins of Public Broadcasting,' 23–4.

50 Prang, 'Origins of Public Broadcasting,' 24. Plaunt papers, file 11-10, copy of George McLaren Brown to Murray, 23 March 1931, and 'B.B.C. statement in answer to enquiry.'

51 Plaunt papers, file 11-21, Spry to Murray, 28 May 1931.

52 LAC, Ottawa, E.A. Weir papers, M-715, typescript note by Weir, 'Interempire Christmas broadcast proposed for Christmas Day 1931'; E. Austin Weir, *The Struggle for National Broadcasting in Canada* (Toronto: McClelland and Stewart, 1965), 141. See also Plaunt papers, file 12-10, 'Memorandum on the cancellation of the empire Christmas broadcast.'

53 Spry papers, vol. 84, file 13, typescript MSS of chapter 4 of unpublished memoirs. See also Vipond, *Listening In*, 265. For a further example of the use to which the affair was put by the CRL see Spry papers, vol. 95, file 12, 'Memorandum presented to the Royal Commission on Railways and Transportation by Graham Spry,' 14 January 1932. Spry later claimed that

he had 'cooked up' the whole affair by suggesting to Murray that the BBC cancel the broadcast and then whipping up Canadian newspaper interest in the resulting debacle. See Weir papers, vol. 6, file 4, Spry to Weir, 11 May 1962. However, other evidence suggests that the cancellation was unplanned, and that the advocates of public broadcasting only subsequently recognized its beneficial consequences. See Plaunt papers, file 11-10, cable from Murray to Spry, 24 December 1931; LAC, Brooke Claxton Fonds, vol. 5, file – Canadian Radio League, 1932–1936, copy of Claxton to Murray, 26 January 1932; Weir papers, vol. 2, file 11, Frank England to Weir, 23 December 1931 and 15 February 1932.

54 Peers, *Politics*, 78.
55 WAC, Reith Diaries, S60/5/3/2, entry for 21 March 1932. Plaunt papers, file 11-24, cable from Spry to Murray, 19 March 1932; file 11-10, cable from Murray to Spry, 21 March 1932; file 3-14, cable Murray to Plaunt, 23 March 1932. University of Toronto Archives and Records Management, Toronto, Vincent Massey papers, box 59, file 3, cable from Plaunt to Massey, 21 March [1932]. O'Brien, 'History of the CRL,' 268–9.
56 Massey papers, box 59, file 3, [Murray], 'Radio Broadcasting – Memorandum submitted as basis of evidence, Ottawa 1932.'
57 Plaunt papers, file 11-25, Spry to Massey, 8 June 1932; Claxton fonds, vol. 5, file – Canadian Radio League, 1932–1936, copy of Claxton to Murray, 14 May 1932; *Toronto Daily Star*, 12 May 1932, quoted by Peers, *Politics*, 86; LAC, RG41, vol. 303, file 14-2-1 (part 1), copy of C.A. Bowman to Donald Manson, 10 January 1949.
58 Vipond, *Listening In*, 264–80; Mary Vipond, 'The Canadian Radio Broadcasting Commission in the 1930s: How Canada's First Public Broadcaster Negotiated "Britishness,"' in Phillip Buckner and R. Douglas Francis, eds, *Canada and the British World: Culture, Migration and Identity* (Vancouver: UBC Press, 2006), 271.
59 WAC, Reith Diaries, S60/5/3/2, entry for 11 November 1932.
60 'The future of British Broadcasting – "I believe the present form will survive" by Sir John Reith,' *London Daily Telegraph*, 15 November 1932.
61 Quoted in Peers, *Politics*, 96.
62 HOC, *Debates*, 18 May 1932, 3035-6, quoted in Weir, 133, and Vipond, *Listening In*, 270.
63 Quoted in Vipond, *Listening In*, 268.
64 Plaunt papers, file 12-3, Alan Plaunt note book, 'Some notes on the Radio League, 25 May 1932.'
65 Plaunt papers, file 12-1, copy of Murray to Claxton, 28 December 1932. Claxton fonds, vol. 5, file – Canadian Radio League, 1932–1936, Copy of

Claxton to Murray, 14 May 1932; C.F. Crandall to Claxton, 18 October 1932. LAC, RG41, vol. 33, file 2-2-3, W. Arthur Steel to W.C. Ronson, 20 May 1933. Weir, *Struggle for National Broadcasting*, 152.

66 HOC *Debates* Session 1932–3, 4858–4917. WAC, Reith Diaries, S60/5/3/2, entry for 16 June 1933.

67 Peers, *Politics*, 109, 122–6. LAC, RG41, vol. 33, file 2-2-3, 'National radio in Canada – report by Major Gladstone Murray,' 25 July 1933.

68 WAC, E15/178, typescript memo by J.C.W. Reith, 'Visit to Canada and the United States of America, November 1933,' 25 November 1933.

69 WAC, E4/48, Murray to Reith, 30 January 1934.

70 Ibid. Malcolm Frost to DBR, 30 December 1933.

71 Peers, *Politics*, 126–36; Nolan, *Foundations*, 110–15, quote at 113.

72 T.J. Allard, *Straight up: Private Broadcasting in Canada, 1918–1958* (Ottawa: Canadian Communications Foundation, 1979), 101–2. Murray had earlier suggested that Grier might appear before the 1932 committee. See Plaunt papers, file 11-10, cable from Murray to Spry, 21 March 1932.

73 *Special Committee on the Operations of the Commission under the Canadian Radio Broadcasting Act, 1932, Minutes and Proceedings* (Ottawa, 1934), 227–37.

74 WAC, E4/48, memo by C.G. Graves, 'Mr. Bennett,' 20 September 1934.

75 Peers, *Politics*, 146–65; Nolan, *Foundations*, 109–22.

76 Plaunt papers, file 1-19, Claxton to Plaunt, 10 December 1935.

77 Ibid. file 7-14, Plaunt to Claxton, 18 November 1935; file 1-19, Claxton to Plaunt, 10 December 1935; file 7-15, Plaunt to Claxton, 14 January 1936.

78 Ibid. file 3-14, Murray to Plaunt, 12 May 1935; file 3-15, Murray to Plaunt, 13 December 1935; O'Brien, 'History of the CRL,' 329–31.

79 Plaunt papers, file 7-14, copy of Plaunt to Howe, 23 December 1935. Peers, *Politics*, 165–70. O'Brien, 'History of the CRL,' 338–44.

80 WAC, Reith Diaries, S60/5/4/3, entry for 15 January 1936.

81 WAC, E4/48, memo by C.G. Graves, 'Mr. Bennett,' 20 September 1934. Vipond, 'The CRBC in the 1930s,' 272–6.

82 Murray fonds, vol. 1, file 'CBC Memoranda and Notes,' typescript MSS, [Murray], 'The Canadian Scene,' n.d. [c. end of 1939].

83 Andrew Boyle, *Only the Wind Will Listen: Reith of the BBC* (London: Hutchinson, 1972), 230.

84 WAC, L2/154/1, extract from memo [from Reith] to Controller and Assistant Controller, n.d. [early 1933]. As early as August 1930 Reith wrote in his diary that he had 'no confidence' in Murray. See WAC, Reith Diaries, S60/5/3/1, entry for 14 August 1930.

85 WAC, L2/154/1, record of interview with Murray, 28 February 1935. WAC, Reith Diaries, S60/5/4/2, entries for 4 February, 1 March, and 9 and 10

April 1935. On the more general frictions within the BBC at this time see Boyle, *Only the Wind*, 255–9.

86 WAC, E1/528, undated copy of cable from Greene to Graves [19 or 20 December 1935]; copy of C.D. Howe to Greene, 19 December 1935; report from Greene to Graves, 27 December 1935.

87 Ibid., copy of cable Graves to Greene, [22 December 1935]; code cable from Greene, received 6 January 1936. In the event, Graves later provided feedback only on minor points: see copy of cable Graves to Greene, sent 6 January 1936. A copy of Greene's report, 'Memorandum on the Future Organization of Radio Broadcasting in Canada,' is also preserved in this file.

88 Plaunt papers, file 3-16, Murray to Plaunt, 2 January 1936.

89 Ibid., file 1-19, Claxton to Plaunt, 17 and 31 January 1936.

90 Massey papers, box 166, file 8. Peers, *Politics*, 170–2. O'Brien, 'History of the CRL,' 349–53.

91 WAC, E1/528, copies of cables from Greene to Graves, 19 and 20 February 1936, and copy of Graves to Sir Edward Harding, 20 February 1936. UKNA, DO35/228/2, file - Canadian Broadcasting, Floud to Harding, 17 January 1936. WAC, Reith Diaries, S60/5/4/3, entry for 22 February 1936.

92 WAC, E1/528, cable from Greene to Graves, 21 February 1936; copy of cable from Graves to Greene, 22 February 1936; record of telephone conversation between Graves and Greene, 24 February 1936; Graves to Reith, 8 January 1936. See also UKNA, DO35/228/2, file – Canadian Broadcasting, extract from H. Batterbee to Floud, 27 March 1936.

93 Peers, *Politics*, 174–5, 183. O'Brien, 'History of the CRL,' 355–60. Plaunt papers, file 1–18, Claxton to Plaunt, 5 March 1936. For Plaunt's published criticisms see Alan B. Plaunt, 'Canadian Radio,' *Saturday Night*, 4 April 1936.

94 Peers, *Politics*, 184–9; Nolan, *Foundations*, 129–34; Vipond, *Listening In*, 41.

95 WAC, E1/528, Harding to Graves, 15 June 1936 and Graves to Harding, 16 June 1936; UKNA, DO35/228/2, file – Interview with Mr Felix Greene at DO, minute by 'C.R.P.,' 29 June 1936.

96 O'Brien, 'History of the CRL,' 365–73; Spry papers, vol. 96, file 2, copy of Plaunt to Claxton, 25 June 1936; Plaunt papers, file 2-2, Crandall to Plaunt, 17 June 1936; file 2-10, J. F. Garrett to Plaunt, 15 June 1936; file 7-22, Plaunt to Garrett, 27 June 1936.

97 WAC, E1/113/2, Graves to Greene, 27 February 1936 plus accompanying note.

98 WAC, L2/154/1, report on Murray by Graves, first quarter, 1936, and 'Note for the PMG – Mr W.E.G. Murray,' 15 December 1936; WAC, Reith Diaries, S60/5/4/3, entry for 14 March 1936.

99   WAC, L2/154/1, Reith's record of interview with Murray, 1 April 1936; Ian McIntyre, 'Murray, (William Ewart) Gladstone (1893–1970),' *Oxford Dictionary of National Biography* (Oxford: Oxford University Press, 2004).

100 Plaunt papers, file 2-2, Crandall to Plaunt, 17 June 1936; file 7-24, Plaunt to Murray, 6 August 1936.

101 WAC, L2/154/1, 'Statement of Major W.E. Gladstone to board of governors and director-general,' 29 April 1936.

102 Plaunt papers, file 3-15, Murray to Plaunt, 1 November 1935.

103 Ibid. file 3-19, Murray to Plaunt, 21 and 22 July 1936. See also file 3-15, Murray to Plaunt, 5 November 1935.

104 WAC, L2/154/1, Murray to Graves, 24 April 1936.

105 UKNA, DO35/228/2, minute by 'C.R.P.,' 29 June 1936. The Dominions Office refused to get involved.

106 Plaunt papers, file 2-13, Greene to Plaunt, 30 May 1936; file 1-7, Greene to Plaunt, 18 September 1936.

107 LAC, W.L.M. King papers, reel C-3685, vol. 213, ff. 184182–3, Charles A. Bowman to King, [n.d.]; reel C-3692 vol. 224, ff. 193420–3, Alan Plaunt to King, 29 July 1936, and f. 193425, Plaunt to King, 5 July 1936. See also Plaunt papers, file 1-20, Claxton to Plaunt, 4 July 1936; file 7-22, Plaunt to Murray, 22 June [1936]; and file 7-24, Plaunt to Claxton, 15 September 1936.

108 Plaunt papers, file 1-20, copy of Claxton to N. McL. Rogers, 16 June 1936; file 13-4, 'Radio League memo – confidential – Re: W.E. Gladstone Murray,' 7 May 1936.

109 WAC, E1/113/2, Greene to Graves, 6 October 1936.

110 Murray fonds, vol. 14, scrapbook, cuttings: 'For the Canadian Ether,' *Liverpool Daily Post*, 24 September 1936; *Wireless World*, 2 October 1936; *Sunday Times*, 27 September 1936.

111 WAC, E1/113/2, Greene to Graves, 6 October 1936. WAC, Reith Diaries, S60/5/4/4, entry for 23 September 1936. On some of Murray's subsequent empire-related activities at the CBC see Simon J. Potter, 'The BBC, the CBC, and the 1939 Royal Tour of Canada,' *Cultural and Social History* 3, no. 4 (October 2006): 424–44.

4 'The Luxury of Moderate Use': Seagram and Moderation Advertising, 1934–1955

DANIEL J. ROBINSON

At a 2005 press conference promoting Dan Aykroyd's investment in an Ontario winery the actor-comedian took an impromptu bathroom break and joked upon returning: 'Everything in moderation. I did have three glasses.'[1] In the 2006 satirical film *Thank You for Smoking*, weekly meetings of the M.O.D. ('Merchants of Death') Squad featured tobacco and firearms lobbyists alongside Polly Bailey, the head of the 'Moderation Council,' who fretted over the effect of fetal alcohol syndrome awareness campaigns on alcohol sales. To work, these jokes required audience knowledge of the close association between alcohol and the merits of moderation, a relationship with a long history in Canada and the United States. The moderation message underpins contemporary understandings of socially acceptable drinking. Today's archetypal 'social' drinker is also a moderate drinker (at least those over thirty), whether imbibing with others or alone. Up to two drinks daily, physicians tell us, improves cholesterol counts, lessens blood clotting, and reduces heart disease. Psychiatrists point to alcohol's 'biphasic' effect: a couple of drinks typically make us cheerful and relaxed, while more than four can unleash feelings of sadness or anger.[2] The moderate drinker, sound of body and mind, exemplifies moral worth and social responsibility; she or he recognizes appropriate limits and (most) always exercises self-restraint.

This paper provides a historical account of alcohol promotion and moderation discourse. In 1934, soon after entering the American market in the wake of the repeal of prohibition, the Canadian distiller Seagram launched its inaugural moderation advertising campaign, a first-of-its-kind appeal for socially responsible liquor consumption.[3] Seagram's moderation advertising, in various forms, continued into the late 1990s, making it one of North America's longest-running advertising campaigns.[4] Despite this longevity, historians of advertising[5] or alcohol[6] have not dealt much with this public relations campaign, either for its influence on the improved social standing of alcohol by the 1950s or for its effect on corporate social responsibility programs in other sectors.[7]

The longevity and enduring appeal of Seagram's moderation advertising derive from more than the resonance of the campaign's core messages – that excessive drinking carries the risk of physical and psychological harm, familial strife, and diminished social standing. The public relations discourse of moderation fitted well with Seagram's overall marketing strategy of promoting premium, blended whisky brands to discriminating consumers who would savour the product sparingly. Political-economic factors were also significant: in all but two Canadian provinces brand advertising for spirits was banned. Moderation's vitality was a function of its mutative and transcendent qualities. The advertising campaign was launched to alleviate social concerns about alcohol abuse after the end of American prohibition, but the moderation theme advanced beyond the act of drinking to promulgate the 'moderate personality' as an ideal type. Against the backdrop of consumer goods rationing during the Second World War, moderation advertising exalted the 'moderate consumer' as a paragon of civic virtue in the struggle against inflation. During the early Cold War years, the campaign expanded to promote the 'moderate citizen' as an exemplar of political reason and common sense. Moderation evolved into an all-encompassing creed, a way of life affecting not only drinking habits, but general temperament, getting and spending, and political outlook.

Moderation advertising was also bound up with the personal ambitions of Sam Bronfman, the Jewish immigrant who rose from humble origins to build up Seagram into a multinational powerhouse. By the early 1950s, it counted $700 million in annual sales, most of which were in the United States.[8] Indeed, Bronfman was a binational presence during much of his career; after the mid-1930s, he typically spent weekdays in New York and weekends in Montreal while pursuing company business. Accordingly, this paper draws interchangeably on Canadian and U.S. examples, in part because of Bronfman's and Seagram's binational presence, but also because similar moderation advertising ran in both countries. Throughout his life, Bronfman craved forms of social recognition which he believed were denied him by anti-Semitism and his association with liquor manufacturing, both during and after prohibition in Canada and the United States. Moderation advertising, with its emphasis on social responsibility, reflected Bronfman's deep-seated desire for social acceptance within reticent, high-society circles.

This paper highlights a type of 'discursive formation' giving rise to moderationist ideas governing alcohol use and corresponding business rationales for its promotion. It is informed by Michel Foucault's interest in the 'practical field' of discursive deployment and the 'law of *existence* of statements' that occur in historically specific contexts.[9] Prohibition and the early post-repeal years provided a singular set of circumstances that enabled the rise and consolidation of a discursive framework concerning the ethical and normative dimensions of alcohol consumption. The moderationist creed, over time, aimed to regulate personal conduct and construct subjective identities while remaining tied to the commercial power of Seagram and the spirits industry in general, the doctrine's primary promulgators. The far-sweeping conceptual embrace of moderationist discourse – advancing idealized notions of drinking, personality, consumption, and citizenship – is reflective of what Nikolas Rose calls a 'technique of the self,' a mode of self-regulation that produces individual subjectivities aligned with larger social and political objectives. Scholars of 'governmentality' have focused on different players that have facilitated this 'regime of the self,' among them the 'psy-' professions, voluntary organizations, and pastoral groups.[10] Largely neglected, however, have been business activities and the role of commercial consumption in general in producing forms of discursive knowledge and accompanying truths.[11]

Background

The son of Jewish refugees fleeing czarist Russia in the late 1880s, Sam Bronfman entered the innkeeping and bar business in 1912 with the purchase of the Bell Hotel in Winnipeg, Manitoba. When during the Great War the rising prohibitionist tide forced the closure of the province's bars, Sam turned to the federally regulated interprovincial liquor trade. In 1918, Ottawa banned this trade while allowing the sale of spirits for medicinal purposes. Consequently, Bronfman and brothers Harry and Allan formed a mail-order company to sell liquor to drugstores nationwide, in effect using the federal postal system to evade provincially mandated prohibition. In 1924, the brothers built a distillery in the Montreal suburb of LaSalle, incorporating that year as Distillers Corporation Ltd. Four years later, it bought Joseph E. Seagram and Sons, an Ontario whisky distillery established in 1857 and known for its 'V.O.' and '83' brands. The name Distillers Corporation-Seagram Limited having been adopted, the company's first-year profits were an impressive $2.2 million, largely the result of American prohibition and the demand for bootleg whisky shipped from Canada. In the early 1920s, the Bronfmans sold whisky to prairie 'export houses,' whose agents then smuggled it into U.S. border states. Enhanced law enforcement curtailed these operations by the late 1920s, when the illicit liquor trade moved east to the waters of the Great Lakes, until it too was stymied by stepped-up border patrols. By the early 1930s, the base for supplying much of the U.S. whisky market had shifted to the French islands of St Pierre and Miquelon, located off the coast of Newfoundland.[12]

During these early years, the Bronfman brothers had frequent run-ins with law enforcement and political officials, though none resulted in serious convictions. Their early operations paid no federal income taxes, which in 1921 resulted in a $200,000 payment to Ottawa for back taxes. While the Bronfmans sold whisky legally to export houses, their agents had widely known ties to American organized crime. Prior to being investigated by the Royal Commission on Customs and Excise in the late 1920s, the Bronfmans destroyed the account books for some of their export companies. In 1930 Harry Bronfman was tried and acquitted by a Saskatchewan jury for bribing a customs officer. In 1935, the Royal Canadian Mounted Police charged Sam and Harry with tax evasion, claiming that they had rerouted U.S.-bound whisky back into Canada in order to save $5 million in custom and excise duties. The brothers were acquitted on these charges.[13] In 1949, the U.S. Justice Department's Anti-Trust Division investigated Seagram and three other distillers for anti-trust violations, though no charges were ever laid. Members of a House of Representatives subcommittee later alleged that charges had been avoided because of irregular political contributions, mostly to Democrats, with the largest of these being a $50,000 donation from Seagram Vice-President James E. Friel and fellow executives.[14] In 1952, the Federal Trade Commission filed charges of conspiracy to fix prices against Seagram and its twenty-one subsidiaries.[15]

While spirits were legal to manufacture and sell in most of Canada by the early 1930s, alcohol use remained highly contested.[16] The Gallup poll arrived in Canada in 1941, and soon after tallies on 'the liquor question' appeared. While just 22 per cent favoured total prohibition in March 1942, 67 per cent of decided opinion backed weekly limits on liquor purchases. Six months later support for prohibition rose to 31 percent; likely more troubling for distillers, however, was the finding that two-thirds of decided respondents favoured nationalizing the manufacture and sale of spirits.[17] Public opinion on alcohol was often divided. When asked if liquor sales should be halted on a hypothetical 'V-Day,' 45 per cent agreed, while 48 per cent were opposed. Opinions were evenly split (43–43 per cent) in September 1945 on whether liquor rationing should be continued after the war. Underscoring this lack of consensus, a Gallup poll in March 1946 noted: 'If you get 100 average Canadians in a room and asked them what they would do about the liquor situation in Canada, you'd probably get a good many more than 100 answers, so diversified is opinion on this issue.' Canadians were evenly divided in 1948 on the merits of liquor advertising in print media and on billboards. Fifty-one per cent of decided opinion was in favour, while 48 per cent was opposed. Gallup pollsters registered a paradoxical finding: 'And such is the perversity of human nature that, in Ontario, where brand advertising of liquor is not permitted, a majority think it should be. In Quebec, which is one of two provinces where brand advertising is permitted, a majority think it should not be.'[18]

The advertising of distilled spirits was highly regulated. In 1948, only British Columbia and Quebec allowed brand and institutional (company) advertising for spirits. Institutional advertising was permitted in Ontario, Manitoba, Alberta, and New Brunswick. Saskatchewan, Nova Scotia, and Prince Edward Island banned all forms of spirits advertising. A 1958 report by Vickers and Benson, Seagram's advertising agency from the 1920s until the 1960s, decried how spirits advertising was 'handcuffed and weighed down by the varying liquor regulations of *all ten* Canadian provinces.' British Columbia and Quebec had the most liberal liquor laws, and many national magazines were printed in Quebec, if not edited there, in order to carry spirits ads. Even in Quebec, one of only two provinces to permit institutional and brand advertising, a 'gentlemen's agreement' prohibited the depiction of bottles, glasses, and drinking scenes in hard liquor advertisements and banned the use of billboards and outdoor posters.[19] N.G. McHardy, the editor of *Wine, Beer and Spirits in Canada*, underscored how social propriety concerns had forced distilled spirits producers to 'exclude from his advertising some of the very qualities which are regarded as praiseworthy when they appear in advertising campaigns waged on behalf of other products.' As a consequence, liquor companies lacked the 'creative freedom' to effectively advertise their products.[20]

With limited advertising options, Seagram secured other means for promoting its products and company name. Event sponsorship, corporate philanthropy, institutional advertising, and goodwill publishing ventures all figured prominently. Seagram sponsored numerous sporting events like boxing matches, running races, swimming contests, snowshoe races, and golf tournaments such as the International Blind Golfers Tournament. In 1936, it became the lead sponsor of the Canadian Open Golf Championship, doubling the prize purse and offering the Seagram Gold Cup.[21] Philanthropic efforts centred on Jewish causes, notably organizations like the Jewish Federation of Charities and Mount Sinai Sanatorium. In 1943, Seagram published and distributed *Canada – The Foundations of Its Future*, a lavishly illustrated history of Canada written by Stephen Leacock. Ten years later, the company published *Cities of Canada*, which featured cityscape paintings from the Seagram art collection. In 1951, the company spent $1 million to establish the Sam Bronfman Foundation to 'perpetuate the ideals of American democracy.' It endowed a chair in Columbia University's Graduate School of Business to promote the 'basic techniques of democratic business activity,' ironically so given Bronfman's notoriously autocratic style of managing.[22] That year, Seagram formed the Seagram Family Achievement Association, a public relations initiative aimed at the company's distributors and their families. The goal was to make the U.S. spirits industry 'as respected as it [is] in Great Britain and other countries abroad.' Members were encouraged to assist charity drives and, when a 'bad liquor situation developed in their communities,' to 'lead the fight against it.'[23] Public relations activities like these were not foreign to North American businesses; General Electric, AT&T, DuPont, and others had adopted similar 'acts of public beneficence' in order to affirm the free enterprise system and the legitimacy of big business when both were under attack during the depression.[24]

For companies like Seagram, public opinion mattered as much as consumer choices. Frank Schwengel, Seagram's president of U.S. operations, observed in 1951 that the liquor industry was a 'creature of legislative process though confirmed by the will of the people,' while 'subject to recall by the same process which gave it birth.'[25] Seagram advertising executive William Wachtel described cultivating close ties with wholesalers, salesmen, retailers, and bar owners, with the goal of 'raising the standards of behaviour' and avoiding 'bad publicity which would damage the image of our industry.'[26] Such concerns were not unwarranted. Soon after the repeal of prohibition, the Roosevelt administration had seriously considered heavy state regulation of the distilling industry, eventually backing off over concerns that such a government agency would become too prone to political influence.[27] In 1942, Washington required the distilling industry to convert to the production of industrial alcohol, with the exception of brief 'liquor holidays' in 1944 and 1945.[28] During the 1940s and 1950s, nine congressional hearings discussed heightened regulations or outright bans involving liquor marketing and advertising. Pennock and Kerr note that dry sentiment 'remained a powerful voice in some regions for several decades after 1933'; as a consequence, no other industry 'policed itself so carefully in an effort to stave off widespread animosity.'[29] Such self-regulation in the United States is seen with the advertising code of the Distilled Spirits Institute, the industry association. It prohibited ads in Sunday newspapers, religious publications, and on radio (and later television). It also banned the depiction of women in advertisements until 1958. Liquor advertising generally did not portray anything 'other than moderate drinking in safe, and usually genteel surroundings.'[30]

Seagram's embrace of moderation in the 1930s was not a new development for the alcohol industry. In Canada during the 1910s and 1920s, 'moderation leagues,' often backed by beer and spirits manufacturers, waged campaigns against dry proponents and prohibition itself. Their arguments focused on lost excise tax revenues and prohibition's radicalization of the drink-deprived working classes. Alcohol bans were cast as 'un-British' and unpatriotic, an affront to the venerable tradition of individual liberty. The leagues recruited heavily among Great War veterans, organizing petition drives and lobbying governments to hold plebiscites on repeal. Moderation was touted as a 'third path' between the extremes of statist prohibition and the unbridled saloon or speakeasy.[31] As Craig Heron argues, the success of the moderation message in helping to overturn prohibition owed to its protean nature:

It captured the yearning of bourgeois Canadians for refined drinking occasions, and an end to lawlessness, and a new era of less politically destabilizing extremism. It embraced the proletarian desire for the right to respectable imbibing and an end to class-biased legislation. It was an appeal to greater personal freedom for sensible, orderly behaviour, under the still watchful eyes of the state. It was an acceptable compromise for the brewing and distilling interests, and it made sense to the majority of the thousands of Canadians who were asked to express an opinion on the continuation or repeal of prohibition between 1919 and 1929.[32]

Similarly, in the United States, the Council for Moderation, whose members included John D. Rockefeller, Jr, and William H. Vanderbilt, lobbied for a 'practical program of temperance education' in which alcohol would be a matter of 'personal responsibility rather than legal prohibition.'[33] And here too moderation appeals would prove effective during the campaign for repeal.[34]

The Moderate Drinker

'We who make whisky say: DRINK MODERATELY,' proclaimed the headline of the Seagram advertisement that ran in dozens of American newspapers and magazines in October 1934 (figure 4.1). In keeping with the solemn message, the inaugural moderation ad contained no image, only a dense page of text.[35] Wisdom through the ages had shown that the 'lasting enjoyment of the pleasures of life depends on *moderation*,' an ethos and approach to drinking absent during the age of excess that was prohibition-era America. The repeal era, however, presented 'threats' to freedom and liberty, since people 'lacked experience' in making sound lifestyle and brand choices about liquor. The moderation message took up concerns that people might forgo milk or bread to purchase liquor. Whisky was a luxury product, not a replacement for basic staples, and luxury items were best enjoyed in moderation. But not all whiskies were luxurious, for only Seagram brands possessed the *'full mellowness, full wholesomeness'* rendered by long aging and skilful blending. Moderation was a call to drink less of a good thing, to avoid the 'empty satisfaction that follows upon profusion of the second rate.' It was a call to 'Drink moderately ... Drink better whiskey,' which, given the ad's syllogism, meant drinking Seagram's products.[36] Moderation and the marketing of premium whisky went down nicely together.

Not surprisingly, Seagram's initial marketing strategy in the United States stressed the superiority of older, blended Canadian rye whiskies over 'straight' bourbon whiskies. In 1934, it launched its Five Crown and Seven Crown labels, which soon grew to be sales leaders in their categories. Brands like King's Plate and, later, Chivas Regal and Crown Royal evoked aristocratic themes, seen as a 'way of moving to the upscale segment of the market' and lending an 'aura of class' to the brands. Advertising campaigns included 'Say Seagram's and Be Sure'

We who make whiskey SAY:
"DRINK MODERATELY"

ON one point all thoughtful men have always agreed. On one point all connoisseurs in the art of enjoyable living have always agreed.

The lasting enjoyment of the pleasures of life depends on *moderation.*

A few weeks will mark the anniversary of Repeal. We think it is appropriate that we who make whiskey should emphasize, to you who drink whiskey, the desirability of moderation.

For a situation exists today which requires us both to take an honest, serious look at the future.

Our own stake in that future is clear—our part in an industry in which we have held an honored position for 77 years.

Your stake is of vital concern.

It involves not only your health, your money expenditures, and your enjoyment of life—but a principle which is the very core and fibre of American history and tradition—your personal liberty.

The Threat to Liberty

When Repeal came, most brand names were unfamiliar. People lacked experience. They didn't know how to choose.

Many bought unwisely. And drank unwisely, too. Because this new whiskey was inexpensive, it was consumed freely. Because of its rawness and harshness, it could not be consumed as whiskey should be—for mellow warmth and flavor.

If we both think honestly and speak frankly, we must admit this condition is not in the tradition of fine living. It is not what any thoughtful person could desire.

What Common Sense Suggests

There is nothing new about drinking whiskey.

Through generations, it has always occupied a natural place in gracious living.

The House of Seagram believes that whiskey, properly used, is deserving of that position. Seagram's has always felt that the proper use of whiskey suggests a pleasure in its aroma, its flavor, its mellowness.

However, these characteristics are *found only in whiskey that has been properly distilled and then brought to full mellowness, full wholesomeness, by aging.*

The real enjoyment which whiskey can add to the pleasures of gracious living is possible only to the man who drinks good, aged whiskey and drinks moderately.

Therefore, the lesson of generations of experience is not inapplicable to problems of today. The principle of moderation is not at variance with what common sense suggests as the right course for us today.

Drink moderately...Drink better whiskey.

Whiskey is a Luxury

Whiskey cannot take the place of milk, bread or meat. The pleasure which good whiskey offers is definitely a luxury.

On our part we feel so strongly that we say— *the House of Seagram does not want a dollar that should be spent for the necessities of life.*

And even to those to whom whiskey does not mean actual deprivation, we say—treat whiskey as a luxury. A pint of good, aged whiskey will bring you more enjoyment, more satisfaction, than a quart of whiskey of dubious quality.

We feel sure that you will agree with us that the desirable way of life is thoughtful, informed by experience, guided by common sense. Realizing this, we feel sure that you will prefer moderation in the enjoyment of the finest to the empty satisfaction that follows upon profusion of the second rate.

THE HOUSE OF

Seagram

FINE WHISKIES SINCE 1857

Joseph E. Seagram & Sons, Inc., Executive Offices: Chrysler Bldg., New York City

Figure 4.1: Seagram's inaugural moderation ad ran in October 1934, the launch of a social responsibility campaign that continued into the 1990s. Hagley Museum and Library.

and the much-discussed[37] 'Men of Distinction' series for Lord Calvert whisky, consisting of endorsements by debonair actors, literary notables, and European royalty. Seagram also sold bottled whisky to distributors, rather than barrel consignments, which ensured greater control over product quality. Sam Bronfman wanted his 'advertising to reflect quality, because he really did believe in quality'; and he was known for issuing maxims like 'Go first class' and 'Take the high road.'[38] In his advertising and personal proselytizing, Bronfman sought to overhaul whisky's lowbrow image, from an association with the hayseed and bootlegger to one embodying cosmopolitanism and regal grace. It may have seemed incongruous that a line of 'modern,' blended whiskies would be married, via branding and advertising, to royal privilege conflating distinctive taste with social lineage. Seagram's approach, however, reflects Roland Marchand's observation that aristocratic themes in interwar advertising were part of a larger strategy for 'providing audiences with fantasies that would buffer their adaptation to modern realities' and assuage anxieties about erosions of individual autonomy and community.[39]

In Canada, the moderation ads appeared shortly after, usually as copies of American ads. The 1937 ad, 'We Don't Want Bread Money' (figure 4.2), showed a pair of withered hands slicing bread. Again, readers were advised that Seagram whiskies were 'luxury' goods, meant only for those who could afford 'the luxury of moderate use.' Moderation was less about deprivation and delayed gratification than about a particular style of consumption for whisky brands connoting social privilege, gracious living, and premium taste. 'Drinking and Driving Do Not Mix' (April 1937) contained a brief plea for 'safer, saner driving' as a public safety measure. But much of the ad *promoted* a category of drinking: 'Whiskey is a luxury and should be treated as such,' the ad intoned. 'When taken moderately ... with a true appreciation of its taste, bouquet and character, fine whiskey brings a sense of friendliness and fellowship to social gatherings.' A year later, 'Pay your Bills First' reiterated that basic amenities – not whisky – should have 'first call' on people's pocketbooks. Moreover, the ad cautioned, the 'very existence of legalized liquor in this country depends upon the civilized manner in which it is consumed.' Reflecting the paternalism of many of these ads, Father's Day formed the backdrop for numerous moderation ads during the late 1930s and 1940s. In 'You're a Hero to Your Son,' fathers who drank immoderately were urged, somewhat naively, to abstain entirely (figure 4.3), The responsibilities of the father-as-moderate-drinker were twofold: he must spare his chil-

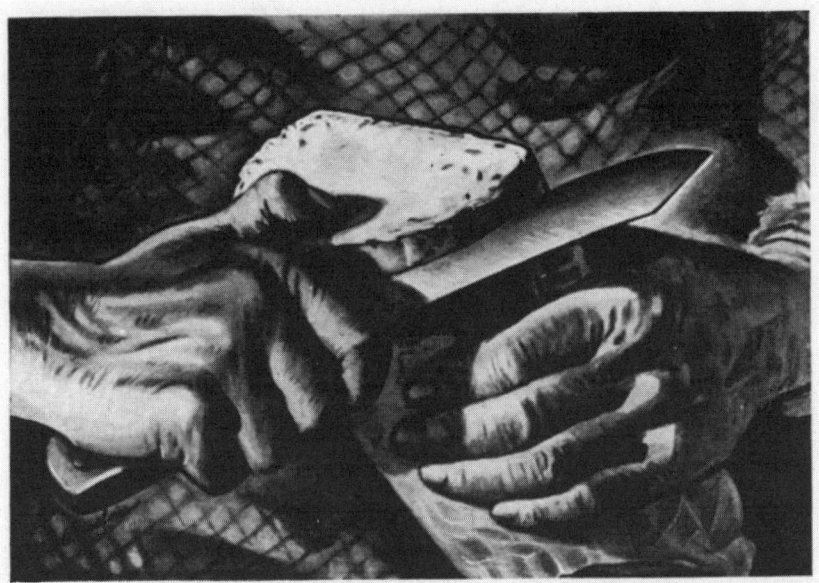

WE DON'T WANT BREAD MONEY

Liquor is one of the luxuries of life, to be bought and enjoyed only after the necessities are provided. Whoever needs bread for himself or his family, should not buy whiskey.

The persons we want for our regular customers have definite incomes and definite obligations. They do not exceed the one nor neglect the other. We make sales to such persons with a clear conscience because Seagram whiskies are well worth all they cost to those who can afford the luxury of moderate use. We don't want to sell whiskey to anyone who buys it at a sacrifice of the necessities or decencies. At this season of the year it seems opportune to again repeat our policy...to again reiterate our sense of social obligation.

"We don't want to sell whiskey to anyone who buys it at a sacrifice of the necessities of life."

SEAGRAM-DISTILLERS CORPORATION, EXECUTIVE OFFICES: N.Y.

THE HOUSE OF SEAGRAM

FINE WHISKIES SINCE 1857

Figure 4.2: Against the backdrop of the depression and temperance sentiment, Seagram, in this 1937 ad, promoted its whiskies as discretionary goods, suitable only for people who could 'afford the luxury of moderate use.' Hagley Museum and Library.

You can obtain a reproduction of the above drawing, suitable for framing, by writing to Seagram-Distillers Corp., Chrysler Building, New York City

YOU'RE A HERO ·· TO YOUR SON

Most boys worship their Dad as a hero whose standards and ideals they gradually acquire as their own.

Nothing is quite so disillusioning to the clear eyes of a youngster as the sight of a man—his own father—who has used liquor unwisely.

The damage goes deeper than momentary shame.

Any man who cannot drink wisely and moderately, owes it to his son . . . his family, not to drink at all.

The coming generation will be less apt to use liquor intemperately if older people will regard it as a luxury and treat it as a contribution to gracious living—to be enjoyed in moderation.

Surely, Father's Day is an appropriate occasion for the House of Seagram, as one of America's leading distillers, to say as we have said for *four* years . . . "Drink Moderately".

··· THE HOUSE OF SEAGRAM ···
Fine Whiskies Since 1857

Seagram-Distillers Corp. Executive Offices, New York

Figure 4.3: Around Father's Day, moderation ads, like this one from 1938, equated restrained drinking with paternal responsibility. Hagley Museum and Library.

dren the ignominy 'that goes deeper than momentary shame' of seeing him drink 'unwisely.' Second, he must set an example and pass on the moderationist torch to his own sons, who, when adults, would uphold whisky 'as a luxury and treat it as a contribution to gracious living.' At its heart, moderation advertising promoted a particular mode of consumption, however restrained, one that affirmed personal dignity and social responsibility, while also licensing a limited form of individual gratification.

The Moderate Personality

In 1936, Seagram published the thirty-seven-page booklet, 'You'll Feel Better,' which trumpeted moderation as the key to 'health and happiness' during one's 'precious Middle Years.' The booklet was a moral treatise on the redemptive qualities of moderation, both as practice and philosophy. Many men in their twenties, it stated, overindulged and behaved recklessly. When in their thirties, these men began to 'take stock of things,' chief among them the embrace of more moderate approaches to living. They were now in search of 'sound habits of thinking and of living,' and, not surprisingly, 'sound habits mean moderate habits.' 'Moderation in thinking' was as important as healthy eating and drinking, for psychologists had shown that 'intemperate thinking' effectively 'poison[ed] the body.' A moderate disposition was the 'magic password to contentment and happiness for everyman,' who would be spared ailments like migraine headaches and chronic dyspepsia, which were the painful effects of 'wrong thinking upon the physical body.'

In the chapter 'Wisdom of the Ages,' the philosophical pedigree of moderation was laid out. Homage was paid to moderation's early disciples – Euripides, Plato, and Seneca – and Spartan thought was praised for its espousal of 'moderation in all things.' Quotations from Socrates ('moderation is but another name for Wisdom') and Confucius ('the superior man is he who errs neither on the side of excess nor of self-denial, but practices moderation in the use of all of his gifts and powers') appeared, as did Benjamin Franklin's choice of moderation as one of his twelve precepts for healthy living. In later chapters, the moderationist creed addressed the emotions, noting how 'uncontrolled emotionalism' fostered greed, jealousy, and vanity. The moderate man must not overindulge in the 'emotion of love,' since this 'may sacrifice his hope of a long and comfortable life.' Similar warnings were issued against excessive levels of work and play. The penultimate chapter discussed moderation and drinking. For those 'especially superior men' who 'work at high tension' jobs and desire to relax at day's end, the answer was simple: 'Drink moderately if you cannot stop thinking and being tense over the day's work.' By doing so, 'You'll Feel Better.'[40]

Part stoic treatise, part personality primer for the mass society, 'You'll Feel Better' was a template for better living in the post-repeal age. It embodied a view of self-realization via consumption, emphasizing the responsible exercise of individual will and admonishing 'excessive' types of indulgence whose 'epitome [was] the alcoholic.'[41] Significantly, the scientific study of alcohol changed during the 1930s, from a previous focus on environmental aspects of alcohol use (e.g., family strife, civic disruption) to one highlighting physiological and psychological questions. Advancing this research agenda was the Research Council on Problems of Alcohol, formed in 1939, which became the precursor to the influential Yale Center for Alcohol Studies. The Research Council was funded by the liquor industry, which, Valverde notes, was keen to demonstrate that 'alcohol was not itself a problem, and that the problems of drinking were really caused by a small minority of people who had pathological patterns of consumption.'[42]

Moderation advertising generated favourable feedback from customers and the press. Bronfman claimed his firm received some 150,000 complimentary letters.[43] A *Canadian Business* article in 1940 noted how Seagram's ad campaign had 'revolutionized relations between a producer of goods and the public' by 'advocating moderation in all things.' The article noted how a recent issue of *Reader's Digest* had reprinted a series of moderation ads under the headline 'A New High in Liquor Advertising.' The campaign earned ad industry awards like the Socrates Award and the Publishers Service Award.[44] In a 1942 editorial, the *Globe and Mail* reiterated the moderationist line when arguing against wartime prohibition: 'The wise use of any potentially dangerous article comes through sound upbringing, good education and self-discipline, and cannot be imparted by law.' Those who 'drink as civilized people, should not be prevented from enjoying the undoubted social advantages of stimulants which overcome diffidence and facilitate social intercourse.'[45] But opposition to the 'liquor trade' during wartime remained strong in certain parts of Canada, notably on the prairies, where the Bronfmans' earlier days as whisky traders were part of popular lore. Editorial writers at the *Moose Jaw Times-Herald* sarcastically attacked opponents of wartime liquor controls in a piece titled, 'Salute to the Bootlegger':

All hail to the Bronfmans, the Regina junk dealers who have become multimillionaires in the whisky business under both 'prohibition' and 'moderation' eras. All hail to the Bronfman plan to educate our rising generation. The Ministers of Education in all the Provinces, in formulating their true temperance education programs, should call in the Bronfman professors![46]

While the general trend in public opinion after 1942 moved progressively against wartime prohibition, there remained strong pockets of anti-drink sentiment in English-speaking Canada, notably among evangelical Protestants, married women, and rural dwellers.

The Moderate Consumer

Dry advocates won a partial victory in December 1942, when Ottawa banned most types of institutional and brand advertising for beer, wine, and spirits.[47] This was done to decrease the demand for beverage alcohol, whose consumption had grown considerably since 1939, and increase the supply of industrial alcohol for the production of war goods like synthetic rubber, smokeless powder, and pharmaceuticals. Alcohol companies could still advertise in support of the war effort, but they could not make direct reference to their roles as beverage alcohol producers. Consequently, Seagram issued a number of ads highlighting the company's role in manufacturing industrial alcohol and the multiple uses for it. As well, the company ran ads promoting war bonds, salvage drives, and closer Canadian–American relations ('We both like Apple Pie and Cheese').[48] A 1943 company memo described how such advertising did 'an outstanding job of creating good will and enhancing the prestige of the House of Seagram.'[49]

Towards war's end, new moderation advertising appeared promoting restrained consumption as a brake on inflation. According to an ad agency report, the moderation campaign was purposely 'broadened to include messages on behalf of controlled spending as a safeguard against unbridled inflation.' The 1945 ad 'Men Who Think of Tomorrow Guard Against Inflation Today' (figure 4.4) counselled Canadians to spend their savings on Victory Bonds, not unnecessary expenditures. The war against fascism was nearly won, but not yet the war against inflation, which had proved costly during and after the Great War. A postwar follow-up ad, 'Men who Think of Tomorrow … Practice Moderation Today!' warned of inflationary pressures linked to 'immoderate and unessential spending.' The ad cautioned against the 'many strange ideas and philosophies that are with us today,' underscoring that 'we think of tomorrow – and be moderate in all we do.' Delayed gratifica-

Figure 4.4: During the Second World War, Seagram's moderation advertising moved beyond alcohol use to emphasize moderate consumption in general as a brake on inflation. Hagley Museum and Library.

tion and thrift – long-standing agrarian and Protestant work ethic values – were now integral features of moderate consumption.[50]

Canada was a moderate nation and Canadians were a moderate people, subsequent ads asserted. 'We Walk the Middle Road' (1946) praised continued government controls on wages and prices in the fight against inflation. Low inflation was attributed to Canadians' embrace of the 'middle road' involving 'moderation in all things – in our thinking, in our actions and in our pleasures.' The ad 'Moderation Promises a Glorious Future' championed the stoicism and restraint of Canadians, who were unwilling to 'give in to the natural desire for immediate enjoyment of everything and anything presently in short supply.' Other ads like 'Who's Lucky?' and 'Moderation: One of Canada's Finest Assets' promoted moderate consumption as the surest hedge against the 'Inflationary Squirrel Cage.' In bolder terms, a 1947 ad, 'Something or Nothing,' proclaimed it better to have a 'moderate "something" ' than to have little in an inflationary economy. This was premised on the view 'that MODERATION is the key to CONTINUED ENJOYMENT, a principle to which the House of Seagram has always subscribed.' Additional ads like 'The Ice Is Still Thin' and 'Moderation Will See Us Through' echoed these points. The reintegration of moderate drinking with moderate consumption was seen in the 1947 ad 'Living Happily.' Here the 'business' of happy living hinged on moderation in 'attitudes,' 'spending,' 'personal habits,' and, when the occasion called for it, drinking whisky. The ad offered one of the fullest accounts of the moderationist creed: 'Along the path of moderation lies peace of mind, the respect of our neighbours, the confidence of our business associates, security and happiness.' Bronfman, who personally vetted each moderation ad, was, at least publicly, also a devotee to the cause: 'If we lived more moderately in everything,' he told the *Vancouver Province* in 1950, 'we'd live a lot longer.'[51] Liberal freedoms and consumer choice must not give licence to the pathology of excessive indulgence. Liquor use and postwar consumption in general required the responsible exercise of individual will.[52]

The Moderate Citizen

Moderation was a way of life, a means of reconciling tensions between self-indulgence and social welfare, between therapeutic release and delayed gratification. It soon branched out to incorporate more overt political meanings. Inflationary fears had waned by the late 1940s, replaced by political concerns related to the emerging Cold War. 'What Makes a Good Citizen?' a 1947 ad asked. The answer was the rejection of political extremes in many forms, notably bigotry. The ideal citizen understood his obligations to community and country, and reflected these by being 'moderate in his thinking and moderate in his actions,' which included drinking. A more political message resided in the 1948 ad, 'Freedom Isn't Free.' Freedom of speech and freedom of worship entailed such responsibilities as tolerance and mutual respect, and so too did the 'freedom to use whisky.' Here the corollary was an obligation to our families and 'to our communities.' In 'What Price Democracy' (1948), Canadians were cautioned against taking for granted democracy and civil liberties (figure 4.5). Preserving these freedoms and ideals would require ongoing vigilance. In service to this cause was moderation, now elevated to being 'one of the chief safeguards of democracy.' By being 'moderate in our thinking, in our actions, and in our pleasures, we are living democratically.' This discourse was in keeping with calls for political moderation offered by Arthur M. Schlesinger, Jr, and others in the late 1940s and early 1950s, in which liberalism was reframed in pragmatic and centrist forms.[53]

The first moderation ads stressed the virtue of self-control when drinking. Their scope soon after widened to espouse the merits of moderate personality types and, during the war, moderate consumption to combat inflation. After 1945, the campaign trumpeted moderate political beliefs, a muted reference to recent advances of democratic socialism and the emerging bipolar world order. What started as a moral message regarding alcohol use came to incorporate other areas of human life: psyche, society, and public sphere, such that one observer could claim in a liquor trade publication in 1956: '[America is] becoming a nation of moderates ... Our taste in clothing, schools, politics, is growing middle-of-the-road, at least for the moment.'[54] Marchand recounts how corporate public relations during the interwar years progressively colonized social, cultural, and political spheres of activity.[55] At stake for Seagram was not the legitimacy of oligopoly capitalism, but rather the social viability of a long-standing – if recently proscribed – pastime and product category.

Jewish Respectability

By all accounts, Bronfman played a hands-on role in Seagram's marketing and advertising. He conferred often and at length with his market-

WHAT PRICE

DEMOCRACY?

Democracy is without price . . . no one can ever take it for granted or assume it is paid for in full. It is an in-heritance we are duty bound to pass on . . . not only to the next generation, but to our fellow-men everywhere who have yet to enjoy its full benefits.

Democracy grew from a great ideal . . . that all men are born free and equal and are deserving of the same privileges. It can live on only if we constantly strive to fulfill this ideal and protect the priceless freedoms won.

Moderation is one of the chief safeguards of democracy. By being moderate in our thinking, in our actions, and in our pleasures, we are living democratically.

As The House of Seagram has so often stated, by being moderate in all things, including the enjoyment of whisky, we are acting for the common good.

Men who Think of Tomorrow
Practice Moderation Today!

THE HOUSE OF SEAGRAM

Prepared by
VICKERS & BENSON LIMITED
Montreal • Toronto
Magazine Advertisement—M-5
9" x 12"
1948

OCTOBER 1948

Figure 4.5: As the Cold War progressed, the moderation message broadened to include centrist political ideas and democratic freedoms. Hagley Museum and Library.

ing staff and those from advertising agencies with respect to branding, product launches, and bottle and label design. He personally approved all Seagram ads until the 1950s. William Wachtel, a former Seagram executive, praised his 'intuitive capacity'[56] for advertising, and fellow company advertiser Robert Sabloff confirmed Bronfman's zealous attachment to promotion; Bronfman made a habit of calling himself 'Salesman Sam' and often affirmed marketing and advertising as the cornerstones of his business. Bronfman took credit for the idea for moderation advertising, once describing how his advertising agency's initial lukewarm response to his suggestion had brought on the retort: 'If you don't have that ad on my [desk] the next time I'm in New York ... I am going to get another agency.'[57] Bronfman was especially proud of the praise for moderation ads issued by clergymen, public officials, editorialists, and ordinary citizens. For someone 'demonized as a bootlegger,' a Bronfman colleague noted, 'it was the ultimate endorsement and vindication.'[58]

Bronfman's wealth did not shield him from anti-Semitism in his business dealings. In 1926, he went to Britain to propose a partnership with Distillers Company Limited (DCL), the pre-eminent Edinburgh distiller. DCL rejected Bronfman's initial proposal, based, in part, on a board-commissioned report concluding that 'the Jews to which the Bronfmans belong are not generally regarded with favour in Canada.' DCL investigators had contacted Montreal businessmen, who advised the firm 'to have no dealings with any of the Jews.'[59] Montreal clubs like the Mount Royal denied entry to Bronfman and other Jews, and only late in his career did McGill University and the Bank of Montreal appoint him to their governing boards, despite his long-standing financial ties to both organizations. For many years a deep-pocketed contributor to the Liberal Party, Bronfman failed to procure a much-coveted Senate appointment, a rejection he partially attributed to anti-Semitism. Seagram sponsored the annual Canadian Open Golf Championship, but the trophy was presented by a descendent of Joseph E. Seagram and not 'Mr Sam,' because, as Sabloff described, 'the name Bronfman doesn't sell any whisky, but the [name] Seagram does.'[60] (Ironically, the name Bronfman is Yiddish for 'whisky man.') Bronfman's fortune and commercial prowess – tainted as they were by their association with new money, Jewish money, and liquor money – did not ensure access to the social environs of Montreal's Protestant business elite.

Bronfman, seemingly, had a conflicted relationship with his Jewish identity. On the one hand, he donated heavily to Jewish organizations and causes and took on leadership roles in the Jewish communities of Montreal and New York throughout his life. He served as president of Jewish Philanthropies of Montreal and was co-chair of the Jewish Immigrant Aid Society. From 1939 to 1962, he was the president of the Canadian Jewish Congress (CJC). On the other hand, he was often dismissive of working-class Jews, the loud, gesticulating men in undershirts on St Urbain Street porches seen during city drives; such public displays, Bronfman charged, were 'awful, just awful for our people.' In an address to the CJC, Bronfman underscored his desire to 'make our people a better people' by having them 'conduct themselves [so] that they will gain the respect of their fellow citizens – the non-Jewish citizens.'[61] Such views are reminiscent of those of Booker T. Washington, the African-American leader who a generation earlier had called on black people to improve their own economic and social circumstances before tackling systemic racial discrimination. Bronfman, according to his daughter Phyllis Lambert, took on the role of a 'judgmental paterfamilias' towards his family and the Jewish community.[62] Mordecai Richler's assessment was considerably harsher, characterizing Bronfman as an 'Uncle Tom who would toady to those who had already rejected him,' seen most tragically in his unwillingness to speak out forcefully against Ottawa's tight restrictions on Jewish immigration during the 1930s and 1940s.[63]

Bronfman's preference for 'Old World' traditions leaned more to the British Isles than to the shtetls of eastern Europe. Seagram's Montreal headquarters were built to resemble a sixteenth-century Scottish castle, complete with turrets and battlements. Bronfman's Westmount mansion displayed suits of armour and he commissioned a coat of arms for his family. He returned from British trips using expressions like 'I say' and 'fancy that.' French governesses cared for his children, and his butler was a veteran of the Danish Royal Guard. Bronfman was 'always very impressed by socially prominent *goyim*,' Leo Kolber observed, noting on one occasion Bronfman's boundless pride in having Senator Hartland Molson fly on his company jet. Kolber also recounted when Bronfman 'finally' gained admittance to an exclusive golf club near his New York State estate: 'When I played golf with him a couple of times ... he was always letting people through, so as not to hold anyone up. It was as if he still wasn't quite sure that he belonged there.'[64] Most tellingly, Bronfman lied about his place and date of birth throughout his life. He claimed to have been born in Brandon, Manitoba, in 1891, but was in fact born in southern Russia in 1889, which even his children did not know until after his death in 1971.

Seagram's brand and moderation advertising also reflected Bronfman's long-standing quest for social recognition. As previously noted, Seagram brand advertising emphasized aristocratic pretence and gracious living, which in turn reflected Bronfman's own cultural aspirations and adopted lifestyle. Moderation's message of social responsibility similarly resonated with Bronfman's own status anxiety, owing to anti-Semitism and his being 'extremely sensitive to the public perception that he'd made his name, and his fortune, as a bootlegger' during prohibition.[65] The previous discussion of moderation ads focused largely on the literal meanings of text and imagery, basic associations which semioticians call denotative meanings. Many ads were text-only, and images, when employed, often reinforced the written text, for example withered hands carving bread to signify a life of harsh poverty (figure 4.2). Connotative meanings, the extended or implied meanings derived from the interplay of text and image, allow for interpretative leaps and, on occasion, the exposure of the 'ideological work' which frames the process of signification and produces 'mythical,' higher-order meanings.[66]

The June 1950 moderation ad 'My Dad Says: We're *All* Americans!' (figure 4.6), which ran to coincide with Father's Day, is rich in connotative meaning. It is analysed here at length as an illustrative case study of semiotic analysis. The text concerns a familiar theme of moderation advertising, that of a father's solemn responsibility to serve as good role model for his sons, which included drinking modestly. Familiar too is the text's alignment of moderate drinking with attributes like 'forbearance' and 'justice,' thus extending the moderationist message to broader social and political realms. The dominant textual message, however, is not paternal responsibility but democratic pluralism, as seen with the header 'We're All Americans!' and the call to jettison the 'intolerances, the hatreds and the prejudices of modern life.' Strikingly absent, however, is any reference – textual or iconographic – to those most marginalized in American public life: African Americans, Asian Americans, Hispanics, to name a few. Instead, ethnocultural diversity is represented by the attire, physical appearance, and placement of the four boys. Three boys sport close haircuts and long-sleeved, collared shirts and are looking up admiringly at a T-shirt-clad boy with tousled, curly hair who is gesticulating while speaking. The T-shirt wearer is a

My Dad says:
"We're <u>All</u> Americans !"

AT EARLY DUSK on the front steps... or in the school yard ... in the friendly chatter of young America... here's where democracy starts. And with a quote from that unquestioned authority on all things, Dad!

What a real job this gives the father of a growing boy. To see that his words, as they come from his son's lips, spell out democracy's truths. That they nip off the intolerances, the hatreds and the prejudices of modern life. That they encourage good will and the democratic decency expressed in the words: "We're all Americans!"

And what an even bigger job for Dad! To see that his words are daily supported by fitting action. That he conducts himself as a good citizen, a good neighbor, a good father who fully lives up to the personal responsibility which every freedom big or small demands.

The freedom to enjoy the luxury of drink is a small freedom. Yet, to abuse it, to forget wise moderation in foolish over-indulgence is to fail to understand the meaning of all and every freedom.

That's why we of The House of Seagram, this Father's Day, add to our many public statements on moderation an earnest salute to every American Dad.

For we know that, be it the practice of moderation, the practice of forbearance, or honor, or justice, he appreciates his responsibilities. He does his job. And does it well.

He understands and he makes his family understand that to enjoy freedom, any freedom, you must deserve it.

Seagram-Distillers Corporation, Chrysler Bldg., N.Y.

THE HOUSE OF SEAGRAM
Fine Whiskies Since 1857

Figure 4.6: This Father's Day moderation ad from 1950 contains conflicting meanings. The text promotes cultural pluralism and political equality, while the imagery suggests racial exclusivity and individual superiority. Hagley Museum and Library.

signifier of 'difference,' if a non-threatening one by virtue of his being both a child and visually not very different from the other boys. The ad enables the viewer to 'read in' suitable social types for democratic inclusion, for example people of Italian, Polish, or Jewish origin, but not the black factory worker, the Chinese-American labourer, or, for that matter, the observant Hasidic Jew. While the text stresses inclusivity, the image suggests exclusivity, allowing the ad both to police the racial boundaries of civic participation and to affirm the principle of democratic pluralism. By rendering these seeming contradictions as ordinary or commonsensical, the ad performs the ideological work of 'naturalizing' a racially and/or ethnoculturally delineated polity, notably so when viewed against the backdrop of Jim Crow America.

The ad mirrors Bronfman's own views on the proper terms for minority acceptance by mainstream society. This should not accrue automatically, by virtue of universal right; it should be earned through hard work, cultural uplift, and social responsibility. In the ad, the T-shirt boy, who seems slightly older than the others, is looked up to by the other boys, literally and figuratively, as seen in the engrossed listening poses of the other boys. He commands their attention, likely too their respect. It was in the post-1945 years that Jews, in the words of one scholar, succeeded in 'becoming white folks,' resulting from the decline of anti-Semitism and that community's strong embrace of higher education and hard work, leading to economic success and social mobility.[67] This ad forms a cultural artefact of that unfolding social drama.

The visual layout of the ad emphasizes individual superiority over democratic egalitarianism. By pointing upward, the camera's point of view affirms a hierarchical mode of authority, one that, in light of the protagonist's appearance and gesturing, evokes more the iconography of Little Caesar than that of the New England Town Hall. The image affirms the primacy of 'getting ahead,' of being on top, which, of course, are mythical American values. The use of photography abets this interpretive process owing to the ideological power of truthful representation inherent in the notion that the 'camera doesn't lie.' By obscuring the 'problems of internal contradiction or irrational association,' photographic images help render divergent themes congruent.[68] As Barthes similarly notes, mythical signs, like the one in this ad, function to organize a 'world which is without contradictions because it is without depth ... it establishes a blissful clarity: things appear to mean something by themselves.' Political and social conflict and accommodation, the products of historical forces, are 'purified' via mythical signification and afforded a 'natural and eternal justification.'[69]

Conclusion

Integrating the themes of responsible drinking and gracious living, Seagram's moderation advertising assuaged public concerns over alcohol's increased availability after prohibition. The campaign counselled people to drink moderately and to consider the ethical, familial, and social implications of liquor use. Ads warned against drinking and driving, buying liquor with bills outstanding, and appearing drunk before one's children. The campaign aligned well with Seagram's general marketing strategy aimed at disassociating whisky from the tavern and the speakeasy, while imbuing Seagram brands with attributes like social responsibility, urbane sophistication, and regal distinction. The double-voiced, polysemic nature of moderation advertising enabled it to promote a category of whisky drinking while articulating limits on alcohol consumption. Moderation advertising fitted well in a country with heavy regulations on liquor promotion. As one marketing report noted, Seagram's moderation advertising proved especially viable in provinces where 'brand advertising is impossible' or in smaller magazines where 'brand promotion is impossible or undesirable.'[70] What began as a moral imperative regarding alcohol use had, by the 1950s, occupied the wider terrain of the psyche, society, and polity. Along the way, the campaign also served as an adaptive metaphor for Sam Bronfman's preoccupation with social mobility and cultural uplift. The moderation ethos provided a discursive framework for the cultural understanding of spirits consumption in the post-repeal age. It aligned a form of personal consumption with social respectability, along with notions of individual uniqueness and normative conduct. It embodied a consumption ethic in which personal gratification and civility were mutually affirming. Less of a good thing like Seagram whisky meant 'more' of consuming pleasure, ethical and social betterment, and commercial reward.

NOTES

For their research assistance or commentary, I am grateful to Gene Allen, Keir Keightley, Jessica McEwan, Susan MacKenzie, and especially the staff at the

Hagley Museum and Library. Research funding was provided by the Social Sciences and Humanities Research Council of Canada.

1 'Aykroyd Invests $1 Million in Ontario Wines,' *Toronto Star*, 30 November 2005.
2 Meldon Kahan, 'When a Nip for the Heart Becomes Harmful,' *Globe and Mail*, 9 January 2007, A13.
3 On Seagram in general, see Michael R. Marrus, *Mr. Sam: The Life and Times of Samuel Bronfman* (Toronto: Viking, 1991); Daniel J. Robinson, 'Seagram Company Ltd.,' in John McDonough and Karen Egolf, eds, *Encyclopedia of Advertising*, vol. 3 (New York: Fitzroy, Dearborn, 2003), 1409–11; Peter C. Newman, *Bronfman Dynasty: The Rothschilds of the New World* (Toronto: McClelland and Stewart, 1978).
4 Before Seagram's dissolution in 2001, the company's website featured moderation ads from each decade beginning in the 1930s. In 1970, Seagram published the brochure 'Moderation Messages by Seagram,' which outlined the history of the campaign. Hagley Museum and Library, Seagram, box 87, file Albert, Borden, Stridsberg ad agency, 'Moderation Case History' (memo), 8 January 1976.
5 For political-economic works on advertising, see Otis Pease, *The Responsibilities of American Advertising: Private Control and Public Influence, 1920–1940* (New Haven: Yale University Press, 1958); Daniel Pope, *The Making of Modern Advertising* (New York: Basic Books, 1983); Stephen Fox, *The Mirror Makers: A History of American Advertising and Its Creators* (New York: Morrow, 1984); James D. Norris, *Advertising and the Transformation of American Society, 1865–1920* (New York: Greenwood Press, 1990); and Russell Johnston, *Selling Themselves: The Emergence of Canadian Advertising* (Toronto: University of Toronto Press, 2000). For culturally informed studies, see Roland Marchand, *Advertising the American Dream: Making Way for Modernity 1920–1940* (Berkeley: University of California Press, 1985); Marchand, *Creating the Corporate Soul: The Rise of Public Relations and Corporate Imagery in American Big Business* (Berkeley: University of California Press, 1998); and Pamela Laird, *Advertising Progress: American Business and the Rise of Consumer Marketing* (Baltimore: Johns Hopkins University Press, 1998). For cultural works drawing heavily on theoretical analysis, see Jackson Lears, *Fables of Abundance: A Cultural History of Advertising in America* (New York: Basic Books, 1994); Richard Ohmann, *Selling Culture: Magazines, Markets, and Class at the Turn of the Century* (London: Verso, 1996); Patricia Johnston, *Real Fantasies: Edward Steichen's Advertising Photography* (Berkeley: University of California Press, 1997); and Paul Rutherford, *Endless Propaganda: The Advertising of Public Goods* (Toronto: University of Toronto Press, 2000).

6 Seagram's moderation campaign is mentioned briefly in Craig Heron, *Booze: A Distilled History* (Toronto: Between the Lines, 2003), 318–19, and Cheryl Krasnick Warsh, 'Smoke and Mirrors: Gender Representation in North American Tobacco and Alcohol Advertisements before 1950,' *Histoire sociale / Social History*, 31 (1999): 183–222. Mariana Valverde's discussion of moderate drinking does not deal with campaigns by liquor manufacturers; *Diseases of the Will: Alcohol and the Dilemmas of Freedom* (Cambridge: Cambridge University Press, 1998), 172–9. For other works on twentieth-century alcohol history see Greg Marquis, 'Alcohol and the Family in Canada,' *Journal of Family History* 29, no. 4 (July 2004): 308–27; Marquis, '"A Reluctant Concession to Modernity": Alcohol and Modernization in the Maritimes, 1945–1980,' *Acadiensis* 32, no. 2 (2003): 31–59; Dan Malleck, 'The Bureaucratization of Moral Regulation: The LCBO and (Not-So) Standard Hotel Licensing in Niagara, 1927–1944,' *Histoire sociale / Social History* 38 (2005): 59–77; Robert A. Campbell, *Sit Down and Drink Your Beer: Regulating Vancouver's Beer Parlours, 1925–1954* (Toronto: University of Toronto Press, 2001); Heron, 'The Boys and Their Booze: Masculinities and Public Drinking in Working-Class Hamilton, 1890–1946,' *Canadian Historical Review* 86, no. 3 (September 2005): 411–52; Cheryl Krasnick Warsh, ed., *Drink in Canada: Historical Essays* (Montreal: McGill-Queen's University Press, 1993); Mariana Valverde, 'A Postcolonial Women's Law? Domestic Violence and the Ontario Liquor Board's "Indian List,"' *Feminist Studies* 30, no. 3 (2004): 566–88. For the U.S., see Pamela E. Pennock and K. Austin Kerr, 'In the Shadow of prohibition: Domestic American Alcohol Policy since 1933,' *Business History* 47, no. 3 (July 2005): 383–400; Catherine Gilbert Murdock, *Domesticating Drink: Women, Men, and Alcohol, 1870–1940* (Baltimore: Johns Hopkins University Press, 1998); Lori Rotskoff, *Love on the Rocks: Men, Women, and Alcohol in Post–World War II America* (Chapel Hill: University of North Carolina Press, 2002); Sara W. Tracy and Caroline Jean Acker, eds, *Altering American Consciousness: The History of Alcohol and Drug Use in the United States, 1800–2000* (Amherst: University of Massachusetts Press, 2004).
7 Rotskoff, *Love on the Rocks*, 37; Heron, *Booze*, 327; On public relations history, see Marchand, *Creating the Corporate Soul*; Karen S. Miller, *The Voice of Business: Hill and Knowlton and Postwar Public Relations* (Chapel Hill: University of North Carolina Press, 1999); and Robert Jackall and Janice M. Hirota, *Image Makers: Advertising, Public Relations, and the Ethos of Advocacy* (Chicago: University of Chicago Press, 2000); Alan P. Loeb, 'Paradigms Lost: A Case Study Analysis of Models of Corporate Responsibility for the Environment,' *Business and Economic History* 28, no. 2 (1998): 95–107; M. Marinetto, 'The Historical Development of Business Philanthropy: Social

Responsibility in the New Corporate Economy,' *Business History* 41, no. 4 (1999): 1–20.

8   Marrus, *Mr. Sam*, 368.

9   Michel Foucault, 'Politics and the Study of Discourse,' in Graham Burchell, Colin Gordon, and Peter Mill, eds, *The Foucault Effect: Studies in Governmentality* (London: Harvester, 1991), 59–61.

10 Rose, *Governing the Soul: The Shaping of the Private Self*, 2nd ed. (London: Free Association, 1999), xx, xxiv.

11 Valverde, *Diseases of the Will*, 13.

12 Marrus, *Mr. Sam*, 236–9, 246–51; Robinson, 'Seagram Company Ltd.,' 1409–10.

13 Marrus, *Mr. Sam*, 72–3, 152–9, 206.

14 'Liquor Gifts Tied to Justice Inquiry,' *New York Times*, 24 October 1952, 24

15 Ibid.; '2 Liquor Concerns Accused by F.T.C.,' *New York Times*, 2 October 1952, 43.

16 The last two provinces to end prohibition were Nova Scotia (1930) and Prince Edward Island (1948). For dates for other provinces, see Heron, *Booze*, 270.

17 Canadian Institute of Public Opinion [CIPO] poll releases: 7 March 1942; 23 September 1942; 26 September 1942. Prime Minister Mackenzie King abstained from drinking alcohol during the Second World War. His diary records him as favouring the 'wiping out of publications which owe their existence to liquor advertising (12 November 1942), believing that 'one of the worst features of the day is the drinking on the part of the younger people' (15 January 1943); he was 'prepared to nationalize the whole brewing business' (12 March 1943). Library and Archives Canada, Diaries of Prime Minister William Lyon Mackenzie King, MG26-J13, www.collectionscanada.gc.ca/databases/king/index-e.html.

18 CIPO releases: 15 November 1944; 5 September 1945; 9 March 1946; 28 August 1948; 15 June 1949.

19 Hagley Museum and Library, Seagram Collection, file, Company History; Vicker and Benson Report, 'Outline and Background of House of Seagram Advertising, From 1940 to 1958,' 1958; CIPO release 28 August 1948; Ronald B. Weir, *The History of the Distillers Company, 1877–1939: Diversification and Growth in Whisky and Chemicals* (Oxford: Oxford University Press, 1995), 261.

20 Cited in 'Outline and Background of House of Seagram Advertising.'

21 'Canadian Open for Seagram Gold Cup,' *Mayfair*, September 1938.

22 '$1,000,000 to Perpetuate Free Ideals,' *Montreal Daily Star*, 3 March 1951.

23 'Liquor Men Start Drive for Respect,' *New York Times*, 14 November 1951, 51; 'Outline and Background of House of Seagram Advertising.'

24 Marchand, *Creating the Corporate Soul*, 167. The editors of a special journal issue on the 'business of dependency' observed that heavy doses of advertising and public relations accompanied the marketing of controversial products. Matthias Kipping and Lina Galvez Munoz, 'The Business of Dependency: An Introduction,' *Business History* 47, no. 3 (July 2005): 334. My work on the marketing of controversial products confirms this point. See Robinson, 'Marketing Gum, Making Meanings: Wrigley in North America, 1890–1930,' *Enterprise and Society* 5, no. 1 (March 2004): 4–44, and 'Marketing and Regulating Cigarettes in Canada, 1957 to 1971,' in Pierre Lanthier and Claude Bellavance, eds, *Les territoires de l'entreprise* (Sainte-Foy: Les Presses de l'Université Laval, 2004), 243–61.

25 Seagram Collection, Biographical Files, box 4, file 1951. Frank R. Schwengel, 'External Problems of the Industry,' address to Seagram Family Achievement Association, November 1951.

26 William Wachtel, *The Anatomy of a Hidden Persuader* (New York: Vantage Press, 1975), 87–8.

27 Pennock and Kerr, 'In the Shadow,' 386–7.

28 Rotskoff, *Love on the Rocks*, 49.

29 Pennock and Kerr, 'In the Shadow,' 390, 389.

30 Pennock and Kerr, 'In the Shadow,' 390; Marrus, *Mr. Sam*, 194–202.

31 Heron, *Booze*, 193–6.

32 Ibid., 269.

33 Seagram, Series – Biographical, vol. 11, file 'Moderation Ads,' booklet, 'The Story of Drink in America and Outline of Educational Program for the Council for Moderation,' 1935.

34 Rotskoff, *Love on the Rocks*, 49; For the Second World War period, Rotskoff writes: 'The assumption that most people drank moderately helped solidify the wets' hegemony in society at large' (50).

35 All ads are drawn from the Seagram Collection at the Hagley Museum and Library.

36 Seagram, Ad series, Box 21a, file 'Seagram Moderation Series.'

37 For one example, see Marshall McLuhan, *The Mechanical Bride: Folklore of Industrial Man* (New York: Vanguard Press, 1951), 56–9.

38 Hagley, Seagram, Biographical – Box 7, file 'Robert Sabloff.' Marrus interview with Robert Sabloff, 23 January 1990. Leo Kolber, *Leo: A Life* (Montreal: McGill-Queen's University Press, 2003), 25, 27; Heron, *Booze*, 301–2.

39 Marchand, *Advertising the American Dream*, xxi, 202.

40 Seagram, Biographical, vol. 11, file 'Moderation Ads,' brochure, 'You'll Feel Better,' 1936. On success manuals, see Judy Hilkey, *Character Is Capital: Success Manuals and Manhood in Gilded Age America* (Chapel Hill: University of North Carolina Press, 1997).

41 Rose, *Governing the Soul*, 266; Rose, *Powers of Freedom: Reframing Political Thought* (Cambridge: Cambridge University Press, 1999), 85–8.
42 Valverde, *Diseases of the Will*, 99.
43 Kolber, *Leo: A Life*, 24.
44 W.A. Lawrence, 'Sales: $103,231,334,' *Canadian Business*, December 1940, 52–4.
45 'Prohibition Not the Remedy,' *Globe and Mail*, 6 June 1942.
46 'Salute to the Bootlegger,' editorial, *Moose Jaw Times-Herald*, 12 December 1942.
47 Seagram, Box 'Government Regulations,' Canada, PC 11374, 16/12/42, 'Wartime Alcoholic Beverages Order, 1942.' On wartime alcohol regulations, see Yves Tremblay, 'La consommation bridée: Contrôle des prix et rationnement durant la Deuxième Guerre Mondiale,' *Revue d'histoire de l'Amérique Français* 58, no. 4 (2005): 569–607.
48 Seagram, 'Outline and Background of House of Seagram Advertising.'
49 Seagram, Box 87, file Scrapbook – House of Seagram Advertising Campaign, 1943, 'To All Seagram Salesmen,' memo, 1943.
50 Before the eighteenth century, consumption carried negative meanings involving wastefulness or destruction. More favourable connotations for the term only began in the nineteenth century. See Raymond Williams, 'Consumer,' in *Keywords: A Vocabulary of Culture and Society* (New York: Oxford University Press, 1976).
51 'Moderate Drinking Urged by Distiller,' *Vancouver Province*, 3 May 1950.
52 Rose, *Governing the Soul*, 266.
53 Arthur M. Schlesinger, Jr, *The Vital Center: The Politics of Freedom* (Boston: Houghton Mifflin, 1949).
54 'Hard Liquor: Nobody Wants It Any More,' *Brief*, May 1956, 52.
55 Marchand, *Creating the Corporate Soul*.
56 Wachtel, *Anatomy of a Hidden Persuader*, 126.
57 Marrus, *Mr. Sam*, 198, 199–200.
58 Kolber, *Leo: A Life*, 24.
59 Cited in Weir, *History of the Distillers Company, 1977–1939*, 263.
60 Hagley, Seagram, Biographical – box 7, file 'Robert Sabloff.' Marrus interview with Robert Sabloff, 23 January 1990.
61 Marrus, *Mr. Sam*, 250, 264.
62 Marrus, *Mr. Sam*, 250.
63 Mordecai Richler, *Belling the Cat: Essays, Reports and Opinions* (Toronto: Knopf Canada, 1998), 33–6.
64 Kolber, *Leo: A Life*, 27.
65 Kolber, *Leo: A Life*, 25.

66 See Roland Barthes, *Mythologies*, trans. A. Lavers (London: Jonathan Cape, 1972); Umberto Eco, *A Theory of Semiotics* (Bloomington: Indiana University Press, 1976), and Ron Beasley, Marcel Danesi, and Paul Perron, *Signs for Sale: An Outline of Semiotic Analysis for Advertisers and Marketers* (Ottawa: Legas, 2000). See also the article by James Cairns, chapter 7 in this collection.

67 Karen Brodkin, *How Jews Became White Folks* (New Brunswick, NJ: Rutgers University Press, 1998). Noel Ignatiev similarly explores how Irish immigrants in the United States used the Catholic Church, Democratic Party, unions, and anti-black violence during the 1830s and 1840s to secure their place within the 'White Republic.' *How the Irish Became White* (New York: Routledge, 1995).

68 Marchand, *Advertising the American Dream*, 154; Robinson, 'Marketing Gum,' 38.

69 Barthes, *Mythologies*, 143.

70 Seagram, Advertising Series, box 21A, file 'Vickers and Benson,' memo 'Outline and Background of House of Seagram Advertising: From 1940 to 1958.'

5 Evelyn Dick, Soap Star: Newspaper Coverage of the Torso Murder Case, 1946–1947

ALISON JACQUES

In 1946 a young woman named Evelyn Dick was accused of killing her husband and one of her children in Hamilton, Ontario. The case came to be known as the torso murder, due to the fact that the body of John Dick, Evelyn's husband, had been dismembered, its head and limbs burned to ashes.[1] John's torso had been dumped over the side of an escarpment; its discovery set in motion a series of murder trials that are still described as some of the most sensational in Canadian history. The grisly treatment of the two victims certainly contributed to the public's fascination: John was shot and then dismembered, and baby Peter was strangled, his corpse encased in cement and locked for two years in a suitcase. However, it was the accused woman, Evelyn, who was the central figure in daily press coverage of the case. Though she never confessed involvement in either murder, she was eventually imprisoned for the manslaughter of her infant son.

It was not only the legal proceedings or Evelyn's role in the crimes that were addressed in the hundreds of news items published during the course of her trials. The defendant's body was routinely scrutinized by the press; specifically, journalists described, and ascribed meaning to, Evelyn's physical appearance, eating habits, and mannerisms. In addition, a great deal of attention was paid to spectators – especially women – who attended the trials, whether they sat in the gallery of the courtroom or gathered outside to watch her come and go. Indeed, in portrayals of the defendant and spectators, gender was at the forefront in the press coverage of this case. Of course, it was relatively uncommon for a woman to be charged with murder in Canada at that time, as has been the case throughout recorded history.[2] It follows that Evelyn's trials would attract intense media attention; after all, it is the extraordinary that is most newsworthy. Moreover, women accused of committing violent acts are invariably portrayed as having done so *as women*; gender and sexuality are at the forefront of public discourse about women's aggression in a way that does not generally occur in talk of violent men.[3]

Not only is the torso murder case seen to be 'as much a part of Hamilton history as Allan MacNab, Isaac Buchanan, the Stelco strike and the Tiger-Cats,' but it has inspired a wide variety of popular cultural texts in the past six decades.[4] Still, the case has received little scholarly attention. Writing in 1996, Robyn Gillam argued that the case, along with some of these subsequent texts, employed generic codes of 'hardboiled' detective fiction and film noir.[5] It is true that the case involved ingredients of these 'masculine' genres, which were emerging at roughly the same time; however, in the telling of the story in the newspapers of the day, these ingredients were used in a melodramatic recipe and turned into soap. That is, the press constructed a 'feminine' narrative comprising elements of soap opera, with a central female 'character,' descriptions of domestic spaces and family relationships, and gossip, wrought largely in emotive language. The story of Evelyn and the torso murder, serialized daily in the press, was a never-ending drama; coverage may have ended when Evelyn went to prison, but the story itself lacked narrative closure.

Evelyn remained Canada's most notorious female killer for nearly fifty years, until the position was usurped by Karla Homolka in the 1990s. This article aims to shed light on a case that provided Canada with 'the first big news story, juicy and scandalous, of the post-war years,'[6] and to determine the ways in which the defendant was put into discourse in the press in 1946 and 1947. While a number of print media sources in Canada and the United States reported on Evelyn's trials, this analysis is limited to coverage in four Canadian daily newspapers: the *Hamilton Spectator* (the only local daily paper), the *Toronto Daily Star*, the (Toronto) *Globe and Mail*, and the *Toronto Evening Telegram*.[7]

The Torso Murder Case

On 16 March 1946, five children were hiking just outside of Hamilton when they found the torso of a man, chest down on the ground, about ten metres below the top of the embankment. The body's arms, legs, and head were missing and appeared to have been sawn off. The torso was soon identified as that of John Dick, a forty-year-old Russian immigrant and driver for the Hamilton Street Railway (HSR). When police informed John's widow of the murder of her husband, twenty-five-year-old Evelyn Dick replied, 'Don't look at me – I don't know anything about it.' She was taken to the local police headquarters for questioning.[8] Over the year that followed, Evelyn appeared as the defendant in three highly publicized murder trials.

Evelyn was the only child of Scottish immigrants Donald and Alexandra MacLean. The lower-middle-class family lived in a modest neighbourhood where Donald worked for the HSR and Alexandra was a homemaker. However, for years Donald allegedly stole money from the streetcar fare boxes, allowing the MacLeans to live beyond their means. In industrial working-class Hamilton, the city's exclusive social 'gentry' comprised only some forty families, but Alexandra was determined that her daughter break into the upper echelon of local society.[9] Evelyn did not excel at her prestigious private high school, but she was pretty and had 'sex appeal.' It may have been Alexandra who saw opportunity in her daughter's attributes and began setting up dates for Evelyn with older men. According to former *Toronto Star* crime reporter Jocko Thomas, by the age of twenty-five Evelyn 'was well known in Hamilton as what was then called a party girl.'[10] (Evelyn would later testify that she had had sexual intercourse with 150 men, including lawyers, businessmen, and 'the scions of two west end families.')[11] Whatever the specifics of these social arrangements, Evelyn was by her mid-twenties a financially stable – and expensively dressed – woman. She never held a legitimate job, and not for lack of opportunity, as jobs were increasingly available to young women during the Second World War.[12]

Evelyn, not yet married, had given birth three times by the time she turned twenty-four: a daughter, Heather Maria, was born in July 1942; a stillborn daughter in June 1943; and a son, Peter David, in September 1944. When Evelyn was pregnant with Peter, her father reportedly made it clear that he did not want a second child in the house where he, Alexandra, Evelyn, and two-year-old Heather lived. After Peter was born, Evelyn did not bring him home; instead, she told her parents that she had turned over her son to the Children's Aid Society, which would arrange his adoption.[13] She continued to live with her parents until June 1945, when she, Heather, and Alexandra moved to an apartment. Donald remained at the family's home on Rosslyn Avenue.

In mid-September 1945, Evelyn announced to her mother that she planned to marry John Dick. Alexandra did not approve; she had never heard of him, and with his blue-collar job and modest income, John was not at all the kind of man for whom she had been training her daughter.[14] The couple were married 4 October, and that night, Evelyn went home to her mother – without her new husband. Within a week, she went out to the theatre with twenty-five-year-old steelworker Bill Bohozuk and 'had sex relations with him at his home after the show.'[15] Evelyn and John did live together briefly. Evelyn bought a house on Carrick Avenue, and she, John, Alexandra, and Heather moved in on 31 October. According to Alexandra, Evelyn and John 'didn't get along at all' and 'they used to argue over women and money' whenever John was at home.[16] John moved out of the house on Christmas Eve and was boarding with a cousin when, on 6 March 1946, he failed to report to work at the HSR.[17] His torso was found on 16 March. Evelyn was living in the Carrick Avenue home with her mother and daughter when she was taken to the police station for questioning on 19 March.

Over the next few weeks, Evelyn provided police with seven different statements about the circumstances surrounding her husband's murder.[18] In some she admitted involvement in the torso's disposal, and she once spoke of being present when John was shot, though she claimed no part in a conspiracy to commit the murder. In one version, 'Italian' gangsters from Windsor had been hired by Bohozuk to 'fix' John; in another, Bohozuk had been the killer. According to Evelyn, Bohozuk had 'started to talk about getting rid of John, because John was scandalizing his name amongst his friends.'[19] On 21 March, Bohozuk was brought before the magistrate's court on charges of vagrancy and having an unregistered revolver.[20]

While Evelyn was held without bail, police searched her house and her father's house. Officers found a number of objects belonging to John Dick, including bloodstained buttons from a streetcar driver's uniform. The discovery of two thousand dollars worth of streetcar tickets at Donald's house prompted police to charge him with theft.[21] A search of Evelyn's attic on 25 March yielded something much more startling: a chunk of cement inside a small suitcase was found to contain the remains of a male infant, inside a zipped-shut leatherette bag and wrapped in a skirt that had on its waistband a label reading 'E. MacLean.'[22] The next day, Evelyn was charged with the murder of her husband. On 29 March, Bohozuk was also charged with John's murder, and both Evelyn and Bohozuk were charged with the murder of the infant, who was identified as Peter David White – the baby born in 1944 whom Evelyn had said was put up for adoption.[23]

The police investigation continued, and on 15 April 1946, murder charges were also brought against sixty-eight-year-old Donald and sixty-one-year-old Alexandra MacLean in connection with John's death. (The charge against Alexandra was later dropped due to insufficient evidence.) Police had uncovered further incriminating evidence at Donald's home, including spent bullet casings, and burnt fragments of human bone and teeth were found in ashes spread on the ground behind the women's house.[24]

Evelyn's first trial for the murder of John Dick opened 7 October 1946 at the Wentworth County Court House in Hamilton; Bohozuk and Donald would be tried at a later date. During the course of the trial, statements that Evelyn had made to police were entered as evidence against her, though none had been made in the presence of an attorney. No physical evidence linked Evelyn directly with the murder, but her statements alone were incriminating in that their inherent contradictions ensured that her 'wickedness' eclipsed the actual evidence.[25] On 16 October, the jury deliberated for just under two hours before returning a guilty verdict; despite the jury's recommendation for mercy, the judge sentenced Evelyn to hang. Her execution was scheduled for 7 January 1947, at which time she would become the first person to hang in Hamilton since 1930 and the first woman ever to face the noose in that city.[26]

While in jail, Evelyn hired Toronto lawyer John J. Robinette, who petitioned the Ontario Court of Appeal for a new trial. He pointed out to the court that police had questioned Evelyn about the murder and obtained statements while she was charged not with murder but only with vagrancy, and that police had not properly warned Evelyn that each of the statements she made could be used against her in a murder trial. On 17 January 1947, the five appeal court justices were unanimous in setting aside Evelyn's conviction and ordered a retrial.[27]

Evelyn's second murder trial opened on 24 February 1947. Again, she was tried alone. This time, her statements were excluded. Robinette argued that the Crown's evidence actually pointed to Donald MacLean and that, while Evelyn may indeed have known of the murder and even been an accessory after the fact, the only charge she faced was murder. On that charge, he stated to the jury, one 'would not hang a dog' on the evidence presented by the Crown. The jury agreed, and Evelyn was acquitted on 6 March.[28]

Evelyn returned to the Wentworth County Court House on 24 March 1947, for her third trial, this time for the murder of baby Peter White.

Robinette pointed out to the jury that all evidence against his client was circumstantial, and he stressed her role as a single mother to four-year-old Heather. The jury returned a guilty verdict on the lesser charge of manslaughter on 25 March.[29] The next day, psychiatrist Robert Finlayson told the court that he had evaluated Evelyn and determined that she had a 'mental age' of thirteen and an IQ in the low eighties. The judge then sentenced Evelyn to life imprisonment – the maximum sentence for a manslaughter conviction – to be served at the Kingston Prison for Women.[30]

By the end of March 1947, Bill Bohozuk had been acquitted of both murders.[31] Donald MacLean pleaded guilty to a charge of being an accessory after the fact to the murder of John Dick, and he was sentenced to a five-year term in Kingston Penitentiary.[32] On 18 July 1947, Evelyn entered the maximum-security women's prison in Kingston.[33] By 9 August of that year, the Crown had exhausted all means of appealing Evelyn's acquittal on the torso murder charge, and the case was over.[34] No further charges were laid or suspects pursued.

Evelyn Dick in the Press

These murder trials took place before the advent of television in Canada.[35] It is no surprise, then, that the newspapers included a great deal of scene-setting description and a great number of photographs. News stories routinely emphasized that Evelyn was a physically attractive woman. Reporters commonly referred to her as 'the pretty defendant' and 'the pretty accused,' as well as 'the dark-haired defendant,' 'the comely young widow,' and so on.[36] Whether or not Evelyn was empirically attractive was, of course, largely subjective, and unimportant. If, as John Berger argues, 'those who are not judged beautiful are *not beautiful*,' then it follows that the opposite is also true: Evelyn was pretty because the press judged her so.[37]

Journalists also described Evelyn's outfits generously and in great detail. For instance, on the opening day of her first trial, she wore 'new shoes with bows trimmed in a gold-like metal,' along with nylon stockings, 'a chic black dress, and black gloves.'[38] The next day, it was reported, her earrings were 'brilliant,' and 'her nail polish was the exact shade of her lipstick.'[39] Evelyn's overall appearance, according to the press coverage, was properly feminine, but more like that of a movie star than a woman facing a murder charge. That is, her appearance was excessive – as was the commentary itself. No doubt such elaborate descriptions appealed mainly to female readers; indeed, such detailed descriptions of Evelyn's dress would not have seemed out of place in the papers' fashion pages, and most were written by women.

Photographs aided in constructing Evelyn's appearance as both familiar and excessive. Day after day she appeared in the papers wearing slight variations on the same outfit. The numerous photographs also contributed to the impression that Evelyn was vain, and she reportedly posed eagerly for photographs (instructing photographers to 'Make this one good!') and enjoyed their publication (asking of the newspapers, 'Are there any good pictures of me?').[40] However, these photographs did not simply reflect how Evelyn 'really' looked or was, any more than the text presented a neutral 'truth.' After all, 'the press photograph is an object that has been worked on, chosen, composed, constructed, treated according to professional, aesthetic, or ideological norms.'[41] Like any image, then, a newspaper photograph is constructed, reflecting the photographers' (and photo editors') 'way of seeing.'[42]

Taken individually, photographs of Evelyn published in the four newspapers are unremarkable. Most are flattering portrayals of a smiling young woman in a fur coat and dark hat. Taken together, though, the sheer number of photos of Evelyn has the effect of compounding what Susan Sontag called 'the tendency inherent in all photographs to accord value to their subjects.'[43] If a single photograph confers importance on its subject, then the near-constant presence of her image during the year of her trials served to elevate Evelyn to celebrity status. These photos would have been published primarily to attract readers, but there may have been a second, underlying explanation for their abundance: according to Sandra Kemp, ever since Pythagoras initiated the formal study of physiognomy, 'the notion that a person's true character is revealed in their physical appearance has remained the definitive concept for the Western imagination.'[44] Accused of committing two unimaginable murders, Evelyn's 'true character' was a mystery indeed; no doubt the public looked to the media for enlightenment.

The focus on Evelyn's image, both in photographs and in text, was intensified by the fact that she had few opportunities to speak, either in or out of court. She testified only twice, at the preliminary hearing in April 1946 and, briefly, at her first trial that October, and reporters were not allowed to print her testimony. Although she made small talk with reporters on occasion, she did not grant formal interviews. Without opportunities to furnish quotable statements, Evelyn was analysed in the press in terms of what could be *seen* of her: her body, which encompassed her clothing, her hairstyle and cosmetics, her facial expression, and her body language. Reporters relied on these physical elements and ascribed meanings to them. The close and continual scrutiny of Evelyn recalls the use in Victorian England of public scrutiny as 'part of a transgressive woman's punishment'; according to Judith Knelman, the Victorian press routinely commented on the femininity of an accused murderess, including the way she 'wore her hair, the movements she made with her hands, the tint of her complexion, the focus of her eyes, the thickness of her lips, the firmness of her step, [and] the construction of her frame.'[45]

The focus on Evelyn's body remained steady throughout the course of her trials, but less and less for its sex appeal than for its changing size; the press was fixated on Evelyn's food intake and continual weight gain. For the duration of the torso murder case, postwar food rationing was in place across Canada, and a general social preoccupation with food was apparent in daily news reports on the fluctuating availability and cost of beef, sugar, butter, and other items.[46] From the start of Evelyn's case, mentions were made of her meals and of her (excessive) appetite. For example, during the April 1946 preliminary hearing, one police officer was overheard saying to another, 'She's always hungry.' Even following her murder conviction, reporters noted, Evelyn never failed to 'scrape the bottom of her porridge bowl.' Highlighting the enthusiasm with which she was seen to consume food, long articles were sometimes punctuated with subheadings such as 'Hearty Appetite,' 'Enjoyed Sandwich,' and 'Ate Chicken Dinner.'[47]

When the first trial began on 7 October 1946, papers reported the news that Evelyn, who had spent the previous six months in jail, had put on ten to fifteen pounds and needed a new dress. Not even a death sentence could dampen her appetite; defence counsel John Sullivan told reporters on 18 October that Evelyn was 'red-eyed and distraught. But she still ... takes an interest in food.' Over the following three months, she reportedly gained a further twenty pounds. On 10 January 1947, while Evelyn was in jail awaiting the outcome of her appeal hearing, Sullivan told reporters, 'She is eating very well, and it is showing on her figure ... She appears to be standing the strain very well.' Reports of her meals and appetite became almost comical, if not downright grotesque. For example, the *Star* described a meal that Evelyn shared with the sheriff and two lawyers, at which 'she finished her hefty chicken dinner before the men, then proceeded to eat four large slices of apple pie.' Evelyn was still, if less regularly, described as 'pretty,' 'comely,' and 'attractive,' but increasingly, descriptions of her size and shape accompanied those of her face, hair, makeup, and clothing. The 'pretty accused' could now also be described as 'short, fat Evelyn.'[48] Implicit was the judgment that Evelyn's eating and weight gain were inappropriate for a woman in her situation, and perhaps for any woman.

Not only did the focus on Evelyn's weight gain allow the papers to objectify and comment on her body – through observations that her usual black dress was now 'skin tight,' her squirrel coat 'tightly buttoned,' and so on – but it was as though her transgression was manifesting itself physically. Evelyn's excessive appetite for food seemed instead to stand in for her other appetites, excesses, and transgressions. The intense focus on her weight gain in jail connoted sexual excess on two levels, suggesting, first, that she could not control any of her appetites, and second, that she overate in response to the frustrations of enforced celibacy.[49] While Sullivan had interpreted Evelyn's appetite as a sign of her 'standing the strain,' a *Telegram* story hypothesized that her 'enormous' weight gain actually indicated 'the extent of her despair.'[50] While it may well have been despair that led Evelyn to overeat in jail, her ever-expanding body functioned as an ever-solidifying site of guilt and transgression. By explaining her weight gain only in terms of eating, reporters held Evelyn solely responsible; an alternative discourse could have questioned, for example, the exercise-time policies of the Barton Street Jail or the nutritional value of the food it served, making Evelyn's weight gain a sign of an institutional problem. Instead, the newspapers pointed only to her seemingly out-of-control appetite.

The papers' preoccupation with Evelyn's physical appearance was also apparent in daily remarks on her every movement and expression. Like the photographs, reports of Evelyn's behaviour were not neutral but selected. Evelyn did not simply glance, or listen, for example; rather, she 'glanced disinterestedly,' and she 'listened impassively' – or, even worse, she 'just [didn't] seem to listen at all.'[51] Over and over, the papers linked Evelyn's movements, posture, body language, and facial expressions to boredom, detachment, and a lack of interest in the proceedings. Again, the adjective-noun pairings are telling, such as the following from just two days of trial coverage: 'nonchalant air,' 'strange stillness,' 'aloof composure,' 'impassive expressionlessness.'[52]

Other stories revolved entirely around the boredom, detachment, and lack of concern that Evelyn's behaviour *seemed* to indicate, particularly in the face of the disturbing and violent nature of some of the court testimony. Amid 'the grimmest testimony,' for instance, Evelyn 'scarcely showed an interest in the statements of the witnesses.' As the pathologist, Dr Deadman, described to the court 'arms and legs being sawed off, the head being removed, and bones being snapped by hand,' Evelyn 'never even blinked.' Such reports often depended on the shock and eager interest of courtroom spectators to constitute Evelyn's own reactions as abnormal. As evidence was presented in court of the terrible violence done to her husband, Evelyn 'seem[ed] more unconcerned than even the spectators from the streets'; indeed, she was seen to be 'the least moved person in the court.'[53] The strength of such depictions lies in their repetition. After all, as Mary Doyle points out, 'it's legal to describe a defendant as listening "impassively" to gruesome evidence but, if she is described in similar words day after day, might not a picture of a cold, callous person capable of murder form itself even unconsciously in the minds of newspaper readers?'[54] Reports of Evelyn's mannerisms in court were remarkably similar to those of the countenance of sixteen-year-old Grace Marks, a servant accused nearly one hundred years earlier of murdering her master in Richmond Hill, Ontario. Marks was described at the time as being 'utterly devoid of expression' and of seeming 'completely unconscious of the awful situation in which she stood.'[55] According to Knelman, such formulaic descriptions were 'derived from English newspaper accounts of women, especially young women, who were not intimidated by rituals of justice.'[56]

While she did not appear to be intimidated, Evelyn was not constructed as physically threatening in any way. Any moral or social threat was neutralized somewhat by the fact that she was said to be childish, characterized over and over again as a 'child' or a 'little girl.' Her defence relied overtly on such a characterization in Evelyn's first murder trial: in Sullivan's address to the jury, he asked the twelve men to consider that 'the cutting up of the body' was a physical task 'beyond the power of this little girl.'[57] More often, though, Evelyn was infantilized on a mental or emotional level, facilitating a suggestion that she was feeble-minded.[58] Such comparisons began to appear in the press during Evelyn's first trial, more than five months before her 'mental age' was officially placed at thirteen. From her first appearances in court, the press depicted Evelyn not as a rational, cold-blooded woman, but as 'a woman with the mind of a hurt, wrought-up young girl.' She was seen to be 'as buoyant and cheerful as a schoolgirl with nothing on her mind but love stories.' Journalists also connected Evelyn's courtroom habit of drawing and note-taking with immaturity and potential feeble-mindedness. For example, reporters noted that Evelyn's penmanship was 'perhaps a little childish in the rounding of the letters and the somewhat spectacular loops,' her drawings 'artless and amateurish, like that done by any public school child.'[59] While a rational woman who appeared to have little interest in her own murder trial might be regarded as a threat, any power – or dignity – granted Evelyn by her refusal to show emotion in court is lost in the newspapers' construction of her as a simple-minded 'schoolgirl.'

Trial Spectators in the Press

During Evelyn's trials and hearings, whenever spectators were present at the courthouse, their presence was noted by the press, in both news items and photographs. Indeed, the *Telegram* was correct in its observation during Evelyn's first trial that 'crowds attracted to the Wentworth County court house for a fleeting glimpse of a 25-year-old Hamilton housewife … have caused almost as much comment as the defendant.'[60]

Two distinct groups of spectators were described in the news coverage: the spectators of the trial itself, within the courtroom; and the spectators of the *spectacle* of the trials, gathered outside the courthouse. The same individuals could occupy both of these positions at different times – a person not admitted to the courtroom one day may have lined up earlier the next day and gotten in – but the two *positions* were constructed in the papers as being quite different. By including the spectators so often in case-related stories and photographs, the media justified their own steady interest; clearly, they could say, the public wants to know. Over the course of the torso murder case, two major themes emerged in the coverage of spectators who were in attendance: first, the oppositional construction of the two groups of spectators as embodying, on the one hand, submission to state authority (inside) and, on the other, a carnivalesque anarchy (outside); and second, the feminization of both groups of spectators, both in photographs and text.

Spectators inside the courtroom were most assuredly subjected to a ritualized display of state power, as was the case for spectators of public executions in eighteenth-century France, as described by Michel Foucault.[61] The austere courtroom itself; the robes worn by the judge and lawyers, and the covered heads required of female spectators; the position of the judge on a raised platform at the head of the room; the traditional, ritual language used during the proceedings – all of these things signify the state's patriarchal authority.[62] Carolyn Strange notes that 'trials close off possibilities,' in that only certain individuals are allowed to speak.[63] Indeed, the newspapers reported several instances in which spectators were warned to keep silent. In light of some 'disturbances' – including 'talking and laughing' – by spectators during Evelyn's first murder trial, the deputy sheriff announced, 'This is not a show, this is a court ... Govern yourselves accordingly.' It was also made clear that spectators were not to be entertained by the proceedings. Chief Justice McRuer opened the second trial with a warning that 'the slightest evidence' that any spectator was 'making light of the proceedings' would lead to that person's eviction from the courtroom; 'It is a shameful thing for anyone to come to this trial and view it as something for their merriment,' he said.[64] Orders such as this served to put the trials into discourse in such a way as to reassert the authority of the state.

While there were a handful of reports on subversive hijinks by spectators, these events occurred during recesses and lunch breaks, or in the halls outside of the courtroom itself. In one instance, the court was cleared for the lunch break to prevent spectators from saving seats for the afternoon session; then, however, 'it occurred to some one [sic] to look into the ladies' washroom beside the court chamber – a small, poky place – and they found there 35 women.' During the jury's two-hour deliberations at the end of Evelyn's first trial, a number of spectators reportedly stayed in the courtroom to wait; they 'lounged' and 'chatted,' and the atmosphere was light. However, when the jury returned, and the session resumed, the spectators turned solemn in deference to the court's authority. When the guilty verdict was announced, 'there was no outcry, scarcely a stir.'[65]

In sharp contrast to 'the dignity of the well-ordered court' was the 'circus atmosphere' of the scene outside.[66] Queues formed early as spectators hoped to gain admission to court, but those who did not get in often stayed to watch for Evelyn's arrival or departure by car. At first, spectators were excited but generally well behaved. The fourth day of the first trial, 10 October 1946, marked the crowd's transformation from a gathering of individuals to a 'running, stumbling, mumbling mass' that 'hurled itself' into Evelyn's path.[67] According to the *Globe and Mail*, 'the crowd went wild. They pushed over one another and trampled and shoved.'[68] A week later, while Evelyn's conviction was met with 'scarcely a stir' inside the austere courtroom, she was confronted by 'a shrieking mob' upon leaving the courthouse.[69] Hyperbolic descriptions of the scene revealed the press to be as caught up in the excitement as any observer. The *Spectator* painted a disorienting picture: 'Photographers' flash bulbs flared intermittently in the dark. People strained forward to look at her. A small child was heard crying.' The *Globe and Mail* reported that 'bobby-soxers and elderly women, children and grown men fought for a glimpse of the convicted woman,' while a 'wave of hysteria swept the crowd.'[70]

A similar scene followed the conclusion of the second trial as well. Following her acquittal on 7 March 1947, Evelyn was greeted by 'boos and derisive shrieks.' By all accounts, the crowds that had demonstrated unrestrained curiosity now displayed a carnivalesque hostility. Police reinforcements were brought in to control the 'disorderly, howling mob' waiting outside the courthouse, which included 'middle-aged women [who] had been making threats and loudly complaining about the verdict.' One member of the crowd was an 'elderly woman' who 'opened her large purse and showed a number of people the contents – several chunks of icy mud she had picked up "to throw at [Evelyn]," she said.'[71]

Had they lined up earlier that day, members of the 'howling mob' could have witnessed Evelyn's acquittal from inside the courtroom, where, most likely, they would have obeyed the judge's orders to sit silently. While spectators inside the courtroom were instructed to respect the seriousness of the proceedings, efforts made outside to subdue the crowds were less successful. Spectators were willing to line up 'in an orderly column of threes' while waiting to be admitted; however, when the doors were opened, 'the charge of the housewives – yes, and businessmen, too – resemble[d] nothing so much as a herd of buffalo.'[72] A number of women were separated from their shoes and their purses in the surging crowd, despite the increased police presence and newly erected rope barricades. Onlookers ran alongside Evelyn's taxi until it left them behind. Bobby-soxers shouted, 'I saw her, I saw her.' Crowds once pressed so hard against a door at the courthouse that it broke from its hinges. A Boy Scout took advantage of the captive audience to raise money selling apples; the *Spectator* printed a photograph of the entrepreneurial boy and one of his customers: the trial judge.[73]

Such reports of the outdoor crowds served to strengthen the press construction of the case as a spectacle. Indeed, the discursive function of the crowds lay not in the fact that they gathered, but in the fact that their gathering was reported in detail and shown in photographs on a daily basis. In turn, coverage of the crowds may have encouraged further spectatorship (and newspaper readership). When asked why she had come to the courthouse in an attempt to gain entry to Evelyn's trial, one 'middle-aged housewife' offered this reply: 'I came because my neighbor got in yesterday, and I wanted to see if I could get in. Now I'm going to see if my picture gets in the papers tomorrow, because hers did.'[74] Spectators of the courtroom proceedings may have been awed by displays of state power, as were the execution witnesses described by Foucault, but those who gathered outside were too busy enjoying the carnivalesque event to be much impressed by the state, recalling instead Thomas Laqueur's analysis of British crowds who watched hangings and beheadings in the seventeenth, eighteenth, and nineteenth centuries. Laqueur argues that public executions represented not 'solemn state theatre,' but rather 'a theatre of far greater fluidity,' at which the boisterous crowd, not the state, was central.[75] Press coverage of the 'shrieking mobs' in Hamilton constructed a raucous collective that literally could not be contained by officialdom. Laqueur's execution scenes depicted 'an overflowing vibrant, alive, noisy, fat, body/body politics overturning itself in all directions.'[76] The newspaper coverage of the crowds attending Evelyn's trials also depicted a carnival crowd: eating, shrieking, booing, cheering, spitting, running, chasing, and bursting through doors and rope barricades. And it was a feminized crowd – yes, there were 'businessmen, too,' but only women were singled out and identified in photographs, and stories regularly commented on the presence, actions, and appearance of female spectators.

Anonymous crowd photographs taken outside the Wentworth County Court House during all three of Evelyn's trials clearly showed the presence of both men and women. However, every photograph that featured one or a small group of individual spectators and/or identified them by name portrayed girls and women. Spectators were not photographed inside the courtroom, but the newspaper reports still focused on the women in attendance, portraying them as being more involved, or having more of an interest, than their male counterparts. A typical description of the crowds gathered outside the courthouse noted that many of those present were 'women who looked as if they had shelved their housework for the day' and 'working girls on their way to offices and shops.' Inside the courtroom, female spectators included 'neatly-packed rows of housewives,' 'elderly women in fussy, beflowered hats, and younger women in suits.'[77] Such feminization of a crowd is not unusual; whatever their proportions of males and females, crowds have long been defined by an excess of stereotypically feminine traits.[78] In the case of Evelyn's trials, press accounts of the spectators as not just feminine but *female* may have been linked to the gender of the defendant. As noted in the previous section, Evelyn's reactions were often measured against those of the 'normal' courtroom spectators. The newspapers' focus on female spectators served to reinforce as deviant Evelyn's own femaleness.

The Case of Evelyn Dick as a Soap-Opera Narrative

Of all the column inches devoted to Evelyn's case in 1946 and 1947, the most expressive and dramatic content was generally found in the papers' 'colour' stories, most notably those written by Marjorie Earl of the *Star* and Eva-Lis Wuorio of the *Globe and Mail*.[79] For the most part, Earl and Wuorio reframed the day-to-day courtroom proceedings as episodes of a continuing human-interest story. Where the front-page 'news' stories recounted what was said, the 'colour' stories elaborated on *how* it was said, or how it felt to hear it said, or what the person who said it was wearing. On occasion, Earl and Wuorio even became participant-observers of the events, reporting on their own interactions with Evelyn and Alexandra. Although not identified explicitly as 'sob sisters,' these female journalists still produced a personal, sentimental, and at times 'hyperexpressive' kind of prose that is associated with the feminized term.[80] I do not mean to suggest that the women's writing style was determined by their gender – in fact, a few of the most over-wrought passages came from Allan Kent of the *Telegram*[81] – but rather that female journalists in the 1940s were most likely given the task of producing 'feminine' content.[82] Overall, the narrative of the torso murder and Evelyn's trials was largely shaped by this content.

These 'colour' stories contained language that could easily be described as 'melodramatic,' in the commonly used sense of the word. According to Peter Brooks, *melodrama* is 'a label that has a bad reputation'; its everyday connotations include 'the indulgence of strong emotionalism; moral polarization and schematization; extreme states of being, situations, actions; overt villainy ... inflated and extravagant expression; dark plottings, suspense, [and] breathtaking peripety.'[83] Within the genre of melodrama, the product with one of the worst reputations is the daytime soap opera. First appearing on radio in the 1920s, and becoming 'entrenched in the American broadcast world' with the 1936 launch of the program *The Guiding Light*, these melodramatic serials were designed to appeal to women in their homes in order to organize them as consumers of household products, which the programs advertised.[84]

Aside from sharing many characteristics of the umbrella genre of melodrama, soap operas did then and continue to feature a number of unique traits. Mary Ellen Brown identifies the following qualities of soap opera, among others: 'the centrality of female characters,' 'the characterization of female characters as powerful,' 'multiple characters and plots as well as multiple points of view,' 'plots that hinge on relationships between people, particularly family and romantic relationships,' and 'serial form that resists narrative closure (never-endingness).'[85] The collective newspaper coverage of the case of Evelyn Dick shares these qualities and can thus be viewed through the lenses of melodrama and, more specifically, soap opera.

Perhaps the single most defining characteristic of soap opera is, as Brown notes, its 'never-endingness'; that is, 'not only do soaps never end, but their beginnings are soon lost sight of,' leaving only a middle that goes on and on.[86] While it is easy to pinpoint the beginning of the *coverage* of the torso murder case – indeed, it was 16 March 1946 when children discovered the torso of John Dick on a wooded mountainside – the *story* started earlier. After all, the appearance of a dead body actually represents the ending of another story. The newspapers reached into Evelyn's past on occasion, appearing to shed light on later events; for example, on the day Evelyn was convicted of murder and sentenced to hang, the *Star* printed a photo of her as a child above a quote by her mother: 'She was such a beautiful baby.'[87] The story of the case also lacked narrative closure. For the murder of John Dick, Evelyn was ultimately acquitted and, while Donald MacLean was convicted as an accessory, no one else served time. In fact, no one can be sure about what actually happened to John. The police failed to solve the case, and the killer or killers declined to confess. There was no neat wrap-up, no concluding chapter that tied up all the loose ends. Then, while Evelyn was found to be legally responsible for the death of baby Peter David White, and did receive the maximum sentence for her manslaughter conviction, an 'ending' was still lacking. She admitted nothing. Her version of events put the blame on Bill Bohozuk, but the court did not buy it, and he was freed. Again, loose ends were left hanging.

Even the press noted the absence of a proper conclusion to the mystery of the infant's death; a *Globe and Mail* reporter evaluated Evelyn's third trial from the perspective of a frustrated moviegoer:

This trial has had all the aspects of a mystery movie. But they do it better in the movies ... The movie detective would have produced the driver who took Evelyn home from the hospital – who knows whether she went straight home – what she did, whom she saw – and the case would have been open and shut.[88]

If the case of Evelyn Dick had been a 'mystery movie,' it may have been open and shut; instead, the case was a soap opera, and it stayed open. In fact, the day before her evocation of a 'mystery movie,' the same reporter explicitly likened the case to a soap opera by comparing its (female) spectators to soap fans; those denied entry to the public gallery reacted like 'a person done out of listening to her favorite soap opera.' She continued:

> They were lined up at 1 o'clock yesterday for the afternoon session which began at 2:30. It was pouring rain, but they didn't care. They had read the synopsis of preceding installments in the newspapers. This would be another thrilling chapter, and even when it ends the story isn't finished … From the curious spectators' standpoint all it seemed to lack was a good commercial.[89]

The reporter's recognition that 'even when it ends the story isn't finished' evokes the 'never-endingness' of the daytime soap opera. As well, presentation of the case in 'installments in the newspapers' created a serial narrative, a distinguishing feature of soap opera. In her analysis of the coverage, Doyle observed that key details of the torso case (e.g., the charges and circumstances of the crimes) were not repeated from day to day, indicating an assumption that readers followed the reports daily, and so already knew the 'back story.'[90]

Clearly a female 'character' was central to this story, although nearly every other figure involved in the case was male. Weaver notes the male domination of the Canadian criminal justice system in the 1940s; as he points out, 'men alone had questioned, charged, tried, defended, and judged Evelyn Dick.'[91] Newspaper readers today might expect that John Dick and baby Peter White, the male victims, would have played significant roles in the story, but they were largely absent. This focus on the accused rather than the victim was not unusual for 1940s news coverage, however; research has found that victims generally played a minor role in crime news prior to the 1960s.[92] A corpse was commonly treated as 'little more than a relic of another's transgression.'[93] And if Evelyn was the leading lady in the story of the murders, her mother was the most prominent member of the supporting cast. Alexandra's testimony against her daughter was twice a sensational highlight of the case, she appeared in dozens of newspaper photographs, and she made herself available to reporters on several occasions, usually to share her reactions to each turn of events. In October 1946, for example, upon learning that Evelyn had been convicted and sentenced to death, Alexandra wept as she was interviewed in her 'tastefully and expensively furnished living room.'[94] When Evelyn was acquitted the following March, Alexandra again received reporters 'in the living room of the now-famous house at 32 Carrick [A]ve.'[95] By inviting the press into her house – the house that actually belonged to Evelyn – Alexandra provided a key soap-opera quality to the narrative, namely, a glimpse into the private, interior domestic space of the women's home. During these interviews, Alexandra and the (usually female) newspaper reporters together realized other classic elements of melodrama and soap opera, such as intimate talk and emotional display:

> 'I loved her so much and she loved me. We were very close until she married John Dick.' ...
> [Alexandra's] grief and terror were so real and so terrible, so pitifully responsive to sympathy, that I wept with her ...
> 'Oh,' she said in a choked voice, suddenly covering her mouth with her hand as though to stifle a scream. Her face contorted and tears streamed down her tired, aged cheeks. Reaching out, she clutched my arm, put her head down on my coatfront and wept.[96]

The press, in turn, by publishing such accounts alongside 'hard news' stories of the case, legitimized and elevated such 'feminine' concerns as interpersonal relationships and family ties. At the same time, though, the struggles of the 'characters' in the Evelyn Dick story make no 'real-life demands' upon the reader, as is also the case with soaps: 'With almost no effort at all, the viewer can participate vicariously in love affairs, friendships, and intrigue that seem intimate but are safely remote.'[97]

Of course, the case involved Evelyn's family from the start: her husband and infant were the victims, and her parents were both charged early on with the murder of their son-in-law. Reporters and lawyers alike – and no doubt the public – speculated at length as to the influence of Evelyn's family life on her transgressions. In his closing remarks to the jury at Evelyn's first trial, defence counsel John J. Sullivan made a point of mentioning that the MacLean family home was 'divided' and lacked 'the harmony and unity that one expects in the average home.'[98]

During the second trial, a 'colour story' framed Evelyn's predicament in terms of her family background and upbringing: 'And you think again, as so often before, of a lower class home. A house on a quiet street, British immigrant parents, the daughter trying to "better" herself, not mentally, but socially. You think of the childhood of the girl, and what it must have been like.'[99] Following Evelyn's manslaughter conviction, a psychiatrist testified not only that Evelyn was nearly a moron, but also that she had been affected by 'constant family trouble,' which included parental bickering and a lack of discipline.[100] Other than the rare mention of 'a lower class home,' this continual focus on Evelyn's home life masked larger social and economic factors, seeking instead to locate responsibility in the family and in the failures of individuals. This discourse illustrates 'domestic melodrama's oft-noted tendency to portray all ideological conflicts in terms of the family.'[101] Regarding the murder of Evelyn's baby, for instance, at no time did journalists address the economic and emotional pressures of single motherhood or issues related to unwanted pregnancy.

Much of the press speculation about the case – particularly that which was concerned with the 'tangled, blood-stained web that [had] been woven around the family'[102] – resembled gossip and, as such, involved a social-control function. Gossip 'serves to remind members of the community of the importance of its norms and values … It may be used to punish those who transgress and, at the same time, to warn everyone else not to transgress, lest they be shunned as well.'[103] Evelyn was the transgressor, of course, and the presence of gossip about her family life reflects the historical context within which her transgressions occurred. At a given time, the subjects of gossip tend to reflect 'conflicting social obligations and expectations' of the period, as in the following example: 'In societies where men are expected to be virile and display their powers by predatory sexual conquests of women, whereas women are expected to be chaste and virginal … gossip frequently concerns sexual liaisons.'[104] It makes sense, then, that Evelyn's trials in 1946 and 1947 generated gossip about domestic conflict, unwed motherhood, and promiscuous sexual activity – not to mention a couple who marry against parental wishes, only to begin living apart immediately. After all, the heterosexual nuclear family was 'a central – if not *the* central – concern of postwar life' and was 'valued as the "traditional" foundation of the Canadian social structure' in those years.[105] Evelyn's alleged involvement in a murder was far from being her only transgression.

Conclusion

Evelyn spent eleven years and three months in the federal Prison for Women in Kingston before she was released under ticket of leave in November 1958 at the age of thirty-eight.[106] She was given a new name and identity and was relocated secretly. Evelyn effectively disappeared, her whereabouts known only to the parole board.[107] In 1985, she applied for and was granted a pardon under federal Royal Prerogative of Mercy provisions, meaning that she no longer had to report to the parole board. She had the same freedoms as any Canadian citizen, and her parole-board record was forever sealed.[108] It is unknown whether she is still alive. In the mid-1990s, Evelyn was effectively replaced by Karla Homolka as Canada's most notorious female killer. Karla herself was aware of Evelyn's case, having read Brian Vallée's 2001 book *The Torso Murder* while in prison; Karla reportedly found Evelyn's ability to 'vaporize' after her own release from prison 'very interesting.'[109] Indeed, it is Evelyn's ultimate 'disappearance' that continues to intrigue journalists and true-crime writers today.

By contrast, it was largely her appearance that fascinated as the case unfolded in the 1940s. An analysis of the discursive construction of Evelyn Dick in the daily news coverage of the torso murder case reveals a gendered focus on both the defendant and the spectators who attended her trials. News items and photographs routinely drew attention to Evelyn's physical beauty, and journalists repeatedly scrutinized her body for clues as to her various transgressions. At the same time, female spectators were continually singled out in descriptions and images of the curious crowds, often representing 'normal' womanhood in contrast to 'abnormal' Evelyn.

More than sixty years have passed since Evelyn went to prison, and it has become common for journalists to describe her, in retrospect, as a 'femme fatale.'[110] The torso murder and resulting trials did take place at the apogee of what came to be known as film noir, a dark cinematic style that commonly featured a deadly woman.[111] However, the *telling* of the story in the newspapers did not follow conventions of noir so much as it adhered to the 'feminine' codes of soap opera. Instead of a dark and dangerous tale that played out in the shadows, driven by the investigation, the press constructed a melodramatic narrative about what would now be called a dysfunctional family, with anxieties about class and status; about babies born out of wedlock in an era when the nuclear family was especially revered; about a house full of women (three generations lived on their own together: Alexandra, Evelyn, and Evelyn's daughter, Heather) at a time when many local households had recently lost their men; about a beautiful young woman with a shocking private life thrust suddenly into the public arena; about the moral outrage and curious gaze of housewives and bobby-soxers. Each instalment that appeared in the newspapers strengthened Evelyn's status as the star.

NOTES

1 Writers commonly use the term 'torso murder' to signify the case as a whole, encompassing the murders of both John Dick and baby Peter White, even though the only torso involved was John's. The term is used this way throughout this article.

2 D. Owen Carrigan, *Crime and Punishment in Canada: A History* (Toronto: McClelland and Stewart, 1991), 262. See also Karlene Faith, *Unruly Women: The Politics of Confinement and Resistance* (Vancouver: Press Gang, 1993); Helen Boritch, *Fallen Women: Female Crime and Criminal Justice in Canada* (Scarborough: ITP Nelson, 1997).

3 Frances Heidensohn, *Women and Crime* (Houndsmills, UK: Macmillan, 1985), 94; Ann Lloyd, *Doubly Deviant, Doubly Damned: Society's Treatment of Violent Women* (London: Penguin, 1995); Bronwyn Naylor, 'Women's Crime and Media Coverage: Making Explanations,' in R. Emerson Dobash, Russell P. Dobash, and Lesley Noaks, eds, *Gender and Crime* (Cardiff: University of Wales Press, 1995), 77–95; Sarah Wight and Alice Myers, 'Introduction,' in Alice Myers and Sarah Wight, eds, *No Angels: Women Who Commit Violence* (London: Pandora, 1996), xi–xvi.

4 Lise Diebel, 'Where Are You, Mrs. Dick?' *Hamilton Spectator*, 10 June 2006, MP61. Texts based on the case range from television dramatizations and a stage play to a punk song; since 2000 alone, the case has inspired a novel, a TV documentary and made-for-TV movie, a non-fiction book, and a short musical film.

5 Robyn A. Gillam, 'Evelyn Dick: Deconstructing a Fictional Body,' *The Mid-Atlantic Almanack: The Journal of the Mid-Atlantic Popular/American Culture Association* 5 (1996): 85–106.

6 Jack Batten, *Robinette: The Dean of Canadian Lawyers* (Toronto: Macmillan, 1984), 70.

7 Throughout this article, the titles of these papers are abbreviated in notes

as follows: *HS* (*Hamilton Spectator*), *TDS* (*Toronto Daily Star*), *GM* (*Globe and Mail*), and *TET* (*Toronto Evening Telegram*).

8 'Produce Bones and Teeth Claimed Taken from Ashes,' *HS*, 25 April 1946, 11; 'Remains on Mountain Side Said Those of John Dick,' *HS*, 19 March 1946, 7; '"Don't Look at Me," Say Evelyn Denied Murder,' *TDS*, 23 April 1947, 1; 'Mrs. Dick, Told of Torso, Said "Don't Look at Me" Insp. Wood Tells Jurors,' *TET*, 12 October 1946, 1.

9 Batten, *Robinette*, 50–2; Jocko Thomas, *From Police Headquarters: True Tales from the Big City Crime Beat* (Toronto: Stoddart, 1990), 91.

10 Thomas, *From Police Headquarters*, 89.

11 Batten, *Robinette*, 70.

12 On wartime conditions for Canadian women, see Ruth Roach Pierson, *'They're Still Women After All': The Second World War and Canadian Womanhood* (Toronto: McClelland and Stewart, 1986).

13 Lex Schrag, '"E. MacLean" Nameband on Skirt Beside Body of Baby, Detective Says,' *GM*, 25 March 1947, 1; 'Evelyn Dick Never Applied to Us, Children's Aid Says,' *TDS*, 25 March 1947, 2.

14 As Alexandra would later testify in court, 'I did not approve of him … He had no money.' 'Daughter Shouted at Her "Keep Your Mouth Shut" Mother of Widow Says,' *TET*, 9 October 1946, 1.

15 Ibid.; '"You Keep Your Mouth Shut," Mrs. MacLean Quotes Accused,' *HS*, 9 October 1946, 12; 'Two of Four Statements "False," Says Evelyn Dick,' *TDS*, 15 October 1946, 11.

16 '"You Keep Your Mouth Shut,"' *HS*, 12.

17 '"Yes, John Dick Is Dead" Mother Quotes Evelyn,' *TDS*, 9 October 1946, 2.

18 The written decision in the appeal of Evelyn's conviction, in January 1947, addressed seven statements attributed to her. The second appeal – the appeal of her acquittal in April 1947 – specified eleven statements; three of these were brief statements that had not been entered into evidence at Evelyn's first trial, and two of the eleven had previously been treated as a single statement. *Rex v. Dick*, O.R. 1947, 105; *Rex v. Dick*, O.R. 1947, 695.

19 'Accused Tells How She Saw "Part of Face, All Smashed,"' *HS*, 15 October 1946, 8; 'Windsor Gangsters Killed Her Husband, Mrs. Dick Charged in Statement to Police,' *GM*, 15 October 1946, 8.

20 'Two, Possibly 3 More Sought in Torso Case,' *TDS*, 21 March 1946, 1.

21 'Police Seizures Occurred on Five Distinct Occasions,' *HS*, 10 January 1947, 7; 'Father of Torso Widow Bailed on Theft Charge,' *TDS*, 23 March 1946, 1.

22 Schrag, '"E. MacLean" Nameband on Skirt,' *GM*, 1, 2.

23 'Joint Accusations Made against Man and Woman,' *HS*, 29 March 1946, 7; 'Evelyn Dick and William Bohozuk Jointly Charged with Two Slay-

ings,' *GM*, 30 March 1946, 15. The surname 'White' belonged to a fictional 'Admiral Norman White,' whom Evelyn had invented as a respectable father for her three babies and an absent husband for herself.

24 'Joint Murder Charge Faces 4 in Hamilton,' *HS*, 16 April 1946, 2; 'Commit 3 in Torso Case[;] Mrs. MacLean Acquitted,' *TDS*, 27 April 1946, 2.

25 John C. Weaver, *Crimes, Constables, and Courts: Order and Transgression in a Canadian City, 1816–1970* (Montreal and Kingston: McGill-Queen's University Press, 1995), 151.

26 Ibid.; 'Evelyn Dick Sentenced to Hang Jan. 7,' *HS*, 17 October 1946, 8.

27 *Rex v. Dick*, O.R. 1947, 105, 128; Alan Randall, 'Ontario Court of Appeal Sets Aside Her Conviction,' *HS*, 17 January 1947, 7; 'Five Judges Unanimous[,] Order New Torso Trial,' *TDS*, 17 January 1947, 1.

28 'Boehler Testimony Termed Fantastic,' *HS*, 5 March 1947, 7, 8; '"Could Not Hang Dog" on Evidence – Robinette,' *TDS*, 5 March 1947, 1.

29 The separate charge of infanticide was not added to the Canadian Criminal Code until 1948, one year after Evelyn's conviction in the death of baby Peter David White. Kirsten Johnson Kramar, *Unwilling Mothers, Unwanted Babies: Infanticide in Canada* (Vancouver: UBC Press, 2005), 3.

30 'Accused Woman Found Mentally Aged 13 Years,' *HS*, 26 March 1947, 7; Lex Schrag, 'Evelyn, Jailed for Life, Subnormal, Doctor Says; Redemption Is Possible,' *GM*, 27 March 1947, 17.

31 Lex Schrag, 'Bohozuk Found Not Guilty of Slaying Newborn Child,' *GM*, 31 March 1947, 1; 'Bohozuk "Not Guilty"[;] Walks Out a Free Man,' *TDS*, 31 March 1947, 1.

32 '5 Years in Pen Donald MacLean Torso Sentence,' *TDS*, 2 April 1947, 1; Wilfred List, 'MacLean Gets Five-Year Term as Accessory,' *GM*, 3 April 1947, 1.

33 'Mrs. Evelyn Dick Taken from Jail to Penitentiary,' *HS*, 18 July 1947, 7; 'Unglamorous Pen Entry by "Glamorous" Evelyn,' *GM*, 19 July 1947, 5.

34 Ben Rose, 'Evelyn Dick Case Ended, Supreme Court Refuses Appeal Plea,' *TDS*, 9 August 1947, 1.

35 On the early history of television in Canada, see Paul Rutherford, *When Television Was Young: Primetime Canada 1952–1967* (Toronto: University of Toronto Press, 1990).

36 See, for example, 'Mrs. Dick Looks up at Clouds Then Says: "What a Difference,"' *TDS*, 8 October 1946, 1; 'Mrs. Dick Looks as if She's Shed Some Tears,' *TDS*, 10 October 1946, 5; 'Curious Crowd Swarms around Accused Woman,' *HS*, 10 October 1946, 7; 'Admit 3 of 4 Statements Said Made by Evelyn Dick,' *TDS*, 12 October 1946, 1; Marjorie Earl, 'Occasionally Evelyn Looks as if She'd Like to Cry,' *TDS*, 4 March 1947, 27.

37 John Berger, *Ways of Seeing* (London: British Broadcasting Corporation, 1972), 52.

38 'Mrs. Dick Faces Separate Trial in Torso Murder,' *TDS*, 7 October 1946, 2.

39 Eva-Lis Wuorio, 'Mrs. Dick Like Unwilling Guest at Tea,' *GM*, 8 October 1946, 3.

40 '"Make This Good!" Smiling Mrs. Dick Urges Camera Men,' *HS*, 27 January 1947, 7; Marjorie Earl, 'Are There Good Pictures of Me? Evelyn Dick's First Question,' *TDS*, 9 October 1946, 3.

41 Roland Barthes, 'The Photographic Message,' in Susan Sontag, ed., *A Barthes Reader* (New York: Hill and Wang, 1982), 198.

42 Berger, *Ways of Seeing*, 10. See also Alan Trachtenberg, *Reading American Photographs: Images as History, Mathew Brady to Walker Evans* (New York: Hill and Wang, 1989), xvi.

43 Susan Sontag, *On Photography* (New York: Farrar, Straus and Giroux, 1977), 28.

44 Sandra Kemp, '"Myra, Myra on the Wall": The Fascination of Faces,' *Critical Quarterly* 40, no. 1 (1998): 40.

45 Judith Knelman, *Twisting in the Wind: The Murderess and the English Press* (Toronto: University of Toronto Press, 1998), 250.

46 On Canadian postwar food rationing, see Jeff Keshen, 'One for All or All for One: Black Marketing in Canada, 1939–1947,' in J.L. Granatstein and Peter Neary, eds, *The Good Fight: Canadians and World War II* (Toronto: Copp Clark, 1995), 263–91.

47 'Tell Court of Disputes between Dick, Wife's Kin,' *TDS*, 25 April 1946, 15; 'Evelyn Happy, Eats Hearty[,] Advises Mates, Pays Fines,' *TDS*, 18 January 1947, 3; Eva-Lis Wuorio, 'Courtroom Bright Spot in Evelyn Dick's Day,' *GM*, 11 October 1946, 15; Wuorio, 'Like Unwilling Guest,' *GM*; 'Mrs. MacLean Posts Surety for Appearance as Witness,' *HS*, 27 April 1946, 10.

48 Ralph Hyman, 'Won't Testify against Pair, Mrs. Dick Says,' *GM*, 18 October 1946, 1; 'Prison Stay Agrees with Evelyn Dick; Adds 20 Pounds,' *GM*, 10 January 1947, 7; 'Evelyn Happy, Eats Hearty,' *TDS*; Eva-Lis Wuorio, 'Hamilton Women Boo Short, Fat Evelyn Dick,' *GM*, 28 January 1947, 3.

49 Writing on film, Anne Bower notes that food is easily 'read' as a stand-in for sex: 'Watching Food: The Production of Food, Film, and Values,' in Anne L. Bower, ed., *Reel Food: Essays on Food and Film* (New York: Routledge, 2004), 6.

50 Allan Kent, 'Evidence in Murder Case Swings from Evelyn Dick[;] Like MacLean's Trial Now,' *TET*, 27 February 1947, 2.

51 Marjorie Earl, 'Scornful Smile Flickers over Evelyn Dick's Lips,' *TDS*, 24

April 1946, 36; Ralph Hyman, 'Expert Tells Details of Grisly Torso Crime,' *GM*, 9 October 1946, 1; Eva-Lis Wuorio, 'Evelyn Dick Carefully Draws Court Figures,' *GM*, 16 October 1946, 8.

52 Wuorio, 'Like Unwilling Guest,' *GM*; 'Daughter Shouted at Her,' *TET*; Eva-Lis Wuorio, 'Evelyn Dick's Composure Shattered as Child Cries on Courthouse Steps,' *GM*, 9 October 1946, 8; Earl, 'Scornful Smile,' *TDS*.

53 'Defence Offers No Evidence in Trial of Mrs. Evelyn Dick,' *HS*, 16 October 1946, 9; 'Daughter Shouted at Her,' *TET*; Wuorio, 'Evelyn Dick's Composure Shattered,' *GM*.

54 Mary C. Doyle, 'Comparison of the Press Coverage of the Peter Demeter Trial with the Press Coverage of the Evelyn Dick Trial' (Master of Journalism major research paper, University of Western Ontario, 1975), 2.

55 This newspaper – quoted in Judith Knelman, 'Can We Believe What the Newspapers Tell Us? Missing Links in *Alias Grace*,' *University of Toronto Quarterly* 68 (spring 1999): 679 – was the *Toronto Star, Transcript and General Advertiser* (1843).

56 Ibid., 679.

57 'Defence Says Mrs. Dick Lived in Dream World[,] Couldn't Commit Crime,' *HS*, 16 October 1946, 10; Ralph Hyman, 'Jury Out 2 Hours; Recommends Mercy,' *GM*, 17 October 1946, 8.

58 Joan Sangster notes that during the interwar period, feeble-mindedness was seen to cause promiscuity and prostitution; this link had weakened by the 1940s, but was still present. On women's conflicts with the law in Ontario, see Sangster, *Regulating Girls and Women: Sexuality, Family, and the Law in Ontario, 1920–1960* (Don Mills, ON: Oxford University Press, 2001).

59 Eva-Lis Wuorio, 'Crowds Early and Late Clamor at Court Doors,' *GM*, 15 October 1946, 9; Marjorie Earl, 'Buy Me Love Stories[,] Smiling Accused Asks,' *TDS*, 12 October 1946, 19; Wuorio, 'Courtroom Bright Spot,' *GM*; 'Mrs. Dick Sleeps Soundly in Hamilton Death Cell,' *TDS*, 17 October 1946, 3.

60 'Curiosity Main Murder Trial Drawing Card,' *TET*, 12 October 1946, 3.

61 Michel Foucault, *Discipline and Punish: The Birth of the Prison*, 2nd ed., trans. Alan Sheridan (New York: Vintage Books, 1995). Foucault's spectators were outdoors, but the site of displays of justice has since shifted from the gallows to the courtroom.

62 John C. Weaver, *Hamilton: An Illustrated History* (Toronto: James Lorimer and National Museums of Canada, 1982), 148.

63 Carolyn Strange, 'Stories of Their Lives: The Historian and the Capital Case File,' in Franca Iacovetta and Wendy Mitchinson, eds, *On the Case: Explorations in Social History* (Toronto: University of Toronto Press, 1998), 36.

64 'Mrs. Dick Had Bandage on Her Hand, Court Told,' *TDS*, 10 October 1946, 2; 'Farmhand Testifies He Saw Man's Leg in Back of Car He Pulled from Mud,' *HS*, 26 February 1947, 8.

65 '35 Women Hide in Tiny Washroom at Trial Lunchtime,' *GM*, 11 October 1946, 15; 'Evelyn Dick Sentenced to Hang,' *HS*.

66 Ibid.

67 'Curious Crowd Swarms,' *HS*.

68 Eva-Lis Wuorio, 'Torso Court Shocked as Evidence Unfolds,' *GM*, 10 October 1946, 3.

69 Fred Egan, 'Shrieking Mob Watches Evelyn Ride to Cell,' *GM*, 17 October 1946, 3.

70 'Evelyn Dick Sentenced to Hang,' *HS*; Egan, 'Shrieking Mob,' *GM*.

71 'Broad Smiles Disappear as Crowd Boos Verdict,' *TET*, 7 March 1947, 3; Eva-Lis Wuorio, 'Tears, Prayers Mark Vigil for Evelyn,' *GM*, 7 March 1947, 1.

72 'Murder Trial Drawing Card,' *TET*.

73 Wuorio, 'Crowds Early and Late,' *GM*; 'Torso Victim's Widow Is Target of Curious Eyes,' *HS*, 8 October 1946, 11; 'Shed Some Tears,' *TDS*; 'Dozen Carnations Sent to Mrs. Dick for Her Birthday,' *HS*, 12 October 1946, 11; 'An Apple for the Judge,' *HS*, 15 October 1946, 7.

74 'Murder Trial Drawing Card,' *TET*.

75 Thomas W. Laqueur, 'Crowds, Carnival and the State in English Executions, 1604-1868,' in A.L. Beier, David Cannadine, and James M. Rosenheim, eds, *The First Modern Society: Essays in English History in Honour of Lawrence Stone* (Cambridge: Cambridge University Press, 1989), 306, 309.

76 Ibid., 348.

77 Earl, 'Scornful Smile,' *TDS*; 'Even Accused Almost Misses Hearing,' *HS*, 7; Wuorio, 'Evelyn Dick's Composure Shattered,' *GM*, 8.

78 See Gustave Le Bon, *The Crowd* (New York: Compass, 1960).

79 Some of the 'colour' coverage of the case was anonymous, and some was attributed to other journalists (including Helen Beattie of the *Globe* and Phyllis Griffiths of the *Telegram*), but Earl and Wuorio were by far the most prolific and regular contributors of this kind of content.

80 The term 'sob sister' was popularized during the sensational 1907 trial of Harry Thaw for the murder of architect Stanford White in New York City; the term was used to refer to the female journalists who covered the trial. For a critical examination of 'sob sisterhood,' see Jean Marie Lutes, 'Sob Sisterhood Revisited,' *American Literary History* 15, no. 3 (2003): 504–32.

81 See, for example, Kent, 'Evelyn Dick Rolls Her Eyes,' *TET*; 'Evelyn Flashes Brief Smile as Court Is Shown Photos of Herself and Boy Friend,' *TET*, 11 October 1946, 3.

82 Jocko Thomas was one of three *Star* reporters assigned to cover Evelyn's first trial; as he later wrote in his memoirs, 'Alf [Tate] and I were to do the running copy of the testimony, while Miss Earl did color stories.' *From Police Headquarters*, 92. For more on Marjorie Earl and sexism in the newsroom, see Patricia Orwen, 'Women of the Star,' *Toronto Star*, 24 May 1992, D1.

83 Peter Brooks, *The Melodramatic Imagination: Balzac, Henry James, Melodrama, and the Mode of Excess* (New Haven, CT: Yale University Press, 1976), 11–12.

84 Mary Ellen Brown, *Soap Opera and Women's Talk: The Pleasure of Resistance* (London: SAGE, 1994), 45, 46.

85 Ibid., 49.

86 Annette Kuhn, 'Women's Genres,' *Screen* 25, no. 1 (1984): 18.

87 Marjorie Earl, '"Only Child, I Idolized Her," Mrs. Dick's Mother Weeps,' *TDS*, 17 October 1946, 3.

88 Helen Beattie, 'Jury Convicts Evelyn; Returns in Five Hours,' *GM*, 26 March 1947, 1.

89 Helen Beattie, '"Soap Opera" Aura at Evelyn's Trial,' *GM*, 25 March 1947, 21.

90 Doyle, 'Comparison of the Press Coverage,' 20.

91 Weaver, *Crimes, Constables, and Courts*, 158.

92 Robert Reiner, Sonia Livingstone, and Jessica Allen, 'No More Happy Endings? The Media and Popular Concern about Crime since the Second World War,' in Tim Hope and Richard Sparks, eds, *Crime, Risk and Insecurity* (London: Routledge, 2000); Reiner, Livingstone, and Allen, 'From Law and Order to Lynch Mobs: Crime News since the Second World War,' in Paul Mason, ed., *Criminal Visions: Media Representations of Crime and Justice* (Cullompton, Devon: Willan, 2003).

93 Sara L. Knox, *Murder: A Tale of Modern American Life* (Durham, NC: Duke University Press, 1998), 15.

94 Earl, '"I Idolized Her,"' *TDS*. See also Eva-Lis Wuorio, 'Evelyn's Mother Weeps in Quiet Hamilton Home,' *GM*, 17 October 1946, 3; Herbert Biggs, 'Knew Evelyn Was "Gone" When Statements Read[,] Tearful Mother Relates,' *TET*, 17 October 1946, 23.

95 'Stoical Mother Doubted Mrs. Dick Would "Get Off,"' *TET*, 7 March 1947, 3.

96 Earl, '"I Idolized Her,"' *TDS*.

97 Ruth Rosen, 'Search for Yesterday,' in Todd Gitlin, ed., *Watching Television* (New York: Pantheon, 1986), 45.

98 'Evelyn Dick Sentenced to Hang,' *HS*.

99 Eva-Lis Wuorio, 'Evelyn Inscrutable Spectator,' *GM*, 6 March 1947, 15.

100 'Mentally Aged 13 Years,' *HS*, 8; 'Evelyn "Cried Like Baby[,]" Knew Right, Wrong – Doctor,' *TDS*, 26 March 1947, 19.

101 Jane Feuer, 'Melodrama, Serial Form and Television Today,' *Screen* 25, no. 1 (1984): 14.

102 'Bohozuk-MacLean Trial Is Postponed to Jan. 27[;] Appeal Outcome Awaited,' *TET*, 15 January 1947, 3.

103 Jack Levin and Arnold Arluke, *Gossip: The Inside Scoop* (New York: Plenum, 1987), 125.

104 Sally Engle Merry, 'Rethinking Gossip and Scandal,' in Donald Black, ed., *Toward a General Theory of Social Control* (Orlando: Academic, 1984), 278.

105 Mary Louise Adams, *The Trouble with Normal: Postwar Youth and the Making of Heterosexuality* (Toronto: University of Toronto Press, 1997), 26, 38.

106 Being 'released under ticket of leave' was the precursor to what is now called being released on parole.

107 Brian Vallée, *The Torso Murder: The Untold Story of Evelyn Dick* (Toronto: Key Porter, 2001), 248–9.

108 Ibid., 277–8.

109 Stephen Williams, *Karla: A Pact with the Devil* (Toronto: Seal, 2003), 493.

110 See, for example, Doug Foley, 'Movie on Evelyn Dick Captures TV Honours,' *HS*, 5 November 2002, A1; Angela Pacienza, 'Slean Takes on Different Role as Femme Fatale in Black Widow,' *Ottawa Citizen*, 19 January 2006, F6.

111 On visual and narrative codes of film noir, see J.A. Place and L.S. Peterson, 'Some Visual Motifs of Film Noir,' *Film Comment* 10, no. 1 (January–February 1974): 30–5; Michael Walker, 'Film Noir: Introduction,' in Ian Cameron, ed., *The Book of Film Noir* (New York: Continuum, 1993), 8–38. On the femme fatale in film noir, see the collected essays in E. Ann Kaplan, ed., *Women in Film Noir*, 2nd ed. (London: BFI, 1998).

6 Variety Show as National Identity: CBC Television and Dominion Day Celebrations, 1958–1980

MATTHEW HAYDAY

Can television be used to bind a nation together or create a national identity? Over the past fifty years, the Canadian government has experimented with different types of events on 1 July, initially known as Dominion Day and now as Canada Day, in an effort to foster a greater sense of national unity and promote certain conceptions of Canadian identity. This involvement often took the form of collaboration between the government and the Canadian Broadcasting Corporation (CBC) to produce a television special, broadcast nationwide, that covered Ottawa-based festivities, sometimes with additional feeds from locations across the country. But what sort of images of Canada did the government want to put forth? Did this change over time? How was this message of Canadian identity constrained by the dictates of the television medium? In this article, I examine these questions in reference to the Dominion Day celebrations organized by the Canadian federal government.

In recent years, many public commentators have discussed televised moments or events watched by huge audiences that created a sense of shared experience (e.g., watching the moon landing) or fostered a sense of national pride (e.g., Paul Henderson's 1972 goal in the Canada–Russia hockey series, or Ben Johnson's win in the 100-metre dash at the 1988 Seoul Olympics). The role played by various forms of media in fostering nationalism and creating community has also been of keen interest for academics. Since the first publication of Benedict Anderson's *Imagined Communities* in 1983, most studies of the development of nationalism and national identities refer to his seminal work. Anderson develops a number of intriguing concepts about how people came to organize and identify themselves as nations. He identifies the development of mass media, initially in the form of print capitalism, as one of the key factors that led to the formation of what he calls 'imagined communities' – communities of people who had never met and likely would never meet each other and yet who felt a sense of belonging to the same community despite the wide distances that separated them. The first manifestations of this, he argues, occurred in the Americas, where Creole communities, governed by locally born elites who had little chance of advancement in the hierarchies of their respective colonial powers, began to identify more firmly with their colonies of residence. They used the local press to reinforce the imagined colonial community, a process which in turn reinforced their status as the colonial elite. This combination of print capitalism and colony–metropole relations fostered the development of nationalisms in the colonies of the Americas, providing a model which would be imitated worldwide.[1]

Canada is notably absent from Anderson's study of nationalism in the Americas. This is not surprising, as the colony of New France lacked a French-language newspaper. Moreover, unlike the United States and Latin American nations, Canada did not experience a revolutionary break from its imperial rulers, but, rather, evolved relatively peacefully towards its independence. As a country, Canada thus lacks some of the more obvious rallying cries of nationhood such as the founding myths discussed by Eric Hobsbawm.[2] Like Anderson, Hobsbawm argues that nationalism has fairly recent roots and further contends that nationalism is often reinforced by traditions that are assumed to have timeless roots but that are actually invented by governments or other elites to serve this nation-building purpose.

In the same period as Anderson was writing *Imagined Communities* and Hobsbawm was developing his theory of invented traditions, communications professor Maurice Charland of Concordia University was arguing that Canada had followed a route towards forging its sense of nationhood which was somewhat different in process to the print capitalism–based nationalism elaborated by Anderson, although similar in outcome.[3] Charland argues that would-be Canadian nation-builders since Confederation have espoused the development of 'technological nationalism.' In essence, this form of nationalism consisted of building transportation and communication networks to bind Canadians together – a process which incidentally served the interests of the railway capitalists and communications professionals who advanced this model of nationhood. Initially, Charland argues, nation-building was accomplished through the construction of the national railway, the

Canadian Pacific Railway, which served as both a physical and discursive tool for developing the Canadian nation-state: physical, because it linked the Canadian provinces together and fostered economic growth; discursive, because it stood as a metaphor for the development of Canada and the linkages between Canadians. In Charland's model, the railway filled the role occupied by print capitalism for Anderson in the cultural construction of the nation.

After the completion of the railway, the Canadian government and English-Canadian nationalists turned to communications networks to further bind Canadians together. As Mary Vipond observes, the federal government established the Canadian Broadcasting Corporation (first as a national radio network, then expanding into television) as a means of fostering national unity and national identity, while also attempting to stave off Americanization. She notes that this was an explicit aim of the government of R.B. Bennett, which wanted to 'use the latest communications technology to unite and bind the nation.'[4] However, Charland argues that this media-based successor model of technological nationalism was much weaker than its railway-based predecessor because it imposed a top-down model of communication rather than inviting popular participation. Moreover, he argues that communications technology alone, in the absence of good content, was insufficient to foster a distinctive Canadian culture.

Historian Robert Cupido draws on both Charland's and Anderson's theories to examine the 1927 radio broadcast of the Diamond Jubilee of Confederation, which was the first time that a nationwide radio broadcast from Parliament Hill was attempted.[5] Cupido examines the conception of Canadian identity that the Liberal government of Mackenzie King was attempting to convey with this broadcast and then attempts to assess the degree to which the broadcast was an effective means of fostering this identity. Ultimately, Cupido argues that the 1927 radio show, rather than helping to overcome divisions in Canada, served to reinforce them. Specifically, he argues that working-class immigrants to Canada would have had neither the language capacity to understand the messages of the broadcast nor the financial means to afford a radio. Moreover, he found that many Canadians opted not to tune in for the day-long broadcast and instead chose to observe Dominion Day in other ways. Although an estimated five million people tuned in to hear part of the radio broadcast, Cupido argues that this did not mean that they necessarily listened to the entire show or took away the messages from the broadcast that its creators intended. I tend to find Cupido's assessment of the 1927 Jubilee broadcast's impact overly pessimistic, given that it did manage to attract an audience that totalled over half the Canadian population.

Thirty years after the Diamond Jubilee, the Canadian government once again became active in attempting to promote Canadian celebrations of Dominion Day and the Canadian nation more broadly. Given the intimate connection between Dominion Day and Canadian identity, the content of these celebrations was highly contentious. Indeed, as Raymond Blake has observed, it took almost forty years and dozens of attempts for the federal government to change the official designation of 1 July from Dominion Day to Canada Day.[6] Even now, more than a quarter-century after the official change passed through Parliament in 1982, many still cling to the original name. Determining the message that the celebrations of this day would attempt to convey was even more problematic, since so many different facets of Canadian identity had to be addressed, from conceptions of Canada as a British nation, to official bilingualism and English-French duality, to newer models which stressed multiculturalism, regionalism, and First Nations. The manner in which these elements were integrated into the broadcast changed over time, as organizers progressively moved away from a British-centric model of Canadian identity to one that was more pluralistic. They also experimented with the degree to which these shows included explicitly political messages, as opposed to attempting to project their preferred vision of Canadian identity more implicitly through the selection of performers at these events.

This paper will examine some aspects of how these themes of Canadian identity were incorporated into the CBC televised broadcasts. My primary focus will be on the logistics of organizing these shows for a nationwide audience and the manner in which the CBC executed this nation-building/nationalism-inspiring task. This will include an examination of decision-making processes, funding questions, and the division of responsibilities between the government and the CBC, using the archival holdings of the CBC, the Secretary of State Department, and the personal papers of some key government mandarins as sources. This article will also analyse how the televised format shaped decisions about who would perform, what impact this had on the image of Canada presented in the shows (videotaped copies of which were viewed), and what strengths and weaknesses the televised format brought to this nation-building effort. While reception analysis of television is difficult,[7] I will also attempt to assess, using both government and CBC polling data and newspaper reports, how well these shows were received by their audience and whether the government's intended messages were conveyed and/or accepted.

To analyse these events, I propose to draw not only on the scholars already mentioned, but also on the methodology of a number of studies of Canadian, American, and Australian commemorative and celebratory events. A growing literature in Canada examines the manner in which large-scale commemorative events have been constructed for popular consumption, although few of these studies to date have addressed recurring annual celebrations.[8] Historians and sociologists such as Len Travers and Lyn Spillman have demonstrated that much can be learned from a longitudinal study of these celebrations by examining changes over time.[9] I will be looking at the celebrations and broadcasts which took place from 1958, the year of the first celebrations organized under the Conservative government of John Diefenbaker, to 1980, following the defeat of the Quebec referendum on sovereignty-association. This twenty-two-year period encompassed the mandates of four prime ministers, representing both Liberal and Conservative governments, and reflected a period of massive political and social change and turmoil in Canada.

A full examination of every year's celebration is beyond the scope of this article. In order to get a comparative perspective, I examine three major subsets of the broadcasts in depth: the initial 1958 and 1960 broadcasts organized by the federal government under Conservative Prime Minister John Diefenbaker; the 1965 and 1966 broadcasts, which were intended as a build-up to the 1967 Centennial celebrations;[10] and the 1977 and 1978 broadcasts, which were a response to the rise of Quebec nationalism and federal government concerns over national unity associated with the impending referendum on sovereignty-association.

Inventing the Tradition of Dominion Day Celebrations: The Diefenbaker Years

The average participant attending the annual noonday and evening Canada Day concerts on Parliament Hill to hear Natalie McMaster, Roch Voisine, Wilfrid Le Bouthillier, Anne Murray, or other Canadian talent, might be surprised to learn that this annual 'tradition' has fairly recent roots and is in fact an invented tradition of the type discussed by Hobsbawm and was initiated by the federal government after the Second World War. Aside from the 1927 Diamond Jubilee of Confederation, the federal government did little to celebrate 1 July for much of the first century after Confederation. It was the governor general who organized the main observances of this day as late as the 1940s and 1950s, and this was in the form of small-scale gatherings, usually garden parties at Rideau Hall intended for the ambassadorial community and other dignitaries.

The governor general also recorded an annual Dominion Day greeting for the nation, broadcast on CBC Radio. As a special event for 1 July 1958, the CBC decided to make Governor General Vincent Massey's Dominion Day speech its first coast-to-coast simultaneous broadcast on CBC Television.[11] Before the advent of official collaboration with the federal government on 1 July activities, CBC Radio celebrated Dominion Day with special programming in a variety of different formats. These ranged from special programs of Canadian songs to a teleplay on the birth of Canada entitled 'We See Thee Rise.'

After the election of John Diefenbaker's Progressive Conservative government in 1957 the federal government took a more active interest in Dominion Day celebrations. Diefenbaker was particularly keen on celebrating Canada's status as a British dominion and had been upset by what he viewed as the progressive severing of Canada's Commonwealth ties and British identity by successive Liberal administrations. No celebrations had been arranged during the tenure of Louis St Laurent, but Diefenbaker arranged to have the Red Ensign flown from the Peace Tower on 1 July 1957 and secured cabinet approval in principle to have 'some suitable public celebration' held on Dominion Day 1958.[12] He appointed a suitably enthusiastic and Anglophilic secretary of state to handle this task: Ellen Fairclough, a member of both the United Empire Loyalists Association and the Imperial Order Daughters of the Empire.

Fairclough raised the issue of an annual official celebration of Dominion Day at the cabinet meetings of 15 and 20 May 1958 and received cabinet authorization to organize these celebrations in coordination with other government ministries.[13] Her ministry intended to make this a rather formal affair, featuring speeches from top government officials and the governor general, military bands, a carillon, and fireworks. The main involvement of CBC Television in this initial government-organized celebration was its nationwide broadcast of Governor General Massey's speech, although clips of the bands and military processions were also included in news broadcasts. The celebratory events on Parliament Hill were thus initially intended for the local Ottawa residents who physically attended.

Formal events for 1959 were overshadowed by the opening of the St

Lawrence Seaway, but Fairclough's department returned to organizing celebrations in 1960. These events were conceived in the framework of her responsibilities as minister for citizenship and immigration. The year 1960 marked the first time that CBC television was actively involved in organizing the Dominion Day activities, as it worked together with the ministry on the creation of a special pre-recorded program. 'Dominion Day: A Day to Remember' was an hour-long television special that traced the paths of six immigrants from their arrival in Canada from different parts of the world (Ukraine, Scotland, France, the United States, Netherlands, and Hong Kong) up to their swearing-in as new Canadian citizens. This latter event was to occur in a special ceremony on Parliament Hill on Dominion Day which would be broadcast live. The show stressed the theme of how immigrants from around the world were contributing to the building of Canada and acculturating to their new home. It was followed by a broadcast of the navy's sunset ceremony performed on Parliament Hill. This early celebration thus stressed strong elements of patriotism, had an explicit narrative arc, and was favourably received by audiences across the country.[14]

Despite the warm reception accorded to the 1960 special, the Secretary of State department moved away from this narrative format for its future television collaborations with CBC, choosing instead to focus on live performances, which performed double duty as entertainment for Ottawa residents and tourists. In the early 1960s, the government also began to incorporate more festive elements into its Dominion Day ceremonies in addition to the formalities of speeches and military processions. Performers such as the Travellers (best known for their Canadian version of the song 'This Land Is Your Land') and Les Feux-Follets were invited to perform songs and dance numbers. CBC and Radio-Canada recorded parts of these live shows on Parliament Hill and rebroadcast them later in the day. These were small-scale events, featuring at most three performing groups. Seeking a more professional approach to the events, the federal government invited the CBC to assume a partial production role, beginning with the 1963 celebrations.

In this earliest phase of inventing a new Canadian tradition of celebrating the nation's founding event, it is clear that the Diefenbaker government, seeking to reaffirm Canada's links to its British heritage, attempted to craft its Dominion Day celebrations with this objective in mind. Its celebrations therefore stressed messages of immigrant integration into a British (and to a lesser extent, French) Canada. Having had some initial success with the televised aspects of these celebrations, the government was now beginning to mobilize the potential of the media more extensively for its nation-building projects.

The Amateur 1960s: Creating the New Symbols of Canada

The mid- to late 1960s would be marked by a major effort on the part of the Pearson and Trudeau Liberal governments to redefine Canada's identity in a more expansive and inclusive fashion. While Diefenbaker's Conservatives had been primarily concerned with restoring a frayed British connection, the Liberal prime ministers were more interested in promoting distinctively Canadian symbols such as a new flag (1965) and official anthem (which was actively debated in this decade, but not formally adopted until 1980). This was also a decade spent coming to terms with French Canadians' demands for recognition of their place in Canada, rising Quebec nationalism, and early demands from multicultural and aboriginal groups for a new place in the Canadian tapestry. Moreover, Canada's impending centennial year was a key opportunity for national unity projects.

In 1964, the Pearson government decided to ramp up the scale of its Dominion Day celebrations in preparation for the Centennial celebrations in 1967. The Secretary of State viewed the CBC as a potential partner that could both improve the quality of these broadcasts and give them broader exposure across the country.[15] Unlike Diefenbaker's government, which still clung to a British model of Canadian identity, Pearson's Liberal government would modify the content of the Diefenbaker-invented tradition of Dominion Day celebrations, moving towards a more pluralistic conception of Canada. It would also more aggressively employ CBC Television as a partner in disseminating this new vision of Canada. These concerns were reflected in both the content and the format of the celebrations.

The federal government gave the CBC a certain degree of creative freedom to design the 1965 broadcast, both in terms of staging and choice of performers. The CBC did have to operate within the funding constraints of the federal government, which was covering the costs of the broadcast, but the show's director was given final say over artistic decisions. The Canadian Folk Arts Council (CFAC) also participated in the selection of performing artists, pre-screening talent in each province, while the CBC made the final cut of choices for the planned broadcast. Both organizations were operating within some broad guidelines from the federal government, which wanted the artists to include representation from all provinces as well as English, French, Native, and ethnic participation. The Secretary of State also preferred that the show not be 'like Ed Sullivan.'[16] Ideally, the government hoped that the CBC would produce 'a showcase of the various ethnic groups which make up the population of Canada, emphasizing the British, French and Indian heritage.'[17]

Coordinating the three main organizers of the show – the government, the CBC, and the CFAC – proved difficult. Secretary of State staff complained that the CBC personnel virtually disappeared for most of April and May, with the result that final decisions, and indeed even auditions, had not taken place by early June. Moreover, power struggles erupted as a result of a lack of clearly defined authority between CBC and the Secretary of State department.[18] Government–CBC relations were hardly improved by the sudden resignation, on 21 June, of Bill Davis, the producer-director of the show, who was upset with the inadequate quality of the local technical crews. In his letter of resignation, Davis claimed that a 'combination of amateur performers and a green crew can only produce an amateur result' and said that he did not want to tarnish his reputation with an amateurish show.[19] This effort to create a slick production to foster national unity was clearly off to a difficult start.

But was the final result as problematic as Davis had feared, or did it meet the federal government's objectives? What type of show did Canadian viewers see on Dominion Day 1965? The broadcast took place from a fixed, octagonal stage on Parliament Hill, with the Centre Block of the Parliament Buildings as a backdrop. A tall pole was erected on each corner of the stage, creating a cage structure. Once the broadcast began, young men in shorts bearing a torch took up a position at each corner. These young men also opened and closed the gate to the stage for each performer as he or she entered. Hosting the show were CBC personalities Alex Trebek and Henri Bergeron, both bilingual, who alternated their introductions to each act in English and French. They introduced the performance as a showcase of 'gifts' brought from across the country, which may be interpreted as an allegorical coming-together of the family of provinces to celebrate Canada's birthday, reinforcing the idea of a nationwide imagined community.

This theme of provincial gifts was reinforced by title cards that were flashed on the television screen bearing the name and images of the province from which the performer came. A wide range of amateur performers was included to meet the federal government's criteria. For aboriginal representation, there was the Cariboo Indian Girls Scottish Pipe Band from the Williams Lake Residential School in British Columbia, and Marlene Jackson, a Cree baton twirler from Manitoba. In addition to Bergeron, francophones were represented by Edith Butler, an Acadian folk singer from New Brunswick, and Les Mirabelles, a choir from Quebec. A wide array of 'ethnic' and visible-minority performers was included, ranging from the Ensemble Montréalaise des Danses Slavianes (a Montreal-based troupe of dancers who, while not Slavic themselves, enjoyed Slavic dances), to the Zemplyn Slovak Folk Dancers from Toronto, a kendo demonstration from British Columbia's Steveson Kendo Club, and a choral presentation by the Dorrington Quartet from Zion Baptist Church in Nova Scotia. Finally, the English-origin component of Canada's heritage was furnished by singer Helen Marquess of Newfoundland, Prince Edward Island's Maida Rogerson from the 1965 cast of the *Anne of Green Gables* musical, and the Calgary Safety Patrol Round-up Singers.

Despite the Secretary of State department's request that the show not be like Ed Sullivan's, government officials were left with the impression that this was the model that had been followed; they expressed concern that the show had been 'undignified' for Parliament Hill and was not a suitable model for future years. Moreover, the format of the show, which highlighted the provincial origins of each performer, also made it easy to notice the absence of a Saskatchewan representative – a fact which led to great anguish and public complaint from that province's viewers.[20] Moreover, as Davis had feared, there were several comments that the show was overly amateurish in quality. Officials in the Secretary of State Department also raised questions about the 'authenticity' of the ethnic performances, particularly the decision to include Slavic dances performed by French Canadians.[21]

Beyond these criticisms raised at the time of the broadcast, a modern analyst would be concerned, in light of the questions about authenticity, by a letter from the British Columbia representative of the CFAC, responding to the desire of Ottawa officials to include a performer of Chinese origin. In this letter he wrote: 'Chinese people do not specialize in dances, music or songs, although we have tried to persuade them to do this so we could include their presentations in the programs of the Folk Society here. They are excellent in parades as they have a very good drill team and specialize in a dragon performance.'[22] The mental image of a government encouraging its ethnic communities to change their traditional performance styles for the purposes of a government-sponsored heritage festival is troubling enough. How might one interpret the selection of aboriginal performers who played Scottish bagpipes and twirled flaming batons? While there was movement in the early Pearson years towards greater inclusion of multicultural groups in Dominion Day celebrations, the same was not true for aboriginal peoples. The 1965 broadcast clearly reflected the assimilationist federal policy towards Canada's aboriginal communities, who were expected to abandon their traditional practices and acculturate to a Euro-Canadian norm. Thus, in seeking to invent new Canadian traditions for an imagined national community, the show's organizers were simultaneously contributing to the destruction or co-option of the traditions of some of Canada's component communities.

The transition from a show intended for an Ottawa audience to one primarily aimed at a national viewership was somewhat problematic, as many spectators complained that their view was obstructed by camera equipment. (Notably, the desire to cater to an imagined national community had trumped the concerns of the live Ottawa community.) These various complaints resulted in some new directives for 1966. A first change was the addition of a half-hour, non-televised pre-show with local talent to appeal to the Ottawa-based crowd. The federal government also set a more detailed schedule of deadlines for selecting performers, added explicit geographic criteria for the selection of performers, and requested that the ethnic communities included in the show be rotated from year to year, although the CBC retained its final say over the program's composition.[23]

Artist selection for the 1966 show was guided by the following three criteria of the Secretary of State: competence and excellence of repertoire; authenticity; and balance between types of performance (choirs, dancers, soloists, etc.) The show itself tended to follow much the same format as it did the year before, with the same co-hosts and the use of amateur talent. However, many of the concerns of 1965 had been rectified. Folk dancers from the Ukrainian, Chinese, Portuguese, Polish, and Russian communities performed, as did representatives from the Anglo-Canadian and French-Canadian communities. First Nations were less obviously represented, although Manitoba representative Diane Landry, who was Miss Canada, did speak of her Métis heritage, and Saskatchewanian Geoff Howard sang his own composition about Métis leader Louis Riel.

With its variety show format and pool of amateur performers, the broadcast still had echoes of Ed Sullivan, even though Sullivan mostly used professionals. But over all, government organizers were much happier with the broadcast and with their collaboration with the CBC.[24] There were, after all, limits to what could be accomplished with a budget of slightly under $5,000 for artists' fees and $57,000 for the entire show, including air time. Using amateur performers also made it possible for the government organizers to incorporate representation from a wide swath of Canadian communities, ethnicities, linguistic groups, and regions. Together this created the image of a diverse Canadian tapestry – described as 'One Big Happy Family' in the theme song performed by Trebek and Bergeron – that the organizers aimed to portray. It should, however, be noted that not all the communities included in this framework were treated equally. The British and French-Canadian communities continued to be central to this image, with immigrant communities contributing the folkloric aspects of their heritage, such as dance, song, or sport. The implicit message about aboriginal Canada (political speeches not playing a significant role in these events) presented in these celebrations was that while these communities continued to exist, they were rapidly acculturating to Euro-Canadian practices and shedding their old traditions by adopting Euro-Canadian pastimes such as playing the bagpipes, twirling batons, or participating in the Miss Canada pageant.

The Dominion Day shows of the mid-1960s effectively served to work out the bugs in the federal government's approach to celebrating Canada in time for the 1967 Centennial Hullabaloo, which benefited from a much larger budget and higher-profile talent than in previous years. In the years following the Centennial, however, this invented tradition started to fade away. In the late 1960s the CBC covered the federally organized Ottawa activities only as part of its news broadcasts, rather than participating in their production. In the 1970s, the CBC began to coordinate its own 1 July specials, without reference to government plans.[25] This occasioned a few comments in government circles about the CBC's lack of patriotism and its unwillingness to shoulder part of the costs of organizing the official 1 July event. But by the mid-1970s even the federal government seemed to be cooling to the idea of state-sponsored celebrations of Canada's birthday. In 1976, faced with a major budget deficit, the Trudeau government decided to eliminate its funding for Dominion Day events. It was an ironic twist of fate that the year in which Ottawa ceased its celebrations of the anniversary of Confederation also witnessed the election of a Quebec government that wanted to undo this pact.

The 1970s: 'A Big Outpouring of Love'

It is an understatement to say that the election of the Parti Québécois sent waves of panic through Ottawa. The 16 November 1976 election of René Lévesque's government had far-reaching ramifications throughout the federal government and forced many to rethink their approach to national unity questions. Certainly, senior civil servants and politicians sought to defeat any referendum on separation or sovereignty-association when it eventually came. While part of this federal effort would be focused on new constitutional talks, the Trudeau government was also determined to compete with its Quebec counterpart on a symbolic level and to compete for the hearts of the people.

In the Secretary of State department, this determination translated into a decision to allocate over $3 million for Canada Day celebrations across the country and a massive televised special. Prime Minister Trudeau appointed senior mandarin Bernard Ostry on 6 April 1977 to coordinate a massive 1 July extravaganza from coast to coast. This was going to be a major challenge for Ostry and his team, since the dwindling infrastructure for organizing Dominion Day events had been completely eliminated the year before. Moreover, the Quebec government was already well underway in planning for its own national holiday celebrations on 24 June. Tapping into the long-running provincial observance of la Fête St-Jean Baptiste, the provincial government had recently modified and renamed this pan-Canadian Catholic tradition to become the secular and Quebec-centred Fête Nationale, in effect conferring on Quebec's national holiday a much longer history and tradition of observance than its federal counterpart. For 1977, a multi-hour concert was already in the works for Montreal. The team assembled by Ostry wanted to do something significant but was conscious that they had to avoid the appearance of direct competition with these events, as they knew they could not compete directly with Quebec's outpouring of genuine emotion.

With the decision to organize a major celebration being made late in the winter of 1977, planning was somewhat chaotic. The hastily assembled Canada's Birthday Secretariat quickly set about planning events for the nation's capital, including parades, street festivals, and entertainment in the city's parks. This was all to culminate with a variety show on Parliament Hill, as had been the case with celebrations over the past two decades. However, Ostry's team and their CBC partners wanted this centerpiece event to be more than just a run-of-the-mill variety show. They started from the rather vague premise of wanting to create a television 'event' that would 'reflect some feeling of national unity' and 'which people across Canada will want to watch.'[26] Lacking a concrete definition of what constituted the identity of the Canadian community, they turned to late-1960s conceptions of how Canadian identity had been constructed and celebrated. Initial concepts of the show envisioned featuring leading Canadians in entertainment and the arts to headline the celebration, and also including folk representations of Canada's cultural diversity.

Some imaginative pairings were considered, such as Anne Murray singing with the Young Acadian Choir. The organizers wanted to 'include the ordinary and extraordinary Canadians who have a positive statement to make about this country' in order to 'allow a unifying theme to emerge from our diversity to create a sense of oneness, a sense of participation, a sense of celebration.'[27] The CBC was again sought out as the key partner in creating this spectacle. Producer John Hirsch was brought on board to produce the broadcast.

The plan developed by CBC for the 1977 celebration of Canada's Birthday (as it was billed, instead of the term Dominion Day, which the government was attempting to legally change to Canada Day) was expansive and extravagant. Hirsch and his team envisioned a three-hour live broadcast, entitled 'Celebrate Canada.' Using all the CBC's technical resources, including its Anik satellite, the show would consist of a series of eight- to fifteen-minute segments from the Ottawa variety show and live segments from coast to coast to coast. The CBC press release promoting the show billed it as 'the largest entertainment spectacle the country has ever seen[;] for three hours, Canadians will be linked together by satellite in an impressive demonstration of faith in vitality of the country, expressed through the talents of Canada's leading performers.'[28] The press release mentioned hook-ups at Anne Murray's home in Springhill, Nova Scotia, the World Gymnastics competition in Edmonton, Ontario Place, and the Northwest Territories. Moreover, the involvement of the government in the celebration was played down, as the release stressed that 'this program has been produced with the participation of Canadians who believe in a country called Canada.' We can see elements of technological nationalism at work here, with the Anik satellite as the linking technology. However, the CBC was also selling 'Celebrate Canada' as a more participatory event than the 1927 radio broadcast, since the show's content would originate in a variety of locations across Canada and would be crafted by Canadian artists and performers, not politicians.

CBC's 'Celebrate Canada' show, funded by the federal government, was over three and a half hours in length, and was broadcast simultaneously on 842 of the 844 radio and television media outlets in Canada (only two independent stations in Quebec held out) and a number of border stations in the United States. This massive distribution was possible because the show was offered free of charge to other networks in order to support this national unity effort. Co-hosted by Betty Williams and Ernie Afaganis, the show alternated between the Ottawa stage and the CBC hook-ups across Canada, ranging from Vancouver to St John's to Yellowknife. While the show did incorporate elements such as a citizenship court, the Drumheller rodeo, and a re-enactment of Champlain's landing at Quebec, its main focus was on the musical and dance stars. These included: English-language stars such as Anne Murray, Bobby Gimby, and Tommy Hunter; French-language and bilingual performances from Ginette Reno, Patsy Gallant, Juliette, and René Simard; Aboriginal and Métis performers Buffy Sainte-Marie, Tom Jackson, and the Delta Dancers in Yellowknife; and a multicultural/ethnic component represented by Salome Bey and the Ukrainian Shumka Dancers. A scheduled ballet performance by Karen Kain was cut at the last minute due to a downpour on Parliament Hill, which meant that pop and folk performances predominated.

Reactions to this show from spectators and organizers were varied. A poll undertaken for Canada's Birthday Committee found that approximately 11.7 million people (just under half the population) watched or listened to all or part of the special broadcast. Fifty per cent of those who watched or listened thought that the celebrations would make it more likely that Canada would remain united (ranging from a high of 54 per cent of Quebec respondents to a low of 38 per cent in the prairies). Forty-seven per cent thought that federal dollars were well spent, versus 34 per cent who did not (Quebeckers were 53 to 27 in favour). The spectators were also impressed by the technical aspects of the show.[29]

The broadcast got a mixed response from the press. Blaik Kirby, writing for the *Globe and Mail*, wryly observed that the show had 'more stars than the Crab nebula, more technical mastery than a Viking space probe and it tried desperately to have more patriotic fervour than Rene Levesque.' Although he thought the show succeeded both technically and in its quantity of stars, 'as for "rousing our hearts to beat for Canada," if they didn't beat yesterday, I doubt they do today.' He also noted the limited representation from French Canada.[30] The *Ottawa Journal* was more optimistic, with Frank Daley noting that the 'celebratory feeling was genuine and pervasive and made the day a whopping success, other than never mentioning New Brunswick in a three-hour telecast.'[31] Organizers were not completely satisfied with the 1977 spectacle either. From a technical standpoint, they expressed concerns that the mix of events staged for live audiences and those explicitly aimed at the television audience did not gel properly. They also worried that the show was somewhat disconnected and unwieldy. Even Secretary of State John Roberts commented that 'neither did many people express satisfaction with the 1977 "collage production"' and that perhaps an in-studio show would be better for the future.[32] While the big-name performers were well received, one official noted in his debriefing document that 'some of the performances broadcast were, sad to say, of only barely acceptable quality.' Others raised concerns that there was something 'American' about the format of the show and that more classical music or dance elements should be added to the more popular entertainments.

Did a coherent vision of a national identity emerge from this collage of Canadian images? Given that the organizers wanted the show to project a vision of an 'outpouring of love' for Canada from all quarters, the results were at best mixed and somewhat uneven. For a show conceived as part of an effort to combat separatism, the francophone elements were problematic. The biggest stars, Reno and Simard, were no longer viewed as 'true Quebeckers' in their home province since their careers had migrated to the United States, and some critics of the show pointed out that Patsy Gallant, a francophone New Brunswicker, did not compensate for this shortfall. Most big-name francophone stars steered clear of the Ottawa events, while others actively participated in the Fête Nationale celebrations. Efforts to ensure a multicultural image of Canada were also problematic because of the gala show's emphasis on topnotch talent. Salome Bey was the sole 'name' performer from a visible minority, and even among the amateur talent, only the Ukrainian Shumka dancers stood out. Aboriginal participation, meanwhile, was greatly improved by the live hook-ups on Manitoba's Broken Head Reserve and in Yellowknife, featuring some performers with name recognition.

Given the massive reserves of technology and funding allocated to the 1977 broadcast and the fairly high viewership numbers, the message of Canadian identity and national unity it created was rather weak and diffuse, which points to the limitations of focusing solely on implicit messages of Canadian unity and identity. The show lacked a strong narrative arc (of the type used in 1960's 'Dominion Day: A Day to Remember') and was practically devoid of explicit statements or speeches about Canadian identity or the state of the nation, with the possible exception of a free-form poem on Canada delivered by Keath Barrie at Ontario Place. It is tempting to interpret the somewhat muddled vision of Canadian identity which emerged from the show as the result of its variety show format, which tends to compartmentalize the individual performers. However, it would have been possible to include speeches from Canadian politicians or other public figures among the various segments. The decision to focus solely on the performing artists, while arguably better from an entertainment perspective, was perhaps too depoliticized to convey the national unity message sought by the government organizers as extensively as they had hoped.

With the referendum looming in the future and Lévesque and Trudeau still in office, Canada's Birthday Secretariat was left in place (although renamed as Festival Canada) for 1978, with former National Arts Centre director G. Hamilton Southam replacing Bernard Ostry at the helm. A similar mandate was set out for the 1 July celebrations, in which 'everything should be coordinated as a national love-feast, giving the people of each Province, or Territory, the feeling that on their particular day their fellow Canadians were thinking of them and wishing them well.'[33]

The CBC and Festival Canada revised the format for the televised spectacle in light of some of the difficulties from the prior year, although this would have been more evident behind the scenes than in the eye of the viewer. From the audience's perspective, the main difference was that all segments were designed for television, although some of the performances were recorded in front of live audiences. The television broadcast capped off a week-long event called 'Festival Canada,' which featured the twinning of Canadian provinces and territories for six days of themed activities and television mini-specials. Festival Canada coordinated all the local events and selection of artists, and contracted with the CBC to handle the technical issues and direct the Ottawa-based variety show.

The content of the 1978 broadcast was in many ways similar to that of 1977, including the local hook-ups across the country and many of the same performers (Simard, Bey, Shumka dancers). This meant a continuation of the fairly heavy focus on folk and pop performances, including such acts as Bruce Cockburn, Tommy Hunter, the Irish Rovers, and Sylvia Tyson. However, Ottawa officials clearly inserted some elements to make the program less like an American variety show, notably through the introduction of more 'high culture' acts and solemn events. These included such classical performances as a ballet pas de deux featuring Karen Kain and the singing of the national anthem by opera singer Maureen Forrester. It also incorporated a citizenship ceremony on Parliament Hill presided over by citizenship court judge Hélène Baillargeon-Côté (formerly of the children's program *Chez Hélène*).

The show proceeded smoothly. The level of francophone and multicultural representation continued to be somewhat low, but the government was generally pleased with the event. Again, there was mixed reaction in the press to this attempt to stimulate nationalism. The variety of performances was wide enough that there was usually at least one element that commentators liked, although there was also extensive criticism of other elements of the show. Ray Conlogue observed in the *Globe and Mail*: 'All-Canadian freedom gives me a bigger lift than all-Canadian disco'[34] (a critique of the bevy of sparkly, spandex-clad dancers accompanying chanteuse Patsy Gallant), while his colleague William Johnson observed that "nationalism may do bad things for the economy and one's sleep but it does wonders for the performing arts.'[35]

In 1979 the scope of the televised Canada's Birthday show was scaled back dramatically, essentially returning to the format of the mid-1960s and broadcasting exclusively from a stage on Parliament Hill. The federal government's overall budget for Canada Day activities remained high, at over $3.8 million, but only $459,000 of this was spent in Ottawa, with the rest allocated to local community celebrations across the country in an effort to promote active celebration of Canada's birthday.[36] The show's budget was still much larger than those of the mid-1960s, permitting organizers to book high-profile talent such as Al Waxman, Donald Sutherland, Caroll Baker, the Canadian Brass, and Maureen Forrester. However, more amateur performers were incorporated into the programming than in the previous two years. Governor General Ed Schreyer was also on hand to give a speech at the beginning of the broadcast and to preside over the citizenship ceremony at the close of the event.

After 1979, the federal government withdrew from its direct involvement in televised events and large variety-show spectacles for the nation's capital. For most of the 1980s, Ottawa instead directed its funding to community-based events across the country and allowed the National Capital Commission to organize smaller-scale events for Ottawa. Not until the late 1980s would a televised Canada Day spectacle again feature in the federal government's plans for 1 July.

Conclusion

A number of conclusions can be drawn regarding this collaborative effort by the CBC and the federal government to invent a new tradition of celebrating the anniversary of Confederation to promote an evolving vision of Canadian identity. The constraints and strengths of the medium of television clearly affected the construction of these celebrations, with a variety of consequences. The collaborative CBC–government Dominion Day television broadcasts rapidly passed through two initial incarnations before settling on a more or less fixed format. After experimenting with a combination of formal speeches and military ceremonies in the late 1950s and early 1960s, and a pre-recorded narrative show in 1960, variants of the variety show format were followed until 1979. Initially this show took place on a fixed stage on Parliament Hill, and then the 'stage' was broadened to encompass several locations in Canada, using satellite technology to bridge the geographic distance separating Canadians. The format, however, remained that of a variety show, with individual performers selected to represent the diverse elements of the Canadian national community.

This variety show format was problematic for many in terms of fostering a coherent vision of the Canadian community. A number of government officials, newspaper critics, and members of the public viewed this format as overly inspired by American television models, particularly *The Ed Sullivan Show*. There was a heavy focus on mass popular or folk culture in the choice of performers for the television broadcasts throughout the 1960s and 1970s, to the detriment of 'high' culture, military bands, or political speeches. Indeed, the near-complete absence of politicians from the stage is striking. Some respondents to government polls observed that the variety show atmosphere was undignified for Parliament Hill and that something more solemn might have been more appropriate for the celebration of Canada's birthday.

This decision to let the artists' 'love for Canada' speak for itself in the show, while making for good entertainment, was also problematic. A number of journalists commented on the lack of overt statements or political messages about Canada. Inclusion of such statements might have been a more direct way of fostering the model of Canadian identity that organizers had in mind. Moreover, there were limitations to what a selection of performers could implicitly convey in terms of a vision of Canada by their presence alone, particularly once the decision was made in the late 1970s to focus on big-name performers. In this

respect, Charland's criticism that the content carried on CBC's infra-
structure could fall short in fostering nationalism and national unity
seems to have some validity. While the CBC's Dominion Day broadcasts featured 'Canadian content,' unlike much of CBC's programming
in earlier decades, by the late 1970s most of English-speaking Canada's
popular music was not all that different from its American counterpart.
Programs composed solely of performances of this music, without more
explicit statements (or even songs) about Canadian identity, were thus
of only limited utility in fostering a unified Canadian community with
an identity distinct from its southern neighbour. Certainly the visual
iconography of the maple leaf and the flag (which were featured prominently on most stages) and some of the token efforts to promote citizenship, such as the citizenship courts, resonated with viewers, who stated
that they felt the shows were useful for promoting Canadian identity.
For many journalists and respondents to the government's evaluation
surveys, however, the 1 July broadcasts were enjoyed more as massive
pop concerts and were less successful in fostering conceptions of Canadian identity.

   In terms of presenting an image of English–French unity, performers' politics became an issue: many high-profile Quebec-based stars,
such as Robert Charlebois and Diane Dufresne, were separatists and
thus refused to participate in federally organized events. Their absence
from these television shows was striking. As for the objective of promoting an image of Canada as a multicultural and diverse society, the
dearth of big-name stars from visible-minority communities meant that
these communities could not be well represented among the performances. While resorting to amateur talent might have filled these gaps,
the CBC producers did not want to do this, as this would have reduced
the show's attraction for viewers. Indeed, only aboriginal Canada fared
better in the 1970s shows than in the 1960s, as the assimilationist over-
tones of earlier broadcasts were replaced by more representative images of aboriginal culture and life in Canada. The use of the Anik satellites
in 1977 and 1978 brought both an aboriginal reserve and the Canadian
north into the living rooms of viewers, which was a particular strength
of this format.

   If these mega-spectacle broadcasts were greeted with mixed reviews
in the English-language media, they certainly did not succeed in winning over Quebec's sovereignist journalists. Gilles Constantineau, writing in Le Devoir on 4 July 1977, called the three-hour mega-spectacle
'[le] flop le plus long, le plus étendu géographiquement, et le plus

poussé techniquement, bref du bide le plus monstrueux qui ait jamais marqué l'histoire universelle de la télévision' and considered its 1978 successor a 'sinistre spectacle.' In 1979, Lise Bissonnette commented in *Le Devoir* that 'c'était aussi tous les gadgets de music hall empruntés sans adaptation à nos voisins du sud, un faux cirque pour employer l'armée de figurants engagés à grands frais. Fallait-il en remettre pour convaincre les Canadiens de verser un larme ... Ce genre de spectacle doit-il cesser? Sous cette forme, sans doute. Tant d'autres formules s'offriraient si on voulait cesser d'acheter à grands frais les plaisirs des rassemblements.'[37]

The decision to abandon the Canada Day variety show for the better part of the 1980s was prompted by the impression among federal officials that there were limits to how far a television show could go in terms of stimulating a sense of national community and fostering a sense of communal celebration of the nation's birthday.[38] Although the televised format adopted in the 1970s with community drop-ins from coast to coast crafted an image of Canada Day which was more participatory than the 1927 Diamond Jubilee broadcasts from Ottawa, the watching of a Dominion Day television show was still a rather passive way of engaging in a celebration of Canada. Recognition of this fact is part of what led to the federal government's late-1970s decision to channel funds through the Canadian Folk Arts Council and the Council on Canadian Unity to provide start-up funding for community groups across the country who wanted to organize celebrations for 1 July. For the period from 1980 to 1987, the federal government abandoned its involvement in national Canada Day television broadcasts and the model of technological nationalism.

In the 1980s, federal officials and politicians hoped that community-based celebrations might more directly stimulate a sense of warmth and feeling towards Canada that was not being fully realized by televised events. Indeed, as our examination has shown, the CBC's conception of what it thought would attract viewers did not always coincide with the image of Canada that the government wanted to project. Even if it were possible to guarantee that the audience would accept the messages about Canada that were being presented in the shows, the message was not always what the government had in mind, nor was it presented in a manner conducive to fostering a sense of strong linkages between Canadians or a sense of shared celebration. This suggests that Charland's assertions about the limits of technological nationalism were partly borne out by the Canadian government's policies towards celebration of 1 July, which came up somewhat short of its aspirations. Responses from government surveys and newspaper reports suggest that, as vehicles for fostering a sense of community and national identity, these variety shows did not do enough to stimulate a clear vision of Canadian identity in viewers' imaginations.

But should these shortcomings be attributed entirely to the format of these shows? The adoption of a depoliticized approach might have weakened the programs' capacity to foster the government's vision of the Canadian imagined community. Yet ultimately, the disjointed, and at times incoherent, images that these broadcasts projected about the Canadian community may have reflected the conflicted nature of Canadian identity more than their organizers intended. These Dominion Day broadcasts deliberately avoided overt, American-style patriotism. Instead, they presented an image of Canadian identity that was pluralistic and inclusive of the diverse elements of Canadian society – a liberal and even individualistic approach that was beginning to replace the traditional British-centric model of Canadian identity that had predominated until the 1950s. Perhaps this vision itself – which did not provide a concrete, easily definable picture of Canadian identity – had as much to do with the failure of the Dominion Day broadcasts to inspire a strong sense of national community as did the shortcomings of the medium that conveyed it. On a more positive note, the emphasis on entertainment over politics did at least lead more Canadians to recognize the founding date of their country. Determining what should be celebrated about Canada, and the extent to which the media could and would contribute to this celebration, would be the subject of additional experimentation and debate in the decades to come.

NOTES

The author would like to acknowledge both the financial support provided for this research by the SSHRC Postdoctoral Fellowship Program and the comments and suggestions of professors Andrew Nurse and Owen Griffiths at Mount Allison University, who kindly read earlier versions of this article.

1 Benedict Anderson, *Imagined Communities: Reflections on the Origin and Spread of Nationalism*, rev. ed. (London: Verso, 1991).
2 E.J. Hobsbawm, *Nations and Nationalism since 1780: Programme, Myth, Reality*, 2nd ed. (Cambridge: Cambridge University Press, 1992). Eric

Hobsbawm and Terence Ranger, eds, *The Invention of Tradition* (Cambridge: Cambridge University Press, 1983).

3 Maurice Charland, 'Technological Nationalism,' *Canadian Journal of Political and Social Theory* 10, no. 1–2 (1986): 196–220. Notably, Charland does not make any reference to Anderson's work.

4 Mary Vipond, *The Mass Media in Canada*, 3rd ed. (Toronto: James Lorimer, 2000), 41.

5 Robert Cupido, 'The Medium, the Message and the Modern: The Jubilee Broadcast of 1927,' *International Journal of Canadian Studies* 26 (Fall 2002): 101–23.

6 Raymond Blake, 'From Dominion Day to Canada Day: A Glimpse of a Changing Canada,' paper presented at the Association for Canadian Studies Annual Conference, Montreal, November 2004.

7 A number of historians and communications specialists have devoted a substantial amount of attention to reception analysis of television, which is largely beyond the scope of this article. Interested readers may wish to consult some of the following titles: Paul Rutherford, *When Television Was Young : Primetime Canada, 1952–1967* (Toronto: University of Toronto Press, 1990); John O'Connor, ed., *Image as Artifact: The Historical Analysis of Film and Television* (Malabar, FL: Robert E. Krieger, 1990); John Fiske and John Hartley, *Reading Television* (London: Methuen, 1978); Sonia Livingstone, *Making Sense of Television: The Psychology of Audience Interpretation* (New York: Routledge, 1998).

8 Jonathan Vance's study of Remembrance Day does adopt a longitudinal perspective in *Death So Noble: Memory, Meaning, and the First World War* (Vancouver: UBC Press, 1997). Other key works include: H.V. Nelles, *The Art of Nation-Building: Pageantry and Spectacle at Quebec's Tercentenary* (Toronto: University of Toronto Press, 1999); Ronald Rudin, *Founding Fathers: The Celebration of Champlain and Laval in the Streets of Quebec, 1878–1908* (Toronto: University of Toronto Press, 2003); Helen Davies, 'The Politics of Participation: A Study of Canada's Centennial Celebration' (PhD diss., University of Manitoba, 1999); Eva Mackey, *The House of Difference : Cultural Politics and National Identity in Canada* (London: Routledge, 1999); Robert Stamp, 'Empire Day in the Schools of Ontario: The Training of Young Imperialists,' *Journal of Canadian Studies* 8, no. 3 (1973): 32–42; Michihisa Hosokawa, 'Making Imperial Canadians: Empire Day in Canada,' paper presented at the British World Conference, Calgary, 10–12 July 2003; Mary Vipond, 'The Mass Media in Canadian History: The Empire Day Broadcast of 1939,' *Journal of the Canadian Historical Association* 14 (2003): 1–22.

9 Len Travers, *Celebrating the Fourth: Independence Day and the Rites of Nationalism in the Early Republic* (Amherst: University of Massachusetts Press, 1997); Lyn Spillman, *Nation and Commemoration: Creating National Identities in the United States and Australia* (Cambridge: Cambridge University Press, 1997).

10 The centennial year of 1967 was marked by massive coast-to-coast events celebrating the one hundredth anniversary of Confederation on a scale that far outstripped any other celebration of 1 July. For this reason, I have excluded it from this particular comparative analysis, although there is a growing literature about 1967 for readers who are interested in this topic.

11 Mary Vipond notes Paul Bruck's observation (*The Genealogy of News-as-Discourse: A Canadian Case Study* [Unpublished manuscript, 1986]) that broadcasters reach new heights of technological accomplishment for events deemed of national importance. Mary Vipond, 'The Beginnings of Public Broadcasting in Canada: The CRBC 1932–1936,' *Canadian Journal of Communication* 19, no. 2 (1994): 151–72.

12 Library and Archives Canada (LAC), RG 2, Privy Council Office, series A-5-a, volume 1892, Cabinet Conclusions 2 July 1957, 2.

13 LAC, RG 2, Privy Council Office, series A-5-a, volume 1898, Cabinet Conclusions 20 May 1958, 5–6.

14 LAC, RG 41 CBC, vol. 917, series A-V-2, file PG 18-21 Special Events Programs, Dominion Day, 1938–1979, file 2 1955–1976, memo from Michael Sadlier, 11 July 1960, memo from Doug Nixon, director of English-language programming, to staff, 7 July 1960.

15 LAC, RG 6 Secretary of State, Acc. 1986–87/419, box 15, file 1-7-4/1-1 pt. 1964: National Celebrations – Dominion Day – Parliament Hill – 1964, letter from the Acting Director of Citizenship & Immigration to H. Measures, 20 April 1964.

16 The documentary record does not clarify what it was specifically about *The Ed Sullivan Show* that the government wanted to avoid. However, it appears that federal officials did not want the show to seem to be modelled after American television and perhaps wanted to avoid a variety show format if possible.

17 LAC, RG 41 CBC, vol. 917, series A-V-2, file PG 18-21 Special Events Programs, Dominion Day, 1938–1979, file 2 1955–1976, internal memo from W. Martin re: Dominion Day Programming, 19 May 1965.

18 LAC, RG 6, Acc. 1986–87/419, box 15, file 1-7-4/1-1 pt. 1965: National Celebrations – Dominion Day – Parliament Hill – 1965, memo from Paul Kellner on the role of the Citizenship Branch in July 1st celebrations, 30 July 1965.

19 LAC, RG 41 CBC, vol. 917, series A-V-2, file PG 18-21 Special Events Programs, Dominion Day, 1938–1979, file 2 1955–1976, letter from Bill Davis, producer-director of TV light entertainment to Thom Benson, CBC, 21 June 1965.
20 Saskatchewan was represented by Robert Fleming, the show's musical director, but this was not evident to the spectators.
21 LAC, RG 6, Acc. 1986–87/419, box 15, file 1-7-4/1-1 pt. 1965: National Celebrations – Dominion Day – Parliament Hill – 1965, memo from Paul Kellner on the role of the Citizenship Branch in July 1st celebrations, 30 July 1965; memo from Claude Brouillard, National Liaison officer, Citizenship Branch to A.J. Cormier, Chief of Liaison, 20 July 1965.
22 LAC, RG 6, Acc. 1986-87/419, box 15, file 1-7-4/1-1 pt. 1965: National Celebrations – Dominion Day – Parliament Hill – 1965, letter from Leo Klepalski to Paul Kellner, 5 May 1965.
23 LAC, RG 6, Acc. 1986-87/419, box 15, file 1-7-4/1-1 pt. 1966: National Celebrations – Dominion Day – Parliament Hill – 1966, memo by Leon Kossar, CFAC, 31 March 1966.
24 LAC, RG 6, Acc. 1986-87/419, box 15, file 1-7-4/1-1 pt. 1966: National Celebrations – Dominion Day – Parliament Hill – 1966, vol. 2, memo from Jean Lagassé, Director of Citizenship Branch, 12 July 1966.
25 A key exception to this was the CBC coverage of the André Gagnon–hosted Dominion Day special from 1972, which created a major flap over the lack of bilingualism for the live audience. Television audiences had the benefit of an English voice-over for Gagnon's French-language introduction.
26 LAC, RG 41 CBC, vol 917, series A-V-2, file PG 18-21 Special Events Programs, Dominion Day, 1938–1979, file 3 1977–1979, internal memo from Jack McAndrew, Area Head, TV Variety to Jack Craine, Director of TV Programming, 6 April 1977.
27 Ibid.
28 LAC, RG 41 CBC, vol 917, series A-V-2, file PG 18-21 Special Events Programs, Dominion Day, 1938–1979, file 3 1977–1979, Press Release – 'Celebrate Canada – a Three-Hour entertainment spectacular live on CBC television on July 1st.'
29 LAC, MG 31 D230 G. Hamilton Southam, vol. 32, file 32: Festival Canada. 'Canada Day 1977: A Report and Recommendations,' 8 September 1977.
30 Blaik Kirby, 'O Canada One TV Show Won't Save the Country,' *Globe and Mail* 2 July 1977, 1.
31 Frank Daley 'The Party Is Over … But Let's Not Call It a Day,' *Ottawa Journal*, 4 July 1977, 21.

32 LAC, MG 31 D230, G. Hamilton Southam, vol 22, file 9: Festival Canada Correspondence 1977–78, Letter from John Roberts to Hamilton Southam, 5 August 1977.

33 LAC, RG 41 CBC, vol 917, series A-V-2, file PG 18-21 Special Events Programs, Dominion Day, 1938–1979, file 3 1977–1979, *Festival Canada 1978, 5th Revision*, 24 October 1977.

34 Ray Conlogue, 'CBC Serves a Dagwood Sandwich instead of a Birthday Cake,' *Globe and Mail*, 3 July 1978, 13.

35 William Johnson, 'Noisy Nationalism – The Cause of Lost Sleep,' *Globe and Mail*, 3 July 1978, 8.

36 LAC, MG 31 D230, G. Hamilton Southam, volume 22, file 34: Festival Canada: Interim Report by G. Hamilton Southam, July 1979.

37 Lise Bissonnette, 'Pitié pour l'année prochaine,' *Le Devoir*, 4 juillet 1979, 4.

38 LAC, RG 6 BAN 2002-01308-X, box 30, file 7215-80, vol. 1, Ceremonies and Celebrations – 1 July 1980, memorandum to Cabinet re: Festival Canada, 22 January 1980.

7 Politics? Fear Not! The Rise of *The Average Superhero* in the Visual Rhetoric of Bill Davis's 1971 Election Pamphlet

JAMES CAIRNS

In contemporary liberal democracies, it is widely taken for granted that powerful politicians pay people to tell them what to wear. The image of the political candidate, 'as conveyed by his or her physical appearance, speech style, and general mode of self-presentation,' is one of the most discussed features of recent elections. Campaign strategists pursue eye-catching photographs with a singular focus, 'even if that means taking the leader to an unwinnable riding just to get the required visuals.' The political scene bears out Boorstin's exclamation: 'The language of images is everywhere. Everywhere it has displaced the language of ideals.' At the start of the twenty-first century, few would dispute the suggestion that concerns about political style have come to matter as much as – some would say more than – questions about political issues. It should be noted, however, that in addition to describing the present, the statement also comments on the past: it implies that the practice of politics has changed over time.[1]

The general election of 1945 was the first in which a Canadian party hired an advertising firm to help construct its public image.[2] Since then, an industry has grown out of people dedicated to what Thompson calls 'the management of visibility,' or the 'branding' of political people and parties.[3] The body of literature on the *spectacularization* of political communication lends scholarly support to what many sense intuitively: that the worlds of politics and entertainment are converging.[4] Yet the bulk of studies on 'the era of image politics' focus on television to the exclusion of other media.[5] By contrast, this paper takes a fresh approach to a common theme and sheds light on the emergence of now-familiar imagery within the political sphere of Ontario by examining an understudied medium – the election campaign pamphlet.

Drawing on Roland Barthes's 'spectral analysis' of print advertising,[6] this paper interprets messages contained in a landmark election pamphlet from early in the era of image politics.[7] Comparing then-premier Bill Davis's 1971 brochure to examples of pamphlets from earlier Ontario elections, the paper addresses the changing relationship between image and text in campaign literature and shows that the Davis pamphlet relies on photographs to make statements which could not be as subtly voiced in its verbal component. Bringing together the linguistic, denotative, and connotative messages of Davis's brochure that articulated a cohesive visual framework, the paper concludes by arguing that the pamphlet exemplifies the rise of *The Average Superhero* within the subtext of political textual propaganda. The concept of *The Average Superhero* is developed through comparison of central messages in Davis's election brochure and central themes in classic superhero comic books.[8] Discussing the use of common imagery and narratives in these two different cultural artefacts (i.e., campaign pamphlets and comic books) allows us to gain insight into the historical emergence of what has become a familiar figure in recent electoral politics.

The Subfield of Election Advertising Research

Election campaigns are widely depicted as helping citizens 'make an informed choice' about people and parties best suited for public office. And as 'political advertising has become the dominant form of communication between politicians and the publics they seek to lead,' an army of scholars has undertaken research on election campaign advertising. After more than a half-century of work, the topic now constitutes its own subfield of political studies.[9] Although the resultant literature resists easy characterization, the following survey outlines four broad categories which organize conceptually the distinguishing features of the subfield and chart the path of this study.

First, research may be characterized by temporal outlook. Every study of election advertising focuses on artefacts and events in its own time, from an earlier time, or some combination of the two.[10] Their simplicity notwithstanding, these subcategories are useful guides and reveal that the majority of studies deal with contemporary election ads. Second, studies can be divided between the mountain of research focusing on television advertisements, and the mound focusing on other marketing media, for example, oratory, print, radio, or more recently, the internet.[11] Third, from a methodological perspective, content analysis of a large sample of ads is the most popular investigative approach, although survey research and other effects-based studies are often used to shed light on how political advertisements influence voter opinion. Although fewer by comparison, the subfield also includes semiotic analyses.[12]

Fourth, and perhaps most important, the literature can be divided using Lazarsfeld's distinction between 'administrative' and 'critical' research.[13] Studies conducted from the administrative perspective are concerned with such issues as: whether negative advertising bolsters or deters voter-turnout, 'whether the claims in advertisements are true or untrue,' or which 'five basic photographs every candidate needs' in his or her campaign material.[14] By contrast, critical approaches interpret election advertising as 'an ellipse of language,' with the potential to evoke 'hidden myths' – part and parcel of 'the wider, and infinitely recursive, discourse constituted by promotional culture as a whole.' The critical perspective views the ad as a cultural practice which serves to 'reinforce and enhance an entire sociopolitical structure that undergirds a political regime and/or system.'[15]

At every turn, the framework above ushers this essay into the minority camp. In stark contrast to the popular administrative content analysis of a large sample of contemporary television ads, this chapter takes a critical, qualitative, historical approach to a single election brochure. The amalgam of unconventional choices is clear; but what reasons suggest that concerted non-conformity will make an instructive guide? First, Schudson's dictum that 'advertising may shape our sense of values even where it does not greatly corrupt our buying [or voting] habits' is a standing call for critical approaches to political marketing.[16] Second, though some disapprove of Barthes's distinction between denotation and connotation,[17] his 'spectral analysis' remains the 'prototypical' method of critically investigating the interplay between image and text in print advertising.[18] Lule's recent application of the model highlights its advantages by reiterating the need to analyse 'the literal meanings of the photograph' as a first step toward understanding 'ideological messages that are hidden by ... the *having-been-there* quality of the photographic image.'[19] Third, one need not hold a Whiggish conception of unending progress to understand that the contemporary world is shot through with the past, and that by turning to history, it becomes easier to assess continuities and changes in social practices and cultural artefacts.[20]

But in the era of TV politics, why a pamphlet? For one thing, although outshone by the ubiquitous glow of the television 'polispot,' print literature remains one of the longest-serving forms of political communication: parties and politicians 'continue to use this form of advertising for campaigns at all levels of office.'[21] It is frequently said that television brought election campaigning into the living room; but however much insight the statement carries, it deprives election brochures of their time-tested portability. The pamphlet has long been in living rooms – not to mention kitchens, postboxes, fairgrounds, and pubs.[22] Rather than being dismissed as old-fashioned, print election material should be considered a bridge between pre-electronic campaign techniques and newer forms. Furthermore, printed campaign literature 'contrasts with the somehow fleeting aspect of the other events of the campaign as picked up by the media and filtered through them. It represents a kind of background noise that contributes to fill in the silent intervals and to keep up a pressure and a presence.' The suggestion is not that pamphlets once performed precisely the same role as television does today, but that differences among campaign media do exist, which makes it imperative that scholars begin to 'take these differences seriously and turn some of their attention to exploring the dynamics of media beyond television.'[23]

In Canada, although several administrative studies have used election pamphlets as part of their evidentiary base, no major empirical work critically discusses the visuality of pamphlets; no study treats the brochure primarily as a cultural artefact, capable of transmitting ideological messages beyond the candidate's obvious 'Vote for Me' strategy.[24] For example, Whitehorn uses pamphlets to report shifts in a party's platform, but he is silent on the form in which promises are presented. Devoted exclusively to extracting issues from the text of the brochure, the study neglects to comment on its visual properties. Taras notes that early twentieth-century campaign literature was 'eye-catching and often very clever'; however, the words do not explore meaning-making through print election material, but introduce a chapter on contemporary campaign methods.[25] The present study does not claim to be original in every respect; but by combining all four minority perspectives in the subfield of election advertising research, concerted non-conformity opens up a space to explore an underexamined medium in the history of Canadian electioneering, with the purpose of critically interpreting messages contained in a groundbreaking political artefact.

Election Pamphlets in Ontario

The earliest election pamphlets in Ontario are virtually a different species than those produced today. Unlike the thin, image-saturated, folded flyer of contemporary campaigns, pamphlets from the province's first decades were bulky, text-based booklets. Brochures with a cover were bound in monochrome paper, their fronts displaying long, descriptive titles in large block letters.[26] In keeping with their substantial weight, early pamphlets were loaded with a public significance that is absent from their twenty-first-century progeny. While it was once commonplace, today it is difficult to imagine pamphlets, in whole or part, being reprinted in newspapers or concerns about an allegedly slanderous pamphlet gripping a campaign.[27] Early pamphlet/booklets were used to: recount a party's legislative performance and detail its policy proposals;[28] refute attacks from rival parties and scrutinize opponents' plans and principles;[29] and report on financial affairs, often through the use of charts and tables.[30] While this paper is not intended to detail every innovation in Ontario pamphleteering, the mention of a few 'firsts' will help to provide comparative context to the discussion of Davis's watershed brochure of 1971.[31]

The first image to mark the cover of an Ontario election pamphlet was the provincial flag. The drawing appeared in 1883, just above the Liberal-Conservative Party's motto: 'With the Party, by the Party, for the Country.'[32] The first time the image of a candidate appeared in a political brochure was the election of 1894[33] (see figure 7.1). However, apart from the two small profile sketches of the Liberal candidates on its front cover and a similarly styled drawing of Premier Oliver Mowat on its back, the pamphlet remained a text-based, detailed description of the party's achievements. The first female face was sketched in a Socialist Party pamphlet for the election of 1902.[34] In 1905, the first photograph of a candidate appeared; yet it was another six years before Liberal Party leader N.W. Rowell became the first candidate to turn his gaze directly toward the camera and engage with the voter eye to eye.[35] In an odd twist, during the 1919 election Premier William Hearst became the first (and perhaps the only) candidate to use campaign literature as a means of downplaying interest in provincial affairs; instead, he distributed a pamphlet which depicted 'the war effort as virtually his sole concern.'[36] It was not until 1943 that an election pamphlet included a photograph of a candidate wearing something other than his or her Sunday best. No doubt, the proto–action shot of Liberal Premier Harry Nixon is staged; but, dressed as he is in a work jacket, fedora, work pants, and gloves, and perched behind the wheel of a tractor, Nixon strikes a casual pose, using the pamphlet photograph in a way never before attempted in an Ontario election campaign.[37] In 1967, further

Figure 7.1: Front cover of *Twenty-Two Years of Reform Government* (1894).

200 James Cairns

This is where the New Democratic Party stands on six of the major issues in this election:

EDUCATION: New Democrats believe that all of Ontario's young people are entitled to the best education possible, an education that will equip them for the changing world they will face when they graduate. To meet this goal, an NDP government will expand the gradeless system, and reduce the size of classes. The teacher training program will be reformed, and there will be a province-wide study of priorities in education.

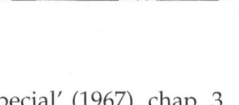

COST OF LIVING: Consumers deserve to get full value for every shopping dollar. To guarantee this, the New Democrats will enact a Consumers' Bill of Rights— the right to be informed, the right to choose, and the right to be heard. The NDP will establish a Prices Review Board to investigate extraordinary price increases, and a Rent Review Board that will seek justification for rent increases. There will be a Truth-in-Business Code, to indicate the true price of goods, real interest rates, and check the quality of products and packaging. Below, the NDP's Supermarket Computer, available now to help you compare prices.

the higher cost of living in the North, including the progressive reduction of sales tax on gasoline sold north of certain points in the province.

Because provincial and federal governments have failed to fight for the interests of our citizens living in the North, a New Democratic government will build a second pipeline in Northern Ontario.

Education: To establish the right priorities in education, an NDP government will launch a single, over-all study of Ontario education. Specifically, the New Democrats would expand the gradeless system, and reduce the size of classes. They would reform the teacher training program, and see to it that Community Colleges can lead to university. Tuition fees will be eliminated. A program of grants and loans will remove barriers for qualified students seeking higher education.

A New Democratic government would provide special financial assistance to adults seeking a second chance at education. University government will be reformed, and the rights of students recognized.

12   NEW DEMOCRAT

Figure 7.2: Excerpt from the *new Democrat*'s 'Election special' (1967), chap. 3, 'The Issues,' 12.

signalling the emergence of image politics in Ontario, the NDP transformed an issue of its publication *new Democrat* into a colourful '16-page campaign magazine.'[38] Adding colour photography to the visual repertoire, the brochure mixes traditional policy promises with new, eye-catching imagery. Built around three four-page chapters on 'The Campaign,' 'The Candidates,' and 'The Issues,' the booklet emphasizes the growing power of the fledgling party and includes a mixture of black-and-white and colour photographs of a full twenty-one NDP candidates (see figure 7.2).

Over the course of the first half of the twentieth century, election pamphlets shrank in size. The long, detailed accounts of party activity and in-depth analysis of the actions of rivals gradually disappeared as the printed brochure became a vehicle for shorter, often point-form promises. By the end of the Second World War, the hundred-plus page pamphlets had disappeared. As pamphlets shrank, their verbal component took on a tone more popular than formal.[39] Importantly, by the mid-1900s, the photograph became a common element of the campaign advertisement. Before the 1967 election in Ontario, all pamphlet photographs were black and white; most were traditionally composed head or head-and-torso shots of the stoic, perfectly groomed, usually white, male candidate; and few pamphlets contained more than one or two images. Nevertheless, acknowledging the danger of constructing too simple a narrative around the progression of pamphlet form and content, it is clear that, between 1875 and 1971, several new methods in creating campaign pamphlets became available, while other older techniques were discontinued.[40]

Bill Davis's Election Pamphlet of 1971

Bill Davis's campaign pamphlet for the 1971 provincial election was a piece of political advertising the likes of which had never been seen in Ontario politics. And it was, indeed, widely seen: the 'glossy pamphlet' was the sole piece of Progressive Conservative Party literature to be distributed in all 117 Ontario ridings.[41] In the days preceding the 21 October vote, newspaper coverage highlighted the 'slick booklet' in stories on the advertising operation being orchestrated by Davis's campaign manager Norman Atkins.[42] Atkins had proven himself a skilful strategist while organizing Allan Lawrence's unsuccessful bid for the party leadership, and in the spring of 1971, shortly after winning the contest and, with it, the title of premier, Davis asked Atkins if he would manage the party's efforts in the upcoming election.[43] 'By this act of conciliation, Davis created the Big Blue Machine, the Conservative organization that was to dominate Ontario politics throughout the Davis years from 1971 to 1985.'[44] Atkins and other members of this select group soon established a secret campaign team known as Ad Hoc Enterprises and began recruiting marketing experts from Toronto firms.[45] This diverse crew would create 'brochures, posters, matchbooks, commercials – everything needed to run an American-style campaign, not just for the leader but for every candidate.'[46]

Laying to rest doubts about the degree to which people involved in the 1971 campaign could sense that the Tories were in the midst of 'taking electioneering to a new level,'[47] top NDP strategist Gerry Caplan recalls:

> I remember that somewhere in the middle, I realized that we were up against a very remarkable foe; and that while we were running a nice, little, sweet, one-dimensional campaign, they had about six or seven dimensions … Every time we turned around, there was something more that we hadn't realized. Whether it was television, radio, or that sixteen page pamphlet … they knew things that we didn't know.[48]

Jonathan Manthorpe notes the strength of the Tories' overall campaign, but concludes that the dominant figure of the marketing strategy

> was Davis, Davis, Davis. Davis in living, breathing colour. Davis barbecuing hamburgers. Davis, his back to the camera, walking pensively on the beach by his cottage in the evening sunlight. Davis among crowds of supporters. Davis walking through the woods with his wife, Kathy. Davis with his family. Davis, Davis, Davis.[49]

To the extent that advertising can determine a party's electoral success – and media coverage from 1971 indicates that Davis's campaign was extremely influential – it is arguable that the efforts of the Big Blue Machine contributed significantly to the Tories' 'landslide victory,' in which they won 78 of 117 seats, an increase of nine from the 1967 contest.[50] In Atkins's recollection, 'it was a storybook campaign.'[51]

Drawing on a single set of images to produce both the party's 'polispots' and its main campaign brochure, the Ad Hoc team created not only a series of lush television commercials (complete with campaign theme song), but also a glitzy, image-laden, highly polished pamphlet –

one that ignores conventions of earlier campaign media.[52] Within the brochure's sixteen pages are set twenty-four colour photographs, with Davis's face appearing in twenty of those shots. One full page of the pamphlet is devoted to photographs of the premier's family: 'six color shots of his wife in jeans and a cardigan, his children, and his dog.'[53] There are eleven direct quotations from the candidate, within which are found twenty first-person references. Davis is referred to by name eight times. From these observations alone, it is clear that Davis's pamphlet was drastically different from the two-tone, single-shot brochures of previous campaigns. Yet, the object of this chapter is not to count textual features, but to apply Barthesian 'spectral analysis' in order to learn more about the messages bound up in Davis's pamphlet.

Recall that, according to Barthes, the advertising image contains three messages. At the level of the linguistic message, text serves two functions. First, it anchors specific symbolic messages to what are always 'polysemous' signifiers; and second, it serves to relay information from the surface level of image and caption to the higher level of the overarching story.[54] Next, Barthes analyses the advertisement's denotative messages, arguing that, distinct from the photograph's ability to transmit a symbolic message, it is also capable of revealing the 'literal' message of the signifiers which fill its frame. Finally, exploring what he calls the 'rhetoric of the image,' Barthes investigates the advertisement's connotative message – the syntagm of culturally constructed symbols and cues that, resting upon the support of the advertisement's literal message, emerge from the interplay between image and text. From here, Barthes observed 'an important historical paradox: the more technology develops the diffusion of information (and notably of images), the more it provides the means of masking the constructed meaning under the appearance of the given meaning.'[55] Thus, despite being socially constructed, culturally specific, and historical in nature, the symbolic message is 'naturalized' by virtue of its intimate connection with the literal message from which it is born.

Linguistic Message: The Expert Humble Servant

The verbal text in Davis's pamphlet provides two conflicting messages about the candidate. On the one hand, the text is used to anchor the potential meanings of the pamphlet's lavish images to an overarching message of humble servitude; on the other, it relays the story of Davis's exceptional talent and leadership. Thus, the linguistic message of Davis's brochure presents the candidate as being simultaneously ordinary and extraordinary.

Following the name 'Bill Davis' (which appears in bold on the brochure's cover), the pamphlet's first words introduce Davis as a regular guy – the type who disdains the pomp and pretence of political office. Running alongside a two-page spread of an open-shirted, 'candid' photograph of Davis's profile, the candidate speaks directly to the voter:

> Some refer to me as Prime Minister and others as Premier. The Opposition calls me the Member from Peel North, among other things. But I've lived with the name Bill for a long time and I prefer that. It's a lot easier.[56]

On this point, it is interesting to note Spiers's contention that, in actual fact, 'an associate as close as [Hugh] Segal only once called [Bill Davis] "Bill," and deduced from the ensuing icy silence that he'd better stick to "Mr. Premier."' A similar concern is raised by Hoy regarding, on one hand, election-pamphlet-Davis's claim to lead a 'political family' that loved to campaign, and on the other, the years Davis spent protecting his family from the public eye.[57] That political candidates are not replicas of the images that appear in campaign advertisements is not an earth-shattering discovery. But the fact that the brochure's opening description of Davis appears to conflict with aspects of his real-life persona is a potent reminder that the pamphlet is being used as a device to fabricate an ideal image of The Politician, not to reflect a party's approach to governance.

Text on the next two pages continues to emphasize Davis's humble character. Atop a collection of photographs of his family and pet dog, Davis explains: 'Every family needs a dog. So do politicians. Ours is Thor. He cost $2.25, new. He's worth a million or so now.' Davis lists his address as 'Main Street, Brampton, Ontario.'[58] (See figure 7.3.) Carrying this 'average-Joe,' or perhaps 'average-Bill,' message into the realm of policy (and remember – the premier is chummy *Bill*, not stuffy *William*), Davis promises to push for 'a greater degree of control by Canadians over their own economy and in the development of their own resources' (8). In the words of his campaign slogan: 'Davis is doing things ... for people' (16). The message throughout is clear: it is the job of government to execute the will of the people; the ideal politician, therefore, will be the average citizen.[59]

It is conceivable that in *middle-of-the-road* Ontario, where 'the requirement of managerial efficiency' in government had long been a cardinal political virtue,[60] voters would have questioned Davis's decision to produce such a flashy campaign brochure. The *Globe and Mail*'s three-part election series, 'Selling the Premier,' expresses concern about the expense of producing elaborate promotional material and indicates that the public was privy to critical assessments of the Big Blue Machine's commercial marketing tactics.[61] The high quality of the television and print advertisements makes obvious their relative high cost; and high levels of campaign spending, especially by a party in power, can easily be seen as wasteful. That threat is lessened, however, by the use of verbal text in the pamphlet to emphasize Davis's down-to-earth approach to politics, his humble lifestyle, and his popular appeal. In Barthes's terminology, the brochure's linguistic message helps to close off other potential connotations of the advertisement by anchoring its images to the narrative of the 'average Bill.'

In competition with this first linguistic message, text is also used to tell of Davis's rise to power. In this narrative, the verbal message drops Davis's common qualities and instead relays information that distinguishes him from other candidates and, by extension, from the 'average-Bill.' In an introduction fit for Street's 'celebrity politician,'[62] Davis's achievements are listed like those of a prizefighter. Emphasizing the candidate's youthful vigour, the pamphlet's faceless narrator gushes that upon entering the Ontario legislature, Davis (then twenty-nine) was 'the youngest member there,' and after becoming minister of education, he was 'the youngest member of the Government.' The voice proceeds: 'in the first 150 days of Davis Government, the Legislature approved 131 bills.'[63] Announcing his strengths as leader and implying his ability to wield influence over fellow party members, not to mention those from other parties, Davis says of his Tory colleagues: 'I've had a hand in choosing some of them, persuading them to make a contribution to public life. Maybe I even twisted a few arms. But we've got a great group of candidates' (11). In this second linguistic message, Davis as modest servant, a man typical of the common voter, is pushed aside by Davis as a young, strong, capable, active, and indeed *expert* politician. These are the traits of the 'highly competent, trustworthy leader' that provided 'decisiveness in the face of strong opposition' by saying 'No' to funding separate schools and cancelling the Spadina Expressway.[64]

When they are placed in direct comparison, the two linguistic messages contradict each other; however, viewed holistically they highlight Davis's diverse positive qualities and his broad electoral appeal.

Although at first glance this strategy may seem disingenuous, if not downright dishonest, when examined against the backcloth of Ontario's dominant political culture, the tension in the linguistic message coincides with the province's tradition of embracing opposing values. Numerous observers note that Ontario politics 'display divergent or even totally contradictory tendencies.'[65] Tracing the origins of this tension back to the pre-Confederation mixture of British Tory and formerly American United Empire Loyalist ideals, MacDonald argues that, for more than two hundred years, the 'basic component of the Ontario political culture' has been 'conservatism with a progressive component.' Wilson calls Ontario 'a red tory province.' Election returns support the claim that, in Ontario, 'political success has stemmed primarily from occupying the centre of the political stage'; and scholars treat Premier Oliver Mowat's brokerage politics as the archetypical example of the successful Ontario politician who integrated competing interests under a single party banner.[66] The point is that while Bill Davis's campaign was the first to employ a particular visual rhetoric in order to project an appeal so broad that Mowat would have blushed in its shadow, the trope upon which 'the expert-humble servant' is constructed is firmly entrenched in Ontario's past politics. The pamphlet builds on Ontario's politico-cultural foundations, carefully articulating and blending what appear to be mutually exclusive qualities.

Denotative Message: A New, Exciting Style

The central theme of the linguistic message – the one that presents Davis as a modest yet omni-talented deal-closer – is also found in what Barthes called the 'literal message' of the advertisement. Recall that at the level of denotation, the image is stripped of all connotations (at least for analytical purposes), leaving the photograph to be interpreted as a 'message without a code.' At this level of analysis, there are two distinct areas for study in Davis's advertisement. The primary focal point is Davis himself – the numerous photographs of the candidate which confirm that Davis is a man of action, each of them containing the message of his literally *'having-been-there.'*[67] Throughout the pamphlet, Davis is pictured in a variety of locations, engaged in various activities. Several photographs show Davis interacting with members of different demographic groups. Here, followed by an entourage of law-enforcement officials and other men in suits (politicians, one presumes), Davis receives applause from a large crowd and reaches to shake hands

Family: "My wife, Kathy, and five children. Neil is 15, Nancy's 13, Cathy's 12, Ian's 9 and Meg is 7. I guess you could say we are a political family. They'll campaign with me and they'll be knocking on doors. They'd like me to win.

"Every family needs a dog. So do politicians. Ours is Thor. He cost $2.25, new. He's worth a million or so now."

Address: "Main Street, Brampton, Ontario."

Figure 7.3: *Bill Davis* election pamphlet (1971), 4–5.

"I believe in a greater degree of control by Canadians over their own economy and in the development of their own resources. That's why we're lending money to Canadian companies and giving preferential treatment to Canadian firms. We've brought in special legislation to protect and encourage our book publishing industry, so that Canadians will continue to write, publish and read books about their own country. We're not mad at anybody, just glad to live in Ontario and have a hand in developing our own land. We want to keep things that way."

with a young boy.[68] Here, he laughs with an elderly woman (11). Here, he stands casually by a lake and talks with another man (8). Here, he sits beside his wife, and listens in an auditorium (9). Here, he is the father, smiling beside his son (9) (see figure 7.4). Here, he sits behind a desk, holding a phone to his ear (6). Nowhere in the verbal text is it announced that Bill Davis is an athlete, but we see evidence of his physical prowess in photographs of Davis wearing a baseball glove and riding a bicycle (9, 14). Also absent from the verbal text is the suggestion that Davis is a contemplative man who enjoys solitary walks along the beach. The direct statement would seem ridiculous in an allegedly serious document intended to explain why a man should be premier. But the information need not be so plainly stated: we can see it for ourselves in a two-page photo spread (12–13). The images serve as visual confirmation, hard evidence for the insinuation that Davis is all things to all people.[69]

A second denoted message comes to light when one takes a holistic approach to the brochure. The aggregate of techniques used to make up Davis's advertisement – colour photography and collage; the mix of third-person narration and first-person testimonials by the candidate; images of a variety of activities and people; even the overall form of the pamphlet, for it is neither a small, single-paged leaflet, nor a thick manifesto like those of the late nineteenth century – must be seen as breaking with the conventional style of campaign literature in Ontario. The ad offers no point-by-point plan designed to teach voters the party platform. This is in contrast to Liberal leader Robert Nixon's official pamphlet from four years earlier, which is composed entirely of bulleted policy promises.[70] Moreover, the formal, if not detached, voice of the earnest public official is replaced by an easy-going, friendly tone. Davis's pamphlet of 1971 denoted – in itself it was *literally* – a new type of visual artefact.

On this reading, at the same time as it conveyed a message about Davis's particular qualities as a candidate for office, the pamphlet also transmitted a message about broader changes in political advertising. True, during the 1967 election, an NDP brochure had used colour photographs and collage, and the Tories had run on the theme of 'Robarts and the record';[71] however, nothing that came before Davis compared with the forcefulness with which the new premier was promoted across the province. The Davis team projected 'an image of the new leader rather than have him explain policies to Ontario voters.'[72] And despite the mechanisms of parliamentary democracy, which compel citizens to vote for candidates in local constituencies, not party leaders, the Big Blue Machine made sure that Davis was the focal point in every riding in Ontario.[73] Whereas the NDP booklet of 1967 devoted a chapter to policy issues, and included images of multiple candidates (not to mention a full page upon which every candidate would place his or her photograph and polling information), the Tory pamphlet was all Davis, all across the province.

Liberal and NDP critics reacted negatively to what they saw as Davis's ostentatious new marketing strategy and 'screamed that American presidential politics had arrived and that the Premier was being sold like a can of tomatoes.' NDP leader Stephen Lewis mocked the Big Blue Machine's 'made-in-Detroit' campaign, accusing it of losing touch with 'the politics of Ontario.' Robert Nixon complained that the PCs were at a huge financial advantage, noting that his Liberal Party had been 'outspent by the Tories in every circumstance I can recall.' In Atkins's recollection: 'We were accused of being "slick." That was the word they used. And ... we were.'[74] Notwithstanding the accuracy of any particular epithet, the shock and disdain bound up in opposition criticism lends further weight to the argument that Davis's pamphlet can be read as a watershed moment in the history of Ontario electioneering.

Connotative Message: The Average Superhero

In our exploration of the brochure's connotative messages, the key question is: What '*other, additional implied meanings*' do we see surfacing from the interplay of image and text? What 'extra-visual leaps' does the pamphlet teach us to make?[75] What ideological themes are embedded in the structure of the advertisement? For starters, though there was 'no catastrophe point, no single historical juncture ... at which we can say that promotion, having previously been "emergent," finally became a "dominant" structuring principle' of the Western world, Davis's election brochure is a clear sign that the essence of 'promotional culture' had seeped into the world of Ontario politics by the early 1970s.[76] True, marketing strategies 'devised to dissect consumers' thoughts and actions' had been used in Canadian politics since the interwar period.[77] Moreover, citing the growing emphasis on party leaders in previous Tory campaigns, Bill Davis himself cautions against interpreting 1971 as a turning point in the history of Ontario electioneering.[78] But from the perspective of visual culture, it is difficult to deny that the pamphlet signified a new and ultimately successful attempt at electoral 'image-altering,' heralding the transition to a type of politics that has since become 'more organized, more professional, more compartmentalized, and less improvised.'[79]

In addition to being an ideal example of the way in which political advertising takes 'complex issues and necessarily reduce[s] them to simple images,'[80] commodifying not only a single candidate for public consumption, but, indeed, the very notion of politics, the pamphlet makes three other crucial connotations. First, it legitimizes and privileges representative democracy and the traditional family unit. Words and images come together to express a message that says, *This is how politics is done: there are rulers and there are ruled. Your job as citizen is to choose the best ruler.* Put differently, one way of doing politics, namely representative democracy – a historically specific, cultural formation – is reified, given a *'natural* image,' in pamphlet form.[81] Of course, the visual support for the myth of representative democracy is in keeping with the political culture of Ontario, for 'civics, as taught in the province's schools, reinforces a view that involvement stops at the ballot box.'[82] Furthermore, the linguistic and literal messages used to introduce Davis's family imply that any good political leader must come from – and by extension, defend – what was popularized as the traditional family unit, consisting of husband, wife, and children. The Ad Hoc group relied heavily upon lessons learned from 'the selling' of John F. Kennedy during the 1960 presidential campaign and the promotion of Pierre Trudeau›s personal qualities during the Liberal Party of Canada's campaign of 1968,[83] deducing from the American and federal experiences an idea that is well known today: successful political advertising 'tells stories people are familiar with.'[84] And what could have been more familiar in 1971 Ontario than the trope of the nuclear family? But in introducing Davis's particular family to the visual landscape of Ontario politics, the pamphlet reproduces – indeed, it celebrates – the idea of Family, and the necessary link between civic leadership and conformity to dominant social norms.

Second, in accordance with the belief that 'enterprises, discoveries and institutions are legitimate only insofar as they contribute to the emancipation of mankind,' the rhetoric of the pamphlet is couched in the myth of inevitable Progress.[85] Whereas the NDP, by comparison, ran a campaign replete with warnings of what might happen under further Conservative rule – one which Stephen Lewis's own executive assistant admits 'couldn't have been better suited to terrify Ontarians about Stephen' – Davis's pamphlet connoted the optimism growing in Ontario since the Drew years and reminded citizens about 'their wealth, their industry, their abundance of everything that the modern world considered best for the good life.'[86] True, it is an election campaign advertisement produced by an incumbent party, so of course it paints a rosy picture about the state of the world. Regardless, justifying the pamphlet's cause for exaggerated optimism does not alter its ideological nature.

Third, the pamphlet upholds the message that politics is rightly the realm of the Great Man. The power of the individual actor underlies the whole piece. In Canada, there is broad agreement that the head of government 'acts more as a team leader than a symbolic embodiment of the government,'[87] but in the pamphlet, it is not the Tories, but Bill Davis who *is doing things* ... for people. In a pamphlet expressly intended to sell one candidate over other parties, Davis's past and potential influence is foregrounded to the exclusion of political realities. The image of Davis on the phone in his office – a veritable staple in modern campaign literature – signifies at once the candidate's strengths as a communicator, his endless availability to the community, his commitment to hard work, and his ability to *get the job done*. Like the famous on-the-phone photographs of President Kennedy during the Cuban missile crisis, the image of Davis is a symbol of the power of the Great Man. Disturbingly, however, as the individual candidate's positive attributes are peddled to the point where there appears to be no limit to his strength, complex social processes are obscured from view. Simultaneously endowing Davis with superpowers – for the candidate is shown to be a friend of all people, and capable of solving all problems – the pamphlet hides the work of a plethora of public servants, sterilizes social problems, ignores intractable disputes, dissolves chronic pain and suffering, and silences alternative forms of political discourse.[88] It is unreasonable to expect a piece of mainstream political propaganda to spread generously credit for civic successes or to concentrate on the undesirable underbelly of politics. Nevertheless, 'spectral analysis' of Davis's pamphlet suggests that the rhetoric of the campaign advertisement serves to defend more than just the good work and intentions of a single candidate. At a deeper level, the pamphlet also accomplishes ideological work, reproducing messages about acceptable political activity and redrawing the normative boundaries of a political community.

On the basis of the foregoing analysis, it is possible to lay the groundwork for a particular way of interpreting the visuality of Davis's landmark political advertisement. What follows is a heuristic device to stimulate new thoughts on the election pamphlet by comparing it with a different textual form – namely, the classic superhero comic book.[89] The argument that this visual metaphor helps to synthesize the collection of observations made up to this point is not meant to suggest that no other metaphor is capable of shedding light upon the pamphlet's discursive properties. That being said, reflecting upon the array of messages in the Davis ad by referring to the signature features of comic book imagery is especially helpful because it provides a framework for pulling together the key features of Davis's pamphlet-constructed persona and the visual attributes of the pamphlet itself. In short the argument is this: Davis's brochure exemplifies the rise of *The Average Superhero* in the visual rhetoric of Ontario election campaigns.

Recall, for instance, the argument that the verbal text in Davis's piece is used to anchor the rich quality of the pamphlet to a message about the candidate's average character. Evocative of the plainclothes costume used in comic books 'to differentiate the private man from the superhero,' text and photographs merge to mask Davis's extraordinary qualities.[90] Yet, working within the same discursive space as the message of the 'average-Bill,' other messages – namely, the narrative of greatness relayed in verbal text, the message of expertise and action denoted by photographic images, and the connotations of the Great Man – have endowed Davis with powers that no mere mortal could possess. In contrast to the narrative of humility, this second set of codes constitutes Davis's cloak of invincibility; it reveals him to be the 'man of steel ... defender of the weak and oppressed, strongest of all men ... noble and gentle – in short, a man far superior to any other human being.'[91] Davis is at once the typical citizen and the consummate politician – he is *The Average Superhero*.[92]

Reflecting on the Tory campaign, Brownsey is right to underline the premium placed upon 'the image of the leader.'[93] However, a more accurate description of the pamphlet itself would use the plural, 'images,' to avoid implying a unity that fails to account for the complex visual representations of election-pamphlet-Davis. The forces driving the Big Blue Machine understood that Davis exuded intelligence and earnestness; their challenge was to cue a 'warm feeling' in Ontario voters by infusing 'folksiness' into the new premier's public presence.[94] The resultant pamphlet-tableau depicted Davis, like his comic book superhero cousins, as possessing discrete identities. By day, he is the accomplished political leader, fighting for the rights and privileges of the citizens of Ontario; by night he is the Family Man. Here, he celebrates 'a diversity of cultures and interests';[95] there, he stands with his wife and children, the incarnation of conservative family values (8, 9). Here, he is the celebrity, surrounded by adoring fans (10, 11); there, he walks by water in solitude at sunset. Even his costume changes: on the phone and at the podium in front of the crowd, he wears a dark suit (the ultimate sign of the establishment), appearing well-groomed and stern-faced (6–7); yet here, his shirt is open, his hair is tousled, and his stubble shows (2–3).

In addition to the manner in which Davis himself personifies *The Average Superhero*, the composition of the pamphlet supports this visual framework. The layout and design of the brochure itself actually resemble a comic book. 'Colour has been a chief selling point of comics' since their introduction, and in much the same way as colourful comic book covers were first used 'to attract buyers,'[96] Davis's colour pamphlet used an emerging technique to appeal to the voter's aesthetic sense. Moreover, breaking with the formal qualities of earlier two-toned, text-based pamphlets, Davis's pamphlet demonstrates the comic-cartoonist's understanding that images are often 'more attractive, and more seductive than written texts.'[97] Yet it is not merely the proliferation of colourful images in both comic and pamphlet that warrants comparison of the two; also noteworthy is the similarity between, on one hand, the complementary use of image and word in Davis's brochure, and on the other, the suggestion that 'what defines narrative in the comic-strip is that picture and text work together to tell *one* story.'[98] Yes, some older pamphlets were also printed on paper and bound in the centre, but they lacked the flashy photos, the catchy quotations, the personal story, the glorification of the Hero, the image-text cohesion, which, packaged together in Davis's pamphlet, offered voters both an easily readable and, most important, new, visually stimulating campaign message.

If we extend the metaphor further, both textual genres perform ideological work. Since the end of the 1930s, superheroes have protected vulnerable masses from supervillains, but in doing so, they have also defended traditional gender roles, war efforts, and the culture of consumption in general.[99] And in much the same way as the comic book superhero is constructed for mass consumption, in the provincial election of 1971, 'the high pressure sales techniques of the Tory campaign had reduced [election-pamphlet-] Davis to the status of a commodity.'[100] In Barthes's language, Davis's pamphlet photograph is a 'mirror,' offering to the voter his or her 'own likeness, but clarified, exalted, superbly elevated into a type.' Gazing into the pamphlet-mirror, voters are 'at once expressed and heroized,' invited by the image to elect themselves.[101] Yet, although *The Average Superhero* can be marketed to the electorate as the embodiment of the ideal politician, he remains a dubious promise, a symbol of Utopia, detached from the complex struggle of the lived experience of the political realm. Achieving the same end as 'symbolic ads' in the commercial sphere, Davis's pamphlet creates 'a world without work, social conflict, or indeed any socially negative features at all.' And in doing so, Davis's glossy booklet evokes the 'prevalent escapist themes of more popular comicbooks.' Facing the instability that defines all things political, *The Average Superhero* declares, *Politics? Fear not!*, for he knows that the classic comic book ends 'with certainties – chaos is vanquished and stability is restored.'[102]

The Average Superhero used an old form of campaign media to establish a new connection between partisan and personal spheres, appealing to each and every Ontarian on informal grounds. And with his superpowers tucked away under the symbols and conventions of an ordinary citizen, he appeared like an approachable fellow; but the fact remains that 'there is no way to interact with an objectified image nor to intervene in the construction of an ad.'[103] Ultimately, his attempt to transcend what previous pamphlets had delimited as the acceptable boundaries for political appeals and engage directly with the voter was a chimera. It carried all the excitement – and with it, all the plausibility – of the plotline of a superhero comic book. Although the contradictions interwoven throughout the pamphlet bear traces of the opposing values that constitute Ontario's political culture, there is no question that *The Average Superhero* himself is anathema to politics.

In conclusion, the notion of *The Average Superhero* provides one way of conceptualizing the totality of the visual and linguistic techniques brought together in a key campaign brochure from early in the era of image politics in Ontario. The intent here is not to suggest that the Davis election brochure *is* a comic book, nor that Davis *is* a superhero. The crucial point is that the Davis pamphlet marketed the candidate in a new way: it placed the man above the party (a transformation that Davis himself acknowledged in the final days of the campaign)[104] and crafted a complex public persona using innovative methods of visual design.

Notwithstanding Atkins's claim that the campaign 'wasn't a question of creating an image, it was a question of getting across to the public who Bill Davis really was,'[105] it would be misleading to conclude that Davis's pamphlet merely publicized never-before-seen parts of

the Ontario politician. The interplay of image and text in the advertisement was constitutive, not revelatory. As campaign strategies born in
the United States during the 1950s and 1960s were imported by the Big
Blue Machine, hastening the 'transformation of visibility' in Ontario
politics, Davis's pamphlet effectively created a new politico-visual
object, one which manufactured the personal (and personality of the)
premier.[106] Similarly to the way text was used to elide Davis's expec-
tation of formality and project instead a non-existent preference for
informality ('Call me Bill' – *only don't!*), the purportedly spontaneous
yet meticulously planned photographs produced – better yet, *they gave
life to* – a species of candidate which had never before run for office in
Ontario.

The Tory campaign of 1971 is often remembered as the first to place
TV 'polispots' at the centre of an Ontario election. Guided by concerted
non-conformity in the subfield of election advertising research, this
paper has shown that while the Big Blue Machine did apply emerging
political marketing techniques, it did not abandon the old printed pamphlet. On the contrary, along with other changes, the Tories transformed
the campaign brochure, too, and distributed the new artefact throughout the province in promoting *The Average Superhero* for premier.

NOTES

The author is grateful to the Social Sciences and Humanities Research Council
of Canada for financial support; to Daniel Robinson, Dennis Denisoff, and
Graham White for commenting on earlier drafts; and to Frederick J. Fletcher
for help accessing television advertisements.

1 Robert S. Wyer, Jr, et al., 'Image, Issues, and Ideology: The Processing of
   Information about Political Candidates,' *Journal of Personality and Social
   Psychology* 61, no. 4 (1991): 533; Joseph Wearing, *Strained Relations: Canadian
   Parties and Voters* (Toronto: McClelland and Stewart, 1988), 100; Daniel
   J. Boorstin, *The Image: A Guide to Pseudo-Events in America* (New York:
   Antheneum, 1972), 183. For the best recent collection of essays on the spec-
   tacularization of politics, see John Corner and Dick Pels, eds, *Media and the
   Restyling of Politics* (London: Sage, 2003).
2 J.L. Granatstein, *The Politics of Survival: The Conservative Party of Canada,
   1939–1945* (Toronto: University of Toronto Press, 1967), 190.
3 John B. Thompson, *The Media and Modernity: A Social Theory of the Media*

(Stanford, CA: Stanford University Press, 1995), 137. For an influential
account of this development, see Larry J. Sabato, *The Rise of Political Consultants: New Ways of Winning Elections* (New York: Basic Books, 1981).
4 See, for example, Bob Franklin, *Packaging Politics: Political Communications
in Britain's Media Democracy* (London: Arnold, 2004); D. Mutz, 'Leading
Horses to Water: Confessions of a *Daily Show* Junkie,' *Journalism and Mass
Communication Educator* 59 (2004): 31–5; F.R. Ankersmit, *Aesthetic Politics*
(Stanford: Stanford University Press, 1996); John Street, 'The Celebrity Politician: Political Style and Popular Culture,' in Corner and Pels, eds, *Media*,
85–98; Liesbet van Zoonen, 'Imagining the Fan Democracy,' *European Journal of Communication* 19, no. 1 (2004): 39–52; Murray Edelman, *Constructing
the Political Spectacle* (Chicago: University of Chicago Press, 1988); R. Lance
Holbert, 'A Typology for the Study of Entertainment Television and Politics,' *American Behavioral Scientist* 49, no. 3 (2005): 436–53; R.L. Holbert, et
al., '*The West Wing* and Depictions of the American Presidency: Expanding
the Theoretical and Empirical Domains of Framing in Political Communication,' *Communication Quarterly* 53 (2005): 505–22.
5 Stephen Kline, 'Image Politics: Negative Advertising Strategies and the
Election Audience,' in M. Nava et al., eds, *Buy This Book: Studies in Advertising and Consumption* (London: Routledge, 1997), 142.
6 Roland Barthes, 'Rhetoric of the Image,' in *Image, Music, Text*, ed. and
trans. S. Heath (New York: Hill and Wang, 1977), 32–51.
7 Throughout the remainder of the paper, unless noted otherwise, the term
'election pamphlet' is used synonymously with the terms 'election brochure,' 'print campaign advertisement,' and 'campaign literature.'
8 For a discussion of the literature on comic books, see below.
9 Daniel Stevens, 'Separate and Unequal Effects: Information, Political
Sophistication and Negative Advertising in American Elections,' *Political
Research Quarterly* 58, no. 3 (2005): 413; Lynda Lee Kaid and Monica Postelnicu, 'Political Advertising in the 2004 Election: Comparison of Traditional
Television and Internet Messages,' *American Behavioral Scientist* 49, no. 2
(1999): 423. The classic political science works in the subfield are from the
United States. See, for example: Bernard R. Berelson, Paul F. Lazarsfeld,
and William N. McPhee, *Voting* (Chicago: University of Chicago Press,
1954); Charles Atkin and Gary Heald, 'Effects of Political Advertising,'
Public Opinion Quarterly 40, no. 2 (1976): 216–28; Dan Nimmo, *The Political
Persuaders: The Techniques of Modern Election Campaigns* (Englewood Cliffs,
NJ: Prentice Hall, 1970); Theodore White, *The Making of the President* (New
York: Atheneum, 1961); and Thomas E. Patterson and Robert D. McClure,
The Unseeing Eye: The Myth of Television Power in National Elections (New

York: Putnam, 1976). For more recent overviews of the subfield, see, for example: Anne Johnston, 'Methodologies for the Study of Political Advertising,' in L.L. Kaid and C. Holtz-Bacha, eds, *The Sage Handbook of Political Advertising* (Thousand Oaks, CA: Sage, 2006), 15–33; David M. Farrell and Rudiger Schmitt-Beck, eds, *Do Political Campaigns Matter? Campaign Effects in Elections and Referendums* (London: Routledge, 2002); Fred Fletcher, ed., *Media, Elections and Democracy*, vol. 19 of the research studies of the Royal Commission on Electoral Reform and Party Financing (Toronto: Dundurn Press, 1992); Nicholas J. O'Shaughnessy, *The Phenomenon of Political Marketing* (London: Macmillan, 1990). For an example of work from a cultural angle, see Glenn W. Richardson, Jr, *Pulp Politics: How Political Advertising Tells the Stories of American Politics* (Lanham, MD: Rowman and Littlefield, 2001); from psychology, see Jennifer Jerit, 'Survival of the Fittest: Rhetoric during the Course of an Election Campaign,' *Political Psychology* 25, no. 4 (2004): 563–75; for an international perspective, see Holtz-Bacha and Kaid, 'Political Advertising in International Comparison,' in Kaid and Holtz-Bacha, eds, *Sage Handbook of Political Advertising*; D.L. Swanson and P. Mancini, eds, *Politics, Media and Modern Democracy. An International Study of Innovations in Electoral Campaigning and Their Consequences* (Westport: Praeger, 1996).

10 For examples of research on phenomena in their own time, see David Sanders and Pippa Norris, 'The Impact of Political Advertising in the 2001 U.K. General Election,' *Political Research Quarterly* 58, no. 4 (2005): 525–36; Gilbert R. Winham and Robert B. Cunningham, 'Party Leader Images in the 1968 Federal Election,' *Canadian Journal of Political Science* 3, no. 1 (1970): 37–55; Shaun Bowler and David M. Farrell, 'Conclusion: The Contemporary Election Campaign,' in S. Bowler and D.M. Farrell, eds, *Electoral Strategies and Political Marketing* (New York: St Martin's Press, 1992), 223–35; Walter C. Soderlund, 'Advertising in the 1993 Federal Election,' *Canadian Parliamentary Review* 18, no. 1 (1995): 16–22. For historical works, see Ian Ward, 'The Early Use of Radio for Political Communication in Australia and Canada: John Henry Austral, Mr Sage and the Man from Mars,' *Australian Journal of Politics and History* 45, no. 3 (1999): 311–329; Joel H. Silbey, *The American Party Battle: Election Campaign Pamphlets, 1828–1876*, 2 vols. (Cambridge, MA: Harvard University Press, 1999). It should be noted that historical studies of electioneering in Canada focus chiefly on party organization and/or key policy debates and, as a result, have tended to treat campaign advertisements, like newspaper coverage, as part of their evidentiary base, not as objects of study in themselves. See, for example: Brian D. Tennyson, 'The Ontario General Election of 1919: The

Beginnings of Agrarian Revolt,' *Journal of Canadian Studies* 4, no. 1 (1969): 26–36; Harold A. Averill, 'The T.N. Gibbs – J. Holden Battle in Ontario South, June, 1873,' *Ontario History* 65, no. 1 (1973): 1–18; Janet B. Kerr, 'Sir Oliver Mowat and the Campaign of 1894,' *Ontario History* 55, no. 1 (1963), 1–13; J.D. Livermore, 'The Ontario Election of 1871: A Case Study of The Transfer of Political Power,' *Ontario History* 71, no. 1 (1979): 39–52; Neil McKenty, S.J., 'Mitchell F. Hepburn and the Ontario Election of 1934,' *Canadian Historical Review* 65, no. 4 (1964): 293–313; Peter Oliver, 'Parties and Elections,' chap. 13 in *G. Howard Ferguson: Ontario Tory* (Toronto: University of Toronto Press, 1977); Robert Cuff, 'The Conservative Party Machine and the Election of 1911 in Ontario,' *Ontario History* 57, no. 3 (1965): 149–56. For longitudinal surveys, see Jay Bryant, 'Paid Media Advertising: Political Communication from the Stone Age to the Present,' in J.A. Thurber and Candice J. Nelson, eds, *Campaigns and Elections: American Style*, 2nd ed. (New York: Westview Press, 2004) , 90–108; Kathleen Hall Jamieson, *Packaging the Presidency: A History and Criticism of Presidential Campaign Advertising*, 3rd ed. (New York: Oxford University Press, 1996); Darrell M. West, *Air Wars: Television Advertising in Election Campaigns, 1952–2004* (Washington: CQ Press, 2005).

11 Perhaps the most commonly cited source on TV 'spot' ads is Edwin Diamond and Stephen Bates, *The Spot: The Rise of Political Advertising on Television*, 3rd ed. (Cambridge, MA: MIT Press, 1992). For an increasingly popular model of analysing television advertising that draws on elements of film and symbolic interactionist theory, see Lynda Lee Kaid and Anne Johnston, *Videostyle in Presidential Campaigns: Style and Content of Televised Political Advertising* (Westport, CT: Praeger, 2001). For a semiotic approach to political advertising on TV, see Frank Biocca, *Television and Political Advertising: Signs, Codes, and Images*, vol. 2 (Hillsdale, NJ: Lawrence Erlbaum Associates, 1991). For a typical content analysis of TV spots in a contemporary campaign, see Lynda Lee Kaid and Daniela V. Dimitrova, 'The Television Advertising Battleground in the 2004 Presidential Election,' *Journalism Studies* 6, no. 2 (2005): 165–75. For a discussion of the use of television in recent Ontario election campaigns, see Robert J. Drummond and Robert MacDermid, 'Elections and Campaigning: "They Blew Our Doors off on the Buy,"' in G. White, ed., *The Government and Politics of Ontario*, 5th ed. (Toronto: University of Toronto Press, 1997), 189–215. For examples of research on other forms of political media, see P. Belanger, R.K. Carty, and M. Eagles, 'The Geography of Canadian Parties' Electoral Campaigns: Leaders' Tours and Constituency Election Results,' *Political Geography* 22 (2003): 439–55; Paul Bradford Raymond, 'Shaping the News: An Analysis

of House Candidates' Campaign Communication,' in J.P. Vermeer, ed., *Campaigns in the News: Mass Media and Congressional Elections* (Westport, CT: Greenwood Press, 1987), 13–29; R.E. Miller and W.M. Richey, 'The Effects of a Campaign Brochure "Drop" in a County-Level Race for State's Attorney,' in D. Nimmo, ed., *Communication Yearbook IV* (New Brunswick, NJ: Transaction Books, 1980), 483–95; William L. Benoit and Kevin A. Stein, 'A Functional Analysis of Presidential Direct Mail Advertising,' *Communication Studies* 56, no. 3 (2005): 221; L. Martin Overby and Jay Barth, 'Radio Advertising in American Political Campaigns: The Persistence, Importance, and Effects of Narrowcasting,' *American Politics Research* 34, no. 4 (2006): 451–78; M. Nolan, 'Canadian Election Broadcasting: Political Practices and Radio Regulation 1919–1938,' *Journal of Broadcasting and Electronic Media* 29, no. 2 (1985): 175–88; Philip N. Howard, *New Media Campaigns and the Managed Citizen* (New York: Cambridge University Press, 2006); Kaid and Postelnicu, 'Political Advertising,' 265–78.

12 For an excellent, recent, comprehensive review of literature on methodological approaches, see Johnston, 'Methodologies,' 18–26. A few notable semiotic approaches: David Sullivan draws on Eco to analyse the 'image strategies' employed by United States Senator Dianne Feinstein; see his 'Images of a Breakthrough Woman Candidate: Dianne Feinstein's 1990, 1992, and 1994 Campaign Television Advertisements,' *Women's Studies in Communication* 21, no. 1 (1998): 7–26. Dan Nimmo and Arthur J. Felsberg use Leymore's semiotic theory as 'an analytical spade ... to explore the hidden myths' in television commercials of a 1978 gubernatorial race; see their 'Hidden Myths in Televised Political Advertising: An Illustration,' in L.L. Kaid, D. Nimmo, and K.R. Sanders, eds, *New Perspectives on Political Advertising* (Carbondale: Southern Illinois University Press, 1986), 248–67. Henri Quere applies Greimas's 'narrative syntax' to election posters published during the 1988 presidential election in France; see his 'French Political Advertising: A Semiological Analysis of Campaign Posters,' in L.L. Kaid, J. Gerstle, and K.R. Sanders, eds, *Mediated Politics in Two Cultures: Presidential Campaigning in the United States and France* (New York: Praeger, 1991), 85–98.

13 Paul F. Lazarsfeld, 'Administrative and Critical Communications Research,' chap. 6 in *Qualitative Analysis: Historical and Critical Essays* (Boston: Allyn and Bacon, 1972). For more recent use of Lazarsfeld's framework, see Dallas W. Smythe and Tran Van Dinh, 'On Critical and Administrative Research: A New Critical Analysis,' *Journal of Communication* 33, no. 3 (1983): 117–27; and Robert E. Babe, *Canadian Communication*

Thought: Ten Foundational Writers (Toronto: University of Toronto Press, 2000), 10–18.

14 Steven E. Finkel and John G. Geer, 'A Spot Check: Casting Doubt on the Demobilizing Effect of Attack Advertising,' *American Journal of Political Science* 42, no. 2 (1998): 592; Ron Facheaux, 'Pictures Perfect: 5 Photos Every Candidate Needs,' *Campaigns and Elections* 20, no. 9 (1999): 33. Treating the 'prevailing political and economic structures as unproblematic, and focus[ing] upon issues that pertain to the functioning of existing political and/or economic processes' (John Corner and Piers Robinson, 'Politics and Mass Media: A Response to John Street,' *Political Studies Review* 4, no. 1 [2006]: 48–54), administrative research that argues that advertising hurts the democratic process includes Stephen Ansolabehere and Shanto Iyengar, *Going Negative: How Attack Ads Shrink and Polarize the Electorate* (New York: Free Press, 1995); and K.S. Johnson-Cartee and G.A. Copeland, *Negative Political Advertising: Coming of Age* (Hillsdale: Erlbaum, 1991). For opposing views on the same issue, see Glenn W. Richardson, Jr, 'Looking for Meaning in All the Wrong Places: Why Negative Advertising Is a Suspect Category,' *Journal of Communication* 51, no. 4 (2001): 775–800; and Stevens, 'Separate.' For professional literature on how to run an effective campaign, see David D. Perlmutter, *The Manship School Guide to Political Communication* (Baton Rouge: Louisiana State University Press, 1999); Bob R.R. Greive, *The Blood, Sweat, and Tears of Political Victory … and Defeat* (Lanham, MD: University of America, Inc., 1999); Edward Schwartzman, *Political Campaign Craftsmanship: A Professional's Candid Guide to Campaigning for Public Office*, 2nd ed. (New York: Van Nostrand Reinhold, 1984); Facheaux, 'Pictures,' 33–4.

15 Barthes, *Mythologies*, trans. A. Lavers (London: Jonathan Cape, 1972), 91; Nimmo and Felsberg, 'Hidden,' 248, 267; Andrew Wernick, *Promotional Culture: Advertising, Ideology and Symbolic Expression* (London: Sage, 1991), 151.

16 Michael Schudson in Wernick, *Promotional Culture*, 188. Doubtless election advertising draws upon as well as appeals to conventional ideas and patterns of behaviour; however, as semiotics teaches, 'it reformulates them to suit its own purposes, not reflecting meaning but rather reconstituting it.' William Leiss, Stephen Kline, and Sut Jhally, *Social Communication in Advertising: Persons, Products and Images of Well-Being* (Toronto: Methuen, 1986), 152.

17 See especially Jean Baudrillard, 'Toward a Critique of the Political Economy of the Sign,' chap. 8 in *For a Critique of the Political Economy of the Sign,*

trans. Charles Levin (St Louis: Telos Press, 1981); Olu Oguibe, 'Photography and the Substance of the Image,' in C. Bell, O. Enwezor, D. Tilkin, and O. Zaya, curators, *In/sight: African Photographers, 1940 to the Present* (New York: Guggenheim Museum Publications, 1996), 237; and Susan Sontag, *On Photography* (New York: Farrar, Strauss and Giroux, 1978).

18 Wernick, *Promotional Culture*, 47n14.

19 Jack Lule, 'Enduring Image of War: Myth and Ideology in a *Newsweek* Cover,' *Journal of Popular Culture* 29, no. 1 (2001): 202–3.

20 For a lively discussion on studying history in the postmodern era, see David Paul Nord, 'The Practice of Historical Research,' in G.H. Stempel III, D. Weaver, and G.C. Wilhoit, eds, *Mass Communication Research and Theory* (Boston: Allyn and Bacon, 2003), 362–85. See also Daniel Robinson's comments on the aims and challenges of historical inquiry in his account of the emergence of opinion polling in Canadian politics, *The Measure of Democracy: Polling, Market Research, and Public Life, 1930–1945* (Toronto: University of Toronto Press, 1999), 8.

21 Benoit and Stein, 'Functional,' 221.

22 For more on the use of some of the earliest examples of campaign pamphlets in the United States and the United Kingdom, see Bernard Bailyn, ed., *Pamphlets of the American Revolution (1750–1776)* (Cambridge, MA: The Belknap Press of Harvard University Press, 1965); Silbey, *American*; and Joad Raymond's excellent *Pamphlets and Pamphleteering in Early Modern Britain* (Cambridge: Cambridge University Press, 2003).

23 Quere, 'French,' 85; Overby and Barth, 'Radio,' 469.

24 For example: Granatstein notes that the Conservative Party sent cigarettes with campaign literature to soldiers overseas during the Second World War; see, *Politics*, 191. On the use of both pro- and anti-CCF campaign literature during the 1940s, see Walter Young, *The Anatomy of a Party: The National CCF, 1932–1961* (Toronto: University of Toronto Press, 1969), 196–205; on the British Columbia Liberals eschewing federal campaign material in favour of their own provincial brand, see Joseph Wearing, *The L-Shaped Party: The Liberal Party of Canada, 1958–1980* (Toronto: McGraw-Hill Ryerson, 1981), 43; on the Progressive Party's reliance on the Canadian Council of Agriculture for election literature, see W.L. Morton, *The Progressive Party in Canada* (Toronto: University of Toronto Press, 1950), 118.

25 Alan Whitehorn, 'The Party in Elections,' chap. 4 in *Canadian Socialism: Essays on the CCF-NDP* (Toronto: Oxford University Press, 1992), acknowledges that television dominates politics today, but his historical survey of CCF/NDP election pamphlets does not stop at the invention of the TV 'polispot.' On the contrary, arguing that the pamphlet is a valuable

indicator of a party's policy platform, printed not for the party faithful, but 'directed to the more skeptical, less sophisticated, mass public' (101n2), he examines election pamphlets to trace shifts in party policy between 1935 and 1984. David Taras, 'In the Eye of the Beholder: The Power of Election Advertising,' chap. 8 in *The Newsmakers: The Media's Influence on Canadian Politics* (Scarborough, ON: Nelson, 1990), 198.

26 For an especially descriptive title, see Archibald McKellar's *An appeal to the electors of Ontario, showing how the Ontario government, as constituted in '81, rewarded the transgressors of the law and punished a detective by legislating $12,533.94 of his fees into their own pockets and into the pockets of other lawyers during the last 9 years* (no pub., 1891).

27 A few brief examples of the *Globe's* use of pamphlets: In the decades straddling the turn of the twentieth century, the newspaper: (1) noted that pamphlets were an effective way of discrediting opponents (e.g., 'Notes and Comments,' 5 June 1894, 4); (2) quoted pamphlets in order to both discredit and promote political positions (e.g., 'The Tory Policy of Reciprocity,' 15 August 1890, 4; 'All the People Some of the Time,' 20 February 1909, 6); and (3) carried no fewer than seven stories in a single month, including three front-page items, on the allegedly slanderous attacks in 'the official campaign pamphlet of the Provincial Conservative party' during the provincial election of 1911 (for the breaking story, see 'A Slanderous Campaign Sheet. Tory Literature May Have to Be Recalled,' 9 May, 1.

28 The *Liberal Conservative hand book on organization and qualification of electors* instructs its candidates that 'the true history of every matter of interest in the contest will be provided in a readable shape and printed for general distribution' (election pamphlet issued by the Liberal-Conservative Union of Ontario, 1887), 6. In fact, many early campaign pamphlets transcribed whole speeches verbatim; see for example the 187-page *Reform Government in the Dominion. Pic-nic speeches, Summer of 1877* (election pamphlet issued by the Reform Association of the Province of Ontario, 1887).

29 See *Mowat and good government. The License question. A Reform pamphlet. The license question – financial, municipal and social; Tory attacks disposed of* (election pamphlet issued by the Reform Association of the Province of Ontario, 1882). The rhetorical functions of the early pamphlet were often executed with a healthy dose of vitriol. For an especially vicious pamphlet attack, in which followers of Mowat are accused of being 'prepared to sacrifice not only their civil but also their religious liberties sooner than be thought to abandon their political leaders,' see *The Lynch-Mowat Concordat. Liberal-Conservative Party pamphlet. The Mowat-Fraser Government accused of being influenced by the 'Romish hierarchy' to substitute an expurgated version of*

the Holy Scripture for use, instead of the original whole Bible, in the schools (election pamphlet issued by the Liberal-Conservative Union of Ontario, 1883), 4.

30 For example, see Adam Crooks, *To the electors of the South Riding of Oxford* (election pamphlet issued by the Reform Party of Ontario, 1875), 15–21. See also the *Globe* article, 'May Not End This Week,' 22 February 1900, 11, which criticizes MPP Marter's claim of a budgetary surplus as listed in 'a Liberal campaign pamphlet.'

31 Regarding all 'firsts' mentioned in this paper: the claim is based upon the collection of pamphlets held at the Archives of Ontario; the Legislative Library at Queen's Park; and the Thomas Fisher Rare Book Library and Robarts Library at the University of Toronto. Incomplete though they may be, the holdings constitute the most extensive collection of provincial election material in Ontario. Judging by the incremental changes in pamphlets over time, it is unlikely that significant omissions from the present analysis would have occurred on account of a handful of lost pamphlets.

32 Liberal-Conservative Party of Ontario, *Ontario elections, 1883: Facts for the people* (election pamphlet issued by the Liberal-Conservative party of Ontario, 1883).

33 J.M. Gibson and J.T. Middleton, *Twenty-Two Years of Reform Government* (election pamphlet issued by the Liberal Party of Ontario, 1894). It is perhaps fitting that a visual breakthrough such as this should have occurred in the provincial campaign in which 'the career of Sir Oliver Mowat achieved its climax.' For more on Mowat's remarkable ability to 'broaden the base of [the Liberal Party's] original support,' see Kerr, 'Sir Oliver Mowat,' 2–3.

34 James Simpson, S.A. Corner, Margaret Haile, and John A. Kelly, *Socialist candidates for the Ontario Legislature* (election pamphlet issued by the Socialist Party of Ontario, 1902).

35 The first photograph was a black-and-white profile shot of Liberal Premier G.W. Ross; see his *The Ross Government has kept Ontario Liberals in the lead: Its record of achievement in the past; its platform of progress for the future* (election pamphlet issued by the Liberal Party of Ontario, 1905). For Rowell, see his *Liberal campaign handbook. New measures and a new leader. General Reform Association for Ontario* (election pamphlet issued by the Ontario Liberal Association, 1911). Over the following two decades, the straight-ahead bust shot became a standard part of the visual vocabulary of Ontario campaign pamphlets. See Rowell's former caucus foe and

newly minted Liberal leader H. Hartley Dewart mimic this pose in 1919: *Ontario Liberal policy: Proceedings of the provincial Liberal convention held at Toronto June 25th–26th, 1919* (election pamphlet issued by the Liberal Party of Ontario, 1919). Despite their opposing views, partisan opponents cast the same straight-on stare in their budget speech pamphlets from 1923: from the United Farmers of Ontario Government, E.C. Drury, *True economy. Common-sense and honesty. Budget address* (Toronto: W.S. Johnston and Co'y Limited, 1923); and from the government-in-waiting, W.F. Nickle, *Financial squandering and bogus surplus. Manipulation of provincial accounts. Speech on the budget* (Liberal-Conservative Association, 1923). Finally, during the year of his loss to Mitchell Hepburn, soon-to-be defeated Premier George S. Henry opted for the straight-on composition – not a surprising choice from a man whose campaign slogan was 'He Ploughs a Straight Furrow.' *Speakers' handbook. The Hon. G.S. Henry, Premier of Ontario* (election pamphlet issued by Liberal-Conservative Party of Ontario, 1934).

36 Peter Oliver, 'Sir William Hearst and the Collapse of the Ontario Conservative Party,' *Canadian Historical Review* 53, no. 1 (1972): 48.

37 Harry Nixon, *Ontario's Premier: 'A man of commonsense'* (election pamphlet issued by the Ontario Liberal Association, 1943).

38 New Democratic Party, *new Democrat: Election special* 7, no. 1 (1967): 1–16. See also 'NDP "weapon": Color photos,' *Toronto Daily Star*, 25 September 1967, 21.

39 Adam Crooks's early brochure (*Electors*, 1875, 2) explains that he has assembled a record of the Reform Government 'which I propose to circulate amongst you in pamphlet form, and which will aid you more fully to fulfill for Ontario all those national and sovereign duties which have been entrusted to it as an independent political authority.' Compare this deferential demeanour with the crass slogan emblazoned on the cover of the Liberal Party's election brochure of 1967: '*Robert Nixon tells you what you're voting for. NOW!*' A rather scary thought, upon literal interpretation. Nixon signs off, 'Sincerely'; Crooks concludes: 'I am, Your obedient servant.'

40 Though their appearance and use have been transformed over the past century, pamphlets were always free of charge: at the dawn of the twentieth century, when British MPs experimented with selling their campaign brochures 'at a penny apiece,' Ontario pamphlets continued to be distributed at no cost. 'Notes and Comments,' *Globe*, 25 November 1903, 6.

41 Eric Dowd, 'Davis Predicts 80 Seats for Tories,' *Toronto Telegram*, 25 September 1971, 4. (Unless otherwise noted, all references to the *Telegram* are from the 'Night Metro' edition.)

42 Sally Barnes, 'Davis: He's Gladhanding,' *Toronto Star*, 9 October 1971, 23.
43 On the Progressive Conservative leadership campaign of April 1971, see David Surplis, 'The Progressive Conservative Leadership Convention of 1971,' in Donald C. MacDonald, ed., *Government and Politics of Ontario* (Toronto: Macmillan, 1975), 64–76.
44 Keith Brownsey, 'The Big Blue Machine: Leadership, Organization, and Faction in the Ontario Progressive Conservative Party, 1971–85,' *Ontario History* 91, no. 1 (1999): 66.
45 Senator Norman Atkins, interview with author, 7 November 2006. In *Bill Davis: A Biography by Claire Hoy* (Toronto: Methuen, 1985), Hugh Macaulay, Roy McMurtry, and, of course, Atkins are identified as the original group from which Ad Hoc Enterprises was born. See chap. 7, 'The Big Blue Machine,' 77–95.
46 Hoy, *Bill*, 87.
47 Atkins, interview.
48 Dr Gerry Caplan, interview by author, 6 November 2006.
49 Jonathan Manthorpe, *The Power and the Tories: Ontario Politics – 1943 to the Present* (Toronto: Macmillan, 1974), 189.
50 Final poll results were as follows: PC, 78 seats (44 per cent pop. vote); Liberal, 20 seats (28 per cent pop. vote); NDP, 19 seats (27 per cent pop. vote). For post-election reviews of the Big Blue campaign, see Vince Devitt, 'The Making of the Premier at Theodore's Restaurant,' *Toronto Star*, 23 October 1971, 21; Fraser Kelly, 'Ads, Jobs and Separate Schools Aided Tory Win,' *Toronto Telegram*, 22 October 1971, 16; Hugh Winsor and Peter Mosher, 'Davis' Ad Campaign Wins Praise from Liberal Strategist,' *Globe and Mail*, 22 October 1971, 10.
51 Atkins, interview.
52 For an especially good journalistic account of the overarching campaign marketing and imaging strategy, see Ross H. Munro, 'What's Happening to Politics?' *Globe and Mail*, 29 October 1971, 1 and 4. John Robarts's election campaign of 1967 also used television commercials, but they were policy-oriented pleas containing relatively few distinct images, and all were shot in black and white. In stark contrast, Davis's television commercials, both the 'free-time' and 'paid' spots, mixed months of colour film footage into a series of ads that include: Davis delivering public speeches (and drinking from a beer mug, on-stage at a rock-concert); Davis walking, talking, and laughing with his family (and dog) at their summer home in Georgian Bay; Davis answering questions in a one-on-one interview setting; as well as 'person-on-the-street' endorsements, in which a plethora

of Ontario voters candidly extol Davis's virtues as a 'trustworthy guy' who 'deserves to lead this province' ('P.C. Party – Bill Davis: 1971 Free-time, Paid Ads and Related Material' [York University Election Broadcast Project, Principal investigator, Fred Fletcher, n.d.]). The catchy tune that played in the background of Davis's TV ads was, according to composer Ben McPeek, 'a combination of The Ballad of the Green Berets and a Place to Stand.' See Ross H. Munro, 'Film Crews Try Hard to Give Davis Warmth but Miss Spontaneous Moments,' *Globe and Mail*, 30 September 1971, 4. Recalling the first time McPeek shared his work with the Ad Hoc group, Atkins says, 'When he came in and played the material, we knew right away – it was a very exciting moment!' Atkins, interview.

53 Hoy, *Bill*, 93.
54 Barthes, 'Rhetoric,' 38–9.
55 Ibid., 42–3.
56 Bill Davis, *Bill Davis* (election pamphlet issued by the Progressive Conservative Party of Ontario, 1971), 2.
57 Rosemary Spiers, *Out of the Blue: The Fall of the Tory Dynasty in Ontario* (Toronto: Macmillan, 1986), 16; Hoy, *Bill*, 94.
58 Davis, *Bill*, 4.
59 The message is familiar, even today. The irony, of course, is that politicians intent on demonstrating their 'averageness' often come from anything but average backgrounds. A recent example of this strategy was demonstrated by George W. Bush – the Governor of Texas and son of a former U.S. president – who won the U.S. general election of 2000 by campaigning as an 'outsider.'
60 Sid Noel, 'The Ontario Political Culture: An Interpretation,' in White, ed., *The Government and Politics of Ontario*, 60.
61 The 'Selling the Premier' series, all written by Ross H. Munro, consists of: Part 1: 'What's Happening to Politics?' 29 September 1971, 1; Part 2: 'Film Crews Try Hard to Give Davis Warmth,' 30 September 1971, 4; and Part 3: 'How Public Opinion Polls Helped to Decide Campaign Strategy,' 1 October 1971, 4. In both news coverage and editorial commentary, the *Toronto Star* repeatedly remarked on the Conservatives' extravagant marketing campaign and criticized party and premier for failing to reveal how much money was at their disposal and how much was being used to sell the premier to the public. See, for example, Editorial, 'Selling a Premier,' *Toronto Star*, 1 October 1971, 6; Jim Robinson, 'Bill Davis: A Candidate Wrapped in Premier's Clothing,' *Toronto Star*, 12 October 1971, 10; see also the *Star*'s political cartoon mocking Davis's excessive marketing job and depicting

Davis atop a mountain, having his face powdered in front of movie cameras, while a man with a megaphone in the background faces a pyramid of choristers and yells, 'Ready with Handel's Hallelujah chorus? OK, Now let's hear it for Bill Davis!' 14 October 1971, 6.

62 Street, 'Celebrity,' 85.

63 Davis, *Bill*, 7.

64 A.K. McDougall, *John P. Robarts: His Life and Government* (Toronto: University of Toronto Press, 1986), 261; Walter G. Pitman, 'The Limits to Diversity: The Separate School Issue in the Politics of Ontario,' in D.C. MacDonald, ed., *Government and Politics of Ontario* (Toronto: Macmillan, 1975), 30. Calling attention to the decisiveness to which many of the 'streeters' refer in Davis's television ads, in the pamphlet, the premier is quoted as saying, 'In the Spadina Expressway decision, we said the cities are for people, not for automobiles.' Davis, *Bill*, 11. One pollster hired by the Ad Hoc group explained that the firmness with which the expressway was stopped was as important as the policy itself, noting that the Spadina move 'gives many people an idea of what kind of guy [Davis] is who would make that kind of decision.' See comments of Robert Teeter in Munro, 'How Public Opinion Polls,' 4.

65 Noel, 'Ontario Political Culture,' 51.

66 Donald C. MacDonald, 'Ontario's Political Culture: Conservatism with a Progressive Component,' *Ontario History* 86, no. 4 (1994): 297; John Wilson, 'The Ontario Political Culture,' in *Government and Politics of Ontario*, ed. D.C. MacDonald, 233; Kerr says of Mowat: 'His stated aim was "to be a friend of all" but to be caught by none,' 'Sir Oliver Mowat,' 3. In Robert Bothwell's opinion, 'none of Mowat's many successors as Liberal leader had the same sure touch, the same ability to compromise or to appeal to widely scattered sections of the province's population' – *A Short History of Ontario* (Edmonton: Hurtig, 1986), 96. As David Mills puts it, 'the 'conservative liberalism of [Mowat's] administration began a tradition that continued to be successful well into the twentieth century' – 'Ontario,' in Doug Orwam, ed., *Canadian History: A Reader's Guide*, vol. 2: *Confederation to the Present* (Toronto: University of Toronto Press, 1994), 335. For the definitive work on Ontario's longest-serving premier, see A. Margaret Evans, *Sir Oliver Mowat* (Toronto: University of Toronto Press, 1992).

67 Barthes, 'Rhetoric,' 42–4; italics in original.

68 Davis, *Bill*, 10.

69 This populist visual landscape complements Davis's explicit 'promises of greater grassroots involvement' in politics which he offered during the

1971 leadership race. Desmond Morton, 'Introduction: People and Politics of Ontario,' in Donald C. MacDonald, ed., *Government and Politics of Ontario*, 8. It should be pointed out that in Morton's opinion, these promises were never delivered.

70 Liberal Party of Ontario, *Robert Nixon Tells You What You're Voting For. NOW!* (1967).

71 Manthorpe, *Power and the Tories*, 71.

72 Brownsey, 'Big Blue Machine,' 67.

73 Atkins, interview. In fact, Atkins admits that the leader-centric campaign may have gone so far as to anger some rank-and-file Tory members at the local level. This is not surprising because, as Hoy recounts, 'everything was *Davis*, not the Conservative party. Local billboards, for example, exhorted, "Joe Blow for Bill Davis"; the party got a tiny credit line'; see, *Bill*, 83. The irony of a leader-centric campaign in a parliamentary democracy was not lost on at least one Ontario newspaper reader. The day before the election, the *Toronto Star* published a letter to the editor from one James Michael III (of Don Mills), which read in part: 'It is a pity that Premier William Davis couldn't declare Ontario a republic so that he could rightfully hold presidential elections under the slogan, "Elect a Davis government."' See 'Why Not Declare Ontario a Republic?' *Toronto Star*, 20 October 1971, 7.

74 Manthorpe, *Power and the Tories*, 189; Jim Robinson, 'Lewis Mocks "Made-In-Detroit" Davis Campaign,' *Toronto Star*, 18 October 1971, 12; 'Leaders Coy on Campaign Cash,' *Toronto Telegram*, 14 September 1971, 28; Atkins, interview.

75 Stuart Hall, 'The Determinations of News Photographs,' in S. Cohen and J. Young, eds, *The Manufacture of News: A Reader* (Beverly Hills, CA: Sage, 1973), 176, italics in original; Ann Reynolds, 'Visual Stories,' in L. Cooke and P. Wollen, eds, *Visual Display: Culture beyond Appearances* (Seattle: Bay Press, 1995), 82–109.

76 The quotation is from Wernick, *Promotional Culture*, 186.

77 Daniel Robinson, *Measure of Democracy*, 163.

78 Hon. Bill Davis, interview by author, 17 November 2006. While both men were fascinating interlocutors, generous with their time and thoughts, here Davis's modesty should be counterbalanced by Atkins's unapologetic (and, indeed, more accurate) statement that 'that campaign was one of the earmark campaigns in Ontario history.' Atkins, interview.

79 Wearing, *Strained Relations*, 95; Bruce I. Newman, *The Mass Marketing of Politics: Democracy in an Age of Manufactured Images* (Thousand Oaks, CA: Sage, 1999), 94.

80 Jonathan W. Rose, *Making 'Pictures in Our Heads': Government Advertising in Canada* (Westport, CT: Praeger, 2000), 2.
81 See Barthes, *Mythologies*, 142–5 (italics in original) for a discussion of myth as 'depoliticized speech.'
82 Morton, 'Introduction,' 11.
83 Although Davis did not have 'the natural ability to communicate with the nation simply by looking into a television camera that had captured the country for Pierre Trudeau three years before' (Manthorpe, *Power and the Tories*, 190), the fact that the federal Liberal Party's 'brilliant, if ambivalent, election campaign' of 1968 (Stephen Clarkson, *The Big Red Machine: How the Liberal Party Dominates Canadian Politics* [Vancouver: UBC Press, 2005], 22) was a source of Tory inspiration in 1971 was pointed out frequently in the journalistic accounts of the Ontario campaign already cited and was mentioned during my interview with Atkins. On Trudeau's campaign of 1968, which, in the words of Liberal strategist Keith Davey, was 'not an election at all, it was a coronation' (quoted in Christina McCall-Newman, *Grits: An Intimate Portrait of the Liberal Party* [Toronto: Macmillan, 1982], 117), see also J. Murray Beck, *Pendulum of Power: Canada's Federal Elections* (Scarborough, ON: Prentice Hall, 1968), 401–17; and Wearing, *L-Shaped Party*, especially 190–2.
84 Richardson, Jr, *Pulp Politics*, 139.
85 See Jean-François Lyotard, 'Defining the Postmodern,' in Lisa Appignanesi, ed., *Postmodernism: ICA Documents* (London: Free Association Books, 1989), 9.
86 Caplan, interview; Bothwell, *Short History of Ontario*, 174.
87 Kline, 'Image Politics,' 147.
88 Raymond Williams offers a thought-provoking insight into one of the recurring themes of image politics, the vision of Utopia: 'If the meanings and values generally operative in the society give no answers to, no means of negotiating, problems of death, lonleliness, frustration, the need for identity and respect, then the magical system [of advertising] must come, mixing its charms and expedients with reality in easily available forms, and binding the weakness to the condition which it has created.' 'Advertising: The Magic System,' in *Culture and Materialism: Selected Essays*, 2nd ed. (London: Verso, 1995), 190.
89 The word 'classic' is used here to distinguish the ideal-type superhero of the Golden Age of comics, whom Wright describes as being 'aligned … squarely on the side of established authority,' from the darker, even self-doubting characters of the Silver Age. See Bradford W. Wright, *Comic Book*

Nation: The Transformation of Youth Culture in America (Baltimore: Johns Hopkins University Press, 2001), 184. For more on this distinction, see Arthur Berger, 'Comics and Culture,' *Journal of Popular Culture* 5, no. 1 (1971): 171–5.

90 Mila Bongco, *Reading Comics: Language, Culture, and the Concept of the Super-hero in Comic Books* (New York: Garland, 2000), 104.

91 Reinhold Reitberger and Wolfgang Fuchs, *Comics: Anatomy of a Mass Medium* (Boston: Little, Brown, 1972), 100.

92 Although Lang and Trimble point out that 'Superman demonstrates that power and humility can exist in one form,' (see 'Whatever Happened to the Man of Tomorrow? An Examination of the American Monomyth and the Comic Book Superhero,' *Journal of Popular Culture* 22, no. 3 [1988]: 160), the fact that 'averageness' is one of the qualities inherent in the superhero's secret identity does not make the word redundant in the Davis metaphor. On the contrary, its threefold purpose is to: (1) remind the reader that the superhero being evoked is the straightforward, classic one of the Golden Era of comics (the *average* one, as opposed to more recent and complex iterations); (2) highlight the attempt to frame Davis as the guy next door. Referring to him simply as a 'superhero' runs the risk of downplaying his ordinary qualities and overemphasizing his extraordinary ones. In fact, it might even be helpful to think of *Averageness* as Davis's signature superpower – he is the mighty *Averageman!* After all, it is by virtue of his unequivocal confession of being average that he becomes invincible; and (3) define election-pamphlet-Davis with an oxymoron, in order to draw out the myriad contradictions in a message that makes a spectacular cel-ebration of humility.

93 Brownsey, 'Big Blue Machine,' 67.

94 Barnes, 'Davis: He's Gladhanding'; Atkins, interview.

95 Davis, *Bill*, 10.

96 Bongco, *Reading Comics*, 104.

97 Robin Varnum and Christina T. Gibbons, 'Introduction,' in R. Varnum and C.T. Gibbons, eds, *The Language of Comics: Word and Image* (Jackson: University Press of Mississippi, 2001), ix.

98 David Carrier, *The Aesthetics of Comics* (University Park: The Pennsylvania State University Press, 2000), 74.

99 Ian Gordon, *Comic Strips and Consumer Culture: 1890–1945* (Washington, DC: Smithsonian Institution Press, 1998), esp. 8–12, and chap. 6, 'The Comic Book: Comics as an Independent Commodity, 1939–1945,' 128–51; Matthew P. McAllister, Edward H. Sewell, Jr, and Ian Gordon, 'Introducing

Comics and Ideology,' in M.P. McAllister, E.H. Sewell, Jr, and I. Gordon, eds, *Comics and Ideology* (New York: Peter Lang, 2001), 1–13; Bongco, *Reading Comics*, esp. 115–18; and Wright, *Comic Book Nation*, esp. 184–5. On a distinctly Canadian comic book superhero who, while in print, 'legitimized the national identity and reinforced the conception of Canada as a "peaceable kingdom,"' see Ryan Edwardson, 'The Many Lives of Captain Canuck: Nationalism, Culture, and the Creation of a Canadian Comic Book Superhero,' *The Journal of Popular Culture* 37, no. 2 (2003): 184–201.

100 Manthorpe, *Power and the Tories*, 212.

101 Barthes, *Mythologies*, 91–2.

102 Wernick, *Promotional Culture*, 35; Bongco, *Reading Comics*, xv, 92.

103 Wernick, *Promotional Culture*, 18.

104 'Davis Claims Party Label Less Relevant,' *Toronto Telegram*, 13 October 1971, 6; 'PC Name Not So Relevant Now,' *Toronto Star* 14 October 1971, 10.

105 Atkins in Devitt, 'Making of the Premier,' 21.

106 For more on the 'transformation of visibility,' see Thompson, *Media and Modernity*, 119–48.

PART TWO

Historiography and Media History

8 Whence and Whither: The Historiography of Canadian Broadcasting

MARY VIPOND

In what state is the history of Canadian broadcasting? Where has it come from, and where should it go in the future? My comments on this broad topic will be a combination of the empirical, the analytical, and the personal. My goal is to provide an overview and assessment of the past and contemporary literature, to point out emphases and lacunae, and to conclude with some thoughts about the directions scholarship in Canadian broadcasting history might move in the future. Although I have gathered a considerable amount of information about the past and current historiography, I make no claim to complete comprehensiveness, and I apologize in advance to those whose work has been inadvertently omitted or underplayed.

I will begin with a reiteration of some observations I have made on various aspects of the historiography of Canadian broadcasting over the past ten years. In 1997 I published an article entitled '"Please Stand By for That Report": The Historiography of Early Canadian Radio,' in *Fréquence/Frequency*, the journal of the late, lamented Association for the Study of Canadian Radio and Television (ASCRT/AERTC). As the title suggests, in that article I examined only the *radio* history produced – in English and in French – prior to the late 1990s. I then followed up more generally on the subject of the historiography of *mass media* in Canada in my presidential address to the Canadian Historical Association (CHA) in 2003.[1] This then is my third foray into this territory; it is not only an update but again has a slightly different focus – I am looking here at the state of the literature on the history of *broadcasting*, radio and television, in Canada at the present moment.[2]

In what follows I will be highlighting the work produced by academically trained historians. This is not because I think that they are the only ones who can do broadcasting history – far from it. The topic lends itself perfectly to multidisciplinary and interdisciplinary approaches, and is obviously of interest to scholars in communications, sociology, literature, and political science, to name just a few other disciplines. But historians are trained in particular skills, especially the assiduous search for and interpretation of archival sources, as well as in certain disciplinary perspectives, particularly the determination to historicize, that is, to contextualize the object of study in its unique time and place. Because I am a historian, I am especially concerned that my colleagues have neglected the field of broadcasting history, and I believe that both the field and the discipline are the poorer for it.

The Historiography of Early Canadian Radio

> Too little radio history has been written in Canada, and too little of it by academic historians.[3]

Serious work on Canadian broadcasting history really began in the 1960s; with one small exception that work was entirely in English.[4] There are several important characteristics of these early works – which include the still-standard studies by Frank Peers and other well-known dissertations, books, and articles by John O'Brien, Austin Weir, and Margaret Prang.[5] To begin with, few of these students of early radio (and to some extent television) history were historians. Frank Peers was an ex-CBC employee and political science professor; Austin Weir's employment with the CBC and its predecessor bodies went back to the 1920s; Jack O'Brien wrote his study of the Canadian Radio League as a dissertation for a communications program. Of this 'classic' list, only Margaret Prang was a historian – and she wrote only one article on radio history. The common theme of all these works was the examination of the political means by which Canadian governments endeavoured to foster the development of national broadcasting in order to combat a perceived cultural threat from the United States. They concentrated on government policy, regulation, and most importantly on the CBC as the alternative model to the evident danger of the 'Americanization' (which was also a code for the 'commercialization') of the Canadian mass media. The sources used by this 'traditional' school were mainly government and newspaper reports, supplemented with some available private papers. With respect to both focus and source material these scholars were very much products of their times. Their stress on the public broadcaster followed from the similar emphasis of the Massey Royal Commission of 1949–51; their unease about the Americanization of Canadian broadcasting also followed from the concerns of the Massey Commission and was part and parcel of the politics, especially the Liberal politics, of the 1960s.[6]

These works laid the foundation for all subsequent Canadian broadcasting history, and we are indebted to them. In retrospect, however, it is easy to see that their range was quite narrow. Basing their research primarily on official documents, these scholars neglected many aspects of historical broadcasting, most especially the program content, the social impact of these new media on audiences, and the tension between regional interests and the centrally based national network of the CBC. These scholars also paid very little attention to private broadcasting, except to cast it in the same negative light as those who had originally promoted the creation of the CBC. The woman from Venus (or indeed from the United States) trying to learn something about Canadian radio and television history in, say, 1980, would have had little inkling that the vast majority of Canadian stations were owned by private broadcasters and that the vast majority of Canadian listeners seemed to prefer their popular and commercialized offerings.[7] Neither would she have known what the broadcast programs were, or how people made sense of them in their lives.

The Second Wave of Canadian Broadcasting Historians

Beginning in the1970s and continuing through the 1980s and early 1990s, a 'second generation' began expanding the focus of broadcasting history, although again it may be noted that not very many academically trained historians were involved. Some of these scholars continued to work on issues of broadcasting policy but offered more sophisticated analyses. Ken Dewar, Marc Raboy, and Michel Filion, for example, threw open to question some of the premises of the first generation, most importantly taking issue with previous assumptions about the virtue and the necessity of the CBC – although they continued to place it at the heart of the story.[8] They used the same kinds of official sources as the earlier generation, but re-examined them, and most particularly in the case of Raboy and Filion introduced troubling questions about the extent to which a centralizing impulse that was at the very least insensitive to the different cultural priorities of francophone Canadians and of the regions was embedded in federal broadcasting policy and in the

CBC. Raboy also challenged the national broadcasting system for its failure to provide a real alternative to either the capitalist corporation or the managerial state. Again, these works tended to be overviews spanning large time periods, they were based mainly on print sources, largely official, and they paid little attention to either programs or listeners.

More innovatively, in the mid-1970s scholars in literature and sociology, in both Quebec and English Canada, began to look beyond policy to radio and television programs and their social impact. In Quebec the names of two literary scholars, Pierre Pagé and Renée Legris,[9] stand out, as does the work of my Concordia colleagues Howard Fink and John Jackson, now retired from the English and sociology departments respectively.[10] This work was more theoretical, more interdisciplinary, and based on the discovery and occasionally the actual salvaging of old program scripts.[11] Most importantly, these scholars began to ask questions about the role of radio in the impact of modernity on Canadian and Quebec society – how it was simultaneously an instrument of progress in democratizing communications, bolstering indigenous popular culture, and fostering artistic experimentation while at the same time often sending mixed or even very traditional messages oriented toward ensuring social stability. These scholars did not concern themselves too much about whether the programs were broadcast by private or public stations, although at least on the English side they tended to use CBC materials because they were more accessible.

One scholar, a former television newscaster who later trained as a historian, falls somewhat between the two schools. Michael J. Nolan's first book, on Alan Plaunt's role in promoting public broadcasting in Canada, was firmly situated in the traditional school.[12] Subsequently, however, he published several articles aimed at broadening the historiography to include commercial, privately owned stations, and his last two books have been a biography of Walter J. Blackburn, owner of the London Free Press and its radio (and television) station CFPL and an institutional study of the CTV network.[13] Although Nolan does not delve much into the literary, the sociological, or the theoretical, he has made an explicit effort through most of his career to attend to something other than the CBC, perhaps because his own journalistic career prior to becoming an academic was in the private sector.

The outstanding name in English-Canadian broadcasting history in what I have termed the period of the 'second generation' is that of Paul Rutherford, whose When Television Was Young: Primetime Canada, 1952–1967, published in 1990, remains the definitive account of early television. *Primetime Canada* is notable for its holistic approach, which combines institutional and intellectual history with program analysis and audience response.[14] Although a very lengthy and very rich book, it is nevertheless not completely comprehensive. Like virtually all the work discussed so far, its focus is on the English national network level, although it includes both the CBC and CTV networks. Rutherford is the first academically trained historian I have mentioned so far who seriously engaged in content analysis. The scope of *When Television Was Young* was so broad that it perhaps had an unfortunate effect: rather than stimulating more interest in media history it may have left a generation of students and their supervisors with the impression that there was nothing more to uncover – that Rutherford had 'done it all.'

The 2003 Survey

As mentioned previously, in 2003 I returned to the topic of the historical literature on the Canadian mass media in an address to the Canadian Historical Association (CHA), focusing particularly on why Canadian academic historians do not seem to be very interested in writing about the history of the mass media. At that time I analysed the Register of Dissertations (both MA and PhD) produced by the CHA to collect all references to the history of newspapers, magazines, film, radio, and television, in English and French, about *any country*. This database mainly – but by no means entirely – picks up theses and dissertations written in history departments. The results were depressing. Out of 3300 in-progress or completed theses, exactly 81 fulfilled my criteria, of which 66 were being written in history departments. I took that as a sign that the historical community does not seem to think that the history of the mass media is very important. Even more astonishing to me was the fact that only *16 out of 3300* involved the study of television, surely the dominant mass medium of the second half of the twentieth century.

Why Is This So?

Canadian historians are suspicious of communication and cultural studies.[15]

Before turning to my survey of the current situation, I would like to pause for a moment to discuss what I think are some of the reasons why the history of the mass media, or more narrowly of broadcasting, has been so neglected, particularly by those trained as historians. I think there are five main factors. First (although this is somewhat less the case in the twenty-first century), for the older generation broadcasting was simply too recent an invention – it wasn't history, but political science. This particularly may explain the lack of serious research into the impact of television on Canadian society. Secondly, interest in any research area is cumulative – if there were few broadcasting historians in one generation, there were few mentors, and therefore few students in the next generation. Given that almost none of the first generation of broadcasting historians worked in history departments, their influence on graduate students was even more attenuated. More importantly, and still a problem, the archival sources were difficult to use; they involved types of interpretation and theoretical considerations that historians were not trained for, and which were often difficult to apply retrospectively. Fourthly, equally importantly, and again still a problem, the sources were difficult to *find*. Broadcasters, especially private broadcasters, rarely saved their programs, especially their everyday 'typical' programs, and historians do need an archive! Finally, I think there was an even more important reason for historians' neglect of broadcasting history until very recently. Radio and television were too *popular*, and too *American*. For historians, to use Paul Attallah's phrase, radio and television have been 'phobic objects.'[16] How many historians wanted to spend years of their lives studying a form that they considered trivial, superficial, artificial, inauthentic, and damaging to all they believed in – whether the Canadian national project, le projet national du Québec, social justice for disadvantaged members of our society, or, at a more immediate level, the willingness of their students to read books and write coherently?[17] Again, it seems this may help explain why those who did indulge in broadcasting history chose to work on public broadcasting, on the CBC. I think this final explanation is particularly important because it also encompasses those who have recently turned to the 'new cultural history' but who seem to prefer to study the 'linguistic turn' as manifest in court trials, advice literature, or museum displays rather. than in radio and television. Even when the mass media are used as sources by those interested in cultural questions, they are often considered to be transparent – that is, the nature, structure, and history of the medium are either ignored or dealt with briefly and superficially; it does not become an element in the analysis. In other words, even those who go to great lengths to use broadcasting sources for their projects still too often fail to focus on either radio or television as *the object of study.*

Why Does It Matter?

> If you are concerned about the environment, if you're concerned about women's rights, health care, foreign policy, Iraq, the economy ... If you're concerned about any of these issues, you MUST be concerned about the media.[18]

John B. Thompson argued in his 1993 book *Media and Modernity* that the development of the media was 'interwoven in fundamental ways' with other development processes to *constitute modernity itself*.[19] The media are central agencies of self- and community-formation in the modern world. Quite simply, the mass media have been one of the major social and political forces in modern societies. Through them we gain much (although certainly not all) of our access to the outside world, much (although again not all) of our entertainment, much (although not all) of our socialization. We live, and have lived since the turn of the twentieth century at least, in a mediatized world. We cannot fully understand that world unless we study, *as objects in and of themselves*, the media in general and broadcast media in particular. To put it another way, as various traditional social institutions such as churches, voluntary organizations, and local communities have withered away throughout the twentieth century, the mass media, and again I would specify television (and at the end of the century, the internet), have grown in influence – indeed, have thrived. Politics, leisure, education, interpersonal communication – I could go on and on – have all been fundamentally transformed in the last century by the flourishing of the broadcast media. We need to know *their* history to understand *our* history.

The Current State of the Field

In preparation for this article, and in order to supplement and broaden my previous survey, I scoured not only the CHA Register of Dissertations but other sources such as the ProQuest dissertations database, *America: History and Life*, the thesis listings and book reviews in the *Canadian Journal of Communication*, the curricula vitae of the members of the Canadian Media History listserve, and the programs of the 2006 conferences of the Canadian Historical Association and the Canadian Communications Association. I limited my search to material written or published between 2000 and 2006, and to academic rather than popular works.[20]

Let me sum up the results of this latest survey in three points. First, while classification and quantification are problematic for a variety of reasons, I was pleasantly surprised at the number of 'hits' I got. The most important caveat is that many of the works that turned up in this survey not only were about radio and TV history, but also often included print history or were more generally about 'communications in Canada.' So, for example, a PhD dissertation on the history of aboriginal media activism in Canada (produced in an anthropology department) has only one chapter on broadcasting, the rest being on print publications.[21] Another PhD dissertation, a biography of Graham Spry (completed in a history department), while of course discussing Spry's role in lobbying for public broadcasting in the 1930s and again in the 1960s and 1970s, also covers many other aspects of his career and his political activism – indeed neither radio nor broadcasting is a 'keyword' for this thesis on the main ProQuest dissertation database.[22]

Secondly, as I mentioned above with respect to the 2003 survey, a number of these works do not actually focus on analysing the broadcast media. So, for example, a book by Magali Deleuze entitled *L'une et l'autre indépendance 1954–1964: les médias au Québec et la guerre d'Algérie* is not really *about* the media per se, but about the various positions of Quebec intellectuals, conservative, liberal, nationalist, and anti-nationalist, on that war.[23] Again, much of the study is based on print sources. My sweep also picked up four other books, all published in 2000, which although not specifically about radio and television, do address issues of communications, culture, and political economy in Canada. These are Gerry Friesen's *Citizens and Nation*, Robert Babe's *Canadian Communication Thought*, Jonathan Rose's *Making 'Pictures in Our Heads,'* and Paul Rutherford's *Endless Propaganda*.[24] These monographs are of interest and relevance to broadcasting scholars, but none of them focuses primarily on the history of Canadian radio and television in any of its facets. The same may be said of some other monographs that have appeared more recently, including Paul Heyer's and J.A. Watson's biographies of Harold Innis.[25]

Nevertheless, there have been several books that do address broadcasting as part of their central problematic; there are articles being written and papers being given, and books are in progress.[26] Moreover there are many more MA and PhD dissertations being completed than my earlier survey uncovered. I cannot claim to have located every last project, but according to my count nine or ten PhD dissertations, five or six MA theses, and twenty-five to thirty articles on Canadian broadcasting history have been produced since 2000. Although there seems to be a temporary dearth of monographs, there is progress in both a quantitative and a qualitative sense. A professor wishing to teach an advanced course on Canadian broadcasting history currently has considerably less difficulty in mounting a curriculum than was the case not too long ago. My third general remark about this new literature unfortunately reiterates one I made about both the earlier periods: the considerable majority of these works are not written by academically trained historians or for history degrees.

A few more specific observations may be made about this most recent crop of works, mostly of a positive nature. To begin with, many of these pieces are about 'cultural' topics – that is, they are about presentation and representation, about *programs*. These are the works that tend often, as with their earlier counterparts, to pay little attention to the medium of radio or television per se, but rather to concentrate on the *subject* of the representation. But many of them do examine radio and TV programs for their aural and visual components, for their mediatized effects, and not simply for their texts. This is progress, because it suggests that scholars and students are becoming more comfortable with semiotic and discourse analysis. Moreover, this trend also suggests that today's broadcasting historians are gaining better access to archives of historical radio and television programs. To cite only two improvements, the reorganization of the audio-visual materials held at Library and Archives Canada has facilitated searches for CBC programming in particular, and the creation of the AV Preservation Trust bodes well for the salvation of more of our historical audio-visual material in both public and private hands.[27]

Among the current crop of monographs, dissertations, theses, and articles that analyse cultural representation, there are a number of subgroups. One particularly strong area is the study of the representation of aboriginal peoples in the media, which includes both how the mainstream media portray First Nations and also how they represent themselves. Of the former I would note several articles by Mary Jane Miller on aboriginals in television drama;[28] of the latter, particular mention must be made of one of the few extended institutional studies in Canadian television history to have appeared in the last six years, Lorna Roth's *Something New in the Air: The Story of First Peoples Television Broadcasting in Canada*.[29] While not strictly historical, there have also been studies of the media presentation of contemporary events involving First Nations peoples, including anthropologist Sandra Lambertus's book on the confrontation at Gustafsen Lake and Roger Larose's PhD dissertation on the televisualization of the Oka affair.[30] This interest in representation of aboriginal peoples is also notable because there seems to have been little or nothing published in the recent past on the historical media portrayal of ethnic minorities in Canada.[31] There is also a decided paucity of works examining the past representation of women in the broadcast media, or of other groups much studied by social historians, such as workers or children or homosexuals. These lacunae are double-barrelled. Not only is there little material on how minorities have been represented in the mainstream media, but there has also been a woeful lack of attention paid to the means by which those under- or misrepresented have been able to gain access to alternative broadcasting outlets such as community radio.[32] One notable and theoretically sophisticated exception to this rule is Patricia Mazepa's PhD dissertation on how various groups of Canadians (socialists, women, religious organizations, etc.) attempted to construct democratic alternatives to both commercial and state media, which deals in part with the broadcast media.[33]

Another group of works study particular programs and series for the ways they both revealed and created the issues and zeitgeists of their eras.[34] E.J. Talbot's article on Robert Choquette's 'urban fables' broadcast on both public and private Montreal radio stations in the 1930s and 1940s is a good example, although the analysis centres entirely on the written texts rather than expanding on the aural experience for which the texts were intended. Some of these pieces, like Robert Cupido's on the famous radio broadcast connected to the Diamond Jubilee of Confederation in 1927, are spin-offs of larger projects; they too vary greatly in the extent to which they take the broadcasting medium into account. Following from their early interest in the role of radio as an instrument of modernization in Quebec, Pierre Pagé and Renée Legris have turned to the study of the representation of the Catholic Church in Quebec media.[35] Their articles in *Études d'histoire religieuse / Historical Studies* in 2002 examine both the form and the content of religious programming in Quebec between the 1930s and the 1970s in the context not only of Quebec but of media history. For the most part these scholars have lacked access to tapes or videos, so have been forced to analyse broadcast programs from the written texts alone (and often even these are difficult to procure). This practice is inevitable, but it multiplies the challenges faced by the broadcasting historian. Some have been more successful than others at reading continuities and scripts with their ultimate purpose as radio or television presentations in mind.

Another area that has been noticeably active, historical in another sense, and that also involves the analysis of representations, is the study of the presentation of history on television. Partly, of course, this has been the result of a surge in such program series, particularly the 'Heritage Minutes' produced with money from the Bronfman Foundation (now Historica), on which there have been at least two PhD dissertations, and the CBC's *Canada: A People's History*, which has (so far) resulted in a crop of opinion pieces by well-known historians (and others) and again at least one thesis, not to mention Mark Starowicz's own book about his vision of the series he produced.[36] On the French side, one may note the PhD dissertation of Frédéric Demers on the popular television series *Les filles de Caleb*, a historical romance.[37]

The contemporary interest in historical broadcast programming extends in other directions as well. David Hogarth's *Documentary Television in Canada: From National Public Service to Global Marketplace* provides a valuable overview of an important genre, and his articles have expanded the analysis to radio documentaries and into a transnational context.[38] Anne MacLennan and Anu Sahota have produced theses (and in MacLennan's case, articles) which analyse radio program schedules and their conceptualization.[39] There have been two PhD theses on the use of broadcast media in educational settings.[40] Although this list of works on historical broadcast programming is undoubtedly not complete, it does indicate that there has been a definite upsurge in interest in examining the cultural meaning of broadcasting. Even if the analysis is not always as medium-specific as it might be, the increasing number of studies examining representations in radio or television programs is a positive sign, and we can hope that at least some of these scholars will begin to guide their own students toward similar essay and thesis topics.

The growing interest in cultural representations does not mean that policy studies have been completely pushed aside. On the contrary, a number of works that investigate broadcasting policy either as the central topic or as part of larger studies on cultural policy have been completed in the last few years. These include PhD dissertations by Norman Fennema on religious broadcasting policy, Ryan Edwardson on Canadian content, and Ira Wagman on audio-visual policy.[41] Political scientists have also shown considerable interest in the impact of television on recent election results.[42] Although not really historical, because they involve 'real-time' analysis, these pieces nevertheless demonstrate the extent to which those who study politics realize that the mass media have fundamentally altered the practice of modern politics. It is unfortunate that historians seem to have lost interest in this intricate reciprocal relationship, which has been significant throughout the broadcasting era.

Last but by no means least, one of the most important developments of the recent past has been the emergence of academic interest in the history of radio and TV in the local context. This is significant in part because local radio (and to a lesser extent television) was historically in the hands of private broadcasters. While the traditional lack of academic interest in Canadian private broadcasting has not been completely overcome, these local studies almost inevitably must pay heed to this sector.[43] Nadine Kozak, Bonnie Wagner, and Stacy Lorenz have all written on aspects of broadcasting on the prairies, and Bradley Kevin Humeniuk on the private radio stations at the Lakehead.[44] One fine thesis looks at television representations of Toronto 'from Hogtown to Megacity,'[45] and on the eastern coast one must make special mention of the ongoing project of Jeff Webb on the history of radio in Newfoundland – by far the most complete examination of radio as both institution and vehicle of regional cultural values yet undertaken in Canada.[46] A second reason for finding this 'on-the-ground' work so encouraging is that it is based in local sources, sometimes including oral history, that can provide a richer and deeper understanding of the meaning of broadcasting in Canadians' daily lives and of how that changed over time. While historical audience studies entail many difficulties, they need to be encouraged, and they are most feasible on the local level.[47] Russell Johnston's new project on the early radio amateurs is another example of an attempt to get at historical audiences by looking at new kinds of sources in two very specific localities.[48]

In concluding this brief survey of the current situation, then, I reiterate that I view as very positive both the growing swell of studies that analyse representations in the broadcast media and the interest being shown within the academy in local broadcasting. I would suggest that both phenomena are the products of the most important trend within the discipline of history in the last twenty years, namely the development of the new cultural history, which has encouraged both the study of representations and a Geertzian focus on the intensive examination of small case studies.[49] There remain some obvious lacunae, however. Most of the works about representations discussed above focus on the texts and, occasionally, on those who wrote those texts. Almost completely lacking, however, is discussion of either those who produced these shows for radio or television, or those who performed in them. Indeed, I uncovered exactly one piece about a Canadian 'performer,' an MA thesis on Pierre Berton which examines some of his television appearances as well as his written oeuvre.[50] Another noticeable gap concerns the application of critical political economy to historical issues; in an era of rapid media consolidation, those interested in critically analysing the political economy of the mass media seem to be targeting the present rather than the past.[51] Similarly, there seems to have been a loss of interest in the 'invasion' of American culture via the mass media. Most importantly, we still lack audience studies. Historical audience studies present many challenges, but they can be done, and they are central to our understanding of the significance of the mass media in our society. Since the 1940s various organizations have been collecting audience statistics, but regretfully the data for the most part remain in their boxes in the archives.[52] In sum, while the new interest in representations and in local contexts is encouraging, the general failure to place those studies within the economic, institutional, and domestic frameworks that govern the production and reception of broadcasting remains regrettable.

Where Should We Go from Here?

In her well-known treatise, *Gender and the Politics of History*, Joan Scott made the argument that traditional women's history, either of the 'great women' or the feminist variety, suffered from isolation from the mainstream of historiography. She argued that the history of women was so important that a new means must be found to make it relevant to the central issues that concern historians, and proposed that an examination of how the discourse on gender-constituted hierarchies of difference was the key to that project.[53] Similarly, I would argue that broadcasting history has been hived off as a small, specialized subfield, rarely impinging on the main concerns of contemporary historians, and also that this practice is equally unacceptable given the centrality of the media to every aspect of modern life. I do not have a wide-ranging and theoretical proposal like Joan Scott's to offer here, but I would suggest a couple of directions in which broadcasting history could move which would make its interconnections with other historiographies more evident.

First, I would propose that broadcasting historians need to make the relevance of their field evident to the social historians who have been so dominant in Canadian university history departments for the past generation. Cultural and social history have many affinities, especially insofar as 'culture' is defined as 'a whole way of life.' In the modern world, broadcast media play a role in fashioning and perpetuating a society's myths and values; those desiring to comprehend how modern societies function and change need to understand how that works. The best Canadian example of this kind of integration of the social and the cultural is Gerry Friesen's *Citizen and Nation*, mentioned above, which tackles the task of writing a Canadian social history that unites rather than divides by focusing on the systems of communications (including in the more recent period, the broadcast media) that enable Canadians to talk to one another, to share stories, and thus to create community. Friesen's book is a synthetic overview dotted with the stories of a few 'real people'; now we need more case studies which build the concept from the ground back up. An excellent American model is the collection entitled *The Radio Reader: Essays in the Cultural History of Radio* edited by Michele Hilmes and Jason Loviglio.[54] While virtually all the essays in this book address the dominant networks during the golden age of radio, they do so in a critical/analytical manner that highlights resistances in and to the mainstream media. Many of the authors, for example, problematize how network radio functioned as a site of power and discourse by analysing how programs presented issues of race, gender, and religion. Here again, then, we have a melding of social history with cultural studies, which it seems to me is the key to 'mainstreaming' broadcasting history.

Even if we use a narrower definition of culture that encompasses only the creative arts, there is plenty of room for cooperation and indeed partnership between social and media historians. Too often historians interested in class have dismissed the mass media of the early twentieth century because they threatened a more 'genuine' working-class culture;[55] now we should persuade them – by showing them – exactly how ordinary people integrated the new media into their everyday lives. What were the popular entertainments of the working class, and how and why were they transformed? More broadly, how do the broadcast media exemplify and promote, for better or for worse, our capitalist economy and our democratic polity? These are questions that address the fundamentals of our historical experience. The media help form our perceptions of the world; in turn our perceptions help determine how we act and live. Thus the broadcast media, their structure, their producers, their programs, and the response of their audiences, are directly relevant to any examination of the history of all sections of modern Canadian society.

A second and equally promising road to the integration of broadcasting history into the mainstream of contemporary historiography is at the pan-national or global level. International interest in world history has skyrocketed in the last decade, and clearly communications, including radio and television, have been among the key agents of globalization. The broadcast media initially arose in the era of nation-building, and each nation developed its own system for organizing and regulating them. To date, most of the scholarship has followed the same pattern, concentrating on analysing the unique attributes of each national case.[56] But broadcasting has historically raised global issues as well, especially regarding regulation of frequencies and more recently of the international flow of programming. From another angle, broadcasting historians everywhere are interested in the same kinds of questions about control, production, representation, and reception of these media. Canada and Canadian scholars should be well-poised to enter into this conversation because of our English, French, and multicultural composition and our long history of awareness of cross-border media penetration. Not only programs but practitioners have moved back and forth across borders since broadcasting began – and so too has the work of major Canadian theorists.[57] We would all understand more about Canadian broadcasting history if we viewed it from a wider and more comparative angle. To date, however, most such work seems to be occurring outside Canada and to be restricted to relationships and comparisons within the English-speaking world, as the work of Michele Hilmes, Simon Potter, and Robert Fortner demonstrates.[58]

Possibly these suggestions for future directions in Canadian broadcasting history will be no more viable than Joan Scott's celebrated proposition, but they are offered in the hope that broadcasting history will cease to be a narrow specialized subfield in which most historians are not much interested and will become as central to the study of the history of modern Canada as radio and television themselves have been to the formation of our modern nation.

NOTES

1 Mary Vipond, 'The Mass Media in Canadian History: The Empire Day Broadcast of 1939,' *Journal of the Canadian Historical Association* 14 (2003): 1–21.
2 The presentation on which this article is based was delivered at the Conference on Media History in Canada (May 2006).

3 Mary Vipond, '"Stand By for That Report": The Historiography of Early
   Canadian Radio,' *Fréquence/Frequency* 7–8 (1997): 13.
4 The one early French study was Institut Canadien d'Éducation des
   Adultes, *La radiodiffusion au Canada depuis ses origines jusqu'à nos jours*
   (Montreal: ICEA, no. 16–17, 1964).
5 Frank W. Peers, *The Politics of Canadian Broadcasting, 1920–1951* (Toronto:
   University of Toronto Press, 1969); Frank W. Peers, *The Public Eye: Televi-
   sion and the Politics of Canadian Broadcasting, 1952–1968* (Toronto: University
   of Toronto Press, 1979); J.E. O'Brien, 'A History of the Canadian Radio
   League, 1930–1936' (PhD diss., University of Southern California, 1964);
   E. Austin Weir, *The Struggle for National Broadcasting in Canada* (Toronto:
   McClelland and Stewart, 1965); M. Prang, 'The Origins of Public Broadcasting in Canada,' *Canadian Historical Review* 46, no. 1 (1965): 1–31.
6 Paul Litt, *The Muses, the Masses and the Massey Commission* (Toronto: University of Toronto Press, 1992), esp. chap. 6; Sylvia Bashevkin, *True Patriot
   Love: The Politics of Canadian Nationalism* (Toronto: Oxford University Press,
   1991).
7 Most of the work on privately owned radio in Canada has been conducted
   by amateur historians, often with personal connections to their topics.
   Among the more useful works are Wayne Schmalz, *On Air: Radio in Saskatchewan* (Regina: Coteau Books, 1990); Betty Large and T. Crothers, *CFCY
   'The Friendly Voice of the Maritimes'* (Charlottetown: Applecross Press, 1989);
   and A.E. Zimmerman, *In the Shadow of the Shield: The Development of Wireless Telegraphy and Radio Broadcasting in Kingston and at Queen's University:
   An Oral and Documentary History, 1902–57* (Kingston: the author, 1991). See
   also Jean du Berger, *La radio au Québec, 1920–1960* (Sainte-Foy: Les Presses
   de l'Université Laval, 1997), which falls somewhere between the scholarly
   and the amateur.
8 K. Dewar, 'The Origins of Public Broadcasting in Canada in Comparative
   Perspective,' *Canadian Journal of Communication* 8, no. 2 (1982): 26–45; Marc
   Raboy, *Missed Opportunities: The Story of Canada's Broadcasting Policy* (Montreal and Kingston: McGill-Queen's University Press, 1990); Michel Filion,
   *Radiodiffusion et société distincte: des origines de la radio jusqu'à la Révolution
   tranquille au Québec* (Laval: Méridien, 1994). Dewar has written only this one
   piece on radio history. He and Filion are both trained as historians, although
   Filion now teaches in a communications program. I would place myself in
   this group in the sense that although my study of the development of Canadian radio in the 1920s was more archivally based, it was almost entirely
   about technological, economic, and regulatory issues; moreover, although it
   was about private stations, it nevertheless 'climaxed' with three chapters on

the beginnings of public broadcasting in Canada, if with a somewhat more sceptical tone than that of the first generation. See Mary Vipond, *Listening In: The First Decade of Canadian Broadcasting, 1922–1932* (Montreal and Kingston: McGill-Queen's University Press, 1992).

9 See, for example, Pierre Pagé (avec la collaboration de Renée Legris et de Louise Blondin), *Répertoire des oeuvres de la littérature radiophonique québécoise, 1930–1970* (Montreal: Fides, 1975); Pierre Pagé avec la collaboration de Renée Legris, *Le comique et l'humour à la radio québécoise: aperçus historiques et textes choisis, 1930–1970*, 2 vols. (Montreal: Éd. La Presse, 1976; Fides, 1979); P. Pagé et R. Legris, *Répertoire des dramatiques québécoises à la télévision, 1952–1977* (Montreal: Fides, 1977); R. Legris, *Robert Choquette, romancier et dramaturge de la radio-télévision* (Montreal: Fides, 1977); R. Legris, *Propagande de guerre et nationalismes dans la radio-feuilleton (1939–1955)* (Montreal: Fides, 1981); Pierre Pagé, *Radiodiffusion et culture savante au Québec (1930-1960)* (Montreal: Éditions Maxime, 1993); Renée Legris, *Hubert Aquin et la radio: une quête d'écriture, 1954–1977* (Montreal: Médiaspaul, 2004). See also E. Lavoie, 'La constitution d'une modernité culturelle populaire dans les médias au Québec (1900–1950),' in Yvan Lamonde et Esther Trépanier, dir., *L'avènement de la modernité culturelle au Québec* (Quebec: IQRC, 1986), 253–98, and, more recently, Michèle Martin, Béatrice Richard, and Dina Salha, 'La pré-modernité de *Radiomonde*: un pas hésitant vers un Québec moderne,' *Histoire Sociale/Social History* 33, no. 65 (2000): 37–57.

10 Howard Fink, 'The Sponsor's vs. The Nation's Choice: North American Radio Drama,' in Peter Lewis, ed., *Radio Drama* (Toronto: Academic Press, 1981); Howard Fink and Brian Morrison with John Jackson, *Canadian National Theatre of the Air, 1962–2000*, 3 vols, http://ccbs.concordia.ca/; Howard Fink and John Jackson, eds, *All the Bright Company: Radio Drama Produced by Andrew Allan* (Kingston and Toronto: Quarry Press and CBC Enterprises, 1987); Howard Fink and John Jackson, eds, *The Road to Victory: Radio Plays of Gerald Noxon* (Waterloo and Kingston: Malcolm Lowry Review Press and Quarry Press, 1989); Howard Fink and John Jackson, 'Jack Bowdery/Jack Ammon: Pioneer Leftist 'Thirties B.C. Radio Dramatist,' *Fréquence/Frequency* 1–2 (1994): 59–71. Other historical works by scholars associated with Concordia's Centre for Broadcasting Studies include Mary Jane Miller's two volumes on CBC television drama, *Turn Up the Contrast: CBC Television Drama since 1952* (Vancouver: UBC Press and CBC Enterprises, 1987), and *Rewind and Search: Conversations with the Makers and Decision Makers of CBC Television Drama* (Montreal and Kingston: McGill-Queen's University Press, 1996), and Greg Marc Nielsen, *Le Canada de*

Radio-Canada: sociologie critique et dialogisme culturel (Toronto: GREF, 1994).

11 Howard Fink's recuperation of CBC radio drama scripts about to be destroyed led to the creation of the CBC Radio Drama Archives, now part of the Concordia Centre for Broadcasting Studies.

12 Michael J. Nolan, *Foundations: Alan Plaunt and the Early Days of CBC Radio* (Montreal: CBC Enterprises, 1986).

13 These works are: 'Canada's Broadcasting Pioneers, 1918–1932,' *Canadian Journal of Communication* 10, no. 3 (1984): 1–26; 'Canadian Election Broadcasting: Political Practices and Radio Regulation 1919–1939,' *Journal of Broadcasting and Electronic Media* 29, no. 2 (1985): 175–88; 'An Infant Industry: Canadian Private Radio, 1919–36,' *Canadian Historical Review* 70, no. 4 (1989): 496–518; *Walter J. Blackburn: A Man for All Media* (Toronto: Macmillan, 1989); *CTV: The Network That Means Business* (Edmonton: University of Alberta Press, 2001).

14 Paul Rutherford, *When Television Was Young: Primetime Canada, 1952–1967* (Toronto: University of Toronto Press, 1990).

15 Russell Johnston, 'Value Added: Recent Books in the History of Communications and Culture,' *Acadiensis* 32, no. 1 (2002): 129.

16 Paul Attallah, 'Review of *Television Studies*, edited by Toby Miller,' *Canadian Journal of Communication* 28, no. 4 (2003): 487.

17 For discussion of various aspects of this problem, see L.W. Levine, *The Unpredictable Past: Explorations in American Cultural History* (New York: Oxford University Press, 1993); Andrew Hoskins, 'New Memory: Mediating History,' *Historical Journal of Film, Radio and Television* 21, no. 4 (2001): 333–46; and Mariana Valverde, 'Some Remarks on the Rise and Fall of Discourse Analysis,' *Histoire sociale / Social History* 65 (2000): 59–77.

18 Bernie Sanders, Independent Member of House of Representatives from Vermont, to conference 'Can Freedom of the Press Survive Media Consolidation,' May 2005, http://www.democracynow.org/2005/5/12/rep_bernie_sanders_on_the_importance (accessed 7 March 2006).

19 John B. Thompson, *The Media and Modernity: A Social Theory of the Media* (Stanford, CA: Stanford University Press, 1993), 3; see also M. Raboy et al., 'Cultural Development and the Open Economy: A Democratic Issue and a Challenge to Public Policy,' *Canadian Journal of Communication* 19, no. 3 (1994): 303.

20 Among recent popular books are Peter Kenter, *TV North: Everything You Wanted to Know about Canadian Television* (North Vancouver: Whitecap Books, 2001); Marilu Walters, *CKUA: Radio Worth Fighting For* (Edmonton: University of Alberta Press, 2002); Stephen Cole, *Here's Looking at Us: Celebrating Fifty Years of CBC-TV* (Toronto: McClelland and Stewart, 2002);

Jean-François Beauchemin, *Ici Radio-Canada: 50 ans de télévision française* (Montreal: Éditions de l'Homme, 2002); Gil Murray, *Nothing On but the Radio: A Look Back at Radio in Canada and How It Changed the World* (Toronto: Dundurn Press, 2003). It is notable that, unlike the earlier period, there seems to be little work being done about local broadcasting stations.

21 Kathleen Buddle-Crowe, 'From Birchbark Talk to Digital Dreamspeaking: A History of Aboriginal Media Activism in Canada' (PhD diss., McMaster University, 2002).

22 David J. Smith, 'Intellectual Activist: Graham Spry, A Biography' (PhD diss., York University, 2003).

23 Montreal: Point de Fuite, 2001.

24 Gerald Friesen, *Citizens and Nation: An Essay on History, Communication, and Canada* (Toronto: University of Toronto Press, 2000); Robert E. Babe, *Canadian Communication Thought: Ten Foundational Writers* (Toronto: University of Toronto Press, 2000); Jonathan W. Rose, *Making 'Pictures in Our Heads': Government Advertising in Canada* (Westport, CT: Praeger, 2000); Paul Rutherford, *Endless Propaganda: The Advertising of Public Goods* (Toronto: University of Toronto Press, 2000). See also the review article by Russell Johnston cited above.

25 Paul Heyer, *Harold Innis* (Lanham, MD: Rowman and Littlefield, 2003); A.J. Watson, *Marginal Man: The Dark Vision of Harold Innis* (Toronto: University of Toronto Press, 2005). The ongoing interest in Innis is also manifest in John Bonnett, 'Communication, Complexity and Empire: The Systemic Thought of Harold Adams Innis' (PhD diss., University of Ottawa, 2002), and in a number of articles in the *Canadian Journal of Communication* 29, no. 2 (2004).

26 Major studies in progress of which I am aware include Gene Allen's project on Canadian Press, part of which looks at CP's involvement in broadcasting radio news; Len Kuffert's work on CBC radio's cultural forms, a follow-up to his *A Great Duty: Canadian Responses to Modern Life and Mass Culture, 1939–1967* (Montreal and Kingston: McGill-Queen's University Press, 2003); Simon Potter's ongoing study of Commonwealth broadcasters; Matthew Hayday's examination of Canada Day celebrations on television; and my own two projects on the Canadian Radio Broadcasting Commission and on the CBC as an 'instrument of war' during the Second World War. See the essays by Allen, Potter, and Hayday elsewhere in this volume. Others who made presentations at the Conference on Media History in Canada in May 2006 are working on topics such as hockey broadcasts, third-language radio, and popular music.

27 See, respectively, the Film, Video and Sound database at http://www.col-

lectionscanada.gc.ca/archivianet/020114_e.html and www.trustav.ca.

28 Mary Jane Miller, 'Where the Spirit Lives: An Influential and Contentious Television Drama about Residential Schools,' *American Review of Canadian Studies* 31 (2001): 71–84; Mary Jane Miller, 'The CBC and Its Presentation of the Native Peoples of Canada in Television Drama,' in H.N. Nicholson, ed., *Screening Culture* (Lanham, MD: Rowman and Littlefield, 2003), 59–73.

29 Montreal and Kingston: McGill-Queen's University Press, 2005.

30 Sandra Lambertus, *Wartime Images, Peacetime Wounds: The Media and the Gustafsen Lake Standoff* (Toronto: University of Toronto Press, 2003); Roger Larose, 'The Oka Crisis on Television: In Praise of the Barbarian' (PhD diss., Concordia University, 2001). See also Pierre Trudel, 'Médias et autochtones: pour une information equilibrée et dépourvu de préjugés,' *Bulletin d'histoire politique* 12, no. 3 (2004): 145–67.

31 For the 1990s see Minelle Mahtani, 'Representing Minorities: Canadian Media and Minority Identities,' *Canadian Ethnic Studies* 33, no. 3 (2001): 99–134.

32 But see the dissertation by Kathleen Buddle-Crowe already cited and also Melissa Benner, 'The Mediated Counterpublics of Canadian Farm Women' (MA thesis, Carleton University, 2004).

33 Patricia Mazepa, 'Battles on the Cultural Front: The (De)Labouring of Culture in Canada, 1914–1944' (PhD diss., Carleton University, 2003).

34 Robert Cupido, 'The Medium, the Message and the Modern: The Jubilee Broadcast of 1927,' *International Journal of Canadian Studies* 26 (2002): 101–23; Peter Neary, 'The CBC "Ventures in Citizenship" Broadcast of 9 November 1938 (Kristalnacht),' *Canadian Jewish Studies* 10 (2002): 109–22; E.J. Talbot, 'Choquette's Urban Fables: Questioning a Certain Modernity,' *Quebec Studies* 34 (Fall-Winter 2002): 47–57; Johanne Trew, 'Conflicting Visions: Don Messer, Liberal Nationalism and the Canadian Unity Debate,' *International Journal of Canadian Studies* 26 (2002): 41–57.

35 R. Legris, 'L'institution ecclesiale et les structures de l'idéologie chrétienne dans les radioromans et les dramatisations historiques (1935–1975),' *Études d'histoire religieuse / Historical Studies* 68 (2002): 41–56; P. Pagé, 'Cinquante ans d'émissions religieuses à la radio québécoise (1931–1981),' ibid., 7–23.

36 Peter Hodgins, 'The Canadian Dream-Work: History, Myth and Nostalgia in the Heritage Minutes' (PhD diss., Carleton University, 2004); Katàrzyna Rukszto, 'Minute by Minute: Canadian History Reimagined for Television Audiences' (PhD diss., York University, 2003); Joe Friesen, '"Canada: A People's History" as "Journalists'" History,' *History Workshop Journal* 56 (2003): 184–203; David Frank, 'Public History and the *People's History*:

A View from Atlantic Canada,' *Acadiensis* 32, no. 2 (2003): 120–33; articles by Margaret Conrad, Patrice Groulx, and Gene Allen in *Histoire sociale / Social History* 34, no. 68 (2001): 377–414; Glenn Brook, '"Canada: A People's History": An Analysis of the Visual Narrative for a Colonial Nation' (MA thesis, Concordia University, 2002); Mark Starowicz, *Making History: The Remarkable Story behind Canada: A People's History* (Toronto: McClelland and Stewart, 2003).

37 Frédéric Demers, 'La mise en scène de l'imaginaire national et historique du Québec francophone dans la téléséries "Les filles de Caleb"' (PhD diss., Université Laval, 2005).

38 David Hogarth, *Documentary Television in Canada: From National Public Service to Global Marketplace* (Montreal and Kingston: McGill-Queen's University Press, 2003); David Hogarth, 'The Other Documentary Tradition: Early Radio Documentaries in Canada,' *Historical Journal of Film, Radio and Television* 21, no. 2 (2001): 123–35; David Hogarth, 'Local Representation in a Global Age: A Case Study of Canadian Documentary Television as a Transnational Genre,' *International Journal of Canadian Studies* 23 (2001): 133–55.

39 Anne F. MacLennan, 'Circumstances beyond Our Control: Canadian Radio Program Schedule Evolution during the 1930s' (PhD diss., Concordia University, 2001); Anne MacLennan, 'What Do the Radio Program Schedules Reveal? Content Analysis versus Accidental Sampling in Early Canadian Radio History,' in Jeff Keshen and Sylvie Perrier, eds, *Bâtir de nouveaux ponts: sources, méthodes et interdisciplinarité / Building New Bridges: Sources, Methods, and Interdisciplinarity* (Ottawa: University of Ottawa Press, 2005), 225–38; Anne MacLennan, 'American Network Broadcasting, the CBC and Canadian Radio Stations during the 1930s: A Content Analysis,' *Journal of Radio Studies* 12, no. 1 (2005): 85–103; Anu Sahota, 'Sermon and Surprise: The Meaning of Scheduling in Broadcast Radio History' (MA essay, Simon Fraser University, 2006).

40 Ronald E. Stotyn, 'Education in the Ether: A Historical Study of "The Alberta School Broadcasts," circa 1929–1959' (PhD diss., Southern Illinois University at Carbondale, 2003); Caroline Boily, 'Les usages scolaires du cinéma, de la radio et de la télévision à la Commission des écoles catholiques de Montréal, 1920–1970' (PhD diss., Université du Québec à Montreal, 2006).

41 Norman Fennema, 'Remote Control: Belief and Canadian Broadcasting – A Case Study of Religion in the Public Square' (PhD diss., University of Victoria, 2003); Ryan Edwardson, 'Canadianization: Canadian Content, Cultural Intervention, and Constructing a National Culture' (PhD diss.,

Queen's University, 2004); Ira Wagman, 'From Spiritual Matters to Economic Facts: Recounting Problems of Knowledge in the History of Canadian Audiovisual Policy, 1928–1961' (PhD diss., McGill University, 2006).

42 See, for example, Colette Brin, 'La télévision publique en campagne: le plan de couverture électorale à la SRC (1997–1998)' (PhD diss., Université Laval, 2003); Catherine Côté, 'TV Coverage and Cynicism: An Analysis of the 2000 Canadian Federal Election' (PhD diss., Queen's University, 2004); E. Gidengil and J. Everitt, 'Conventional Coverage/Unconventional Politicians: Gender and Media Coverage of Canadian Leaders' Debates, 1993, 1997, 2000,' *Canadian Journal of Political Science* 36, no. 3 (2003): 559–77.

43 But see Michael Nolan's book on CTV, cited above, and also Ken Easton, *Building an Industry: A History of Cable Television and Its Development in Canada* (Lawrencetown Beach, NS: Pottersfield Press, 2000). Knowlton Nash's more popular *Swashbucklers: The Story of Canada's Battling Broadcasters* (Toronto: McClelland and Stewart, 2001) might also be noted.

44 Nadine Kozak, '"Among the Necessities": A Social History of Communication Technology on the Canadian Prairies, 1900 to 1950' (MA thesis, Carleton University, 2000); Bonnie Wagner, 'We Proudly Begin Our Broadcast Day: Saskatchewan and the Arrival of Television, 1945–1969' (MA thesis, University of Saskatchewan, 2004); Stacy Lorenz, '"A Lively Interest on the Prairies": Western Canada, the Mass Media, and a "World of Sport," 1870–1939,' *Journal of Sport History* 27, no. 2 (2000): 195–227; Bradley Kevin Humeniuk, 'Constructing Local Culture in a Near Media Monopoly' (MA thesis, Lakehead University, 2003).

45 Sarah A. Matheson, 'Televising Toronto from Hogtown to Megacity' (PhD diss., University of Southern California, 2003).

46 Jeff A. Webb, 'The Invention of Radio Broadcasting in Newfoundland and the Maritime Provinces, 1922–1939' (PhD diss., University of New Brunswick, 1995); 'The Origins of Public Broadcasting: The Commission of Government and the Creation of the Broadcasting Corporation of Newfoundland,' *Acadiensis* 24, no. 2 (1994); 'Constructing Community and Consumers: Joseph R. Smallwood's *Barrelman* Radio Program,' *Journal of the CHA*, n.s., 8 (1997): 165–86; 'VOUS: Armed Forces Radio Service (AFRS) in Newfoundland,' *Journal of Radio Studies* 11, no. 1 (2004): 87–99; 'Who Speaks for the Public? The Debate over Government or Private Broadcasting in Newfoundland, 1939–49,' *Acadiensis* 35, no. 1 (2005); 'Embracing the Modern and the Authentic: Musical Culture upon Radio Station VONF' (unpublished paper delivered to Canadian Historical Association Conference, Toronto, 2006). Webb has also published 'Canada's Moose River

Mine Disaster (1936): Radio-Newspaper Competition in the Business of News,' *Historical Journal of Film, Radio and Television* 16, no. 3 (1996): 365–76.

47 See Mary Vipond, 'Desperately Seeking the Audience for Early Canadian Radio,' in M. Behiels and M. Martel, eds, *Nation, Ideas, Identities* (Don Mills, ON: Oxford University Press, 2000), 86–96.

48 Russell Johnston, 'Canadian Radio Amateurs and Early Broadcasting,' paper delivered to the Conference on Media History in Canada, Ryerson University, Toronto, 31 May 2006.

49 Arif Dirlik, 'Whither History? Encounters with Historism, Postmodernism, Postcolonialism,' in A. Dirlik et al., eds, *History after the Three Worlds* (Lanham, MD: Rowman and Littlefield, 2000), 241–57. See also chapter 9 in this volume.

50 Mathieu Roy, 'Pierre Berton: grand parolier de l'identité canadienne' (MA thesis, Université Laval, 2004).

51 See, for example, David Skinner, James R. Compton, and Michael Gasher, eds, *Converging Media, Diverging Politics: A Political Economy of News Media in the United States and Canada* (Lanham, MD: Lexington Books, 2005).

52 There is a considerable amount of CBC audience research data available, and BBM material is also accessible, although for more recent years. See Ross Eaman, *Channels of Influence: CBC Audience Research and the Canadian Public* (Toronto: University of Toronto Press, 1994).

53 Joan Wallach Scott, *Gender and the Politics of History* (New York: Columbia University Press, rev. ed., 1999), 10.

54 New York: Routledge, 2002.

55 See, for example, Bryan Palmer, *Working Class Experience: The Rise and Reconstitution of Canadian Labour, 1800–1980* (Toronto: McClelland and Stewart, 1983), 194–5, 228–9, 278–9. An interesting example of how this can be done using unexpected sources is Lizbeth Cohen, 'Encountering Mass Culture at the Grassroots: The Experience of Chicago Workers in the 1920s,' *American Quarterly* 41, no. 1 (1989): 6–33.

56 Michele Hilmes, 'Radio Nations: The Importance of Transnational Media Study,' in N. Finzsch and U. Lehmkuhl, eds, *Atlantic Communications: The Media in American and German History from the Seventeenth to the Twentieth Century* (Oxford and New York: Berg, 2004), 301.

57 The current work of Michele Hilmes as demonstrated in her keynote address to the Conference on Media History in Canada analyses some of these exchanges within what she calls the 'Anglosphere.' See Hilmes, 'Front Line Family: "Women's Culture" Comes to the BBC,' *Media Culture and Society* 29, no.1 (2007): 5–29

58 Potter, who is based in the history department at the National University of Ireland, Galway, has recently published, among others, 'Strengthening the Bonds of the Commonwealth: The Imperial Relations Trust and Australian, New Zealand, and Canadian Broadcasting Personnel in Britain, 1946–52,' *Media History* 11, no. 3 (2005): 193–205, and 'The BBC, the CBC, and the 1939 Royal Tour of Canada,' *Cultural and Social History* 3, no. 4 (October 2006): 424–44. See also Robert S. Fortner, *Radio, Morality, and Culture: Britain, Canada and the United States, 1919–1945* (Carbondale: Southern Illinois University Press, 2005). Fortner teaches Communications at Calvin College, Grand Rapids, Michigan. One good point of access to academic literature on global media is the new journal *Global Media and Communications*.

9 Recent Trends in Research on the History of the Press in Quebec: Towards a Cultural History

FERNANDE ROY

(TRANSLATED BY PATRICIA SMART)

A few years ago, at the beginning of this century, Jean de Bonville and I produced an overview of research on the history of the Quebec press.[1] It was our impression at the time that the field was fairly underdeveloped, even taking into account works published in the previous three or four decades. And in fact I do not believe that this state of underdevelopment was limited to Quebec. Unfortunately, little has changed since then: I would still conclude today that there has been a gap in historiography as far as research on the press is concerned, in spite of a few excellent pieces of work that have appeared in the last few years.

This diagnosis of a 'historiographical gap' was, of course, a product of our frustrated expectations. Our article was both an overview and a proposal for future research; it argued for a social history of the press that would put social actors at the centre of its analysis, while at the same time taking the whole media landscape into account. We emphasized the relationships of dependency and feedback among the producers of messages, the messages themselves, and those at whom they were aimed in any given period. We were struck by the disproportion between the large number of studies which *made use of* the press and the very small number which considered *the press itself* to be a phenomenon worth studying. In that 2000 article, Jean de Bonville and I were seeking to change the relationship between historians and the press. For in general, historians have always treated the press as a source of the various data, information, ideas, or ideologies they are interested in rather than turning their attention to the history of that system itself. In calling for historians of the press to change that situation, my colleague and I were probably being either ambitious or naive. Today I would not make such an appeal, for it seems obvious that there would be no point to it. Historians seem not to have assimilated McLuhan's aphorism that 'the medium is the message,' and they continue to read nineteenth- and twentieth-century newspapers solely in terms of their content.

Still, historians of the press can at least make a minimal amount of history of the press available to students and other historians, in order to help them avoid methodological errors in their treatment of what will always be a prime and often an essential source. There are still too many content analyses that accept without question everything that is found in newspapers or make no distinction between editorials and news coverage. There is a need for a methodological guide that would lay out the possibilities and limitations of what can be gleaned from old or contemporary newspapers. The lack of such a manual is a sign of the embryonic state of research on the history of the press in Quebec.

To provide a sense of some of the recent tendencies that do exist, I have·tried to locate all the work done on the history of the press in Quebec between 2000 and 2006 – not only monographs but MA and PhD theses completed or in progress in Quebec universities. As well, I did a content analysis of the following twelve periodicals: *Bulletin d'histoire politique, Cahiers des Dix, Canadian Historical Review, Communication, Études d'histoire religieuse, Globe, Histoire sociale / Social History, Mens, revue d'histoire intellectuelle de l'Amérique française, Recherches sociographiques, Revue d'études canadiennes, Revue d'histoire de l'Amérique française,* and *Revue internationale d'études québécoises.* While my cut-off point is admittedly somewhat arbitrary, I chose not to consider work dealing with the last fifteen years as 'historical.' The results of my research are as follows.

AS FAR AS *research tools* are concerned, there has unfortunately been little progress since 2000. Bibliographical tools like those of de Bonville and Sotiron[2] have not been updated, and the inventory *La presse québécoise* (usually referred to as 'Beaulieu and Hamelin') stopped appearing over fifteen years ago and only covers the period up to 1975.[3] The huge proliferation of new titles has made this inventory into a project beyond the scope of a small research team. And, since granting agencies do not support this type of work, it appears likely that this essential research tool will remain unfinished for the foreseeable future. In order for it to be completed and corrected (for, in spite of its usefulness, it is full of errors), funding from an institution such as Bibliothèque et Archives Nationales du Québec, perhaps in collaboration with Library and Archives Canada, would be necessary. But the budgets of these institutions are not unlimited, and, at least so far, the history of the press has not been one of their priorities. On the other hand, real progress has been made in recent years as far as access to old newspapers is concerned: several are now available online, thanks in large part to the national libraries.

Another glaring lack is a work of *synthesis* covering books and articles on the history of the Quebec press. Preparing such a synthesis is doubtless seen by most researchers as a daunting task, but if one existed it would be an indispensable tool for further research. As far as the present day is concerned, the recent editions of Mary Vipond's work on mass media in Canada[4] and Mark Raboy's on the Quebec media[5] are extremely useful. For previous centuries, there is a substantial article by Fernand Harvey on the development of the periodical press in the city of Quebec from 1764 to 1940,[6] presenting what he describes as 'an overview of a cultural process.' But the press of Montreal and the rest of the province is still awaiting its historian.

There is, however, one overview that exists, but on a *theoretical* rather than an empirical level. And unfortunately historians in general seem uninterested in theories of communication. In fact, I know of only one historian who *is* passionate about communications theory – Jean de Bonville. With his colleague Jean Charron, he has written several articles in this field, and their research has given rise to one of the major works of recent years: *Nature et mutations du journalisme: théories et recherches empiriques*, published in 2004 under the direction of Colette Brin, Jean Charron, and Jean de Bonville.[7]

Indifferent to trends or popularity, de Bonville and Charron continue to explore and deepen their theoretical model, based on the succession of journalistic paradigms (from the journalism of transmission of the eighteenth-century gazettes through the journalism of opinion and information of subsequent periods to the journalism of communication of the present day). As well, they propose a theoretical model of change in journalism and a historical typology of journalistic practices. My own experience as a professor suggests that these texts, in spite of their importance, are perceived by students as very difficult to understand. Jean de Bonville's empirical research has had a much greater impact on historians, in particular his classic and indispensable *Genèse d'un média de masse*.[8]

ALMOST ALL THE THESES and articles in learned journals since 2000 which deal in any way with the history of the press turn out to be, in one way or another, *content analysis*. Within this body of work it is possible to discern certain thematic constellations.

One very popular theme is *war*: the First and Second World Wars, the Algerian War,[9] the Spanish Civil War,[10] and the American Civil War.[11] Fascism and its practitioners (figures like Marshal Pétain and Adrien Arcand) have attracted several researchers.[12] As well, although it was not war (even though there were soldiers patrolling the streets of Montreal), I have allowed myself to include in this category a study examining Claude Ryan and the violence of power during the October crisis of 1970,[13] as well as a study of perceptions of the October crisis over the last thirty years (unfortunately only in the francophone press).[14] In most cases, only the opinions of French Canadians or francophone Quebeckers have been looked at. The authors are interested in comparing such things as conservative and liberal newspapers, or the opinions of members of the clergy or of politicians, but the much more relevant question of comparisons between the anglophone and francophone press has hardly been touched. As well, these studies tend to use a fairly traditional political history approach.

An exception is Jérôme Coutard's PhD thesis: through an examination of the press and propaganda from 1914 to 1918, he seeks to reveal the culture of war.[15] Such an approach is close to the present tendencies of cultural history. Myriam Levert's research on press censorship in the First World War is in a similar vein; while she focuses primarily on the French-language press, Levert is aware of the heuristic potential of a comparative English-/French-Canadian approach.[16]

The work done on *women* continues the direction of previous decades. For example, Isabelle Dornic's doctoral thesis analyses women's quest for identity in the feminist periodical *La Bonne parole* from 1913 to 1958.[17] Literary scholars like Simone Pilon and Julie Roy have begun to recover women's writings in the nineteenth-century press, writings whose authors were often disguised under pseudonyms, sometimes male pseudonyms.[18] The discoveries of this type of research have been more numerous than one might have imagined and have become extremely valuable as tools for uncovering the beginnings of women's journalism. Marie-Josée Béchard has studied the representation of men in the magazine *L'Actualité*,[19] while France Fouquet, using an approach that is more social than cultural, has examined the press as a 'reflection of the evolution of the Quebec family.'[20]

In addition, it would seem that *nationalism* has fallen out of fashion in Quebec, at least as far as analyses of press content are concerned.

Only one study of nationalism – an attempt to understand how Claude Ryan reconciled his liberal, nationalist, and Catholic principles – deals with a daily newspaper.[21] Another thesis in progress examines the representation of nationalism in the press, but the nationalism it deals with is not Québécois, but Basque.[22] In recent works, identity appears to be more fragmented: some researchers, as we have seen, are interested in women's identity, others in gay and lesbian identity,[23] and still other in regional identities.[24] But in general the traditional theme of national identity is only marginally, if at all, included in work being done on the press, and comparisons between the francophone and anglophone press are rare. An exception is Julie Perrone's attempt to analyse the construction of Maurice Richard as a hero in the daily press of Montreal, Quebec, and Toronto – a study of the meaning of a mythical figure who was originally French Canadian but who over time became a pan-Canadian symbol.[25]

Religious questions have given rise to new work: for example, studies of the relationship between church and state in France in 1905 as perceived by the Quebec press,[26] the relationship between Catholic bishops and the media,[27] the tribulations of Quebec Catholicism as reflected in the religious periodicals of the 1960s,[28] media coverage of Vatican II,[29] religious radio programs,[30] and even nuns who were filmmakers.[31] Certain scientific subjects are looked at from a moral perspective, whether specialized topics like euthanasia or more general ones like the journalistic treatment of bioethical issues in the daily press.[32]

The most dominant theme of these content analyses seems to me to be *culture*. Research teams under Bernard Andrès at the Université du Québec à Montréal[33] and Micheline Cambron at the Université de Montréal[34] are continuing their examinations of the press in the eighteenth and nineteenth centuries, providing new looks at topics we thought were well covered. For example, there is now an MA thesis on Valentin Jautard and the *Gazette littéraire de Montréal* in 1778 and 1779.[35] For the twentieth century, there are stimulating new studies reconstituting the literary and journalistic networks that gravitated around reviews like *La Relève*[36] or dailies like *Le Bien public*.[37]

Other studies bring together different media, dealing with topics like the place of music in the press, media discourse on the cinema[38] or theatre,[39] especially in the belle époque, and finally, an analysis of *Radiomonde*, a specialized periodical on radio.[40]

Humour and caricature are generally popular topics with professors and their students. On this theme, one has the choice between 'laughing on an empty stomach' (a study of humour in the popular press during the Great Depression);[41] the combination of humour and politics in the work of Napoléon Aubin[42] or of Hector Berthelot in nineteenth-century funny pages;[43] or the radio humour of the twentieth century.[44] One researcher has also begun to study *faits divers* in a publication dominated by crime news, *Allô police*.[45]

The studies mentioned so far show that the overwhelming tendency in recent work on the press is the same as it has always been: historians are interested above all in content analysis, and the study of the container is generally ignored. There has, however, been a renewal of the ways in which content is treated, with a new interest in long-neglected contents and in cultural approaches. In a certain sense, the media reservoir is unlimited and inexhaustible, for there will always be the perception that there are new contents to be explored.

THE HISTORY OF the press and the media as corporations is a much less active field, except perhaps for *Le Devoir*; it is certainly the most studied newspaper from all points of view,[46] and has been since it was founded. Researchers seem no more interested than they used to be in socio-economic monographs on press corporations. Most Quebec dailies have still not been the object of specific studies of this type.

Nor has the historical influence of the business world on the press been sufficiently studied (for example, there are no studies of pressures exerted on editors by advertisers or directly by newspaper owners). When will we have a study of the multiple enterprises of the publisher/politician Jacob Nicol, for example?

In this regard, the doctoral research of Dominique Marquis represents an exception. Not only does Marquis analyse a particular category of newspapers (the Catholic press), but she looks in depth at one particular firm, the daily newspaper *L'Action catholique*, taking into account not only the *Action catholique* journalists as a group, but also their journalistic practices.[47] As well, Marquis (along with Magali Deleuze) is among the rare researchers to analyse how newspaper content is presented through layout.

Marquis has also included in her work the study of advertising, comparing the advertising policies and practices of *L'Action catholique*, *Le Soleil*, and *La Presse*. But the most important work in this area for the period in question is that of Luc Côté and Jean-Guy Daigle,[48] which looks at the economic and cultural evolution of Quebec towards the 'American way of life' by analysing the advertising content of three dailies, *La Presse*, *Le Soleil*, and the *Montreal Star*. Their book, which traces the gradual emergence of a North American identity in Quebec, is an innovative and rigorous example of the possibilities offered by a cultural studies approach.

The last two works mentioned give an idea of the heuristic potential of comparison in the history of the press. Somewhat in the same spirit, other recent works group newspapers by type rather than studying a single newspaper in isolation: in addition to the already-mentioned study of the Catholic press, there are analyses of the contemporary daily press,[49] the regional press (for example, that of Trois-Rivières),[50] the anarchist press,[51] the musical press,[52] and the humorous press.[53] In all these areas the tendency is to search for the cultural or sociocultural characteristics of different types of newspapers rather than their economic similarities or differences.

ANOTHER RESEARCH AREA, of course, concerns *journalists* themselves. The numerous studies published before 2000 in this area were, on the whole, biographies of individual journalists. Since then such studies have become less common, however. While there are still a few fascinating monographs aimed at the general public on topics like 'the unknown Pierre Péladeau,'[54] they are the exception rather than the rule.

Journalism as a practice has obviously existed since the beginnings of the press, but its existence as a profession only goes back about a century. And it is the profession of journalism that intrigues many present-day historians. One of the first studies in this area – an analysis of the first fifty years of unionization at *Le Soleil* – indicates this approach in its subtitle, 'A Struggle for the Profession.'[55] More ambitious is the important doctoral thesis by Florence Le Cam,[56] which analyses the historical construction of the identity of journalists and the discursive strategies used in the construction of that identity since the last quarter of the nineteenth century. What is particularly gratifying about this study is its long historical perspective; it is an excellent example of the relevance of historical studies for a better understanding of present-day challenges.

Related to the question of professionalization are questions of journalistic standards and *ethics*. Several studies on these topics have appeared in recent years,[57] among them Armande Saint-Jean's analysis of 'Ethics of Information: Foundations and Practices in Quebec since 1960,' based on her 1993 doctoral thesis.[58] More recent studies, in contrast, trace journalists' ethical concerns to well before the advent of the Quiet Revolution.[59]

Finally, a word on *freedom of the press*. It is traditionally believed that this freedom is one of the fruits of democracy and that it was obtained in large measure as a result of the repeated demands of journalists. While there is undoubtedly a measure of truth in this reassuring and typically liberal account of things, I am personally interested in revisiting these questions and in looking more closely at the ideological use that has been made of this call to freedom. From being a legitimate defence of individual and collective rights, this famous freedom has at times become an almost transcendent principle for journalists, one that is open to all kinds of abuse. This research is in progress.

Conclusion

While there have historically been a number of specifically Québécois ways of practising journalism, I am not convinced that the ways in which these practices have been analysed are specific to Quebec. From this overview of recent and ongoing research on the history of the Quebec press, one tendency emerges as particularly clear: francophone Québécois researchers are moving more and more in the direction of cultural history in their research themes, their perspectives, and their interpretations. Without perhaps being totally conscious of it, they, like researchers everywhere, have gone through a sort of 'cultural turn.'[60] In this area as in so many others, cultural history has become the dominant paradigm – even a sort of grab bag, it sometimes seems, in that absolutely everything is seen as susceptible to being clarified by a cultural approach. In my opinion, however, this dominant perspective should not make us forget other possible and even necessary ways of approaching the subject. In history, explanatory factors are always numerous, and the broadest perspective is always desirable. A cultural history of the press should never, for example, neglect dimensions like the social context and economic importance of the press, or its crucial importance in power relationships. It is important that the interpretative landscape not become monochromatic.

I suspect that if I had been looking at the history of the media in a broader sense, and not just at the history of the press, this 'cultural turn' would have been even more apparent. While the broader history of the media is beyond my area of competence, I am struck by the fact that francophone historians in Quebec have barely touched the surface of this area (except perhaps for the history of cinema), preferring to leave media history to communications specialists and other social scientists.

The last part of my conclusion specifically concerns the question of interdisciplinarity. In 2000, Jean de Bonville and I wrote that the history of the press had not been much enhanced by other disciplines. This is no longer the case at all. The study of the eighteenth and nineteenth centuries, even the early twentieth century, has been enriched by the work of literary scholars. In fact, I would say that the recent large-scale, pan-Canadian research projects on the history of the book and publishing have done a great deal to bring scholars together.[61] I do not believe, however, that this is the case for works dealing with the last half of the twentieth century, numerous as they are in Quebec and in the rest of Canada. For this period, the paths followed by literary scholars and historians diverge, and the latter seem not to have found new partners. In the francophone milieu, at least, professors of communication, for example, and historians remain in their respective departments and do not often cross paths at conferences or even in academic journals. In this respect, the Conference on Media History in Canada, held in Toronto in 2006, is without doubt a step in the right direction.

NOTES

1 Fernande Roy and Jean de Bonville, 'La recherche sur l'histoire de la presse québécoise: bilan et perspectives,' *Recherches sociographiques* 61, no. 1 (2000): 15–51.

2 Jean de Bonville, *La presse québécoise de 1764 à 1914: bibliographie analytique* (Sainte-Foy: Presses de l'Université Laval, 1995); Minko Sotiron, *An Annotated Bibliography of Works on Daily Newspapers in Canada, 1914–1983 / Une bibliographie annotée des ouvrages portant sur les quotidiens canadiens, 1914–1983* (Montreal: M. Sotiron, 1987).

3 André Beaulieu and Jean Hamelin, eds, *La presse québécoise des origines à nos jours*, 10 vols. (Sainte-Foy: Presses de l'Université Laval, 1971–90).

4 Mary Vipond, *The Mass Media in Canada*, 3rd ed. (Toronto: James Lorimer, 2000).

5 Marc Raboy, with Geneviève Grimard, *Les médias québécois: presse, radio, télévision, inforoute*, 2nd rev. ed. (Montreal: Gaston Miron, 2000).

6 Fernand Harvey, 'La presse périodique à Québec de 1794 à 1940. Vue d'ensemble d'un processus culturel,' *Les cahiers des Dix* 58 (2004): 213–50.

7 Colette Brin, Jean Charron, and Jean de Bonville, eds, *Nature et mutations du journalisme: théorie et recherches empiriques* (Sainte-Foy: Presses de l'Université Laval, 2004).

8 Jean de Bonville, *La presse québécoise de 1884 à 1914: genèse d'un média de masse* (Sainte-Foy: Presses de l'Université Laval, 1988).

9 Magali Deleuze, 'L'étude des journaux en histoire internationale: le Québec et la guerre d'Algérie,' *Globe. Revue internationale d'études québécoises* 6, no. 2 (2003): 23–50; Magali Deleuze, *L'une et l'autre indépendance, 1954–1964: les médias au Québec et la guerre d'Algérie* (Montreal: Point de Fuite, 2001).

10 Caroline Désy, 'Discours hégémonique et contre-discours sur la guerre d'Espagne dans le Québec des années trente' (PhD diss., Université du Québec à Montréal, 1999); Catherine Pomeyrols, 'Le Devoir et la guerre d'Espagne. Les usages de la référence française,' *Revue d'histoire de l'Amérique française* 58, no. 3 (hiver 2005): 347–87.

11 Philippe Fortin, 'Le journal *Le Pays* et la guerre de Sécession, 1861–1865' (MA thesis, Université du Québec à Montréal, 2000); Philippe Fortin, 'Les sources de renseignement du journal *Le Pays* lors de la guerre de Sécession (1861–1865)' *Communication* 20, no. 2 (hiver-printemps 2001): 118–31.

12 Annabelle Patault, 'La doctrine nazie vue par quatre journaux canadiens-français des années trente: *L'Ordre, Clarté, La Nation, Le Jour*, 1934–1939' (MA thesis, University of Maine, 2002); David Philipps, *Arcand ou la vérité retrouvée* (Saint-Léonard: Éditions Béluga, 2002); Patrick Poirier, 'La représentation du régime hitlérien par *La Patrie* (1933–1939),' *Mens, revue d'histoire intellectuelle de l'Amérique française* 4, no. 1 (automne 2003): 69–93; Patrick Poirier, 'La représentation du régime hitlérien par les éditorialistes du quotidien *La Patrie*, 1933–1939' (MA thesis, Université du Québec à Montréal, 2000); Lise Quirion, 'La presse québécoise d'expression française face au procès du maréchal Pétain,' *Bulletin d'histoire politique* 7, no. 2 (hiver 1999): 43–58.

13 Guy Lachapelle, *Claude Ryan et la violence du pouvoir: Le Devoir et la crise d'octobre, ou le combat de journalistes démocrates* (Sainte-Foy: Presses de l'Université Laval, 2005).

14 Manon Leroux, 'Le discours des acteurs de la crise d'octobre 1970 dans la presse francophone de Montréal, 1971–2000' (MA thesis, Université du Québec à Montréal, 2001).

15 Jérôme Coutard, 'Des valeurs en guerre: presse, propagande et culture de guerre au Québec, 1914–1918,' 2 vols. (PhD diss., Université Laval, 1999); Jérôme Coutard, 'Presse, censure et propagande en 1914–1918: la construction d'une culture de guerre,' *Bulletin d'histoire politique* 8, no. 2–3 (hiver-printemps 2000): 150–71.

16 Myriam Levert, 'La censure de la presse d'expression française du Québec durant la Première Guerre mondiale' (MA thesis, Université du Québec à Montréal, 2001); Myriam Levert, 'Le Québec sous le règne d'Anastasie:

l'expérience censoriale durant la Première Guerre mondiale,' *Revue d'histoire de l'Amérique française* 57, no. 3 (hiver 2004): 333–64.

17 Isabelle Dornic, 'Hier ne meurt jamais: vision et désillusion d'une quête identitaire féminine au Québec: *La Bonne parole*, organe de la Fédération nationale Saint-Jean-Baptiste, 1913–1958,' 2 vols. (PhD diss., Université Laval, 2004).

18 Simone Pilon, 'Constitution du corpus des écrits des femmes dans la presse canadienne-française entre 1883 et 1893 et analyse de l'usage des pseudonymes,' 2 vols. (PhD diss., Université Laval, 1999); Julie Roy, 'Stratégies épistolaires et écritures féminines: les Canadiennes à la conquête des lettres, 1639–1839,' 2 vols. (PhD diss, Université du Québec à Montréal, 2003).

19 Marie-Josée Béchard, 'Les hommes en transformation? une analyse des représentations des hommes au Québec à travers le magazine *Actualité*, 1960–1976' (MA thesis, Université du Québec à Montréal, 2003).

20 France Fouquet, 'La presse écrite: reflet de l'évolution de la famille québécoise de 1972 à 1995' (MA thesis, Université du Québec à Trois-Rivières, 2001).

21 Olivier Marcil, 'La question linguistique dans la pensée de Claude Ryan au *Devoir* (1962–1978): la difficile conciliation des principes nationalistes et libéraux,' *Mens, revue d'histoire intellectuelle de l'Amérique française* 2, no. 2 (printemps 2002): 193–231; Olivier Marcil, *La raison et l'équilibre: libéralisme, nationalisme et catholicisme dans la pensée de Claude Ryan au Devoir, 1962– 1978* (Montreal: Varia, 2002).

22 Éloïse Cassista, 'Le nationalisme du pays basque espagnol dans la presse québécoise (1966–1982)' (MA thesis, Université du Québec à Montréal, in progress).

23 Olivier Shareck, 'Évolution de l'opinion publique face à la reconnaissance des droits des gais et des lesbiennes au Québec telle que vue dans les journaux montréalais et dans les sondages, 1967–1994' (MA thesis, Université du Québec à Montréal, 2003).

24 Marie-Josée Thibault, 'L'évolution des journaux communautaires au Québec' (MA thesis, Université de Sherbrooke, 2000).

25 Julie Perrone, 'Le processus d'héroïsation du Rocket' (MA thesis, Université du Québec à Montréal, 2008).

26 Fabien Gabillet, 'La vraie France est au Canada! Les échos de la séparation de l'Église et de l'État de 1905 dans la presse canadienne-française' (MA thesis, Université Laval, 2000).

27 Dominique Marquis, 'Un nouveau combat pour l'Église: la presse catholique d'information (1907–1940),' *Études d'histoire religieuse* 68 (2002): 73–88.

28 Janice Thériault, 'D'un catholicisme à l'autre: trois ordres catholiques au
    Québec et leurs revues face à l'*Aggiornamento*, 1962–1970,' *Mens, revue
    d'histoire intellectuelle de l'Amérique française* 5, no. 1 (automne 2004): 7–71.
29 Gilles Routhier, 'Assurer la couverture médiatique de Vatican II au
    Canada: les initiatives de l'épiscopat canadien,' *Études d'histoire religieuse*
    68 (2002): 57–72.
30 Pierre Pagé, 'Cinquante ans d'émissions religieuses à la radio québécoise
    (1931–1983). De l'apologétique au dialogue avec les grandes religions,'
    Études d'histoire religieuse 68 (2002): 7–23.
31 Jocelyne Denault, 'Des religieuses cinéastes et des films à découvrir,' *Études*
    d'histoire religieuse 68 (2002): 89–94.
32 Brigitte Massé, 'L'évolution du traitement journalistique des enjeux
    bioéthiques dans la presse quotidienne québécoise de 1972 à 1995' (MA
    thesis, Université Laval, 1999).
33 Julie Roy and Nova Doyon, eds, *Le littéraire à l'oeuvre dans les périodiques
    québécois du XIXe siècle: projet Archibald* (Montreal: Crilcq, Université de
    Montréal, 2005).
34 Micheline Cambron, 'Sur les traces de la vie culturelle. Des périodiques
    comme source première,' in Micheline Cambron, ed., *La vie culturelle à
    Montréal vers 1900* (Montreal: Fides, 2005), 319–33.
35 Nova Doyon, 'Valentin Jautard (1736–1787) et la *Gazette littéraire de Mon-
    tréal* (1778–1779): vers un paradigme du littéraire' (MA thesis, Université
    du Québec à Montréal, 2002).
36 Nancy Houle, 'Origine et consolidation d'un réseau littéraire au XXe siècle:
    le réseau associé à la revue *La Relève*' (MA thesis, Université de Sher-
    brooke, 2001).
37 Maude Roux-Pratte, '*Le Bien public* (1933–1978): la réussite d'une entreprise
    mauricienne à travers ses réseaux' (PhD diss., Université du Québec à
    Montréal, 2008).
38 Marie-France Boucher, 'La construction du discours médiatique sur le
    cinéma au Québec, 1896–1939' (MA thesis, Université Laval, 2000); André
    Gaudreault and Jean-Pierre Sirois-Trahan, *La vie ou du moins ses apparences;
    émergence du cinéma dans la presse de la Belle Époque (1894–1910): anthologie*
    (Montreal: Cinémathèque québécoise, Grafics, 2002).
39 Hervé Guay, 'Les discours sur le théâtre dans la presse hebdomadaire
    montréalaise de langue française de 1898 à 1914: des genres journalistiques
    et des composantes identitaires en compétition' (PhD diss., Université du
    Québec à Montréal, 2005).
40 Michèle Martin, Béatrice Richard, and Dina Salha, 'La pré-modernité de

Radiomonde: un pas hésitant vers un Québec moderne,' *Histoire sociale /
Social History* 33, no. 65 (mai 2000): 37–57.

41 Guillaume Lefrançois, 'Rire le ventre vide: la caricature et les illustrations
dans les quotidiens québécois pendant la Crise des années 1930' (MA the-
sis, Université du Québec à Montréal, 2007).

42 Lucie Villeneuve, 'Rire et rébellion dans *Le Fantasque* de Napoléon Aubin
(1837–1845) ou comment se payer la tête à "lord du rhum,"' *Bulletin
d'histoire politique* 13, no. 2 (hiver 2005): 51–62.

43 Micheline Cambron, 'Humour et politique dans la presse québécoise du
XIXe siècle. Des formes journalistiques comme sources d'humour,' *Bulletin
d'histoire politique* 13, no. 2 (hiver 2005): 31–50; Sophie Gosselin, 'L'humour,
instrument journalistique dans l'oeuvre d'Hector Berthelot' (MA thesis,
Université du Québec à Montréal, 2008).

44 Pierre Pagé, 'Quelques aspects socio-politiques de l'humour radiopho-
nique (1940–1970),' *Bulletin d'histoire politique* 13, no. 2 (hiver 2005): 63–78.

45 Mathieu-Olivier Côté, 'La représentation du crime dans la presse écrite
québécoise: le cas d'*Allô Police*' (MA thesis, Université Laval, 2002). There
is no simple English translation of *faits divers*. The term refers to short news
items about crime, accidents, scandals, oddities, etc., that are generally
considered as frivolous or non-serious news.

46 Dominique Marquis, '*Le Devoir*: un produit unique,' *Les Cahiers du journal-
isme* 8 (2000): 60–74.

47 Dominique Marquis, *Un quotidien pour l'Église: L'Action catholique, 1910–
1940* (Montreal: Leméac, 2004). See also her article on the Catholic press in
chapter 1 of this volume.

48 Luc Côté and Jean-Guy Daigle, *Publicité de masse et masse publicitaire:
le marché québécois des années 1920 aux années 1960* (Ottawa: Presses de
l'Université d'Ottawa, 1999).

49 Louis Jacob, 'Histoire de la presse quotidienne au Québec de 1945 à 1995'
(MA thesis, Université de Montréal, 2003).

50 Mélanie Couture, 'L'appareil de presse trifluvien entre 1850 et 1920' (MA
thesis, Université du Québec à Montréal, 2008).

51 Marc-André Cyr, 'La presse anarchiste au Québec, 1976–2001' (MA thesis,
Université du Québec à Montréal, 2004).

52 Jean-Philippe Tremblay, 'Par-delà la ténacité et l'abnégation: la presse mu-
sicale au Québec, 1890–1959' (MA thesis, Université du Québec à Montréal,
2006).

53 Sophie Gosselin, 'L'humour, instrument journalistique.'

54 Bernard Bujold, *Pierre Péladeau, cet inconnu* (Montreal: Trait d'union, 2003).

55 Louis Fradet, *Les 50 ans du Syndicat de la rédaction du* Soleil, *1950–2000: un combat pour la profession* (Sillery: Septentrion, 2001).

56 Florence Le Cam, 'L'identité du groupe des journalistes du Québec au défi d'Internet,' 2 vols. (PhD diss., Université Laval and Université de Rennes, 2005). To be published by Leméac éditeur, Fall 2009.

57 Marc-François Bernier, *Éthique et déontologie du journalisme*, 2nd ed., rev. (Sainte-Foy: Presses de l'Université Laval, 2004); Patrick J. Brunet, ed. *L'éthique dans la société de l'information* (Sainte-Foy: Presses de l'Université Laval; Paris: L'Harmattan, 2001).

58 Armande Saint-Jean, *Éthique de l'information: fondements et pratiques au Québec depuis 1960* (Montreal: Presses de l'Université de Montréal, 2002).

59 Marie-Pier Frappier, 'Le discours des journalistes canadiens-français de 1945 à 1960 sur les normes journalistiques' (MA thesis, Université du Québec à Montréal, in progress).

60 Quebecois historians of culture have been inspired by work that has enriched French cultural history, including that by Daniel Roche, Roger Chartier, Robert Darnton, Jean-Yves Mollier, Dominique Kalifa, and others. See, for example, Robert Darnton, 'An Early Information Society: News and the Media in Eighteenth-Century Paris,' *American Historical Review* 105, no. 1 (February 2000): 1–35; Dominique Kalifa et Alain Vaillant, 'Pour une histoire culturelle et littéraire de la presse française au XIXe siècle,' *Le Temps des médias* 1, no. 2 (2004): 197–214; Jean-Yves Mollier, 'La naissance de la culture médiatique à la Belle Époque,' *Études littéraires* 30, no. 1 (automne 1997): 15–26.

61 Patricia Lockhart Fleming and Yvan Lamonde, general eds, *Histoire du livre et de l'imprimé au Canada / History of the Book in Canada*, 3 vols. (Montreal and Toronto: Presses de l'Université de Montréal/University of Toronto Press, 2004–7).

10 Encounters with Theory

PAUL RUTHERFORD

S[tudent] – But I have lots of descriptions already! I'm drowning in them. That's just my problem. That's why I'm lost and that's why I thought it would be useful to come to you. Can't ANT help me with this mass of data? I need a framework!

P[rofessor] – 'My Kingdom for a frame!' Very moving; I think I understand your desperation.[1]

This essay is about my search for a frame. Personal narratives may now be in fashion once again because they capture actual experience. Nonetheless this essay requires a modicum of justification. It grew out of a short conference paper I presented in a plenary session devoted to considering the issue 'What Is Media History (and what is it useful for)?' I had once looked upon media history as the study of print and broadcasting institutions, a kind of project which ought to demonstrate the role of the media as active and significant players in the events of the past. I still think that is a reasonable answer to the questions posed in the session. But it is not my answer any more. I now regard media history as a form of cultural history, more properly a part of the study of meanings and signification, where it is crucial to understanding the networks of pleasure and power that organize life. I explored this proposition, again in very personal terms, by reflecting on my own experiences as well as my most recent research project, a monograph that I completed in the spring of 2006.

This essay follows a similar course, except that it deals even more with the issue of theory, which to my mind is the most important change that has overcome the humanities and social sciences since I began work in the early 1970s. I have added an extended list of foot-notes to elaborate and extend my personal narrative, sometimes to contradict my idiosyncratic views, always to highlight other sources or views that might assist a further exploration of cultural theory and its applications. I have also included a brief reflection on the virtues of theory, especially in the context of Canadian media history. For I write this at a time when the theory wave is apparently receding, when cultural theory is under attack in some quarters.[2] And I write in response to what seems to me an overreaction against the postmodern excesses of the immediate past.

A few definitions are in order. I regard theory as a linked series of fundamental insights into how people, their relations, and their arte-facts operate in the world at large. Its purpose is to render intelligible the human condition, although to be sure its acolytes have earned an unenviable reputation as the purveyors of jargon.[3] There are a few mas-ters of high theory, all European, all male: notably Mikhail Bakhtin, Jür-gen Habermas, and Michel Foucault, each of whom had an enormous impact on shaping the intellectual world after 1970. But the empire of theory has drawn widely from anthropology (Clifford Geertz), sociol-ogy (Pierre Bourdieu), literary studies (Terry Eagleton) and visual stud-ies (Guy Debord), British Marxism (Raymond Williams) and American feminism (Judith Butler), linguistics and semiotics (A.J. Greimas).[4] It is, above all, a branch of philosophy because it seeks knowledge about the principles and causes of life. Cultural theory, my main concern here, explores the symbolic foundation of everyday life. I look upon culture as a dynamic relationship among symbols, meanings, and practices. The authors of cultural history focus on texts and images, on signs and discourses, to discover how the culture fashions power and pleas-ure, the body and the self, a sense of time and place.[5] So the histori-cal dimension of cultural studies involves exploring what one might term 'the history behind History,' the foundations out of which are built all kinds of distinct subfields, whether social or economic, political or international history.

Supposedly everyone has a theory, even if they do not acknowledge the fact. But that is beside the point. What counts is engagement, or in the case of the historian the application of the insights of theory to the understanding of character and circumstance in times past. I was trained as a Canadian historian at the University of Toronto in the late 1960s, which meant I was taught that history depended, first and fore-most, on the archives. That explained why as a doctoral student I spent long hours in the National Library in Ottawa reading the editorial pages of one newspaper after another, all in an attempt to understand the character of popular nationalism in the late nineteenth century. I have never shed the view that useful studies, whether about the media or not, must be rooted in primary research. What this training did not do was give me any appreciation of the need for theory, some mode of understanding the significance of all the ideas and ideologies at play. In short I was strong on descriptions, like Bruno Latour's putative student, but lacking a frame. It was only slowly that I came to realize this was a major problem.

The issue that exercised me then was the failure to admit the significance of the press as anything more than a record of what happened, an expression of public opinion, or a channel for the views of politicians and churchmen. At the time, media history, in Canada anyway, was mostly composed of biographies of political journalists and, something very similar, accounts of individual newspapers or like institutions.[6] It was a branch of intellectual history, and not an especially honoured branch. Indeed my initial obsession with the editorial pages was a sign of this conception of newspapers as vehicles of some doctrine or another. The one special research instrument employed by newspaper historians, mostly outside Canada, was called content analysis, which amounted to counting the number of times a particular word or set of words appeared in a carefully defined group of records. Unfortunately, this technique was both enormously time-consuming and usually sterile because it missed the complexities of meaning. It assumed that a word like 'nation' had a fixed meaning, akin to an arithmetic figure, so its frequency in the textual record might be used to determine its significance in the broader world of discourse. Here history had been subsumed in statistics.[7]

There was an alternative approach of sorts: that pioneered by Harold Innis and hyped by Marshall McLuhan, where, putting this very simply, the medium was the message.[8] The view of Innis and McLuhan in my circles in the 1970s was mostly dismissive, even though McLuhan was still active on campus at the University of Toronto. Still, when I began to worry about the need for a frame, I took the time to read carefully through the works of both theorists. The trouble I found with their approach was not just that it seemed so deterministic, and unlikely, but that I did not know how to go about operationalizing the insights, which you could argue was just a failure of imagination on my part.[9] (I can recall my surprise when one doctoral student explained how he intended to employ the insights of both Marx and Innis to explore Toronto newspapers in the late nineteenth century.) Beyond that, it seemed to me that the approach neglected the most interesting parts of any study, namely the content, what was said or written or shown. I argued as much in my first book *The Making of the Canadian Media*,[10] which was meant in part to show that neither Innis nor McLuhan was of much use: 'far more important is the content of messages and the phenomenon of mass communication' than 'the primacy of communications technology in the making of civilization,' or so I concluded then (124).

How fitting that *The Making of the Canadian Media* appeared in a pioneering series devoted to the sociology of Canada.[11] In large part I had derived the frame for my history from the writings of sociologists and communications scholars, British as well as American, such as Joseph Klapper,[12] Dennis McQuail,[13] or Melvin DeFleur and Sandra Ball-Rockeach.[14] On my reading, and there was a bit of misreading as well, the sociology of mass communications demonstrated the utility of the media as vital and autonomous institutions which served to inform and shape their host society. I concluded that they might be 'the masters of consciousness' but not 'the masters of fate' (124), a contrast which in the light of my later work appears bizarre, signifying an impossible opposition. Whatever the virtues of the book as description, I was a proponent of a kind of functionalism, and of something later labelled neoliberalism, that often evaded issues of power and pleasure, especially of what people actually did with the messages of the media. Indeed *The Making of the Canadian Media* was very much a biography of an institution: it did not, and given its slim size could not, deal at any length with the content of newspapers, radio, or television. Instead the book described the career of the media sympathetically as a part of the larger story of nation-building and the development of an open society.

I did not break away from this loose frame when I set out to convert my dissertation on national ideas into a monograph on the emergence of the daily press in Canada. *A Victorian Authority*[15] was also heavy on description, though in this case the account rested on a close reading of news, editorials, advertising, and entertainment. I even indulged in some statistical analysis of the broader categories of information, about life, about the world, about the nation, that were made available to Canadian readers by different sorts of newspapers. More novel, or so I thought at the time, was my flirtation with a brand of semiotics, inspired by the first of the many French theorists I would come to honour, Roland Barthes. I was especially taken by his book of essays entitled *Mythologies*,[16] less so his *Elements of Semiology*,[17] a much more theoretical work which did not suit my empirical temperament at the time. These books, of course, were decades old when I came to them, evidence of how slowly the diffusion of theory could be unless it fell on fertile minds. In any case I endeavoured, albeit modestly, to employ the concept of signs as well as notions of myth to explain just what it was the daily press was doing in the country's big cities.

In the early 1980s, I determined to investigate the first two decades of Canadian television programming. I was moved by that typical desire of the archival historian, namely to explore a topic few others had tackled, at least in any depth.[18] What became *When Television Was Young*[19] treated this story as a noble experiment which succeeded in French Quebec but failed in English Canada. In effect it was an institutional study, albeit one that included both public and private services. As before, the project required extensive research in the archives to pore over CBC files, programming and audience reports, magazine reviews, as well as to view a wide selection of offerings. Once more, the project conformed to the sociological paradigm. I had set out to answer Harold Lasswell's famous question, 'Who says what, how, to whom, with what effect?'[20] The emphasis was on the 'Who' and the 'What,' so I was most concerned with the production side of broadcasting, which meant that a lot of effort went into charting the history of the CBC (since CTV and the independents did not produce much that seemed of any significance). Running through the analysis was that old theme of nation-building, seemingly the default for many a Canadian historian.

But as time went on I had become increasingly interested in other dimensions of the story. One of these was what I termed 'McLuhan's Question (with a little help from Harold Innis): what happens to society when a new medium of communication enters the picture?' I decided that the short answer was not much, or rather a process more of 'adjustment than revolution' (6). At the end of the book, I did offer a more nuanced discussion, based on the experience across the Western world, where I emphasized 'the contrary nature of television' (486), its capacity to buttress authority as well as to cause upset, to educate and to entertain, to foster cynicism as well as conformity, and so on. Television became a 'failed revolution,' its potential for change never realized, because other institutions, notably the state and business, moved to control its development. Had the sober presumptions of sociology once more trumped the wild speculations of the two communications gurus?[21] Not quite: it did occur to me that television had brought such momentous changes to culture and context that authority of all sorts was affected, not to mention the ordinary life of so many people, now conditioned by the profusion of images.[22] I sought refuge in mythology, resurrecting that two-faced Roman god Janus as the appropriate symbol of·modern television.

But the task of researching the television archive had led me to make what would prove a more momentous intellectual discovery, namely the burgeoning fields of cultural studies and the then 'new' cultural history. I wanted to write 'a viewers' history.' I hoped to understand how people appreciated TV programming, something I found the sociological paradigm, even the so-called 'uses and gratifications' variant, did not really do.[23] Cultural studies purported to offer another way of approaching this general problem of popular understanding. In the mid-1980s cultural studies was still a British invention then rapidly spreading through the North American academy among younger scholars who wished to analyse how class, gender, and race marked the artefacts of popular culture.[24] I did read the work of such ethnographers of television as David Morley and Ien Ang, although applying their findings to a history project that had mere ratings data to work with proved challenging.[25] (Only years later, when researching *Weapons of Mass Persuasion*[26] on the selling of the invasion of Iraq, was I able to conduct a small experiment in ethnography by interviewing in depth a sample of television viewers.) I was, for a time, most taken by the writings of John Fiske and John Hartley (notably *Reading Television*):[27] they played around with notions of preferred readings, 'aberrant decoding,' and its replacement 'polysemy,' a semiotic concept which emphasized how often a text was best described as a contested site full of multiple and contradictory meanings.[28] Meanwhile the 'new' cultural history, driven by American academics, was developing similar kinds of tools to understand the nature and the meanings of written and visual artefacts in the past.[29]

Increasingly the kind of text that most intrigued me was the television commercial. I had found the chapter on advertising in *When Television Was Young* a particular pleasure to research and write. After much additional reading, I concluded that we, meaning the affluent West, had recently entered into the era of 'marketing's moment,' when advertising and propaganda had become the most prominent discourse in the public sphere. I wanted to research the origins and the trajectory of this moment, which required that I move away from Canadian history proper to explore the philosophy and techniques of marketing in a much broader context.[30] That said, I did not wholly break with my past, always trying to incorporate some Canadian content in my projects – one of my ongoing peeves was how too often outsiders neglected Canada and how Canadian historians worried too little about what happened elsewhere.[31] Consequently my analysis of television commercials included a fair chunk of material on the Bessies, award-winning ads authored in English Canada, which illuminated aspects of a Canadian sensibility.

I planned what was published as *The New Icons? The Art of Television Advertising* in the tradition of cultural studies.[32] I no longer worried about the sociological paradigm, the mechanics of production and distribution, even the economics of the whole endeavour. Rather I was caught up in the joys of the discourse: I avidly consumed the ads themselves, worrying about their shape, their design, their narratives, how they used sounds and above all images, sometimes contradictory, to fashion appeals. I also probed what people thought of ads, using not only a variety of industry data but the responses of the students I surveyed in my own classes on advertising history. I reasoned that TV commercials constituted a living, if lesser, art that embodied the powerful ideology of consumerism, making these akin to medieval icons (an earlier form of promotion) in their cultural significance. The result was something of a 'fan's history' of commercials, full of that passion for the object which so easily afflicted writers who caught the virus of postmodernism. (No wonder the paperback cover of the initial edition sported an endorsement from a famous Canadian ad maker, Jerry Goodis: 'For anyone who owns a TV set.')

I still had not found a satisfying frame. The overall study of advertising and popular culture was much stronger on techniques of analysis than on schemes of interpretation and explanation. But cultural studies did prove the gateway into cultural theory. Fiske and company were forever citing a whole gamut of European theorists, especially the French variety. It was their example which led me to the study of hegemony, notably the prison writings of the Italian Marxist Antonio Gramsci and the much later British Marxist Raymond Williams.[33] The trouble with the concept of hegemony, though, was that it seemed too 'total' and too reductive, presuming the existence somewhere (in big business, in government, in the media?) of a self-conscious headquarters which masterminded events. In particular it deprived most of the people most of the time of any agency, except it seemed to consent or, occasionally, to resist.[34]

But, fortunately, there were many other theorists to choose from in the repertoire of cultural studies. I went back to semiotics, to Roland Barthes and Umberto Eco especially, who illustrated how systems of signs operated through and across institutions. Most important to my endeavours, I tackled the works of such luminaries as Jürgen Habermas, Mikhail Bakhtin, Paul Ricoeur, Jean Baudrillard, but above all Michel Foucault. The Habermas I was interested in was the historian of the public sphere[35] who outlined a theory of politics where not the practice of voting or the system of parties but the character of discourse, the way people talked and wrote, determined the nature of democracy.[36] Bakhtin offered insights into the world of the carnivalesque (*Rabelais and His World*, 1984), the meaning of high and low in cultural practice, and the persistence of subversion throughout history.[37] He fitted well with my reading of Ricoeur: I was not so much interested in what Ricoeur said about, say, sin or metaphor, on which much of his fame rested, but about utopia and ideology,[38] and how these formations played out a complicated exchange in theory and life. Likewise what I took from Baudrillard was his notion of simulacra, the idea that many agencies, though most especially media, constructed free-floating images that worked on the world of the real.[39] For me, Foucault (about whom much more in a moment) talked of power and pleasure. I still recall the excitement, that moment of epiphany, which strange to say occurred on a cruise, when Foucault's introductory *The History of Sexuality*[40] first made compelling sense. Perhaps the Caribbean air eased the understanding of his theory? (In any case I have made this a habit, most recently bringing Paul Virilio and Jean-Paul Sartre to the North Atlantic.) These works provided me with techniques of analysis and frameworks of interpretation which came to alter my view of what was media history.

I must underline the fact that none of this reading, really a program of self-education, was complete. I did not treat the full oeuvre of these theorists, except in the case of Foucault. I selected, I sampled. The reason is the criterion of utility. Except for a brief time, theory for its own sake did not interest me. My encounters with theory have nearly always been selfish. I read philosophy as a historian in search of insights, agendas, vocabularies which would advance the progress of my own work. So I never explored in depth Habermas's arguments about communicative action since these seemed too abstracted from the messiness of history. I discarded Jacques Derrida early on, and later Jacques Lacan as well, because their arguments seemed so opaque as to be perverse.[41] I am willing to admit that such an approach to theory encourages a kind of misreading, hopefully a creative misreading. The point is that theory is not gospel, that getting it right is not the most important task of a cultural historian. Rather this scholar needs to find those tools which will meet his or her need for a frame. From this standpoint, theory amounts to a resource out of which the historian constructs an intellectual toolbox.

I still read articles and essays in the field of mass communication studies when these pertained to whatever I was researching. But I found that the sociological paradigm, and especially the variant that was common in marketing studies, all too often generated little results of slight importance, whether on matters of content or impact, unless these were refashioned in the wider context of myth, sign, and discourse, or more generally what have been called symbolic practices. Later, particularly after I had read Bruno Latour, it became clear that the literature on mass communications had an unfortunate tendency to presume finished projects and stable products.[42] Instead, the meaning of texts was never constant since that depended on a process of negotiation between producer and consumer. Indeed the media subject was always in a state of construction (and sometimes deconstruction?), an unfinished work so to speak, just as the communications situation was an assemblage of time, mood, design, and accident, among much else. There was much more flux and uncertainty than the sociological paradigm allowed.

Little of the reading I completed in the early 1990s had a direct impact on *The New Icons*, though. The reason was the way I generate research projects, which always reflect my knowledge at the moment of inception. I was still locked into the mode of cultural studies when I designed the research on television advertising. I finally worked cultural theory into the next stage of my account of the history of 'marketing's moment,' namely the rise of advocacy advertising, which became *Endless Propaganda*.[43] Ironically I could not settle on one theory. I was then caught up in the happy chaos of postmodernism, convinced it was best to avoid announcing truth by consciously employing different theories of explanation. So, when writing, I borrowed the frames and the vocabulary of Habermas, Gramsci, Foucault, Ricoeur, and Baudrillard (among others) to assess various dimensions of the propaganda in question. That was almost a recipe for disaster. One of the assessors of the manuscript, apparently rooted in an older tradition of propaganda studies, was mightily disturbed by my taste for philosophers he/she thought were irrelevant to the understanding of this brand of culture.[44] Another assessor, this one in the tradition of cultural studies, found the manuscript's ambivalence more a form of incoherence. It was all a lesson in the dangers of applying theory too liberally: you can easily run into a reader who does not like your choice or the way you have employed theory. What saved *Endless Propaganda* was the wealth of empirical detail, in short extensive work in the archives on social and issue ads, corporate advocacy, public service announcements, and political campaigns. The fun aspect of the project, the play with theory, that was a liability.

In short, I had got theory, perhaps too much theory. One consequence of reading lots of poststructuralism, especially French theory of the likes of Jean-Paul Lyotard and Jean Baudrillard, was that I came to define myself as a postmodern, intent on discovering how culture embodied particular subject positions and relations of power. Nowadays that credo seems to me a fatal disease for a historian since if the profession is not in the business of seeking the 'truth' about the past, something a postmodern must see as impossible, then why do we bother researching and writing our tomes? Better we should try historical fiction.[45]

My use of theory was much more focused when I turned to the story of what I have called 'the Eros project,' now published as *A World Made Sexy*. The book explained how the world of bodies and objects, sometimes places as well, was eroticized during the course of the twentieth century. I would not have considered this project an appropriate topic back when I started writing media history in the mid-1970s. But now it seemed yet another example of a regime of authority (à la Foucault) shaped by the emergence of 'marketing's moment.' I had become convinced that the encounter with theory was one major route to writing good history, and not just at the stage of writing.[46] Latour's student sought inspiration too late in the game. Far better to engage with theory before launching the research project, to employ the theory to shape the character of the research.

Indeed *A World Made Sexy* derives from some passing comments Foucault made in an interview relating to his own history of sexuality, which was just about to appear.[47] His book concentrated chiefly on the nineteenth century. Things had changed dramatically in the course of the next century. The past practice of 'heavy, ponderous, meticulous and constant' discipline over the body no longer suited the type of capitalist society which had emerged by the 1960s, he asserted. 'Then it was discovered that control of sexuality could be attenuated and given new forms.' All of which led to a novel process of governance, specifically a reworking of the power of the erotic and the erotics of power. 'We find a new mode of investment [in the body] which presents itself no longer in the form of control by repression but that of control by stimulation.' Witness the 'economic (and perhaps also ideological) exploitation of eroticisation, from sun-tan products to pornographic films. "Get undressed – but be slim, good-looking, tanned!"'[48] It was this process I set out to chronicle. Here was a case where a work of theory inspired a historical investigation which, in the end, led me to try to stretch the theorist's notion of biopolitics (on which more later) to encompass matters he had never discussed in detail.

The study of 'the Eros project' is probably not the last of my works on marketing's moment, though it has proved the most adventurous so far. The research carried me a good distance from the analysis of media institutions as such. But it focused upon what were obviously vehicles of publicity, of a particular kind of persuasive communications that sought to construct the viewer as a desiring subject. I conducted research in, for example, sex museums in Europe, New York, and Shanghai. I spent time in galleries viewing exhibitions of erotic and surrealist art, and viewing the responses to such material by visitors. I read widely in the works of Freud and the Freudo-Marxists, studied the Barbie campaigns and *Playboy* in the 1950s and 1960s, watched a marvellous array of James Bond movies and trailers, as well as photographed street and wall posters from Rome to Beijing.

The largest chunk of time was spent collecting and assessing what I call displays of sin and fables of lust. These are the best expressions of publicity as erotica where the ad makers draw on the repertoire of pornography to attach an erotic charge to a brand.[49] Consider just two examples, both commercials for jeans, a product that is often rendered sexy. A 1988 British spot called 'Climate' (Levi's 501 jeans) built a narrative of male display where a stunningly handsome man slowly put on his jeans in front of an admiring audience of young and old, men and women, in a diner somewhere in the American west. By contrast, 'X-Rated,' a South African ad (1999) for Soviet jeans, depicted the lovemaking of two beautiful people which ended when the woman, having tied her partner to the bed, stole his jeans and escaped with the prize. There was a tale of true lust.

My analysis of these commercials and the rest of my research material employed techniques and concepts developed to read culture. So, for instance, I appropriated the approach Barthes used to understand the fashion system: in the book I analysed in depth a hundred commercials which were extreme and/or distinct examples of the full variety of erotic ads in common circulation and which worked to highlight nearly all the possible differences in the signs of sex.[50] I used the insights of Bakhtin on the representation of the 'high' and 'low' bodies and the expression of the carnivalesque to assess such items as Maidenform bra ads and Madonna's videos.[51] I borrowed from both Barthes on myth and Baudrillard on simulacra to interpret particular kinds of visual performances. I surveyed the literature on marketing, especially that influenced by cultural theory, to discern how people take possession of what they see and read.[52] The point is that cultural theory has supplied me with the tools to satisfy my aesthetic and analytical priorities, that is, to understand the actual content of the media as well as what people do with it.

I turned to Foucault to provide the overall structure of interpretation. I did investigate other approaches, of course, particularly that of Herbert Marcuse, one of the most famous members of the Frankfurt School. Marcuse talked about the media much more than did Foucault. Marcuse's most famous concept was 'repressive desublimation,' derived from Marx and Freud, whereby authority harnessed the libido to the task of legitimating capitalism and war. It did so by offering all manner of sensual and sexual gratifications, linked to material goods: 'Pleasure, thus adjusted, generates submission,' he lamented.[53] It is obvious how central advertising and the mass media were to such a transformation. But even if you accepted his Freudian notion of a pre-existing sexual desire, outside of history as it were, which I did not, there were too many problems with Marcuse's concept, including its assumption that the public was effectively programmed. His views remained important and his moral qualms apposite, but neither were sufficient to explain what happened.

Foucault's great dramas of sexuality and power offered a more complex and so more subtle theory which suited how the Eros project worked – and did not work. True, at one point in his career, particularly in *Discipline and Punish: The Birth of the Prison*,[54] he had fashioned a bleak view of authority in which the individual seemed caught in a box, unable to escape the trammels of power, forever lacking agency. His take on power, however, became much more nuanced after the mid-1970s, when he turned to the study of biopolitics and governmentality.[55] Biopolitics involved the effort to command the life and the health of populations.[56] Biopolitical enterprises operated on desire; they functioned more through persuasion, even seduction, than coercion. They worked to intensify the process of circulation: the purpose of biopolitics was to induce the acceleration of goods, ideas, innovations, emotions, and orders through the social body, indeed to mobilize the public to attain some kind of commercial, political, moral, or social progress.[57] The approach has the virtue of directing attention to the mechanisms and discourses of rule, the details of governance, in a way which I find superior to its rivals, especially the notion of hegemony. Indeed Foucault pointed to the existence of grand technologies of power and understanding that have operated to shape life throughout the West. These could take a singular form as 'regulated and concerted systems,' and he instanced 'educational institutions.'[58]

The Eros project was one of these biopolitical enterprises in which a special arrangement of technologies generated both pleasure and power. Let me outline the system:

1. a technology of production, embedded in the realm of things: the rise of a libidinal economy, the motive force of the enterprise, that fashioned and distributed an expanding variety of sexy brands, especially after 1970, in search of national and eventually global markets;
2. a technology of domination, involving various techniques of control: the emergence of a regime of stimulation, linked closely to the marketing industry and financed by business, which deployed the techniques of surveillance and even more spectacle to determine the conduct of consumers;
3. a technology of communication, about the domain of signs: the escalating growth of publicity as erotica, the most important technology, delivered by magazines, television commercials, movie trailers, ad posters, music videos, and the like to huge audiences that soon extended well beyond the affluent zone of countries;
4. a technology of the self, pertinent to the realm of belief and action: the spread of an eroticism that enticed individuals to devote themselves to the pursuit of pleasure, to seek happiness and perfection through the consumption of sights, places, and commodities. This technology of the self was the reason the project also counted as a form of emancipation (as well as domination): the erotic being was a 'knowing subject,' not just a creature of appetite or a victim of programming, but an active rather than a passive individual, engaged in 'a practice of self-formation.'[59]

In this interpretation, the media, communication, and signification play the crucial role as agents in a common effort to generate a particular subjectivity, that erotic being who is, of course, a historical artefact, the result of discursive labours. Publicity was the key instrument of circulation. This publicity transformed desire into a series of wants and needs. It was through marketing that a regime of stimulation emerged. It was through a series of different modes of communication that publicity as erotica reached out to construct consumers and markets. It was these publics as watchers and listeners who possessed the Barbie ads or the Madonna narratives and the like to fashion their own play or identity.

All of which brings me back to the notion of the media as a technology of signification. These media are broadly defined here to encompass a whole range of vehicles that radiate and propagate eroticism: not just newspapers or television but also art, museums, and clothes. A slightly modified version of Harold Lasswell's old question still remains central to the research agenda and to the framework of interpretation in media history: Who controls the media, why do they communicate, what are the messages (preferred and otherwise), how are they distributed, to whom, and what effect do they have, and especially what do people do with the messages? But the central issue is always the content, the variety of messages, in a word the text, how it is composed and consumed, how it links to the dominant system of ideas as well as its rivals. This history of the text, again I say my kind of media history, is very much a part of the cultural history of modernity.

I make no claim that I have found the Holy Grail – except for myself. Foucault is not for everyone. The effects of the postmodern infection linger: there is no one theory that suits all cases. In which case one might wonder what justifies this personal narrative? Because my experience speaks to what has been called the cultural turn in the social sciences and the humanities over the past generation. The turn has finally begun to bear fruit in Canadian history with the publication of a series of works that investigate aspects of popular or public culture, some of which employ a variety of theories.[60] Among this collection are three excellent books on communications, each published by the University of Toronto Press, all in 2000. Jeffrey McNairn's *The Capacity to Judge*[61] employed the idea of the public sphere to frame a study of the rise of a 'deliberative democracy' in Ontario in the first half of the nineteenth century. It amounts to an exploration of a Canadian version of the grand story of the Enlightenment. Valerie Korineck's *Roughing It in the Suburbs*[62] drew on cultural studies, Foucault, and feminism to analyse the evolution and character of *Chatelaine* magazine and its audiences during the 1950s and 1960s. She charted here the organization of a particular and vibrant kind of women's culture and community. Gerald Friesen replayed the part of Innis in *Citizens and Nation* to show how successive systems of communication organized the sense of time and space upon which ordinary people built their lives. He amply realized his purpose: 'to explain in new terms why "Canada" is a meaningful public identity.'[63] Each of the authors use different kinds of conceptions drawn from cultural theory to present compelling and novel explanations of important events in the history of the Canadian media. Together, they serve with the other exemplars of cultural history as a vehicle for a new and fuller understanding, both of the trajectory of the Canadian project and of the public narratives that have given its communities a different shape and character over the course of the past two centuries.

In the end the point is not whether Foucault or Habermas or any of the other luminaries are right but whether they are useful. The crucial virtue of theory is that it enables the practising historian to put his work in the broader context of culture. The particular concepts must have at least two features, as Richard Ohmann has put it: they must serve as 'a theory of how history happens rather than an ad hoc matching of causes and effects,' and these concepts must assign 'priority to some agents and forces.' That second feature is essential. Lacking it, the theory 'will either dissolve into an agnostic muddle – history is just one damn thing after another – or it will raise itself into a metaphysical principle that explains everything and hence nothing (usually through a tacit appeal to values that show "us" to be the chosen people).'[64] The useful theory guides the historian in the task of setting a research agenda and designing research instruments. It offers explanations. It serves as a kind of lingua franca to link otherwise disparate projects.[65] Or, as Latour's student realized, it can supply the frame which makes all the archival work meaningful.

NOTES

1 Part of a dialogue between two fictional souls on the virtues of Actor Network Theory (ANT), authored by Bruno Latour (published online, available October 2008, at http://www.bruno-latour.fr/articles/article/090.html). In fact Latour went on to claim that ANT would not serve the student's purpose: 'But no, ANT is pretty useless for that. Its main tenet is that actors themselves make everything, including their own frames, their

own theories, their own contexts, their own metaphysics, even their own ontologies ... So the direction to follow would be more descriptions, I am afraid.'

2 One sign of this retreat was when Terry Eagleton, a major figure in literary theory, published *After Theory* (London: Allen Lane 2003). This work, meant for students and general readers, opened with the bold declaration, 'The golden age of cultural theory is long past' (1). The book was much influenced by Eagleton's distaste for postmodernism and what that creed (or was it just a mood?) had done to the academy in the past two decades. Eagleton had written an earlier attack on this creed, *The Illusions of Postmodernism* (Oxford and Cambridge, MA: Blackwell 1996). My own impression is that Eagleton's disenchantment was rooted in his socialist and especially Marxist views that hardly fit with the present moment in political life.

3 Réal Fillion provides a brief, useful description of the character of theorizing in a discussion of the work of Michael Hardt and Antonio Negri, two theorists who came to fame because their ideas, especially the book *Empire*, seemed so appropriate to understanding the world after 9/11. Fillion's argument drew on the arguments of the philosopher Michael Oakeshott. Fillion, 'Moving beyond Biopower: Hardt and Negri's Post-Foucauldian Philosophy of History,' *History and Theory* 44 (December 2005): 48–9.

4 Other scholars, of course, would make different choices of leading theorists, and of the significant works of these theorists. My comment refers, in particular, to these books: Clifford Geertz, *The Interpretation of Cultures: Selected Essays* (New York: Basic Books, 1973), where he outlines his notion of culture as text and performance; Pierre Bourdieu, *Distinction: A Social Critique of the Judgment of Taste*, trans. Richard Nice (Cambridge, MA: Harvard University Press 1984), which explores ideas of cultural capital and lifestyle; Terry Eagleton, *Ideology: An Introduction* (London and New York: Verso, 1991), an account of how ideology and hegemony organize life; Guy Debord, *The Society of the Spectacle*, trans. Donald Nicholson-Smith (New York: Zone Books 1995), a wild ride of the 1960s that portrayed capitalism as a visual field; Raymond Williams, *Keywords* (London: Fontana 1976), a fund of provocative definitions of crucial terms in contemporary use; Judith Butler, *Bodies That Matter: On the Discursive Limits of 'Sex'* (New York and London: Routledge, 1993), a critique of the prevailing ideas of sex and gender; and A.J. Greimas and Jacques Fontanille, *The Semiotics of Passions: From States of Affairs to States of Feeling*, trans. Paul Perron and Frank Collins (Minneapolis and London: University of Minnesota Press, 1993), which explores the expression of emotions. Williams, Eagleton, and

Debord were each, in very different ways, in the Marxist camp: indeed cultural theory was in the beginning heavily imprinted with Marxian notions.

5 There are many works that outline the nature of cultural history. I have found most useful two books organized, in part, by Lynn Hunt, herself a major figure in the field in the United States. Lynn Hunt, ed., *The New Cultural History* (Berkeley: University of California Press, 1989), and Victoria Bonnell and Lynn Hunt, eds, *Beyond the Cultural Turn: New Directions in the Study of Society and Culture* (Berkeley: University of California Press, 1999).

6 Which does not mean that these works lacked merit. Rather there were some fine studies of powerful editors, notably Maurice Careless's two volume *Brown of the Globe* (Toronto: Macmillan, 1959–63) and Ramsay Cook's *The Politics of John W. Dafoe and the Free Press* (Toronto: University of Toronto Press, 1963). In a different vein was that outstanding investigation of the details of press debate, P.B. Waite's *The Life and Times of Confederation: Politics, Newspapers and the Union of British North America* (Toronto: University of Toronto Press, 1963). These works retained their value because they were grounded in careful, empirical research and thoughtful analysis of what the record revealed.

7 Of course many other scholars have found content analysis a useful tool, especially when mixed with, say, semiotics. See, for example, William Leiss, Stephen Kline, and Sut Jhally, *Social Communication in Advertising: Persons, Products and Images of Well-Being*, 2nd ed. (Scarborough, ON: Nelson, 1990).

8 I am referring, in particular, to Innis's two works, *Empire and Communications* (Oxford: Clarendon, 1950) and *The Bias of Communication* (Toronto: University of Toronto Press, 1951), and to McLuhan's two books *The Gutenberg Galaxy: The Making of Typographic Man* (Toronto: University of Toronto Press, 1962) and *Understanding Media: The Extensions of Man* (New York and Toronto: McGraw-Hill, 1964).

9 Indeed it was a failure of imagination, at least in the case of Innis, as I learned much later when I became familiar with the work of James W. Carey: see, in particular, his collection *Communication as Culture: Essays on Media and Society* (Boston: Unwin Hyman, 1989).

10 *The Making of the Canadian Media* (Toronto: McGraw-Hill Ryerson, 1978).

11 The series was the 'McGraw-Hill Ryerson Series in Canadian Sociology,' edited by Lorne Tepperman.

12 *The Effects of Mass Communication* (Glencoe, IL: Free Press, 1960).

13 *Toward a Sociology of Mass Communications* (London : Collier-Macmillan, 1969)

14 *Theories of Mass Communication*, 3rd ed. (New York: David McKay, 1975).
15 *A Victorian Authority: The Daily Press in Late Nineteenth-Century Canada* (Toronto: University of Toronto Press, 1982).
16 *Mythologies*, trans. A. Lavers (London: Jonathan Cape, 1972).
17 *Elements of Semiology*, trans. Annette Lavers and Colin Smith (New York: Hill and Wang, 1968).
18 At the time, there was an important exception: Frank W. Peers, *The Public Eye: Television and the Politics of Canadian Broadcasting 1952–1968* (Toronto: University of Toronto Press 1979). Peers's study focused on policy and administration, mostly by government and the broadcasting authorities. By the time I had finished my project, there were two other major works on the story of broadcasting: Marc Raboy's *Missed Opportunities: The Story of Canada's Broadcasting Policy* (Montreal: McGill-Queen's University Press, 1990) and Richard Collins's *Culture, Communication, and National Identity: The Case of Canadian Television* (Toronto: University of Toronto Press, 1990). Collins also studied the actual programming, among many other aspects of broadcasting, although his focus was on the period after 1970.
19 *When Television Was Young: Primetime Canada, 1952–1967* (Toronto: Uiversity of Toronto Press, 1990).
20 Likely I was introduced to Lasswell's formulation at an early stage in my work on communications: see H.D Lasswell, 'The Structure and Function of Communication in Society,' in L. Bryson, ed., *The Communication of Ideas* (New York: Harper and Row, 1948), 37–51. Lasswell was a prominent American political scientist of the 1930s and 1940s, famous for his work on propaganda and opinion making. But I recall that I became aware of its significance indirectly, through a critique by Raymond Williams, *Television: Technology and Cultural Form* (Glasgow: Fontana/Collins, 1974), 120–6, who argued that what was missing from the equation was the question of 'Why' – or, as Williams put it, the final phrase 'and for what purpose?' Sometimes theory works its magic in a complicated fashion.
21 I had, in fact, included a section in the book on 'McLunacy' which harshly critiqued McLuhan's take on television: *When Television Was Young*, 26–37.
22 Looking back, especially perusing the endnotes, the place where all scholars leave their mentors, I can see that *When Television Was Young* was influenced by two very different works of theory and analysis that emphasized the cultural import of the medium: Raymond Williams's *Television* and Joshua Merowitz's *No Sense of Place: The Impact of the Electronic Media on Social Behavior* (New York: Oxford University Press, 1985).
23 'Uses and gratifications' theory emphasized what people do with media. There is a brief, critical, but effective definition of the approach in Tim

O'Sullivan et al., *Key Concepts in Communication and Cultural Studies*, 2nd ed. (London and New York: Routledge, 1994), 325–7.

24 What shortly thereafter became the crucial text in the United States was Lawrence Grossberg, Cary Nelson, and Paula Treichler, eds, *Cultural Studies* (New York and London: Routledge, 1992), which contained a wide range of essays mixing theory, textual readings, and audience analyses.

25 David Morley, *Family Television: Cultural Power and Domestic Leisure* (London: Comedia, 1986) and Ien Ang, *Watching Dallas: Soap Opera and the Melodramatic Imagination* (London and New York: Methuen, 1985).

26 *Weapons of Mass Persuasion: Marketing the War against Iraq* (Toronto: University of Toronto Press, 2004).

27 *Reading Television* (London: Methuen, 1978).

28 John Fiske is a major figure in cultural studies, author of a series of impressive and useful works: *Introduction to Communication Studies* (London and New York: Methuen, 1982); *Television Culture* (London and New York: Methuen, 1987); plus the companion volumes *Understanding Popular Culture* and *Reading the Popular* (Boston: Unwin Hyman, 1989). *Reading Television* was one of those books mentioned a number of times in the endnotes of *When Television Was Young*.

29 I was particularly taken by Robert Darnton's famous article, 'Worker's Revolt: The Great Cat Massacre of the Rue Saint-Séverin,' which appeared in his *The Great Cat Massacre and Other Episodes in French Cultural History* (New York: Basic Books, 1984). Here he had employed a popular text, the account of a strange event that occurred in Paris in the 1730s, to unpack the thought and life of early modern Europe.

30 The outstanding work of the American historian Roland Marchand was especially influential at this time. His *Advertising the American Dream: Making Way for Modernity 1920–1940* (Berkeley: University of California Press, 1985) legitimized the field. Marchand was not especially interested in theory as such (though he did make some use of Erving Goffman's insights about the performance of gender). But Marchand definitely was part of the cultural turn, a historian who successfully treated ads as social texts.

31 For the record, though, I plead guilty to largely neglecting Canada in my most recent project, *A World Made Sexy: Freud to Madonna* (Toronto: University of Toronto Press, 2007), which concentrates on things American and European.

32 *The New Icons? The Art of Television Advertising* (Toronto: University of Toronto Press, 1994). All kinds of scholars were then investigating advertising from the standpoint of cultural theory. My approach was influenced by Varda Langholz Leymore, *Hidden Myth: Structure and Symbolism in*

Advertising (New York: Basic Books, 1975), a work of extreme reductionism based on the binary logic of structural anthropology; Judith Williamson, *Decoding Advertisements: Ideology and Meaning in Advertising* (London: Marion Boyars, 1978), a much more compelling account that drew heavily on semiotics; Guy Cook, *The Discourse of Advertising* (London and New York: Routledge, 1992), a work based on linguistics and discourse analysis; and Andrew Wernick, *Promotional Culture: Advertising, Ideology and Symbolic Expression* (London: Sage, 1991), a book written by a self-declared professor of cultural studies. The point is that many scholars (the list above is hardly complete) were exploring the character and import of advertising as cultural texts which both expressed and shaped ideas of pleasure and relations of power. In some measure they were following the pioneering lead of Marshall McLuhan, who, in *The Mechanical Bride: Folklore of Industrial Man* (New York: Vanguard Press, 1951), had first assessed advertising as the 'folklore of industrial man.' It was at this time, by the way, that I came to a better appreciation of the genius of McLuhan.

33 Particularly Gramsci's *Selections from the Prison Notebooks* (New York: International Publishers, 1971) and Williams's *Problems in Materialism and Culture* (London: Verso, 1980), where Williams included a very significant article on advertising. Jackson Lears had introduced the concept of hegemony to American history in the 1980s: 'The Concept of Cultural Hegemony: Problems and Possibilities,' *American Historical Review* 90, no.3 (June 1985): 567–93, and 'A Matter of Taste: Corporate Cultural Hegemony in a Mass-Consumption Society,' in Lary May, ed., *Recasting America: Culture and Politics in the Age of the Cold War* (Chicago: University of Chicago Press 1989), 38–57. Ironically it has been argued since then that the notion of hegemony which took hold in British and American circles was not true to Gramsci's own conception of the term: Peter Ghosh, 'Gramscian Hegemony: An Absolutely Historicist Approach,' *History of European Ideas* 27 (2001): 1–43.

34 That judgment was not shared by many other media historians, however. Todd Gitlin had employed the concept of hegemony to much acclaim in *The Whole World Is Watching: Mass Media in the Making and Unmaking of the New Left* (Berkeley: University of California Press, 1980). Much later, Richard Ohmann wrote a particularly successful account of the rise of the mass magazine in America that rested on the idea of hegemony: *Selling Culture: Magazines, Markets, and Class at the Turn of the Century* (London and New York: Verso, 1996). The fact is that the concept of hegemony, like other theories with any merit, can be, indeed must be, tailored to suit the needs of analysis and interpretation to suit the historical problem under consideration.

35 Jürgen Habermas, *The Structural Transformation of the Public Sphere: An In-quiry into a Category of Bourgeois Society*, trans. Thomas Burger (Cambridge, MA: MIT Press, 1989).

36 Although Habermas had published the work thirty years earlier, it was only after its appearance in English that this book began to have a major effect on British and North American work. Of particular importance was the arrival of Craig Calhoun, ed., *Habermas and the Public Sphere* (Cambridge, MA, and London: MIT Press 1992), which contained a raft of excellent essays (and one by Habermas updating his views) that employed and refashioned the notion of the public sphere. The concept had obvious appeal to students of the media because it focused attention on the power of the press and provided a set of criteria (about rationality, accessibility, universality, etc.) to judge their messages. One recent, successful example of how the concept worked as a tool of interpretation can be found in a textbook: Asa Briggs and Peter Burke, *A Social History of the Media: From Gutenberg to the Internet*, 2nd ed. (Cambridge: Polity 2005), 60–87.

37 Bakhtin enjoyed considerable fame in the circles of literary studies. One book in particular spread this fame into many other areas of academe: Peter Stallybrass and Allon White, *The Politics and Poetics of Transgression* (London: Methuen, 1986) – these authors modified the concepts of carnival and the carnivalesque, high and low, and employed these to assess the cultural history of Western Europe in the post-medieval period. But it was Jackson Lears who demonstrated so successfully how Bakhtin could serve media history. He used the concept of the carnivalesque (he had shed the idea of hegemony he once touted) to explain the nature and appeal of advertising in the United States of the nineteenth century: Lears, *Fables of Abundance: A Cultural History of Advertising in America* (New York: Basic Books, 1994).

38 *Lectures on Ideology and Utopia*, ed. George H. Taylor (New York: Columbia University Press, 1986).

39 The work I refer to here is 'The Precession of Simulacra,' in *Simulacra and Simulation*, trans. Sheila Faria Glaser (Ann Arbor: University of Michigan Press, 1994), 1–42. Baudrillard also wrote a text in 1968 that dealt extensively with advertising: *The System of Objects*, trans. James Benedict (London: Verso, 1996). I have analysed this book in *A World Made Sexy*, 134–9. There was an intriguing application of Baudrillard's ideas to television commercials written by Mark Poster, one of Baudrillard's most prominent exponents in America: see *The Mode of Information: Poststructuralism and Social Context* (Chicago: University of Chicago Press, 1990), 43–68.

40 *The History of Sexuality*, vol. 1: *An Introduction*, trans. Robert Hurley (New York: Vintage, 1990).

41 That judgment is purely idiosyncratic, simply because I have read little of their work. Both theorists are of interest to media scholars: so, for example, essays by Lacan and Derrida are included in Paul Cobley, ed., *The Communication Theory Reader* (London and New York: Routledge, 1996). But it is necessary to make choices, and I found reading a few pieces of Derrida and Lacan extremely difficult and of little value, at least to my project of the moment. By contrast I was willing to read the work of Judith Butler, another theorist notorious for her demanding prose, because her arguments did have more obvious applicability to my interests.

42 I am referring here not only to his signal work *We Have Never Been Modern* (Cambridge, MA: Harvard University Press, 1993) but also to a series of papers he wrote which appeared on his website (http://www.bruno-latour.fr/articles). I was also influenced by those two wild theorists, Gilles Deleuze and Félix Guattari, who developed the concept of assemblages in *A Thousand Plateaus: Capitalism and Schizophrenia* (Minneapolis and London: University of Minnesota Press 1987).

43 *Endless Propaganda: The Advertising of Public Goods* (Toronto: University of Toronto Press, 2000).

44 An additional problem was that I had panned the work of Jacques Ellul – *Propaganda: The Formation of Men's Attitudes*, trans. Konrad Kellen and Jean Lerner (New York: Knopf, 1965) – which the assessor clearly favoured. It remains my view that Ellul's take on propaganda was simple-minded, often unproven, and occasionally ludicrous: see *Endless Propaganda*, 20–1.

45 I was ultimately persuaded by a somewhat belated reading of the critique of PoMo history by Perez Zagorin: 'History, the Referent, and Narrative: Reflections on Postmodernism Now,' *History and Theory* 38 (1999): 1–24. That provoked a rebuttal by Keith Jenkins, one of the leading proponents of postmodern history: 'A Postmodern Reply to Perez Zagorin,' *History and Theory* 39 (2000): 181–200. Then Zagorin responded: 'Rejoinder to a Postmodernist,' *History and Theory* 39 (2000): 201–9. The exchange made for very interesting reading. But I decided Zagorin had the best argument, a decision which likely had much to do with the more personal concern about what I thought I was achieving in the archives and in my books.

46 An encounter with theory, or engaging with theory, does not mean accepting that theory. Consider the case of Paul Starr. He has written a fine book which explores how politics and the state worked to constitute the American media: *The Creation of the Media: Political Origins of Modern Communications* (New York: Basic Books, 2004). You will not find in his index a separate reference to Habermas (or to Foucault or Bakhtin). But if you look for the term 'public sphere,' you will find many references, including

to Habermas's view, which is critiqued in the endnotes. Starr appropriated the term but disagreed with its author, using his own and others' research to dispute Habermas's account of how things happened. That amounts to an 'encounter.'

47 Foucault, *The History of Sexuality*. Foucault's book had been published in French as *La volenté de savoir* in 1976 and in English two years later. His argument that sexuality was a technology of power caused a sensation at the time (as did his view that a focus on Victorian repression was misleading) and established sexual history as a new brand of cultural history.

48 Foucault, 'Body/Power,' in *Power/Knowledge: Selected Interviews and Other Writings 1972–1977*, ed. Colin Gordon (New York: Pantheon, 1980), 57–8. Foucault did talk on other occasions about the contemporary scene, mostly criticizing the notion of liberation. But he never did explore in any depth what had happened to the apparatus of sexuality in the twentieth century.

49 The phenomenon of pornography had become one special concern of scholars of cultural studies, especially, so it seemed, feminist scholars: see Linda Williams, *Hard Core: Power, Pleasure, and the 'Frenzy of the Visible'* (Berkeley: University of California Press, 1992), and Pamela Church Gibson and Roma Gibson, eds, *Dirty Looks: Women, Pornography, Power* (London: British Film Institute, 1993). But my understanding of pornography was also influenced by cultural history, notably Lynn Hunt, ed., *The Invention of Pornography* (New York: Zone Books, 1993), and Carolyn J. Dean, *The Frail Social Body: Pornography, Homosexuality, and Other Fantasies in Interwar France* (Berkeley: University of California Press, 2000).

50 See Roland Barthes, 'Written Clothing,' in Chandra Mukerji and Michael Schudson, eds, *Rethinking Popular Culture: Contemporary Perspectives in Cultural Studies* (Berkeley and Oxford: University of California Press, 1991), 438. This is excerpted from his book, *The Fashion System*, trans. Matthew Ward and Richard Howard (Berkeley: University of California Press, 1990). I had explicitly not employed the approach more common in the social sciences where the researcher is interested in the typical rather than the extreme.

51 I also benefited from the past efforts of cultural studies scholars, notably John Fiske, who had explored in some depth aspects of the story of Madonna: see Fiske, *Television Culture*; *Reading the Popular*; and 'British Cultural Studies and Television,' in Robert Allen, ed., *Channels of Discourse, Reassembled: Television and Contemporary Criticism*, 2nd ed. (Chapel Hill: University of North Carolina Press, 1992), 284–326. Equally useful were the various essays in Cathy Schwichtenberg, ed., *The Madonna Connection: Representational Politics, Subcultural Identities, and Cultural Theory* (Boulder, CO: Westview Press, 1993).

52 See, for instance, the pieces in Stephen Brown and Darach Turley, eds, *Consumer Research: Postcards from the Edge* (London and New York: Routledge, 1997). In fact there is a very active school of such market researchers who publish in the mainstream journals in the field. Here too the cultural turn has had a major impact on academic work.

53 Marcuse, *One-Dimensional Man* (Boston: Beacon Press, 1964), 75. Marcuse had also written earlier, in the 1950s, *Eros and Civilization: A Philosophical Inquiry into Freud* (Boston: Beacon Press, 1974), something of a utopian (and dystopian) text, which is the subject of an analysis in *A World Made Sexy*. .

54 *Discipline and Punish: The Birth of the Prison*, trans. Alan Sheridan (London: A. Lane, 1977).

55 The concept of governmentality focused on the management of conduct by various public and private authorities acting through legal, disciplinary, and security apparatuses. Foucault used the concept chiefly in his lectures at the Collège de France during the late 1970s. The concept was effectively introduced to English-speaking audiences with the publication of *The Foucault Effect: Studies in Governmentality*, ed. Graham Burchell, Colin Gordon, and Peter Miller (Chicago: University of Chicago Press, 1991), which included a key lecture by Foucault. Since then, the insight has generated an enormous literature, some of which is historical. And at least one historian has recently noted how governmentality has begun to take the place of hegemony as an explanatory tool and an interpretive frame: Simon Gunn, 'From Hegemony to Governmentality: Changing Conceptions of Power in Social History,' *Journal of Social History* 39, no. 3 (Spring 2006): 705–20.

56 Biopolitics 'centered not upon the body but upon life: a technology which brings together the mass effects characteristic of a population, which tries to control the series of random events that can occur in a living mass, a technology which tries to predict the probability of those events (by modifying it, if necessary), or at least to compensate for their effects.' Foucault, *'Society Must Be Defended': Lectures at the Collège de France, 1975–76*, ed. Mauro Bertani and Alessandro Fontana, trans. David Macey (New York: Picador, 2003), 249. Foucault dealt at length with the concept only in the last lecture of his 1976 series, the final pages in his *The History of Sexuality*, and the first four lectures of 1978, now published as *Security, Territory, Population: Lectures at the Collège de France, 1977–78*, ed. Michel Senellart, trans. Graham Burchell (New York: Palgrave Macmillan, 2007).

57 In the past decade the concept of biopolitics has attracted more and more attention from the academy, partly because it was used (or, as some critics claimed, misused) by a new group of theorists, notably Giorgio Agamben –

Homo Sacer: Sovereign Power and Bare Life, trans. Daniel Heller-Roazen
(Stanford, CA: Stanford University Press, 1998) – as well as Michael Hardt
and Antonio Negri, *Empire* (Cambridge, MA: Harvard University Press,
2001), to critique modern life. But the concept has had some impact on
the understanding of history. One fine example of a study of governmentality which treated the history of social and cultural life, in this case of
nineteenth-century Britain, is a book by Patrick Joyce, *The Rule of Freedom:
Liberalism and the Modern City* (London: Verso, 2003). For a more general
treatment, however, see Edward Ross Dickinson, 'Biopolitics, Fascism,
Democracy: Some Reflections on Our Discourse about "Modernity,"' *Central European History* 37, no.1 (2004): 1–48, which concentrates on German
historiography. For an excellent overview of the use and future of the concept in the social sciences, see Paul Rabinow and Nikolas Rose, 'Biopower
Today,' *BioSocieties* 1, no. 2 (June 2006): 195–217.

58 See, in particular, 'The Subject and Power,' in *Power*, ed. James D. Faubion
(New York: The New Press, 2000), 326–48, especially 337–9. The essay was
first published in English in 1982.

59 These terms are employed in a number of essays: see Foucault, *Ethics:
Subjectivity and Truth*, ed. Paul Rabinow (New York: The New Press, 1997),
87–92, 201, 282. The phenomenon of self-fashioning has been the focus of
attention from a number of scholars influenced by Foucault's work: see, in
particular, Nikolas Rose, *Inventing Our Selves: Psychology, Power, and Personhood* (Cambridge: Cambridge University Press 1998).

60 I list only some examples of books published in English: Jonathan Vance,
Death So Noble: Memory, Meaning, and the First World War (Vancouver:
UBC Press, 1997); Keith Walden, *Becoming Modern in Toronto: The Industrial
Exhibition and the Shaping of a Late Victorian Culture* (Toronto: University
of Toronto Press, 1997); H.V. Nelles, *The Art of Nation-Building: Pageantry
and Spectacle at Quebec's Tercentenary* (Toronto: University of Toronto Press,
1999); Daniel Robinson, *The Measure of Democracy: Polling, Market Research,
and Public Life, 1930–1945* (Toronto: University of Toronto Press, 1999); E.A.
Heaman, *The Inglorious Arts of Peace: Exhibitions in Canadian Society during
the Nineteenth Century* (Toronto: University of Toronto Press, 1999); Ian
Radforth, *Royal Spectacle: The 1860 Visit of the Prince of Wales to Canada and
the United States* (Toronto: University of Toronto Press, 2004); Craig Heron
and Steve Penfold, *The Workers' Festival: A History of Labour Day in Canada*
(Toronto: University of Toronto Press, 2005); José Igartua, *The Other Quiet
Revolution: National Identities in English Canada, 1945–71* (Vancouver: UBC
Press, 2006); and Michael Gauvreau and Ollivier Hubert, eds, *The Churches
and Social Order in Nineteenth- and Twentieth-Century Canada* (Montreal

and Kingston: McGill-Queen's University Press, 2006). Of these, Walden's book shows the most self-conscious engagement with cultural theory. On a grander scale, though, see Ian McKay, 'The Liberal Order Framework: A Prospectus for a Reconnaissance of Canadian History,' *Canadian Historical Review* 81, no 4 (December 2002): 617–45, which draws on the concepts of hegemony and governmentality to assess the story of Canada.

61 *The Capacity to Judge: Public Opinion and Deliberative Democracy in Upper Canada, 1791–1854* (Toronto: University of Toronto Press, 2000).

62 *Roughing It in the Suburbs: Reading Chatelaine Magazine in the Fifties and Sixties* (Toronto: University of Toronto Press, 2000).

63 Friesen, *Citizens and Nation: An Essay on History, Communication, and Canada* (Toronto: University of Toronto Press, 2000), 227. Friesen's work is not an application of Innis's views, however. Moreover, Friesen takes up ideas of other cultural theorists, notably those of Raymond Williams. In particular he incorporates the responses of ordinary people to the events and forces shaping their lives.

64 Ohmann, *Selling Culture*, 37.

65 This is particularly true in the case of the literature on governmentality and biopolitics. That cuts across a range of disciplinary boundaries, notably including work in the realms of geography, history, sociology, political science, and cultural studies. It also includes topics as diverse as, say, the governing of the nineteenth-century city in England, the organization of citizenship education in nationalist China, or the rise and fall of eugenics in Western Europe. But the issue of theory's ability to break down the barriers our specialties have produced could easily form the basis for another paper (and probably has).

Bibliography

Acland, Charles R. 'Histories of Place and Power: Innis in Canadian Cultural Studies.' In *Harold Innis in the New Century: Reflections and Refractions*, ed. Charles R. Acland and William J. Buxton, 243–60. Montreal: McGill-Queen's University Press, 1999.

Adams, Mary Louise. *The Trouble with Normal: Postwar Youth and the Making of Heterosexuality.* Toronto: University of Toronto Press, 1997.

Agamben, Giorgio. *Homo Sacer: Sovereign Power and Bare Life.* Trans. Daniel Heller-Roazen. Stanford, CA: Stanford University Press, 1998.

Agar, Jon. 'Medium Meets Message: Can Media History and the History of Technology Communicate?' *Journal of Contemporary History* 40, no. 4 (2005): 793–803.

Aird Project Menaces the Trade and Commerce of Radio – On Guard against the Nationalization of Radio. Montreal, 1929.

Allard T.J. *Straight Up: Private Broadcasting in Canada, 1918–1958.* Ottawa: Canadian Communications Foundation, 1979.

Allen, Gene. 'Monopolies of News: Harold Innis, the Telegraph and Wire Services.' In *The Toronto School of Communications Theory: Interpretations, Extensions, Applications*, ed. Menaham Blondheim and Rita Watson, 170–98. Toronto and Jerusalem: University of Toronto Press/Magnes Press, 2008.

– 'News across the Border: Associated Press in Canada, 1893–1917.' *Journalism History* 31, no. 4 (Winter 2006): 206–16.

Anderson, Benedict. *Imagined Communities: Reflections on the Origin and Spread of Nationalism*, rev. ed. New York and London: Verso, 1991.

Ang, Ien. *Watching Dallas: Soap Opera and the Melodramatic Imagination.* London and New York: Methuen 1985.

Ankersmit F.R. *Aesthetic Politics.* Stanford: Stanford University Press, 1996.

Ansolabehere, Stephen, and Shanto Iyengar. *Going Negative: How Attack Ads Shrink and Polarize the Electorate.* New York: Free Press, 1995.

Arblaster, Paul. 'Posts, Newsletters, Newspapers: England in a European System of Communications.' *Media History* 11, no. 1/2 (2005): 21–36.

Ashcroft, R.W. 'Government vs. Private Ownership of Canadian Radio.' Toronto, 1931.

Atkin, Charles, and Gary Heald. 'Effects of Political Advertising.' *Public Opinion Quarterly* 40, no. 2 (1976): 216–28.

Attallah, Paul. 'Review of *Television Studies*, edited by Toby Miller.' *Canadian Journal of Communication* 28, no. 4 (2003): 482.

Averill, Harold A. 'The T.N. Gibbs–J. Holden Battle in Ontario South, June, 1873.'
    Ontario History 65, no. 1 (1973): 1–18.
Babe, Robert E. *Canadian Communication Thought: Ten Foundational Writers.* Toronto:
    University of Toronto Press, 2000.
Bailyn, Bernard, ed. *Pamphlets of the American Revolution (1750–1776).* Cambridge, MA:
    The Belknap Press of Harvard University Press, 1965.
Barthes, Roland. *Elements of Semiology.* Trans. Annette Lavers and Colin Smith. New
    York: Hill and Wang, 1968.
– *Mythologies.* Trans. A. Lavers. London: Jonathan Cape, 1972.
– 'Rhetoric of the Image.' In *Image, Music, Text,* ed. and trans. S. Heath, 32–51. New
    York: Hill and Wang, 1977.
– 'The Photographic Message.' In *A Barthes Reader,* ed. Susan Sontag, 194–210. New
    York: Hill and Wang, 1982.
– *The Fashion System.* Trans. Matthew Ward and Richard Howard. Berkeley: University
    of California Press, 1990.
– 'Written Clothing.' In *Rethinking Popular Culture: Contemporary Perspectives in Cultural
    Studies,* ed. Chandra Mukerji and Michael Schudson, 432–45. Berkeley: University of
    California Press, 1991.
Bashevkin, Sylvia. *True Patriot Love: The Politics of Canadian Nationalism.* Toronto: Oxford
    University Press, 1991.
Batten, Jack. *Robinette: The Dean of Canadian Lawyers.* Toronto: Macmillan, 1984.
Baudrillard, Jean. 'Toward a Critique of the Political Economy of the Sign.' Chap. 8 in *For a
    Critique of the Political Economy of the Sign.* Trans. Charles Levin. St Louis: Telos Press, 1981.
– 'The Precession of Simulacra.' In *Simulacra and Simulation,* trans. Sheila Faria Glaser,
    1–42. Ann Arbor: University of Michigan Press, 1994.
– *The System of Objects.* Trans. James Benedict. London: Verso 1996.
Beasley, Ron, Marcel Danesi, and Paul Perron. *Signs for Sale: An Outline of Semiotic
    Analysis for Advertisers and Marketers.* Ottawa: Legas, 2000.
Beauchemin, Jean-François. *Ici Radio-Canada: 50 ans de télévision française.* Montreal: Édi-
    tions de l'Homme, 2002.
Beaulieu, André, and Jean Hamelin, eds. *La presse québécoise des origines à nos jours.* 10
    vols. Sainte-Foy: Presses de l'Université Laval, 1971–90.
Béchard, Marie-Josée. 'Les hommes en transformation? une analyse des représenta-
    tions des hommes au Québec à travers le magazine *Actualité,* 1960–1976.' MA thesis,
    Université du Québec à Montréal, 2003.
Beck, J. Murray. *Pendulum of Power: Canada's Federal Elections.* Scarborough, ON: Prentice
    Hall, 1968.
Belanger, P., R.K. Carty, and M. Eagles. 'The Geography of Canadian Parties' Electoral
    Campaigns: Leaders' Tours and Constituency Election Results.' *Political Geography* 22
    (2003): 439–55.
Beninger, James R. *The Control Revolution: Technological and Economic Origins of the Infor-
    mation Society.* Cambridge, MA: Harvard University Press, 1986.
Benner, Melissa. 'The Mediated Counterpublics of Canadian Farm Women.' MA thesis,
    Carleton University, 2004.
Benoit, William L., and Kevin A. Stein. 'A Functional Analysis of Presidential Direct
    Mail Advertising.' *Communication Studies* 56, no. 3 (2005).
Berelson, Bernard R., Paul F. Lazarsfeld, and William N. McPhee. *Voting.* Chicago: Uni-
    versity of Chicago Press, 1954.

Berger, Arthur. 'Comics and Culture.' *Journal of Popular Culture* 5, no. 1 (1971): 171–5.
Berger, Carl. *The Sense of Power: Studies in the Ideas of Canadian Imperialism, 1867–1914.* Toronto: University of Toronto Press, 1970.
– *The Writing of Canadian History: Aspects of English-Canadian Historical Writing, 1900–1970,* 2nd ed. Toronto: University of Toronto Press, 1986.
Berger, John. *Ways of Seeing.* London: British Broadcasting Corporation, 1972.
Bernier, Marc-François. *Éthique et déontologie du journalisme,* 2nd ed, rev. Sainte-Foy: Presses de l'Université Laval, 2004.
Biocca, Frank. *Television and Political Advertising: Signs, Codes, and Images,* vol. 2. Hillsdale, NJ: Lawrence Erlbaum Associates, 1991.
Blake, Raymond. 'From Dominion Day to Canada Day: A Glimpse of a Changing Canada.' Paper presented at the Association for Canadian Studies Annual Conference, Montreal, November 2004.
Blondheim, Menahem. *News over the Wires: The Telegraph and the Flow of Public Information in America, 1844–1897.* Cambridge, MA: Harvard University Press, 1994.
Blondheim, Menaham, and Rita Watson, eds. *The Toronto School of Communications Theory: Interpretations, Extensions, Applications.* Toronto and Jerusalem: University of Toronto Press/Magnes Press, 2008.
Boily, Caroline. 'Les usages scolaires du cinéma, de la radio et de la télévision à la Commission des écoles catholiques de Montréal, 1920–1970.' PhD diss., Université du Québec à Montréal, 2006.
Bongco, Mila. *Reading Comics: Language, Culture, and the Concept of the Superhero in Comic Books.* New York: Garland, 2000.
Bonnell, Victoria, and Lynn Hunt, eds. *Beyond the Cultural Turn: New Directions in the Study of Society and Culture.* Berkeley: University of California Press, 1999.
Bonnett, John. 'Communication, Complexity and Empire: The Systemic Thought of Harold Adams Innis.' PhD diss., University of Ottawa, 2002.
Boorstin, Daniel J. *The Image: A Guide to Pseudo-Events in America.* New York: Antheneum, 1972.
Boritch, Helen. *Fallen Women: Female Crime and Criminal Justice in Canada.* Scarborough, ON: ITP Nelson, 1997.
Bothwell, Robert. *A Short History of Ontario.* Edmonton: Hurtig, 1986.
Boucher, Marie-France 'La construction du discours médiatique sur le cinéma au Québec, 1896–1939.' MA thesis, Université Laval, 2000.
Bourdieu, Pierre. *Distinction: A Social Critique of the Judgment of Taste.* Trans. Richard Nice. Cambridge, MA: Harvard University Press, 1984.
Bower, Anne L. 'Watching Food: The Production of Food, Film, and Values.' In *Reel Food: Essays on Food and Film,* ed. Anne L. Bower, 1–13. New York: Routledge, 2004.
Bowler, Shaun, and David M. Farrell. 'Conclusion: The Contemporary Election Campaign.' In *Electoral Strategies and Political Marketing,* ed. S. Bowler and D.M. Farrell, 223–35. New York: St Martin's Press, 1992.
Bowman, Charles A. *Ottawa Editor.* Sidney, BC: Gray's Publishing, 1966.
– *Radio Public Service for Canada: Some Objections Answered.* Ottawa, 1930.
Boyle, Andrew. *Only the Wind Will Listen: Reith of the BBC.* London: Hutchinson, 1972.
Briggs, Asa, and Peter Burke. *A Social History of the Media: From Gutenberg to the Internet,* 2nd ed. Cambridge: Polity, 2005.
Brin, Colette. 'La télévision publique en campagne: le plan de couverture électorale à la SRC (1997–1998).' PhD diss., Université Laval, 2003.

Brin, Colette, Jean Charron, and Jean de Bonville, eds. *Nature et mutations du journalisme: théorie et recherches empiriques*. Sainte-Foy: Presses de l'Université Laval, 2004.

Brodkin, Karen. *How Jews Became White Folks*. New Brunswick, NJ: Rutgers University Press, 1998.

Brook, Glenn. '"Canada: A People's History"': An Analysis of the Visual Narrative for a Colonial Nation.' MA thesis, Concordia University, 2002.

Brooks, Peter. *The Melodramatic Imagination: Balzac, Henry James, Melodrama, and the Mode of Excess*. New Haven, CT: Yale University Press, 1976.

Brown, Mary Ellen. *Soap Opera and Women's Talk: The Pleasure of Resistance*. London: Sage, 1994.

Brown, Richard D. 'Early American Origins of the Information Age.' In *A Nation Transformed by Information: How Information has Shaped the United States from Colonial Times to the Present*, ed. Alfred D. Chandler, Jr, and James W. Cortada, 39–53. New York: Oxford University Press, 2000.

Brown, Stephen, and Darach Turley, eds. *Consumer Research: Postcards from the Edge*. London and New York: Routledge, 1997.

Brownsey, Keith. 'The Big Blue Machine: Leadership, Organization, and Faction in the Ontario Progressive Conservative Party, 1971–85.' *Ontario History* 91, no. 1 (1999): 63–86.

Brunet, Patrick J., ed. *L'éthique dans la société de l'information*. Sainte-Foy: Presses de l'Université Laval / Paris: L'Harmattan, 2001.

Bryant, Jay. 'Paid Media Advertising: Political Communication from the Stone Age to the Present.' In *Campaigns and Elections: American Style*, 2nd ed., ed. J.A. Thurber and Candice J. Nelson, 90–108. New York: Westview Press, 2004.

Buckner, Phillip, ed. *Canada and the End of Empire*. Vancouver: UBC Press, 2004.

Buddle-Crowe, Kathleen. 'From Birchbark Talk to Digital Dreamspeaking: A History of Aboriginal Media Activism in Canada.' PhD diss., McMaster University, 2002.

Bujold, Bernard. *Pierre Péladeau, cet inconnu*. Montreal: Trait d'union, 2003.

Burchell, Graham, Colin Gordon, and Peter Miller, eds. *The Foucault Effect: Studies in Governmentality*. Chicago: University of Chicago Press, 1991.

Butler, Judith. *Bodies That Matter: On the Discursive Limits of 'Sex.'* New York and London: Routledge 1993.

Butsch, Richard. *The Making of American Audiences: From Stage to Television, 1750–1990*. New York: Cambridge University Press, 2000.

Calhoun, Craig., ed. *Habermas and the Public Sphere*. Cambridge, MA: MIT Press, 1992.

Cambron, Micheline. 'Sur les traces de la vie culturelle. Des périodiques comme source première.' In *La vie culturelle à Montréal vers 1900*, ed. Micheline Cambro, 319–33. Montreal: Fides, 2005.

– 'Humour et politique dans la presse québécoise du XIXe siècle. Des formes journalistiques comme sources d'humour.' *Bulletin d'histoire politique* 13, no. 2 (hiver 2005): 31–50.

Campagna, Christiane. 'Le rôle de la presse selon les propriétaires et rédacteurs des journaux montréalais (1830–1880).' MA thesis, History, Université du Québec à Montréal, 1998.

Campbell, Robert A. *Sit Down and Drink Your Beer: Regulating Vancouver's Beer Parlours, 1925–1954*. Toronto: University of Toronto Press, 2001.

Canada. Parliament. House of Commons. *Special Committee on the Operations of the Commission under the Canadian Radio Broadcasting Act, 1932, Minutes and Proceedings*. Ottawa, 1934.

Canada. Royal Commission on Radio Broadcasting. *Report of the Royal Commission on Radio Broadcasting*. Ottawa, 1929.

Careless, Maurice. *Brown of the Globe*. Toronto: Macmillan, 1959–63.

Carey, James W. *Communication as Culture: Essays on Media and Society*. New York: Routledge, 1992; first published 1989.

Carrier, David. *The Aesthetics of Comics*. University Park: Pennsylvania State University Press, 2000.

Carrigan, D. Owen. *Crime and Punishment in Canada: A History*. Toronto: McClelland and Stewart, 1991.

Cassista, Éloïse. 'Le nationalisme du pays basque espagnol dans la presse québécoise (1966–1982).' MA thesis, Université du Québec à Montréal, in progress.

Charland, Maurice. 'Technological Nationalism.' *Canadian Journal of Political and Social Theory* 10, no. 1–2 (1986): 196–220.

Charron, Jean, and Jean de Bonville. 'Le paradigme du journalisme de communication: essai de définition.' *Communication* 17, no. 2 (décembre 1996): 51–97.

– 'La notion de paradigme journalistique: aspects théorique et empirique.' In *Nature et transformation du journalisme. Théorie et recherches empiriques*, ed. Colette Brin, Jean Charron, and Jean de Bonville, 33–55. Quebec: Les Presses de l'Université Laval, 2004.

Clark, Charles E. *The Public Prints: The Newspaper in Anglo-American Culture, 1665–1740*. New York: Oxford University Press, 1994.

Clarkson, Stephen. *The Big Red Machine: How the Liberal Party Dominates Canadian Politics*. Vancouver: UBC Press, 2005.

Cobley, Paul, ed. *The Communication Theory Reader*. London and New York: Routledge, 1996.

Codell, Julie F., ed. *Imperial Co-Histories: National Identities and the British and Colonial Press*. Madison, NJ: Fairleigh Dickinson University Press, 2003.

Cohen, Lizbeth. 'Encountering Mass Culture at the Grassroots: The Experience of Chicago Workers in the 1920s.' *American Quarterly* 41, no. 1 (1989): 6–33.

Cole, Douglas. 'The Problem of "Nationalism" and "Imperialism" in British Settlement Colonies.' *Journal of British Studies* 10, no. 2 (May 1971): 160–82.

Cole, Stephen. *Here's Looking at Us: Celebrating Fifty Years of CBC-TV*. Toronto: McClelland and Stewart, 2002.

Collins, Richard. *Culture, Communication, and National Identity: The Case of Canadian Television*. Toronto: University of Toronto Press, 1990.

Cook, Guy. *The Discourse of Advertising*. London and New York: Routledge, 1992.

Cook, Ramsay. *The Politics of John W. Dafoe and the Free Press*. Toronto: University of Toronto Press, 1963.

Corner, John, and Dick Pels, eds. *Media and the Restyling of Politics*. London: Sage, 2003.

Corner, John, and Piers Robinson. 'Politics and Mass Media: A Response to John Street.' *Political Studies Review* 4, no. 1 (2006): 48–54

Côté, Catherine. 'TV Coverage and Cynicism: An Analysis of the 2000 Canadian Federal Election.' PhD diss., Queen's University, 2004.

Côté, Luc, and Jean-Guy Daigle. *Publicité de masse et masse publicitaire: le marché québécois des années 1920 aux années 1960*. Ottawa: Presses de l'Université d'Ottawa, 1999.

Côté, Mathieu-Olivier. 'La représentation du crime dans la presse écrite québécoise: le cas d'*Allô Police*.' MA thesis, Université Laval, 2002.

Coutard, Jérôme. 'Des valeurs en guerre: presse, propagande et culture de guerre au Québec, 1914–1918,' 2 vols. PhD diss., Université Laval, 1999.

– 'Presse, censure et propagande en 1914–1918: la construction d'une culture de guerre.' *Bulletin d'histoire politique* 8, no. 2–3 (hiver-printemps 2000): 150–71.

Couture, Mélanie. 'L'appareil de presse trifluvien entre 1850 et 1920.' MA thesis, Université du Québec à Montréal, 2008.

Crooks, Adam. *To the Electors of the South Riding of Oxford.* Election pamphlet issued by the Reform Party of Ontario, 1875.

Cuff, Robert. 'The Conservative Party Machine and the Election of 1911 in Ontario.' *Ontario History* 57, no. 3 (1965): 149–56.

Cupido, Robert. 'The Medium, the Message and the Modern: The Jubilee Broadcast of 1927.' *International Journal of Canadian Studies* 26 (Fall 2002): 101–23.

Curran, James. *Media and Power.* London and New York: Routledge, 2002.

– 'Media and the Making of British Society, c. 1700–2000.' *Media History* 8, no. 2 (2002).

Cyr, Marc-André. 'La presse anarchiste au Québec, 1976–2001.' MA thesis, Université du Québec à Montréal, 2004.

Dahl, Hans Fredrick. 'The Pursuit of Media History.' *Media, Culture and Society* 16 (1994): 551–63.

Darnton, Robert. 'Worker's Revolt: The Great Cat Massacre of the Rue Saint-Séverin.' In *The Great Cat Massacre and Other Episodes in French Cultural History.* New York: Basic Books, 1984.

– 'An Early Information Society: News and the Media in Eighteenth-Century Paris.' *American Historical Review* 105, no. 1 (February 2000): 1–35.

Darwin, John. 'A Third British Empire? The Dominion Idea in Imperial Politics.' In *The Oxford History of the British Empire*, vol. 4: *The Twentieth Century*, ed. Judith M. Brown and Wm. Roger Louis, 64–87. Oxford: Oxford University Press, 1999.

Davies, Helen. 'The Politics of Participation: A Study of Canada's Centennial Celebration.' PhD diss., University of Manitoba, 1999.

Dean, Carolyn J. *The Frail Social Body: Pornography, Homosexuality, and Other Fantasies in Interwar France.* Berkeley: University of California Press, 2000.

de Bonville, Jean. *La presse québécoise de 1884 à 1914: genèse d'un média de masse.* Quebec: Les Presses de l'Université Laval, 1988.

– *La presse québécoise de 1764 à 1914: bibliographie analytique.* Sainte-Foy: Presses de l'Université Laval, 1995.

– *Les quotidiens montréalais de 1945 à 1985: morphologie et contenu.* Quebec: Institut québécois de recherche sur la culture, 1995.

Debord, Guy. *The Society of the Spectacle.* Trans. Donald Nicholson-Smith. New York: Zone Books, 1995.

DeFleur, Melvin, and Sandra Ball-Rockeach. *Theories of Mass Communication*, 3rd ed. New York: David McKay, 1975.

Deleuze, Gilles, and Félix Guattari. *A Thousand Plateaus: Capitalism and Schizophrenia.* Minneapolis: University of Minnesota Press, 1987.

Deleuze, Magali. *L'une et l'autre indépendance 1954–1964: les médias au Québec et la guerre d'Algérie.* Montreal: Point de Fuite, 2001.

– 'L'étude des journaux en histoire internationale. Le Québec et la guerre d'Algérie.' *Globe. Revue internationale d'études québécoises* 6, no. 2 (2003): 23–50.

Demers, Frédéric. 'La mise en scène de l'imaginaire national et historique du Québec francophone dans la télésérie "Les filles de Caleb."' PhD diss., Université Laval, 2005.

Denault, Jocelyne. 'Des religieuses cinéastes et des films à découvrir.' *Études d'histoire religieuse* 68 (2002): 89–94.

Désy, Caroline. 'Discours hégémonique et contre-discours sur la guerre d'Espagne dans le Québec des années trente.' PhD diss., Université du Québec à Montréal, 1999.

Dewar, Kenneth C. 'The Origins of Public Broadcasting in Canada in Comparative Perspective.' *Canadian Journal of Communication* 8, no. 2 (January 1982): 26–45.

Diamond, Edwin, and Stephen Bates. *The Spot: The Rise of Political Advertising on Television*, 3rd ed. Cambridge, MA: MIT Press, 1992.

DiCenzo, Maria. 'Feminist Media and History: A Response to James Curran.' *Media History* 10, no. 1 (2004): 43–9.

Dickinson, Edward Ross. 'Biopolitics, Fascism, Democracy: Some Reflections on Our Discourse about "Modernity."' *Central European History* 37, no. 1 (2004): 1–48.

Dirlik, Arif. 'Whither History? Encounters with Historism, Postmodernism, Postcolonialism.' In *History after the Three Worlds*, ed. A. Dirlik et al., 241–57. Lanham, MD: Rowman and Littlefield, 2000.

Dooley, Brendan. *The Social History of Skepticism: Experience and Doubt in Early Modern Culture*. Baltimore: Johns Hopkins University Press, 1999.

Dornic, Isabelle. 'Hier ne meurt jamais: vision et désillusion d'une quête identitaire féminine au Québec: *La Bonne parole*, organe de la Fédération nationale Saint-Jean-Baptiste, 1913–1958,' 2 vols. PhD diss., Université Laval, 2004.

Doyon, Nova. 'Valentin Jautard (1736–1787) et la *Gazette littéraire de Montréal* (1778–1779): vers un paradigme du littéraire.' MA thesis, Université du Québec à Montréal, 2002.

Drache, Daniel. 'Harold Innis and Canadian Capitalist Development.' *Canadian Journal of Political and Social Theory* 6, no. 1–2 (Winter/Spring 1982): 35–60.

Drummond, Robert J., and Robert MacDermid. 'Elections and Campaigning: "They Blew Our Doors off on the Buy."' In *The Government and Politics of Ontario*, 5th ed., ed. G. White, 189–215. Toronto: University of Toronto Press, 1997.

Drury, E. C. *True economy. Common-sense and honesty. Budget address*. Toronto: W.S. Johnston, 1923.

du Berger, Jean. *La Radio au Québec, 1920–1960*. Sainte-Foy: Les Presses de l'Université Laval, 1997.

Durocher, Eric. 'Critical Interests in Broadcasting Policy: Fashioning the Public Interest in the 1932 Broadcasting Act.' MA thesis, Concordia University, 1995.

Eagleton, Terry. *Ideology: An Introduction*. London and New York: Verso 1991.

– *The Illusions of Postmodernism*. Oxford: Blackwell 1996.

– *After Theory*. London: Allen Lane, 2003.

Eaman, Ross. *Channels of Influence: CBC Audience Research and the Canadian Public*. Toronto: University of Toronto Press, 1994.

Easton, Ken. *Building an Industry: A History of Cable Television and Its Development in Canada*. Lawrencetown Beach, NS: Pottersfield Press, 2000.

Eco, Umberto. *A Theory of Semiotics*. Bloomington: Indiana University Press, 1976.

Edelman, Murray. *Constructing the Political Spectacle*. Chicago: University of Chicago Press, 1988.

Edwardson, Ryan. 'The Many Lives of Captain Canuck: Nationalism, Culture, and the Creation of a Canadian Comic Book Superhero.' *The Journal of Popular Culture* 37, no. 2 (2003): 184–201.

– 'Canadianization: Canadian Content, Cultural Intervention, and Constructing a National Culture.' PhD diss., Queen's University, 2004.

Eisenstein, Elizabeth L. 'AHR Forum: An Unacknowledged Revolution Revisited.' *American Historical Review* 107, no. 1 (February 2002): 87–105.

Ellis, David. *Evolution of the Canadian Broadcasting System: Objectives and Realities, 1928–1968*. Ottawa: Department of Communications, 1979.

Ellul, Jacques. *Propaganda: The Formation of Men's Attitudes*. Trans. Konrad Kellen and Jean Lerner. New York: Knopf, 1965.

Emery, Michael, Edwin Emery, and Nancy Roberts. *The Press and America: An Interpretive History of the Mass Media*. Needham Heights, MA: Allyn and Bacon, 2000.

Evans, A. Margaret. *Sir Oliver Mowat*. Toronto: University of Toronto Press, 1992.

Facheaux, Ron. 'Pictures Perfect: 5 Photos Every Candidate Needs.' *Campaigns and Elections* 20, no. 9 (1999): 33–4.

Facts Respecting Radio Broadcasting Under Private Ownership – Issued by Canadian Association of Broadcasters (1929).

Faith, Karlene. *Unruly Women: The Politics of Confinement and Resistance*. Vancouver: Press Gang, 1993.

Farrell, David M., and Rudiger Schmitt-Beck, eds. *Do Political Campaigns Matter? Campaign Effects in Elections and Referendums*. London: Routledge, 2002.

Fennema, Norman. 'Remote Control: Belief and Canadian Broadcasting – A Case Study of Religion in the Public Square.' PhD diss., University of Victoria, 2003.

Feuer, Jane. 'Melodrama, Serial Form and Television Today.' *Screen* 25, no. 1 (1984): 4–17.

Filion, Michel. *Radiodiffusion et société distincte: des origines de la radio jusqu'à la Révolution tranquille au Québec*. Laval: Méridien, 1994.

Fillion, Réal. 'Moving Beyond Biopower: Hardt and Negri's Post-Foucauldian Philosophy of History.' *History and Theory* 44, no. 4 (December 2005): 47–72.

Fink, Howard. 'The Sponsor's vs. The Nation's Choice: North American Radio Drama.' In *Radio Drama*, ed. Peter Lewis, 185–243. Toronto: Academic Press, 1981.

Fink, Howard, and John Jackson. 'Jack Bowdery/Jack Ammon: Pioneer Leftist 'Thirties B.C. Radio Dramatist.' *Fréquence/Frequency* 1–2 (1994): 59–71.

Fink, Howard, and John Jackson, eds. *All the Bright Company: Radio Drama Produced by Andrew Allan*. Kingston and Toronto: Quarry Press and CBC Enterprises, 1987.

– *The Road to Victory: Radio Plays of Gerald Noxon*. Waterloo and Kingston: Malcolm Lowry Review Press and Quarry Press, 1989.

Fink, Howard, and Brian Morrison with John Jackson. *Canadian National Theatre of the Air, 1962–2000*, 3 vols. http://ccbs.concordia.ca/.

Finkel, Steven E., and John G. Geer, 'A Spot Check: Casting Doubt on the Demobilizing Effect of Attack Advertising.' *American Journal of Political Science* 42, no. 2 (1998): 573–95.

Fish, Stanley. *Is There a Text in This Class? The Authority of Interpretive Communities*. Cambridge, MA: Harvard University Press, 1980.

Fiske, John. *Introduction to Communication Studies*. London and New York: Methuen 1982.

– *Television Culture*. London and New York: Methuen 1987.

– *Reading the Popular*. Boston: Unwin Hyman, 1989.

– *Understanding Popular Culture*. Boston: Unwin Hyman, 1989.

– 'British Cultural Studies and Television.' In *Channels of Discourse, Reassembled: Television and Contemporary Criticism*, 2nd ed., ed. Robert Allen, 284–326. Chapel Hill: University of North Carolina Press, 1992.

Fiske, John, and John Hartley. *Reading Television*. London: Methuen, 1978.

Fleming, Patricia Lockhart, and Yvan Lamonde, general eds. *Histoire du livre et de l'imprimé au Canada/History of the Book in Canada*, 3 vols. Montreal and Toronto: Presses de l'Université de Montréal / University of Toronto Press, 2004–7.

Fletcher, Fred, ed. *Media, Elections and Democracy*. Vol. 19 of the research studies of the Royal Commission on Electoral Reform and Party Financing. Toronto: Dundurn Press, 1992.

Fortin, Philippe. 'Le journal *Le Pays* et la guerre de Sécession, 1861–1865.' MA thesis, Université du Québec à Montréal, 2000.

– 'Les sources de renseignement du journal *Le Pays* lors de la guerre de Sécession (1861–1865).' *Communication* 20, no. 2 (hiver-printemps 2001): 118–31.

Fortner, Robert S. *Radio, Morality, and Culture: Britain, Canada and the United States, 1919–1945*. Carbondale, IL: Southern Illinois University Press, 2005.

Foucault, Michel. *Discipline and Punish: The Birth of the Prison*, 2nd ed. Trans. Alan Sheridan. New York: Vintage Books, 1995.

– 'Body/Power.' In *Power/Knowledge: Selected Interviews and Other Writings 1972–1977*, ed. Colin Gordon, 55–62. New York: Pantheon Books, 1980.

– *The History of Sexuality*, vol. 1: *An Introduction*. Trans. Robert Hurley. New York: Vintage 1990.

– 'Politics and the Study of Discourse.' In *The Foucault Effect: Studies in Governmentality*, ed. Graham Burchell, Colin Gordon, and Peter Mill, 53–72. London: Harvester, 1991.

– *Ethics: Subjectivity and Truth*. Ed. Paul Rabinow. New York: New Press, 1997.

– 'The Subject and Power.' In *Power*, ed. James D. Faubion, 326–48. New York: New Press, 2000.

– *'Society Must Be Defended': Lectures at the Collège de France, 1975–76*. Ed. Mauro Bertani and Alessandro Fontana. Trans. David Macey. New York: Picador, 2003.

– *Security, Territory, Population: Lectures at the Collège de France, 1977–78*. Ed. Michel Senellart. Trans. Graham Burchell. New York: Palgrave Macmillan, 2007.

Fouquet, France. 'La presse écrite: reflet de l'évolution de la famille québécoise de 1972 à 1995.' MA thesis, Université du Québec à Trois-Rivières, 2001.

Fox, Stephen. *The Mirror Makers: A History of American Advertising and Its Creators*. New York: Morrow, 1984.

Fradet, Louis. *Les 50 ans du Syndicat de la rédaction du Soleil, 1950–2000: un combat pour la profession*. Sillery: Septentrion, 2001.

Frank, David. 'Public History and the *People's History*: A View from Atlantic Canada.' *Acadiensis* 32, no. 2 (2003): 120–33.

Franklin, Bob. *Packaging Politics: Political Communications in Britain's Media Democracy*. London: Arnold, 2004.

Frappier, Marie-Pier 'Le discours des journalistes canadiens-français de 1945 à 1960 sur les normes journalistiques.' MA thesis, Université du Québec à Montréal, in progress.

Friesen, Gerald. *Citizens and Nation: An Essay on History, Communication, and Canada*. Toronto: University of Toronto Press, 2000.

Friesen, Joe. '"Canada: A People's History" as "Journalists" History.' *History Workshop Journal* 56 (2003): 184–203.

Frigon, Augustin. *The Organization of Radio Broadcasting in Canada: Extrait de la Revue Trimestrielle Canadienne, Septembre 1929*. Montreal, 1929.

Gabillet, Fabien. 'La vraie France est au Canada! Les échos de la séparation de l'Église et de l'État de 1905 dans la presse canadienne-française.' MA thesis, Université Laval, 2000.

Gaudreault, André, and Jean-Pierre Sirois-Trahan. *La vie ou du moins ses apparences; émergence du cinéma dans la presse de la Belle Époque (1894–1910): anthologie*. Montreal: Cinémathèque québécoise, Grafics, 2002.

Gauvreau, Michael, and Ollivier Hubert, eds. *The Churches and Social Order in Nineteenth- and Twentieth-Century Canada*. Montreal and Kingston: McGill-Queen's University Press, 2006.

Geertz, Clifford. *The Interpretation of Cultures: Selected Essays*. New York: Basic Books 1973.

Ghosh, Peter. 'Gramscian Hegemony: An Absolutely Historicist Approach.' *History of European Ideas* 27 (2001): 1–43.

Gibbon, John Murray. 'Radio as a Fine Art.' *Canadian Forum*, March 1931.

Gibson, J.M., and J.T. Middleton. *Twenty-Two Years of Reform Government*. Election pamphlet issued by the Liberal Party of Ontario, 1894.

Gibson, Pamela Church, and Roma Gibson, eds. *Dirty Looks: Women, Pornography, Power*. London: British Film Institute, 1993.

Gidengil, E., and J. Everitt. 'Conventional Coverage/Unconventional Politicians: Gender and Media Coverage of Canadian Leaders' Debates, 1993, 1997, 2000.' *Canadian Journal of Political Science* 36, no. 3 (2003): 559–77.

Gillam, Robyn A. 'Evelyn Dick: Deconstructing a Fictional Body.' *The Mid-Atlantic Almanack: The Journal of the Mid-Atlantic Popular/American Culture Association* 5 (1996): 85–106.

Gitelman, Lisa. *Always Already New: Media, History and the Data of Culture*. Cambridge, MA: MIT Press, 2006.

Gitlin, Todd. *The Whole World Is Watching: Mass Media in the Making and Unmaking of the New Left*. Berkeley: University of California Press, 1980.

Gordon, Ian. *Comic Strips and Consumer Culture: 1890–1945*. Washington: Smithsonian, 1998.

Gorman, Daniel. *Imperial Citizenship: Empire and the Question of Belonging*. Manchester: Manchester University Press, 2006.

Gosselin, Sophie. 'L'humour, instrument journalistique dans l'oeuvre d'Hector Berthelot.' MA thesis, Université du Québec à Montréal, 2008.

Gramsci, Antonio. *Selections from the Prison Notebooks*. New York: International Publishers, 1971.

Granatstein, J.L. *The Politics of Survival: The Conservative Party of Canada, 1939–1945*. Toronto: University of Toronto Press, 1967.

Grant, George. *Technology and Justice*. Toronto: Anansi, 1986.

Greimas, A.J., and Jacques Fontanille. *The Semiotics of Passions: From States of Affairs to States of Feeling*. Trans. Paul Perron and Frank Collins. Minneapolis: University of Minnesota Press, 1993.

Greive, Bob R.R. *The Blood, Sweat, and Tears of Political Victory … and Defeat*. Lanham, MD: University of America, 1999.

Grossberg, Lawrence, Cary Nelson, and Paula Treichler, eds. *Cultural Studies*. New York and London: Routledge, 1992.

Guay, Hervé. 'Les discours sur le théâtre dans la presse hebdomadaire montréalaise de langue française de 1898 à 1914: des genres journalistiques et des composantes identitaires en compétition.' PhD diss., Université du Québec à Montréal, 2005.

Gunn, Simon. 'From Hegemony to Governmentality: Changing Conceptions of Power in Social History.' *Journal of Social History* 39, no. 3 (Spring 2006): 705–20.

Habermas, Jurgen. *The Structural Transformation of the Public Sphere: An Inquiry into a Category of Bourgeois Society*. Trans. Thomas Burger. Cambridge, MA: MIT Press, 1989.

Hall, Stuart. 'The Determinations of News Photographs.' In *The Manufacture of News: A Reader*, ed. S. Cohen and J. Young. Beverly Hills: Sage, 1973.

Hampton, Mark. 'Media Studies and the Mainstreaming of Media History.' *Media History* 11, no. 3 (2005): 239–46.

Hardt, Michael, and Antonio Negri. *Empire*. Cambridge, MA: Harvard University Press, 2001.

Hartley, John. *Popular Reality: Journalism, Modernity, Popular Culture*. London and New York: Arnold, 1996.

Harvey, Fernand. 'La presse périodique à Québec de 1794 à 1940. Vue d'ensemble d'un processus culturel.' *Les Cahiers des Dix* 58 (2004): 213–50.

Heaman, E.A. *The Inglorious Arts of Peace: Exhibitions in Canadian Society during the Nineteenth Century*. Toronto: University of Toronto Press, 1999.

Heidensohn, Frances. *Women and Crime*. Houndsmills, UK: Macmillan, 1985.

Held, David, Anthony McGrew, David Goldblatt, and Jonathan Perraton. *Global Transformations: Politics, Economics and Culture*. Stanford, CA: Stanford University Press, 1999.

Herman, Edward S., and Robert W. McChesney. *The Global Media: The New Missionaries of Corporate Capitalism*. London and New York: Cassell, 1997.

Heron, Craig. *Booze: A Distilled History*. Toronto: Between the Lines, 2003.

– 'The Boys and Their Booze: Masculinities and Public Drinking in Working-Class Hamilton, 1890–1946.' *Canadian Historical Review* 86, no. 3 (September 2005): 411–52.

Heron, Craig, and Steve Penfold. *The Workers' Festival: A History of Labour Day in Canada*. Toronto: University of Toronto Press, 2005.

Heyer, Paul. *Harold Innis*. Lanham, MD: Rowman and Littlefield, 2003.

Heyer, Paul, and David Crowley, 'Introduction.' In Harold A. Innis, *The Bias of Communication*. Toronto: University of Toronto Press, 1991.

Hilkey, Judy. *Character Is Capital: Success Manuals and Manhood in Gilded Age America*. Chapel Hill: University of North Carolina Press, 1997.

Hilmes, Michele. *Radio Voices: American Broadcasting, 1922–1952*. Minneapolis: University of Minnesota Press, 1997.

– 'Who We Are, Who We Are Not: Battle of the Global Paradigms.' In *Planet TV: A Global Television Reader*, ed. Lisa Parks and Shanti Kumar, 53–73. New York and London: New York University Press, 2003.

– ed. *The Television History Book*. London: British Film Institute, 2003.

– 'Radio Nations: The Importance of Transnational Media Study.' In *Atlantic Communications: The Media in American and German History from the Seventeenth to the Twentieth Century*, ed. N. Finzsch and U. Lehmkuhl, 299–308. Oxford and New York: Berg, 2004.

– 'Front Line Family: "Women's Culture" Comes to the BBC.' *Media Culture and Society* 29, no. 1 (2007): 5–29.

Hilmes, Michele, and Jason Loviglio, eds. *The Radio Reader: Essays in the Cultural History of Radio*. New York: Routledge, 2002.

Hobsbawm, Eric. *Nations and Nationalism since 1780: Programme, Myth, Reality*, 2nd ed. Cambridge: Cambridge University Press, 1992.

Hobsbawm, Eric, and Terence Ranger, eds. *The Invention of Tradition*. Cambridge: Cambridge University Press, 1983.

Hodgins, Peter. 'The Canadian Dream-work: History, Myth and Nostalgia in the Heritage Minutes.' PhD diss., Carleton University, 2004.

Hogarth, David. 'Local Representation in a Global Age: A Case Study of Canadian Documentary Television as a Transnational Genre.' *International Journal of Canadian Studies* 23 (2001): 133–55.

– 'The Other Documentary Tradition: Early Radio Documentaries in Canada.' *Historical Journal of Film, Radio and Television* 21, no. 2 (2001): 123–35.

– *Documentary Television in Canada: From National Public Service to Global Marketplace.* Montreal and Kingston: McGill-Queen's University Press, 2003.

Holbert, R. Lance. 'A Typology for the Study of Entertainment Television and Politics.' *American Behavioral Scientist* 49, no. 3 (2005): 436–53.

Holbert, R.L., et. al. '*The West Wing* and Depictions of the American Presidency: Expanding the Theoretical and Empirical Domains of Framing in Political Communication.' *Communication Quarterly* 53 (2005): 505–22.

Holtz-Bacha, Christina, and Lynda Lee Kaid. 'Political Advertising in International Comparison.' In *The Sage Handbook of Political Advertising*, ed. L.L. Kaid and C. Holtz-Bacha, 3–13. Thousand Oaks: Sage, 2006.

Hoskins, Andrew. 'New Memory: Mediating History.' *Historical Journal of Film, Radio and Television* 21, no. 4 (2001): 333–46.

Hosokawa, Michihisa. 'Making Imperial Canadians: Empire Day in Canada.' Paper presented at the British World Conference, Calgary, 10–12 July 2003.

Houle, Nancy. 'Origine et consolidation d'un réseau littéraire au XXe siècle: le réseau associé à la revue *La Relève*.' MA thesis, Université de Sherbrooke, 2001.

Howard, Philip N. *New Media Campaigns and the Managed Citizen.* New York: Cambridge University Press, 2006.

Hoy, Claire. *Bill Davis: A Biography by Claire Hoy.* Toronto: Methuen, 1985.

Huffman, James. *Creating a Public: People and Press in Meiji Japan.* Honolulu: University of Hawaii Press, 1997.

Humeniuk, Bradley Kevin. 'Constructing Local Culture in a Near Media Monopoly.' MA thesis, Lakehead University, 2003.

Hunt, Lynn, ed. *The New Cultural History.* Berkeley: University of California Press, 1989.

– *The Invention of Pornography.* New York: Zone Books, 1993.

Igartua, José. *The Other Quiet Revolution: National Identities in English Canada, 1945–71.* Vancouver: UBC Press, 2006.

Ignatiev, Noel. *How the Irish Became White.* New York: Routledge, 1995.

Innis, Harold A. *Empire and Communications.* Oxford: Clarendon, 1950.

– *The Bias of Communication.* Toronto: University of Toronto Press, 1951.

– 'The Concept of Monopoly and Civilization.' In Innis, *Staples, Markets and Cultural Change: Selected Essays*, ed. Daniel Drache, 384–9. Montreal and Kingston: McGill-Queen's University Press, 1995.

Institut canadien d'éducation des adultes, *La radiodiffusion au Canada depuis ses origines jusqu'à nos jours.* Montreal: ICEA, 1964, no. 16–17.

Jackall, Robert, and Janice M. Hirota. *Image Makers: Advertising, Public Relations, and the Ethos of Advocacy.* Chicago: University of Chicago Press, 2000.

Jackaway, Gwenyth L. *Media at War: Radio's Challenge to the Newspapers, 1924–1939.* Westport, CT: Praeger, 1995.

Jacob, Louis. 'Histoire de la presse quotidienne au Québec de 1945 à 1995.' MA thesis, Université de Montréal, 2003.

Jamieson, Kathleen Hall. *Packaging the Presidency: A History and Criticism of Presidential Campaign Advertising*, 3rd ed. New York: Oxford University Press, 1996.

Jenkins, Keith. 'A Postmodern Reply to Perez Zagorin.' *History and Theory* 39 (2000): 181–200.

Jerit, Jennifer. 'Survival of the Fittest: Rhetoric during the Course of an Election Campaign.' *Political Psychology* 25, no. 4 (2004): 563–75.

John, Richard R. *Spreading the News: The American Postal System from Franklin to Morse.* Cambridge, MA: Harvard University Press, 1998.

Johns, Adrian. 'AHR Forum: How to Acknowledge a Revolution.' *American Historical Review* 107, no. 1 (February 2002): 106–25.

Johnson-Cartee, K.S., and G.A. Copeland. *Negative Political Advertising: Coming of Age.* Hillsdale: Erlbaum, 1991.

Johnston, Anne. 'Methodologies for the Study of Political Advertising.' In *The Sage Handbook of Political Advertising,* ed. L.L. Kaid and C. Holtz-Bacha, 15–33. Thousand Oaks, CA: Sage, 2006.

Johnston, Patricia. *Real Fantasies: Edward Steichen's Advertising Photography.* Berkeley: University of California Press, 1997.

Johnston, Russell. 'The Origins of Public Broadcasting in Canada Reconsidered: The Radio Branch and Cultural Administration, 1922–1932.' MA thesis, Queen's University, 1992.

– *Selling Themselves: The Emergence of Canadian Advertising.* Toronto: University of Toronto Press, 2000.

– 'Value Added: Recent Books in the History of Communications and Culture.' *Acadiensis* 32, no. 1 (2002): 129–39.

– 'Canadian Radio Amateurs and Early Broadcasting.' Paper delivered to the Conference on Media History in Canada, Ryerson University, Toronto, 31 May 2006.

Joyce, Patrick. *The Rule of Freedom: Liberalism and the Modern City.* London: Verso, 2003.

Kaid, Lynda Lee, and Anne Johnston. *Videostyle in Presidential Campaigns: Style and Content of Televised Political Advertising.* Westport, CT: Praeger, 2001.

Kaid, Lynda Lee, and Daniela V. Dimitrova. 'The Television Advertising Battleground in the 2004 Presidential Election.' *Journalism Studies* 6, no. 2 (2005): 165–75.

Kaid, Lynda Lee, and Monica Postelnicu. 'Political Advertising in the 2004 Election: Comparison of Traditional Television and Internet Messages.' *American Behavioral Scientist* 49, no. 2 (1999): 265–78.

Kalifa, Dominique, and Alain Vaillant. 'Pour une histoire culturelle et littéraire de la presse française au XIXe siècle.' *Le temps des médias* 1, no. 2 (2004): 197–214.

Kaplan, E. Ann, ed. *Women in Film Noir,* 2nd ed. London: British Film Institute, 1998.

Kaplan, Richard L. *Politics and the American Press: The Rise of Objectivity, 1865–1920.* Cambridge: Cambridge University Press, 2002.

Kaukiainen, Yrjö. 'Shrinking the World: Improvements in the Speed of Information Transmission, c. 1820–1870.' *European Review of Economic History* 5, no. 1 (2001): 1–28.

Kaul, Chandrika. *Reporting the Raj: The British Press and India, c. 1880–1922.* Manchester: Manchester University Press, 2003.

– ed. *Media and the British Empire.* Basingstoke: Palgrave Macmillan, 2006.

Kayser. Jacques. *Le quotidien français.* Paris: Armand Colin, 1963.

Keightley, Keir. 'Long Play: Adult-Oriented Popular Music and the Temporal Logics of the Post-War Sound Recording Industry in the USA.' *Media, Culture and Society* 26, no. 3 (2004): 375–91.

Kemp, Sandra. '"Myra, Myra on the Wall": The Fascination of Faces.' *Critical Quarterly* 40, no. 1 (1998): 38–69.

Kenter, Peter. *TV North: Everything You Wanted to Know about Canadian Television.* North Vancouver: Whitecap Books, 2001.

Kerr, Janet B. 'Sir Oliver Mowat and the Campaign of 1894.' *Ontario History* 55, no. 1 (1963): 1–13.

Keshen, Jeff. 'One for All or All for One: Black Marketing in Canada, 1939–1947.' In *The Good Fight: Canadians and World War II,* ed. J.L. Granatstein and Peter Neary. Toronto: Copp Clark, 1995.

Kielbowicz, Richard B. *News in the Mail: The Press, Post Office, and Public Information, 1700–1860s.* New York: Greenwood Press, 1989.

Kipping, Matthias, and Lina Galvez Munoz. 'The Business of Dependency: An Introduction.' *Business History* 47, no. 3 (July 2005): 331–6.

Klapper, Joseph. *The Effects of Mass Communication.* Glencoe, IL: Free Press, 1960.

Kline, Stephen. 'Image Politics: Negative Advertising Strategies and the Election Audience.' In *Buy This Book: Studies in Advertising and Consumption,* ed. M. Nava et al., 139–56. London: Routledge, 1997.

Knelman, Judith. *Twisting in the Wind: The Murderess and the English Press.* Toronto: University of Toronto Press, 1998.

– 'Can We Believe What the Newspapers Tell Us? Missing Links in *Alias Grace.' University of Toronto Quarterly* 68, no. 2 (Spring 1999): 677–86.

Knox, Sara L. *Murder: A Tale of Modern American Life.* Durham, NC: Duke University Press, 1998.

Kolber, Leo. *Leo: A Life.* Montreal: McGill-Queen's University Press, 2003.

Korinek, Valerie. *Roughing It in the Suburbs: Reading Chatelaine Magazine in the Fifties and Sixties.* Toronto: University of Toronto Press, 2000.

Kozak, Nadine. '"Among the Necessities": A Social History of Communication Technology on the Canadian Prairies, 1900 to 1950.' MA thesis, Carleton University, 2000.

Kramar, Kirsten Johnson. *Unwilling Mothers, Unwanted Babies: Infanticide in Canada.* Vancouver: UBC Press, 2005.

Kuffert, Len. *A Great Duty: Canadian Responses to Modern Life and Mass Culture, 1939–1967.* Montreal and Kingston: McGill-Queen's University Press, 2003.

Kuhn, Annette. 'Women's Genres.' *Screen* 25, no. 1 (1984): 18–28.

Lachapelle, Guy. *Claude Ryan et la violence du pouvoir:* Le Devoir *et la crise d'octobre, ou le combat de journalistes démocrates.* Sainte-Foy: Presses de l'Université Laval, 2005.

L'action sociale catholique et l'oeuvre de la presse catholique. Quebec: Imprimerie Éd. Marcotte, 1907.

Laird, Pamela. *Advertising Progress: American Business and the Rise of Consumer Marketing.* Baltimore: Johns Hopkins University Press, 1998.

Lambertus, Sandra. *Wartime Images, Peacetime Wounds: The Media and the Gustafsen Lake Standoff.* Toronto: University of Toronto Press, 2003.

Lang, Jeffrey S., and Patrick Trimble. 'Whatever Happened to the Man of Tomorrow? An Examination of the American Monomyth and the Comic Book Superhero.' *Journal of Popular Culture* 22, no. 3 (1988): 157–73.

Laqueur, Thomas W. 'Crowds, Carnival and the State in English Executions, 1604–1868.' In *The First Modern Society: Essays in English History in Honour of Lawrence Stone,* ed. A. L. Beier, David Cannadine, and James M. Rosenheim, 305–55. Cambridge: Cambridge University Press, 1989.

Large, Betty, and T. Crothers. CFCY *'The Friendly Voice of the Maritimes.'* Charlottetown, PEI: Applecross Press, 1989.

Larose, Roger. 'The Oka Crisis on Television: In Praise of the Barbarian.' PhD diss., Concordia University, 2001.

Lasswell, H.D. 'The Structure and Function of Communication in Society.' In *The Communication of Ideas*, ed. L. Bryson, 37–51. New York: Harper and Row, 1948.

Latour, Bruno. *We Have Never Been Modern*. Cambridge, MA: Harvard University Press, 1993.

Lavoie, E. 'La Constitution d'une modernité culturelle populaire dans les médias au Québec (1900–1950).' In *L'Avènement de la modernité culturelle au Québec*, dir. Yvan Lamonde et Esther Trépanier, 253–98. Quebec: IQRC, 1986.

Lazarsfeld, Paul F. 'Administrative and Critical Communications Research.' Chap. 6 in *Qualitative Analysis: Historical and Critical Essays*. Boston: Allyn and Bacon, 1972.

Lears, Jackson. 'The Concept of Cultural Hegemony: Problems and Possibilities.' *American Historical Review* 90, no. 3 (June 1985): 567–93.

– 'A Matter of Taste: Corporate Cultural Hegemony in a Mass-Consumption Society.' In *Recasting America: Culture and Politics in the Age of the Cold War*, ed. Lary May, 38–57. Chicago: University of Chicago Press, 1989.

– *Fables of Abundance: A Cultural History of Advertising in America*. New York: Basic Books, 1994.

Le Bon, Gustave. *The Crowd*. New York: Compass, 1960.

Le Cam, Florence. 'L'identité du groupe des journalistes du Québec au défi d'Internet,' 2 vols. PhD diss., Université Laval and Université de Rennes, 2005.

Lefrançois, Guillaume. 'Rire le ventre vide: la caricature et les illustrations dans les quotidiens québécois pendant la Crise des années 1930.' MA thesis, Université du Québec à Montréal, 2007.

Legris, Renée. *Robert Choquette, romancier et dramaturge de la radio-télévision*. Montreal: Fides, 1977.

– *Propagande de guerre et nationalismes dans la radio-feuilleton (1939–1955)*. Montreal: Fides, 1981.

– 'L'Institution ecclesiale et les structures de l'idéologie chrétienne dans les radioromans et les dramatisations historiques (1935–1975).' *Études d'histoire religieuse / Historical Studies* 68 (2002): 41–56.

– *Hubert Aquin et la radio: une quête d'écriture, 1954–1977*. Montreal: Médiaspaul, 2004.

Leiss, William, Stephen Kline, and Sut Jhally. *Social Communication in Advertising: Persons, Products and Images of Well-Being*. Toronto: Methuen, 1986.

Leonard, Thomas C. *News for All: America's Coming-of-Age with the Press*. New York and Toronto : Oxford University Press, 1995.

Leroux, Manon. 'Le discours des acteurs de la crise d'octobre 1970 dans la presse francophone de Montréal, 1971–2000.' MA thesis, Université du Québec à Montréal, 2001.

Levert, Myriam. 'La censure de la presse d'expression française du Québec durant la Première Guerre mondiale.' MA thesis, Université du Québec à Montréal, 2001.

– 'Le Québec sous le règne d'Anastasie: l'expérience censoriale durant la Première Guerre mondiale.' *Revue d'histoire de l'Amérique française* 57, no. 3 (hiver 2004): 333–64.

Levin, Jack, and Arnold Arluke. *Gossip: The Inside Scoop*. New York: Plenum, 1987.

Levine, L.W. *The Unpredictable Past: Explorations in American Cultural History*. New York: Oxford University Press, 1993.

Leymore, Varda Langholz. *Hidden Myth: Structure and Symbolism in Advertising*. New York: Basic Books, 1975.

Liberal Campaign Handbook. New Measures and a New Leader. General Reform Association for Ontario. Election pamphlet issued by the Ontario Liberal Association, 1911.

Liberal Conservative Hand Book on Organization and Qualification of Electors. Election pamphlet issued by the Liberal-Conservative Union of Ontario, 1887.

Liberal Party of Ontario. *Robert Nixon Tells You What You're Voting For. NOW!* (1967).

Liberal-Conservative Party of Ontario. *Ontario Elections, 1883: Facts for the People.* Election pamphlet issued by the Liberal-Conservative party of Ontario, 1883.

Litt, Paul. *The Muses, the Masses and the Massey Commission.* Toronto: University of Toronto Press, 1992.

Livermore, J.D. 'The Ontario Election of 1871: A Case Study of the Transfer of Political Power.' *Ontario History* 71, no. 1 (1979): 39–52.

Livingstone, Sonia. *Making Sense of Television: The Psychology of Audience Interpretation.* New York: Routledge, 1998.

Lloyd, Ann. *Doubly Deviant, Doubly Damned: Society's Treatment of Violent Women.* London: Penguin, 1995.

Loeb, Alan P. 'Paradigms Lost: A Case Study Analysis of Models of Corporate Responsibility for the Environment.' *Business and Economic History* 28, no. 2 (1998): 95–107.

Lorenz, Stacy. '"A Lively Interest on the Prairies": Western Canada, the Mass Media, and a "World of Sport," 1870–1939.' *Journal of Sport History* 27, no. 2 (2000): 195–227.

Lule, Jack. 'Enduring Image of War: Myth and Ideology in a *Newsweek* Cover.' *Journal of Popular Culture* 29, no. 1 (2001): 199–211.

Lutes, Jean Marie. 'Sob Sisterhood Revisited.' *American Literary History* 15, no. 3 (2003): 504–32.

Lyotard, Jean-François. 'Defining the Postmodern.' In *Postmodernism: ICA Documents,* ed. Lisa Appignanesi. London: Free Association Books, 1989.

MacDonald, Donald C. 'Ontario's Political Culture: Conservatism with a Progressive Component.' *Ontario History* 86, no. 4 (1994): 297–317.

MacKenzie, David. 'Canada, the North Atlantic Triangle, and the Empire.' In *The Oxford History of the British Empire* vol. 4, *The Twentieth Century,* ed. Judith M. Brown and W. Roger Louis, 574–96. Oxford: Oxford University Press, 1999.

Mackey, Eva. *The House of Difference : Cultural Politics and National Identity in Canada.* London: Routledge, 1999.

MacLennan, Anne. 'Circumstances beyond Our Control: Canadian Radio Program Schedule Evolution during the 1930s.' PhD diss., Concordia University, 2001.

– 'American Network Broadcasting, the CBC and Canadian Radio Stations During the 1930s: A Content Analysis.' *Journal of Radio Studies* 12, no. 1 (2005): 85–103.

– 'What Do the Radio Program Schedules Reveal? Content Analysis Versus Accidental Sampling in Early Canadian Radio History.' In *Bâtir de nouveaux ponts: sources, méthodes et interdisciplinarité / Building New Bridges: Sources, Methods, and Interdisciplinarity,* ed. Jeff Keshen and Sylvie Perrier, 225–38. Ottawa: University of Ottawa Press, 2005.

Mahtani, Minelle. 'Representing Minorities: Canadian Media and Minority Identities.' *Canadian Ethnic Studies,* 33, no. 3 (2001): 99–134.

Malleck, Dan. 'The Bureaucratization of Moral Regulation: The LCBO and (Not-So) Standard Hotel Licensing in Niagara, 1927–1944.' *Histoire sociale / Social History* 38 (2005): 59–77.

Manthorpe, Jonathan. *The Power and the Tories: Ontario Politics – 1943 to the Present.* Toronto: Macmillan, 1974.

Marchand, Roland. *Advertising the American Dream: Making Way for Modernity 1920–1940.* Berkeley: University of California Press, 1985.

– *Creating the Corporate Soul: The Rise of Public Relations and Corporate Imagery in American Big Business.* Berkeley: University of California Press, 1998.

Marcil, Olivier. 'La question linguistique dans la pensée de Claude Ryan au *Devoir* (1962–1978): la difficile conciliation des principes nationalistes et libéraux.' *Mens, revue d'histoire intellectuelle de l'Amérique française* 2, no. 2 (printemps 2002): 193–231.

– *La raison et l'équilibre: libéralisme, nationalisme et catholicisme dans la pensée de Claude Ryan au Devoir, 1962–1978.* Montreal: Varia, 2002.

Marcuse, Herbert. *One-Dimensional Man.* Boston: Beacon Press, 1964.

– *Eros and Civilization: A Philosophical Inquiry into Freud.* Boston: Beacon Press, 1974.

Marinetto, M. 'The Historical Development of Business Philanthropy: Social Responsibility in the New Corporate Economy.' *Business History* 41, no. 4 (1999): 1–20

Marquis, Dominique. 'La presse catholique au Québec, 1910–1940.' PhD thesis, History, Université du Québec à Montréal, 1999.

– 'Le Devoir, un produit unique.' *Les Cahiers du journalisme* 8 (December 2000): 60–74.

– 'Un nouveau combat pour l'Église: la presse catholique d'information (1907–1940).' *Études d'histoire religieuse* 68 (2002): 73–88.

– *Un quotidien pour l'Église: L'Action catholique, 1910–1940.* Montreal: Leméac, 2004.

Marquis, Greg. '"A Reluctant Concession to Modernity": Alcohol and Modernization in the Maritimes, 1945–1980.' *Acadiensis* 32, no. 2 (2003): 31–59.

– 'Alcohol and the Family in Canada.' *Journal of Family History* 29, no. 4 (July 2004): 308–27.

Marrus, Michael R. *Mr. Sam: The Life and Times of Samuel Bronfman.* Toronto: Viking, 1991.

Martin, Michèle, Béatrice Richard, and Dina Salha. 'La pré-modernité de *Radiomonde*: un pas hésitant vers un Québec moderne.' *Histoire sociale / Social History* 33, no. 65 (2000): 37–57.

Marvin, Carolyn. *When Old Technologies Were New: Thinking about Electric Communication in the Late Nineteenth Century.* New York: Oxford University Press, 1988.

Massé, Brigitte. 'L'évolution du traitement journalistique des enjeux bioéthiques dans la presse quotidienne québécoise de 1972 à 1995.' MA thesis, Université Laval, 1999.

Matheson, Sarah A. 'Televising Toronto from Hogtown to Megacity.' PhD diss., University of Southern California, 2003.

Mattelart, Armand. *The Invention of Communication,* Trans. Susan Emanual. Minneapolis: University of Minnesota Press, 1996.

Mazepa, Patricia. 'Battles on the Cultural Front: The (De)Labouring of Culture in Canada, 1914–1944.' PhD diss., Carleton University, 2003.

McAllister, Matthew P., Edward H. Sewell, Jr, and Ian Gordon. 'Introducing Comics and Ideology.' In *Comics and Ideology,* ed. M.P. McAllister, E.H. Sewell, Jr, and I. Gordon, 1–13. New York: Peter Lang, 2001.

McCall-Newman, Christina. *Grits: An Intimate Portrait of the Liberal Party.* Toronto: Macmillan, 1982.

McChesney, Robert W. *Telecommunications, Mass Media, and Democracy: The Battle for the Control of U.S. Broadcasting, 1928–1935.* New York: Oxford University Press, 1993.

– 'Graham Spry and the Future of Public Broadcasting.' *Canadian Journal of Communication* 24, no. 1 (1999): 25–48.

McDougall A.K. *John P. Robarts: His Life and Government.* Toronto: University of Toronto Press, 1986.

McIntyre, Ian. 'Murray, (William Ewart) Gladstone (1893–1970).' *Oxford Dictionary of National Biography.* Oxford: Oxford University Press, 2004.

McKay, Ian. 'The Liberal Order Framework: A Prospectus for a Reconnaissance of Canadian History.' *Canadian Historical Review* 81, no 4 (December 2002): 617–45.

McKellar, Archibald. *An appeal to the electors of Ontario, showing how the Ontario government, as constituted in '81, rewarded the transgressors of the law and punished a detective by legislating $12,533.94 of his fees into their own pockets and into the pockets of other lawyers during the last 9 years* (1891).

McKenty, Neil, S.J. 'Mitchell F. Hepburn and the Ontario Election of 1934.' *Canadian Historical Review* 65, no. 4 (1964): 293–313.

McLuhan, Marshall. *The Mechanical Bride: Folklore of Industrial Man.* New York: Vanguard Press, 1951.

– *The Gutenberg Galaxy: The Making of Typographic Man.* Toronto: University of Toronto Press, 1962.

– *Understanding Media: The Extensions of Man.* New York and Toronto: McGraw-Hill, 1964.

McNairn, Jeffrey L. *The Capacity To Judge: Public Opinion and Deliberative Democracy in Upper Canada, 1791–1854.* Toronto: University of Toronto Press, 2000.

McQuail, Dennis. *Toward a Sociology of Mass Communications.* London: Collier-Macmillan, 1969.

Meyrowitz, Joshua. *No Sense of Place: The Impact of the Electronic Media on Social Behavior.* New York: Oxford University Press, 1985.

Merry, Sally Engle. 'Rethinking Gossip and Scandal.' In *Toward a General Theory of Social Control,* ed. Donald Black, 271–302. Orlando: Academic, 1984.

Miller, Carman. *Painting the Map Red: Canada and the South African War, 1899–1902.* Ottawa: Canadian War Museum, 1993.

Miller, Karen S. *The Voice of Business: Hill and Knowlton and Postwar Public Relations.* Chapel Hill: University of North Carolina Press, 1999.

Miller, Mary Jane. *Turn Up the Contrast: CBC Television Drama since 1952.* Vancouver: UBC Press and CBC Enterprises, 1987.

– *Rewind and Search: Conversations with the Makers and Decision Makers of CBC Television Drama.* Montreal and Kingston: McGill-Queen's University Press, 1996.

– 'Where the Spirit Lives: An Influential and Contentious Television Drama about Residential Schools.' *American Review of Canadian Studies* 31 (2001): 71–84.

– 'The CBC and Its Presentation of the Native Peoples of Canada in Television Drama.' In *Screening Culture,* ed. H.N. Nicholson, 59–73. Lanham, MD: Rowman and Littlefield, 2003.

Miller, R.E., and W.M. Richey. 'The Effects of a Campaign Brochure "Drop" in a County-Level Race for State's Attorney.' In *Communication Yearbook IV,* ed. D. Nimmo, 483–95. New Brunswick, NJ: Transaction Books, 1980.

Mills, David. 'Ontario.' In *Canadian History: A Reader's Guide,* vol. 2: *Confederation to the Present,* ed. Doug Owram, 296–340. Toronto: University of Toronto Press, 1994.

Mollier, Jean-Yves 'La naissance de la culture médiatique à la Belle Époque.' *Études littéraires* 30, no. 1 (automne 1997): 15–26.

Morley, David. *Family Television: Cultural Power and Domestic Leisure.* London: Comedia 1986.

Morton, Desmond. 'Introduction: People and Politics of Ontario.' In *Government and Politics of Ontario,* ed. D.C. MacDonald. Toronto: Macmillan, 1975.

Morton, W.L. *The Progressive Party in Canada.* Toronto: University of Toronto Press, 1950.

Mouillaud, Maurice. 'Le système des journaux (Théorie et méthodes pour l'analyse de presse).' *Langages* 11 (1968): 61–83.

Mowat and Good Government. The License Question. A Reform Pamphlet. The License Ques-

tion – Financial, Municipal and Social; Tory Attacks Disposed Of. Election pamphlet issued by the Reform Association of the Province of Ontario, 1882.

Mukerji, Chandra, and Michael Schudson. 'Introduction: Rethinking Popular Culture.' In *Rethinking Popular Culture: Contemporary Perspectives in Cultural Studies,* ed. Mukerji and Schudson, 1–61. Berkeley and Los Angeles: University of California Press, 1991.

Murdock, Catherine Gilbert. *Domesticating Drink: Women, Men, and Alcohol, 1870–1940.* Baltimore: Johns Hopkins University Press, 1998.

Murray, Gil. *Nothing On but the Radio: A Look Back at Radio in Canada and How It Changed the World.* Toronto: Dundurn Press, 2003.

Mutz, D. 'Leading Horses to Water: Confessions of a *Daily Show* Junkie.' *Journalism and Mass Communication Educator* 59 (2004): 31–5.

Nash, Knowlton. *Swashbucklers: The Story of Canada's Battling Broadcasters.* Toronto: McClelland and Stewart, 2001.

Naylor, Bronwyn. 'Women's Crime and Media Coverage: Making Explanations.' In *Gender and Crime,* ed. R. Emerson Dobash, Russell P. Dobash, and Lesley Noaks, 77–95. Cardiff: University of Wales Press, 1995.

Neary, Peter. 'The CBC "Ventures in Citizenship" Broadcast of 9 November 1938 (Kristalnacht).' *Canadian Jewish Studies* 10 (2002): 109–22.

Nelles H.V. *The Art of Nation-Building: Pageantry and Spectacle at Quebec's Tercentenary.* Toronto: University of Toronto Press, 1999.

Nerone, John C. 'A Local History of the U.S. Press: Cincinatti, 1793–1858.' In *Ruthless Criticism: New Perspectives in U.S. Communication History,* ed. William S. Solomon and Robert W. McChesney, 38–65. Minneapolis: University of Minnesota Press, 1993.

– 'Approaches to Media History.' In *A Companion to Media Studies,* ed. Angharad N. Valdivia, 93–111. Malden, MA: Blackwell, 2005.

New Democratic Party. *new Democrat: Election special* 7, no. 1 (1967): 1–16.

Newman, Bruce I. *The Mass Marketing of Politics: Democracy in an Age of Manufactured Images.* Thousand Oaks, CA: Sage, 1999.

Newman, Peter C. *Bronfman Dynasty: The Rothschilds of the New World.* Toronto: McClelland and Stewart, 1978.

Nicholas, Sian. 'All the News That's Fit to Broadcast: The Popular Press versus the BBC, 1922–45.' In *Northcliffe's Legacy: Aspects of the British Popular Press, 1896–1996,* ed. Peter Catterall, Colin Seymour-Ure, and Adrian Smith, 121–148. London: Macmillan, 2000.

Nichols, M.E. *(CP): The Story of The Canadian Press.* Toronto: Ryerson Press, 1948.

Nickle, W.F. *Financial squandering and bogus surplus. Manipulation of provincial accounts. Speech on the budget.* Liberal-Conservative Association, 1923.

Nielsen, Greg M. *Le Canada de Radio-Canada: Sociologie Critique et dialogisme culturel.* Toronto: GREF, 1994.

Nimmo, Dan. *The Political Persuaders: The Techniques of Modern Election Campaigns.* Englewood Cliffs, NJ: Prentice Hall, 1970.

Nimmo, Dan, and Arthur J. Felsberg. 'Hidden Myths in Televised Political Advertising: An Illustration.' In *New Perspectives on Political Advertising,* ed. L.L. Kaid, D. Nimmo, and K.R. Sanders, 248–67. Carbondale: Southern Illinois University Press, 1986.

Nixon, Harry. *Ontario's Premier: 'A Man of Commonsense.'* Election pamphlet issued by the Ontario Liberal Association, 1943.

Noel, Sid. 'The Ontario Political Culture: An Interpretation.' In *The Government and Politics of Ontario,* ed. G. White, 49–68. Toronto: University of Toronto Press, 1997.

Nolan, Michael J. 'Canada's Broadcasting Pioneers, 1918–1932.' *Canadian Journal of Communication* 10, no. 3 (1984): 1–26.
– 'Canadian Election Broadcasting: Political Practices and Radio Regulation 1919–1939.' *Journal of Broadcasting and Electronic Media* 29, no. 2 (1985): 175–88.
– *Foundations: Alan Plaunt and the Early Days of CBC Radio.* Toronto: CBC Enterprises, 1986.
– 'An Infant Industry: Canadian Private Radio, 1919–36.' *Canadian Historical Review* 70, no. 4 (December 1989): 496–518.
– *Walter J. Blackburn: A Man for All Media.* Toronto: Macmillan, 1989.
– *CTV: The Network that Means Business.* Edmonton: University of Alberta Press, 2001.
Nord, David Paul. *Communities of Journalism: A History of American Newspapers and Their Readers.* Urbana: University of Illinois Press, 2001.
– 'The Practice of Historical Research.' In *Mass Communication Research and Theory*, ed. G.H. Stempel III, D. Weaver, and G.C. Wilhoit, 362–85. Boston: Allyn and Bacon, 2003.
Norris, James D. *Advertising and the Transformation of American Society, 1865–1920.* New York: Greenwood Press, 1990.
O'Brien, John Egli. 'A History of the Canadian Radio League, 1930–1936.' PhD diss., University of Southern California, 1964.
O'Connor, John, ed. *Image as Artifact: The Historical Analysis of Film and Television.* Malabar, FL: Robert E. Krieger, 1990.
Oguibe, Olu. 'Photography and the Substance of the Image.' In *In/sight: African Photographers, 1940 to the Present*, curated by C. Bell, O. Enwezor, D. Tilkin, and O. Zaya, 231–52. New York: Guggenheim Museum, 1996.
Ohmann, Richard. *Selling Culture: Magazines, Markets, and Class at the Turn of the Century.* London: Verso, 1996.
Oliver, Peter. 'Sir William Hearst and the Collapse of the Ontario Conservative Party.' *Canadian Historical Review* 53, no. 1 (1972): 21–50.
– 'Parties and Elections.' Chap. 13 in *G. Howard Ferguson: Ontario Tory.* Toronto: University of Toronto Press, 1977.
O'Malley, Thomas. 'Media History and Media Studies: Aspects of the Development of the Study of Media History in the UK, 1945–2000.' *Media History* 8, no. 2 (2002): 155–73.
Ontario Liberal Policy: Proceedings of the Provincial Liberal Convention Held at Toronto June 25th–26th, 1919. Election pamphlet issued by the Liberal party of Ontario, 1919.
O'Shaughnessy, Nicholas J. *The Phenomenon of Political Marketing.* London: Macmillan, 1990.
O'Sullivan, Tim, et al. *Key Concepts in Communication and Cultural Studies*, 2nd ed. London and New York: Routledge, 1994.
Overby, L. Martin, and Jay Barth. 'Radio Advertising in American Political Campaigns: The Persistence, Importance, and Effects of Narrowcasting.' *American Politics Research* 34, no. 4 (2006): 451–78.
Owram, D.R. 'Canada and the Empire.' In *The Oxford History of the British Empire*, vol. 5: *Historiography*, ed. Robin W. Winks. Oxford: Oxford University Press, 1999.
Pagé, Pierre. *Radiodiffusion et culture savante au Québec (1930–1960).* Montreal: Éditions Maxime, 1993.
– 'Cinquante ans d'émissions religieuses à la radio québécoise (1931–1981). De l'apologétique au dialogue avec les grandes religions.' *Études d'histoire religieuse* 68. (2002): 7–23.
– 'Quelques aspects socio-politiques de l'humour radiophonique (1940–1970).' *Bulletin d'histoire politique* 13, no. 2 (hiver 2005): 63–78.

Pagé, Pierre, and Renée Legris, *Répertoire des dramatiques québécoises à la télévision, 1952–1977*. Montreal: Fides, 1977.

Pagé, Pierre, avec la collaboration de Renée Legris. *Le Comique et l'humour à la radio québécoise: aperçus historiques et textes choisis, 1930–1970*, 2 vols. Montreal: Éd. La Presse, 1976, Fides, 1979.

Pagé, Pierre, avec la collaboration de Renée Legris et de Louise Blondin. *Répertoire des oeuvres de la littérature radiophonique québécoise, 1930–1970*. Montreal: Fides, 1975.

Palmer, Bryan. *Working Class Experience: The Rise and Reconstitution of Canadian Labour, 1800–1980*. Toronto: McClelland and Stewart, 1983.

Parks, Lisa, and Shanti Kumar, eds. *Planet TV: A Global Television Reader*. New York and London: New York University Press, 2003.

Patault, Annabelle. 'La doctrine nazie vue par quatre journaux canadiens-français des années trente: *L'Ordre, Clarté, La Nation, Le Jour*, 1934–1939.' MA thesis, University of Maine, 2002.

Patterson, Graeme. *History and Communications: Harold Innis, Marshall McLuhan, the Interpretation of History*. Toronto: University of Toronto Press, 1990.

Patterson, Thomas E., and Robert D. McClure. *The Unseeing Eye: The Myth of Television Power in National Elections*. New York: Putnam, 1976.

Pease, Otis. *The Responsibilities of American Advertising: Private Control and Public Influence, 1920–1940*. New Haven: Yale University Press, 1958.

Peers, Frank W. *The Politics of Canadian Broadcasting, 1920–1951*. Toronto: University of Toronto Press, 1969.

– *The Public Eye: Television and the Politics of Canadian Broadcasting, 1952–1968*. Toronto: University of Toronto Press, 1979.

Penlington, Norman. *Canada and Imperialism, 1896–1899*. Toronto: University of Toronto Press, 1965.

Pennock, Pamela E., and K. Austin Kerr. 'In the Shadow of Prohibition: Domestic American Alcohol Policy since 1933.' *Business History* 47, no. 3 (July 2005): 383–400.

Perlmutter, David D. *The Manship School Guide to Political Communication*. Baton Rouge: Louisiana State University Press, 1999.

Perrone, Julie. 'Le processus d'héroïsation du Rocket.' MA thesis, Université du Québec à Montréal, 2008.

Perry, Adele. 'The Historian and the Theorist Revisited.' *Histoire sociale / Social History* 65 (2000): 145–51.

Peters, John Durham. *Speaking into the Air: A History of the Idea of Communication*. Chicago: University of Chicago Press, 1999.

Philipps, David. *Arcand ou la vérité retrouvée*. Saint-Léonard: Éditions Béluga, 2002.

Pierson, Ruth Roach. *'They're Still Women after All': The Second World War and Canadian Womanhood*. Toronto: McClelland and Stewart, 1986.

Pike, Robert, and Dwayne Winseck. 'The Politics of Global Media Reform, 1907–23.' *Media, Culture and Society* 26, no. 5 (September 2004): 643–75.

Pilon, Simone. 'Constitution du corpus des écrits des femmes dans la presse canadienne-française entre 1883 et 1893 et analyse de l'usage des pseudonymes.' 2 vols. PhD diss., Université Laval, 1999.

Pitman, Walter G. 'The Limits to Diversity: The Separate School Issue in the Politics of Ontario.' In *Government and Politics of Ontario*, ed. D.C. MacDonald. Toronto: Macmillan, 1975.

Place, J.A., and L.S. Peterson. 'Some Visual Motifs of Film Noir.' *Film Comment* 10, no. 1 (January–February 1974): 30–5.

Poirier, Patrick. 'La représentation du régime hitlérien par les éditorialistes du quotidien *La Patrie*, 1933–1939.' MA thesis, Université du Québec à Montréal, 2000.

– 'La représentation du régime hitlérien par *La Patrie* (1933–1939).' *Mens, revue d'histoire intellectuelle de l'Amérique française* 4, no. 1 (automne 2003): 69–93

Pomeyrols, Catherine. '*Le Devoir* et la guerre d'Espagne. Les usages de la référence française.' *Revue d'histoire de l'Amérique française* 58, no. 3 (hiver 2005): 347–87.

Pope, Daniel. *The Making of Modern Advertising*. New York: Basic Books, 1983.

Popkin, Jeremy D. *Revolutionary News: The Press in France, 1789–1799*. Durham, NC: Duke University Press, 1990.

Poster, Mark. *The Mode of Information: Poststructuralism and Social Context*. Chicago: University of Chicago Press, 1990.

Potter, Simon J. *News and the British World: The Emergence of an Imperial Press System, 1876–1922*. Oxford: Oxford University Press, 2003.

– ed. *Newspapers and Empire in Ireland and Britain: Reporting the British Empire, c. 1857–1921*. Dublin: Four Courts, 2004.

– 'Strengthening the Bonds of the Commonwealth: The Imperial Relations Trust and Australian, New Zealand, and Canadian Broadcasting Personnel in Britain, 1946–52.' *Media History* 11, no. 3 (December 2005): 193–205.

– 'The BBC, the CBC, and the 1939 Royal Tour of Canada.' *Cultural and Social History* 3, no. 4 (October 2006): 424–44.

– 'Richard Jebb, John S. Ewart, and the Round Table, 1898–1926.' *English Historical Review* 122, no. 495 (February 2007): 105–132.

– 'Webs, Networks, and Systems: Globalization and the Mass Media in the Nineteenth- and Twentieth-Century British Empire.' *Journal of British Studies*, 46, no. 3 (July 2007): 621–46.

Prang, Margaret. 'The Origins of Public Broadcasting in Canada.' *Canadian Historical Review* 46, no. 1 (March 1965): 1–31.

Pratte, Alf. 'Going along for the Ride on the Prosperity Bandwagon: Peaceful Annexation, Not War, between the Editors and Radio, 1923–1941.' *Journal of Radio Studies* 2 (1993): 123–39.

Quere, Henri. 'French Political Advertising: A Semiological Analysis of Campaign Posters.' In *Mediated Politics in Two Cultures: Presidential Campaigning in the United States and France*, ed. L.L. Kaid, J. Gerstle, and K.R. Sanders, 85–98. New York: Praeger, 1991.

Quirion, Lise. 'La presse québécoise d'expression française face au procès du maréchal Pétain.' *Bulletin d'histoire politique* 7, no. 2 (hiver 1999): 43–58.

Rabinow, Paul, and Nikolas Rose. 'Biopower Today.' *BioSocieties* 1, no. 2 (June 2006): 195–217.

Raboy, Marc. *Missed Opportunities: The Story of Canada's Broadcasting Policy*. Montreal and Kingston: McGill-Queen's University Press, 1990.

Raboy, Marc, with Geneviève Grimard. *Les médias québécois: presse, radio, télévision, inforoute*, 2nd rev. ed. Montreal: Gaston Miron, 2000.

Raboy, Marc, et al. 'Cultural Development and the Open Economy: A Democratic Issue and a Challenge to Public Policy.' *Canadian Journal of Communication* 19, no. 3 (1994): 291–316.

Radforth, Ian. *Royal Spectacle: The 1860 Visit of the Prince of Wales to Canada and the United States*. Toronto: University of Toronto Press, 2004.

Raymond, Joad. *Pamphlets and Pamphleteering in Early Modern Britain*. Cambridge: Cambridge University Press, 2003.

– 'Introduction: Networks, Communication, Practice.' *Media History* 11, no. 1/2 (2005): 3–19.

Raymond, Paul Bradford. 'Shaping the News: An Analysis of House Candidates' Campaign Communication.' In *Campaigns in the News: Mass Media and Congressional Elections*, ed. J.P. Vermeer, 13–29. Westport, CT: Greenwood Press, 1987.

Reform Government in the Dominion. Pic-nic speeches, Summer of 1877. Election pamphlet issued by the Reform Association of the Province of Ontario, 1887.

Reiner, Robert, Sonia Livingstone, and Jessica Allen. 'No More Happy Endings? The Media and Popular Concern about Crime since the Second World War.' In *Crime, Risk and Insecurity*, ed. Tim Hope and Richard Sparks, 107–25. London: Routledge, 2000.

– 'From Law and Order to Lynch Mobs: Crime News since the Second World War.' In *Criminal Visions: Media Representations of Crime and Justice*, ed. Paul Mason, 13–32. Cullompton, Devon: Willan, 2003.

Reitberger, Reinhold, and Wolfgang Fuchs. *Comics: Anatomy of a Mass Medium*. Boston: Little, Brown, 1972.

Reynolds, Ann. 'Visual Stories.' In *Visual Display: Culture beyond Appearances*, ed. L. Cooke and P. Wollen, 82–109. Seattle: Bay Press, 1995.

Richardson, Glenn W., Jr. 'Looking for Meaning in All the Wrong Places: Why Negative Advertising Is a Suspect Category.' *Journal of Communication* 51, no. 4 (2001): 775–800.

– *Pulp Politics: How Political Advertising Tells the Stories of American Politics*. Lanham, MD: Rowman and Littlefield, 2001.

Richler, Mordecai. *Belling the Cat: Essays, Reports and Opinions*. Toronto: Knopf, 1998.

Ricoeur, Paul. *Lectures on Ideology and Utopia*. Ed. George H. Taylor. New York: Columbia University Press, 1986.

Robinson, Daniel J. *The Measure of Democracy: Polling, Market Research, and Public Life, 1930–1945*. Toronto: University of Toronto Press, 1999.

– 'Seagram Company Ltd.' In *Encyclopedia of Advertising*, vol. 3, ed. John McDonough and Karen Egolf, 1409–11. New York: Fitzroy, Dearborn, 2003.

– 'Marketing and Regulating Cigarettes in Canada, 1957 to 1971.' In *Les territoires de l'entreprise*, ed. Pierre Lanthier and Claude Bellavance, 243–61. Sainte-Foy: Les Presses de l'Université Laval, 2004.

– 'Marketing Gum, Making Meanings: Wrigley in North America, 1890–1930.' *Enterprise and Society* 5, no. 1 (March 2004): 4–44.

– ed. *Communication History in Canada*. Toronto: Oxford University Press, 2004.

Rodgers, Daniel T. *Atlantic Crossings: Social Politics in a Progressive Age*. Cambridge, MA: Belknap Press of Harvard University Press, 1998.

Rose, Jonathan W. *Making 'Pictures in Our Heads': Government Advertising in Canada*. Westport, CT: Praeger, 2000.

Rose, Nikolas. *Inventing Our Selves: Psychology, Power, and Personhood*. Cambridge: Cambridge University Press, 1998.

– *Governing the Soul: The Shaping of the Private Self*, 2nd ed. London: Free Association, 1999.

– *Powers of Freedom: Reframing Political Thought*. Cambridge: Cambridge University Press, 1999.

Rosen, Ruth. 'Search for Yesterday.' In *Watching Television*, ed. Todd Gitlin, 42–67. New York: Pantheon, 1986.

Roth, Lorna. *Something New in the Air: The Story of First Peoples Television Broadcasting in Canada*. Montreal and Kingston: McGill-Queen's University Press, 2005.

Rotskoff, Lori. *Love on the Rocks: Men, Women, and Alcohol in Post–World War II America.* Chapel Hill: University of North Carolina Press, 2002.

Routhier, Gilles. 'Assurer la couverture médiatique de Vatican II au Canada: les initiatives de l'épiscopat canadien.' *Études d'histoire religieuse* 68 (2002): 57–72.

Roux-Pratte, Maude. *'Le Bien public* (1933–1978): la réussite d'une entreprise mauricienne à travers ses réseaux.' PhD diss., Université du Québec à Montréal, 2008.

Roy, Fernande, and Jean de Bonville. 'La recherche sur l'histoire de la presse québécoise: bilan et perspectives.' *Recherches sociographiques* 41, no. 1 (2000): 15–51.

Roy, Julie. 'Stratégies épistolaires et écritures féminines: les Canadiennes à la conquête des lettres, 1639–1839.' 2 vols. PhD diss, Université du Québec à Montréal, 2003.

Roy, Julie, and Nova Doyon, eds. *Le littéraire à l'oeuvre dans les périodiques québécois du XIXe siècle: projet Archibald.* Montreal: Crilcq, Université de Montréal, 2005.

Roy, Mathieu. 'Pierre Berton: grand parolier de l'identité canadienne.' MA thesis, Université Laval, 2004.

Rudin, Ronald. *Founding Fathers: The Celebration of Champlain and Laval in the Streets of Quebec, 1878–1908.* Toronto: University of Toronto Press, 2003.

Rukszto, Katarzyna. 'Minute by Minute: Canadian History Reimagined for Television Audiences.' PhD diss., York University, 2003.

Rutherford, Paul. *The Making of the Canadian Media.* Toronto: McGraw-Hill Ryerson, 1978.

– *A Victorian Authority: The Daily Press in Late Nineteenth-Century Canada.* Toronto: University of Toronto Press, 1982.

– *When Television Was Young: Primetime Canada 1952–1967.* Toronto: University of Toronto Press, 1990.

– *The New Icons?: The Art of Television Advertising.* Toronto: University of Toronto Press, 1994.

– *Endless Propaganda: The Advertising of Public Goods.* Toronto: University of Toronto Press, 2000.

– *Weapons of Mass Persuasion: Marketing the War against Iraq.* Toronto: University of Toronto Press, 2004.

– *A World Made Sexy: Freud to Madonna.* Toronto: University of Toronto Press, 2007.

Sabato, Larry J. *The Rise of Political Consultants: New Ways of Winning Elections.* New York: Basic Books, 1981.

Sahota, Anu. 'Sermon and Surprise: The Meaning of Scheduling in Broadcast Radio History.' MA essay, Simon Fraser University, 2006.

Saint-Jean, Armande. *Éthique de l'information: fondements et pratiques au Québec depuis 1960.* Montreal: Presses de l'Université de Montréal, 2002.

Sanders, David, and Pippa Norris, 'The Impact of Political Advertising in the 2001 U.K. General Election.' *Political Research Quarterly* 58, no. 4 (2005): 525–36.

Sangster, Joan. *Regulating Girls and Women: Sexuality, Family, and the Law in Ontario, 1920–1960.* Don Mills, ON: Oxford University Press, 2001.

Schlesinger, Arthur M., Jr. *The Vital Center: The Politics of Freedom.* Boston: Houghton Mifflin, 1949.

Schmalz, Wayne. *On Air: Radio in Saskatchewan.* Regina: Coteau Books, 1990.

Schudson, Michael. *The Power of News.* Cambridge, MA: Harvard University Press, 1995.

– 'Toward a Troubleshooting Manual for Journalism History.' *Journalism and Mass Communication Quarterly* 74, no. 3 (Autumn 1997): 463–6.

Schwartzman, Edward. *Political Campaign Craftsmanship: A Professional's Candid Guide to Campaigning for Public Office*, 2nd ed. New York: Van Nostrand Reinhold, 1984.

Schwarzlose, Richard A. *The Nation's Newsbrokers*, vol. 2: *The Rush to Institution*. Evanston, IL: Northwestern University Press, 1990.

Schwichtenberg, Cathy, ed. *The Madonna Connection: Representational Politics, Subcultural Identities, and Cultural Theory*. Boulder, CO: Westview Press, 1993.

Scott, Joan Wallach. *Gender and the Politics of History*, rev. ed. New York: Columbia University Press, 1999.

Shareck, Olivier. 'Évolution de l'opinion publique face à la reconnaissance des droits des gais et des lesbiennes au Québec telle que vue dans les journaux montréalais et dans les sondages, 1967–1994.' MA thesis, Université du Québec à Montréal, 2003.

Silbey, Joel H. *The American Party Battle: Election Campaign Pamphlets, 1828–1876*, 2 vols. Cambridge, MA: Harvard University Press, 1999.

Simpson, James, S.A. Corner, Margaret Haile, and John A. Kelly. *Socialist candidates for the Ontario Legislature*. Election pamphlet issued by the Socialist Party of Ontario, 1902.

Skinner, David, James R. Compton, and Michael Gasher, eds. *Converging Media, Diverging Politics: A Political Economy of News Media in the United States and Canada*. Lanham, MD: Lexington Books, 2005.

Smith, David J. 'Intellectual Activist: Graham Spry, A Biography.' PhD diss., York University, 2003.

Smythe, Dallas W., and Tran Van Dinh. 'On Critical and Administrative Research: A New Critical Analysis.' *Journal of Communication* 33, no. 3 (1983): 117–27.

Soderlund, Walter C. 'Advertising in the 1993 Federal Election.' *Canadian Parliamentary Review* 18, no. 1 (1995): 16–22.

Sommerville, John. *The News Revolution in England: Cultural Dynamics of Daily Information*. New York and Oxford: Oxford University Press, 1996.

Sontag, Susan. *On Photography*. New York: Farrar, Straus and Giroux, 1977.

Sotiron, Minko. *An Annotated Bibliography of Works on Daily Newspapers in Canada, 1914–1983 / Une bibliographie annotée des ouvrages portant sur les quotidiens canadiens, 1914–1983*. Montreal: M. Sotiron, 1987.

Speakers' Handbook. The Hon. G.S. Henry, Premier of Ontario. Election pamphlet issued by Liberal-Conservative Party of Ontario, 1934.

Spiers, Rosemary. *Out of the Blue: The Fall of the Tory Dynasty in Ontario*. Toronto: Macmillan, 1986.

Spigel, Lynn. *Make Room for TV: Television and the Family Ideal in Postwar America*. Chicago: University of Chicago Press, 1992.

Spillman, Lyn. *Nation and Commemoration: Creating National Identities in the United States and Australia*. Cambridge: Cambridge University Press, 1997.

Spry, Graham. 'The Canadian Broadcasting Issue.' *Canadian Forum*, April 1931.

– 'The Origins of Public Broadcasting in Canada: A Comment.' *Canadian Historical Review* 46, no. 2 (June 1965): 134–41.

– 'Public Policy and Private Pressures: The Canadian Radio League 1930–6 and Countervailing Power.' In *On Canada: Essays in Honour of Frank H. Underhill*, ed. Norman Penlington, 24–36. Toronto: University of Toronto Press, 1971.

Stallybrass, Peter, and Allon White. *The Politics and Poetics of Transgression*. London: Methuen 1986.

Stamp, Robert. 'Empire Day in the Schools of Ontario: The Training of Young Imperialists.' *Journal of Canadian Studies* 8, no. 3 (1973): 32–42.

Starowicz, Mark. *Making History: The Remarkable Story Behind Canada: A People's History*.
Toronto: McClelland and Stewart, 2003.

Starr, Paul. *The Creation of the Media: Political Origins of Modern Communications*. New
York: Basic Books, 2004.

Stevens, Daniel. 'Separate and Unequal Effects: Information, Political Sophistication
and Negative Advertising in American Elections.' *Political Research Quarterly* 58, no. 3
(2005): 413–25.

Stöber, Rudolph. 'What Media Evolution Is: A Theoretical Approach to the History of
New Media.' *European Journal of Communication* 19, no. 4 (2004): 483–505.

Stotyn, Ronald E. 'Education in the Ether: A Historical Study of "The Alberta School Broadcasts," circa 1929–1959.' PhD diss., Southern Illinois University at Carbondale, 2003.

Strange, Carolyn. 'Stories of Their Lives: The Historian and the Capital Case File.' In *On
the Case: Explorations in Social History*, ed. Franca Iacovetta and Wendy Mitchinson,
25–48. Toronto: University of Toronto Press, 1998.

Street, John. 'The Celebrity Politician: Political Style and Popular Culture.' In *Media and
the Restyling of Politics*, ed. John Corner and Dick Pels, 85–98. London: Sage, 2003.

Sullivan, David. 'Images of a Breakthrough Woman Candidate: Dianne Feinstein's 1990,
1992, and 1994 Campaign Television Advertisements.' *Women's Studies in Communication* 21, no. 1 (1998): 7–26.

Surplis, David. 'The Progressive Conservative Leadership Convention of 1971.' In *Government and Politics of Ontario*, ed. Donald C. MacDonald, 64–76. Toronto: Macmillan,
1975.

Swanson, D.L., and P. Mancini, eds. *Politics, Media and Modern Democracy. An International Study of Innovations in Electoral Campaigning and Their Consequences*. Westport,
CT: Praeger, 1996.

Talbot, E.J. 'Choquette's Urban Fables: Questioning a Certain Modernity.' *Quebec Studies*
34 (Fall-Winter 2002): 47–57.

Taras, David. 'In the Eye of the Beholder: The Power of Election Advertising.' Chap. 8 in
The Newsmakers: The Media's Influence on Canadian Politics. Scarborough, ON: Nelson,
1990.

Tennyson, Brian D. 'The Ontario General Election of 1919: The Beginnings of Agrarian
Revolt.' *Journal of Canadian Studies* 4, no. 1 (1969): 26–36.

The Canadian Radio League: Objects, Information, National Support. Ottawa, 1932.

*The Lynch-Mowat Concordat. Liberal-Conservative Party pamphlet. The Mowat-Fraser Govern-
ment accused of being influenced by the 'Romish hierarchy' to substitute an expurgated version of the Holy Scripture for use, instead of the original whole Bible, in the schools*. Election
pamphlet issued by the Liberal-Conservative Union of Ontario, 1883.

Thériault, Janice. 'D'un catholicisme à l'autre: trois ordres catholiques au Québec et
leurs revues face à l'*Aggiornamento*, 1962–1970.' *Mens, revue d'histoire intellectuelle de
l'Amérique française* 5, no. 1 (automne 2004): 7–71.

*The Ross Government has kept Ontario Liberals in the lead: Its record of achievement in the past;
its platform of progress for the future*. Election pamphlet issued by the Liberal Party of
Ontario, 1905.

Thibault, Marie-Josée. 'L'évolution des journaux communautaires au Québec.' MA
thesis, Université de Sherbrooke, 2000.

Thomas, Jocko. *From Police Headquarters: True Tales from the Big City Crime Beat.* Toronto: Stoddart, 1990.

Thompson, John B. *The Media and Modernity: A Social Theory of the Media.* Stanford, CA: Stanford University Press, 1995.

Tompkins, Jane. 'Introduction to Reader-Response Criticism.' In *Reader-Response Criticism: From Formalism to Post-Structuralism,* ed. Jane Tompkins, ix–xxvi. Baltimore: Johns Hopkins University Press, 1980.

Trachtenberg, Alan. *Reading American Photographs: Images as History, Mathew Brady to Walker Evans.* New York: Hill and Wang, 1989.

Tracy, Sara W., and Caroline Jean Acker, eds. *Altering American Consciousness: The History of Alcohol and Drug Use in the United States, 1800–2000.* Amherst: University of Massachusetts Press, 2004.

Travers, Len. *Celebrating the Fourth: Independence Day and the Rites of Nationalism in the Early Republic.* Amherst: University of Massachusetts Press, 1997.

Tremblay, Jean-Philippe. 'Par-delà la ténacité et l'abnégation: la presse musicale au Québec, 1890–1959.' MA thesis, Université du Québec à Montréal, 2006.

Tremblay, Yves. 'La consommation bridée: contrôle des prix et rationnement durant la Deuxième Guerre Mondiale.' *Revue d'histoire de l'Amérique Français* 58, no. 4 (2005): 569–607.

Trew, Johanne. 'Conflicting Visions: Don Messer, Liberal Nationalism and the Canadian Unity Debate.' *International Journal of Canadian Studies* 26 (2002): 41–57.

Trudel, Pierre. 'Médias et autochtones: pour une information equilibrée et dépourvu de préjugés.' *Bulletin d'histoire politique*, 12, no. 3 (2004): 145–67.

Valleé, Brian. *The Torso Murder: The Untold Story of Evelyn Dick.* Toronto: Key Porter, 2001.

Valverde, Mariana. *Diseases of the Will: Alcohol and the Dilemmas of Freedom,.* Cambridge: Cambridge University Press, 1998.

– 'Some Remarks on the Rise and Fall of Discourse Analysis.' *Histoire sociale / Social History* 65 (2000): 59–77.

– 'A Postcolonial Women's Law? Domestic Violence and the Ontario Liquor Board's "Indian List."' *Feminist Studies* 30, no. 3 (2004): 566–88.

Vance, Jonathan *Death So Noble: Memory, Meaning, and the First World War.* Vancouver: UBC Press, 1997.

van Zoonen, Liesbet. 'Imagining the Fan Democracy.' *European Journal of Communication* 19, no. 1 (2004): 39–52.

Varnum, Robin, and Christina T. Gibbons. 'Introduction.' In *The Language of Comics: Word and Image*, ed. R. Varnum and C.T. Gibbons, ix–xix. Jackson: University Press of Mississippi, 2001.

Villeneuve, Lucie. 'Rire et rébellion dans *Le Fantasque* de Napoléon Aubin (1837–1845) ou comment se payer la tête à "lord du rhum."' *Bulletin d'histoire politique* 13, no. 2 (hiver 2005): 51–62.

Vipond, Mary. 'The Nationalist Network: English Canada's Intellectuals and Artists in the 1920s.' *Canadian Review of Studies in Nationalism* 7, no. 1 (Spring 1980): 32–52.

– *Listening In: The First Decade of Canadian Broadcasting, 1922–1932.* Montreal and Kingston: McGill-Queen's University Press, 1992.

– 'The Beginnings of Public Broadcasting in Canada: The CRBC 1932–1936.' *Canadian Journal of Communication* 19, no. 2 (1994): 151–72.

- '"Please Stand by for That Report": The Historiography of Early Canadian Radio.' *Fréquence/Frequency* 7–8 (1997): 13–32.
- 'The Continental Marketplace: Authority, Advertisers and Audiences in Canadian News Broadcasting, 1932–1936.' *Journal of Radio Studies* 6, no. 1 (1999): 169–84.
- 'Desperately Seeking the Audience for Early Canadian Radio.' In *Nations, Ideas, Identities: Essays in Honour of Ramsay Cook*, ed. M. Behiels and M. Martel, 86–96. Don Mills, ON: Oxford University Press, 2000.
- *The Mass Media in Canada*, 3rd ed. Toronto: James Lorimer, 2000.
- 'The Mass Media in Canadian History: The Empire Day Broadcast of 1939.' *Journal of the Canadian Historical Association* 14 (2003): 1–21.
- 'The Canadian Radio Broadcasting Commission in the 1930s: How Canada's First Public Broadcaster Negotiated "Britishness."' In *Canada and the British World: Culture, Migration and Identity*, Phillip Buckner and R. Douglas Francis, 270–87. Vancouver: UBC Press, 2006.
- Wachtel, William. *The Anatomy of a Hidden Persuader*. New York: Vantage Press, 1975.
- Wagman, Ira. 'From Spiritual Matters to Economic Facts: Recounting Problems of Knowledge in the History of Canadian Audiovisual Policy, 1928–1961.' PhD diss., McGill University, 2006.
- Wagner, Bonnie. 'We Proudly Begin Our Broadcast Day: Saskatchewan and the Arrival of Television, 1945–1969.' MA thesis, University of Saskatchewan, 2004.
- Waite, P.B. *The Life and Times of Confederation: Politics, Newspapers and the Union of British North America*. Toronto: University of Toronto Press, 1963.
- Walden, Keith. *Becoming Modern in Toronto: The Industrial Exhibition and the Shaping of a Late Victorian Culture*. Toronto: University of Toronto Press, 1997.
- Walker, Michael. 'Film Noir: Introduction.' In *The Book of Film Noir*, ed. Ian Cameron, 8–38. New York: Continuum, 1993.
- Walkom, Thomas L. 'The Daily Newspaper Industry in Ontario's Developing Capitalistic Economy: Toronto and Ottawa, 1871–1911.' PhD diss., University of Toronto, 1983.
- Walters, Marilu. *CKUA: Radio Worth Fighting For*. Edmonton: University of Alberta Press, 2002.
- Ward, Ian. 'The Early Use of Radio For Political Communication in Australia and Canada: John Henry Austral, Mr Sage and the Man from Mars.' *Australian Journal of Politics and History* 45, no. 3 (1999): 311–29.
- Warsh, Cheryl Krasnick, ed. *Drink in Canada: Historical Essays*. Montreal: McGill-Queen's University Press, 1993.
- 'Smoke and Mirrors: Gender Representation in North American Tobacco and Alcohol Advertisements before 1950.' *Histoire sociale / Social History*, 31 (1999): 183–222.
- Watson A.J. *Marginal Man: The Dark Vision of Harold Innis*. Toronto: University of Toronto Press, 2005.
- Wearing, Joseph. *The L-Shaped Party: The Liberal Party of Canada, 1958–1980*. Toronto: McGraw-Hill Ryerson, 1981.
- *Strained Relations: Canadian Parties and Voters*. Toronto: McClelland and Stewart, 1988.
- Weaver, John C. *Hamilton: An Illustrated History*. Toronto: James Lorimer and National Museums of Canada, 1982.
- *Crimes, Constables, and Courts: Order and Transgression in a Canadian City, 1816–1970*. Montreal and Kingston: McGill-Queen's University Press, 1995.
- Webb, Jeff A. 'The Origins of Public Broadcasting: The Commission of Government and

the Creation of the Broadcasting Corporation of Newfoundland.' *Acadiensis* 24, no. 2 (1994): 88–106.
– 'The Invention of Radio Broadcasting in Newfoundland and the Maritime Provinces, 1922–1939.' PhD diss., University of New Brunswick, 1995.
– 'Canada's Moose River Mine Disaster (1936): Radio–Newspaper Competition in the Business of News.' *Historical Journal of Film, Radio and Television* 16, no. 3 (1996): 365–76.
– 'Constructing Community and Consumers: Joseph R. Smallwood's *Barrelman* Radio Program.' *Journal of the CHA*, n.s., 8 (1997): 165–86.
– 'VOUS: Armed Forces Radio Service (AFRS) in Newfoundland.' *Journal of Radio Studies* 11, no. 1 (2004): 87–99.
– 'Who Speaks for the Public? The Debate over Government or Private Broadcasting in Newfoundland, 1939–49.' *Acadiensis* 35, no. 1 (2005): 74–93.
– 'Embracing the Modern and the Authentic: Musical Culture upon Radio Station VONF.' Paper delivered to Canadian Historical Association Conference, Toronto, 2006.
Weir, E. Austin. *The Struggle for National Broadcasting in Canada*. Toronto: McClelland and Stewart, 1965.
Weir, Ronald B. *The History of the Distillers Company, 1877–1939: Diversification and Growth in Whisky and Chemicals*. Oxford: Oxford University Press, 1995.
Wernick, Andrew. *Promotional Culture: Advertising, Ideology and Symbolic Expression*. London: Sage, 1991.
West, Darrell M. *Air Wars: Television Advertising in Election Campaigns, 1952–2004*. Washington: CQ Press, 2005.
White, Theodore. *The Making of the President*. New York: Atheneum, 1961.
Whitehorn, Alan. 'The Party in Elections.' Chap. 4 in *Canadian Socialism: Essays on the CCF–NDP*. Toronto: Oxford University Press, 1992.
Wight, Sarah, and Alice Myers. 'Introduction.' In *No Angels: Women Who Commit Violence*, ed. Alice Myers and Sarah Wight, xi–xvi. London: Pandora, 1996.
Williams, Linda. *Hard Core: Power, Pleasure, and the 'Frenzy of the Visible.'* Berkeley: University of California Press, 1992.
Williams, Raymond. *Television: Technology and Cultural Form*. Glasgow: Fontana/Collins, 1974.
– *Keywords*. New York: Oxford University Press, 1976.
– *Problems in Materialism and Culture*. London: Verso, 1980.
– 'Advertising: The Magic System.' In *Culture and Materialism: Selected Essays*, 2nd ed. London: Verso, 1995.
Williams, Stephen. *Karla: A Pact With the Devil*. Toronto: Seal, 2003.
Williamson, Judith. *Decoding Advertisements: Ideology and Meaning in Advertising*. London: Marion Boyars, 1978.
Willis, John, ed. *More Than Words: Readings in Transport, Communication and the History of Postal Communication*. Gatineau: Canadian Museum of Civilization, 2007.
Wilson, John. 'The Ontario Political Culture.' In *Government and Politics of Ontario*, ed. D.C. MacDonald, 211–33. Toronto: Macmillan, 1975.
Winham, Gilbert R., and Robert B. Cunningham. 'Party Leader Images in the 1968 Federal Election.' *Canadian Journal of Political Science* 3, no. 1 (1970): 37–55.
Winseck, Dwayne. 'Back to the Future: Telecommunications, Online Information Services and Convergence from 1840 to 1910.' *Media History* 5, no. 2 (1999): 137–57.

Winseck, Dwayne, and Robert M. Pike. *Communication and Empire: Media, Markets and Globalization, 1860–1930*. Durham, NC: Duke University Press, 2007.

Wright, Bradford W. *Comic Book Nation: The Transformation of Youth Culture in America*. Baltimore: Johns Hopkins University Press, 2001.

Wyer, Robert S., Jr, et al. 'Image, Issues, and Ideology: The Processing of Information about Political Candidates.' *Journal of Personality and Social Psychology* 61, no. 4 (1991): 533–45.

Young, Walter. *The Anatomy of a Party: The National CCF, 1932–1961*. Toronto: University of Toronto Press, 1969.

Zagorin, Perez. 'History, the Referent, and Narrative: Reflections on Postmodernism Now.' *History and Theory* 38 (1999): 1–24.

– 'Rejoinder to a Postmodernist.' *History and Theory* 39 (2000): 201–9.

Zimmerman A.E. *In the Shadow of the Shield: The Development of Wireless Telegraphy and Radio Broadcasting in Kingston and at Queen's University: An Oral and Documentary History, 1902–57*. Kingston: the author, 1991.

Contributors

Gene Allen is Associate Professor in the School of Journalism and Director of the Master of Journalism program at Ryerson University.

Daniel J. Robinson is Associate Professor in the Faculty of Information and Media Studies at the University of Western Ontario.

James Cairns is Assistant Professor in the Contemporary Studies program at Wilfrid Laurier University in Brantford, ON.

Matthew Hayday is Assistant Professor of History at the University of Guelph.

Alison Jacques is a PhD candidate in Communication Studies at McGill University.

Dominique Marquis is Professor of History at l'Université du Québec à Montréal.

Simon J. Potter is Lecturer in History at the National University of Ireland, Galway.

Fernande Roy is Professor and Director of Graduate Studies in History at l'Université du Québec à Montréal.

Paul Rutherford is Professor of History at the University of Toronto.

Patricia Smart (translator) is Chancellor's Professor Emerita of French at Carleton University.

Mary Vipond is Professor Emeritus of History at Concordia University.